Meeting and Understanding People

Chris L. Kleinke

W. H. Freeman and Company
New York

To Gerry LeJeune and her family

Library of Congress Cataloging-in-Publication Data

Kleinke, Chris L.
Meeting and understanding people.

Bibliography: p.
Includes index.
1. Interpersonal relations.   2. Interpersonal attraction.
I. Title

HM132.K47   1986   302.3′4   85-31142
ISBN 0-7167-1763-8
ISBN 0-7167-1764-6 (pbk.)

Printed in the United States of America.

1 2 3 4 5 6 7 8 9 0   MP   4 3 2 1 0 8 9 8 7 6

MEETING AND UNDERSTANDING PEOPLE

Table of Contents

Preface

Poets, novelists, and philosophers have been inspired for centuries to write about their observations of human encounters. Psychologists and sociologists have conducted research studies to understand the factors influencing people's perceptions of one another. During the course of your life you will have thousands of human encounters. From them you will develop an understanding about how you interpret people's motives and personalities. Sometimes you will find that your first impressions of others are accurate. On other occasions your initial perceptions will be disproved. When you talk with friends and acquaintances about how you form first impressions, you will be interested to learn about the similarities and differences in your respective styles and methods for evaluating people around you. As you become more attentive to personal interactions you are likely to reflect with fascination on the human experience of "presenting" oneself and forming impressions of others.

My goal in writing this book is to report the results of psychological studies on the ways we perceive people in a way that you can relate to your own life. Such research covers a wide range of topics including nonverbal communication, liking and attraction, social skills, judgments about intentions and motives, stereotyping and biases, and strategies for gaining favor from others. Some of the conclusions about factors influencing first impressions will correspond with your personal experiences, and many of the suggestions about how to make a good first impression will probably be similar to the approaches you already use. Other conclusions will be surprising and may heighten your awareness in your relationships and arouse your curiosity about them. If exploring our ways of perceiving people is as intriguing to you as it is to me, your life will be enriched as you compare psychological research findings with your own experiences interacting with others.

I wish to express gratitude to my friends at the Boston Pain Center of Spaulding Rehabilitation Hospital for their warmth, good humor, and loving support.

Chris L. Kleinke
Anchorage, Alaska

MEETING AND UNDERSTANDING PEOPLE

Overcoming Shyness
and
Perfecting Social Skills

Psychology students are often surprised to discover how much their lives and personal actions are influenced by external circumstances. Psychologists and sociologists have known for a long time that environmental factors affect even such intensely personal matters as choice of dating and marriage partners. In his book *Beyond Freedom and Dignity*, B. F. Skinner attempts to reconcile the environmental influences in our lives with the desire to attribute our actions to choice and free will.[1] He argues that people can broaden their behavioral options by modifying their environments. This insight will be used later to arrive at suggestions for expanding social contacts and potentialities for meeting other people. First, however, it will be useful to learn about some of the factors regulating our social lives. Dramatic examples of how marriage partners can be determined by external forces are seen in cultures in which marriages are arranged. A Kwakiutl Indian of Vancouver Island gave the following description of his marriage:

> When I was old enough to get a wife ... my brother looked for a girl in the same position that I and my brothers had. Without my consent, they picked a wife for me. ... The one I wanted was prettier than the one they chose for me, but she was in a lower position than me, so they wouldn't let me marry her. I argued about it and was very angry with my brother, but I couldn't do anything.

In Japan, an arranged marriage is called a *miai*:

> I was the youngest among my brothers and sisters. They were all married and I was left alone as a single woman. My mother got high blood pressure from worry about my being unmarried. My family were anxious to arrange a marriage as soon as possible and showed my mother the picture of my prospective husband. I was thus in a haste to marry. After the miai, I did not love my partner but I married him. It was not for my sake but because I wanted to relieve my mother and my family of their anxiety that I decided to marry.[2]

Unless you were raised in a culture with arranged marriages, it is unlikely that you would accept the idea of someone else deciding whom you will marry. But how much choice of dating and marriage partners do you actually have? In addition to the limiting influence of social networks, which will be discussed later, there is the problem of shyness. If you are like most people you have probably missed the opportunity to meet someone special because you were feeling shy.

Shyness

Shyness can be defined as being fearful about meeting people and suffering discomfort in their presence. Although you probably recognize shyness in yourself, it might come as a surprise to learn that over 80 percent of Americans in a recent survey cited by Philip Zimbardo in his book *Shyness* said they were shy at some point in their lives.[3] Only 7 percent claimed that they had never experienced shyness. Zimbardo reports that feelings of shyness are prevalent among some of the most seemingly outgoing television and movie personalities. According to Zimbardo, shy people describe themselves as having trouble making conversation and maintaining eye contact and as experiencing discomfort when attempting to initiate interactions with others. People report that they experience shyness primarily when they are with strangers, members of the opposite sex, and authority figures. Zimbardo describes some advantages offered by shyness, such as the opportunity to stand back and observe an interaction before jumping in in an inappropriate manner. Shyness also provides a feeling of individuality and safety from interpersonal conflicts. Moreover, many traits associated with shyness have favorable connotations. Shy people are often described as being modest, polite, and unassuming. In spite of these advantages, however, most people surveyed by Zimbardo said they would prefer to be less shy. This chapter will explore a number of methods you can use for overcoming shyness. First, it will take time to study the psychology of loneliness.

Loneliness

Sociologists such as David Riesman and Philip Slater have described how American values of competition, independence, and individuality result in feelings of loneliness and isolation.[4] In one national survey, 26 percent of Americans surveyed reported that they recently felt "very lonely and remote from other people." Loneliness is an experience viewed by most people as lacking in redeeming value. A survey by a university student health service reported that college students ranked loneliness as one of their most common health problems.[5] People responding to a newspaper survey in New York City described the following reactions to loneliness:

Desperation, panic, helplessness

Depression, sadness, emptiness

Impatience, boredom, anger

Self-depreciation, shame, insecurity

People in the same survey said they responded to loneliness in the following ways:

Crying, sleeping, overeating, taking drugs

Studying, working, exercising, going to a movie

Spending money, going shopping

Calling a friend, visiting someone[6]

MEASURING LONELINESS

Loneliness is experienced by people who feel that their relationships with others are less satisfying than they would like them to be. Loneliness is related less to the quantity of personal interactions than to their meaningfulness.[7] Check whether you agree with the following statements:

1. *I feel in tune with the people around me.*

2. *I do not feel alone.*

3. *I can find companionship when I want it.*

4. *I feel left out.*

5. *No one really knows me well.*

6. *People are around me but not with me.*

The above statements come from the revised UCLA loneliness scale.[8] Lonely people tend to disagree with the first three statements and to agree with the last three. High scores on loneliness are found in people who report spending much time alone, having few friends, and being involved in few social activities. Lonely people are scared to take social risks, and they experience negative feelings about their interactions with others.

HOW PEOPLE EXPLAIN THEIR LONELINESS

Social psychologists have studied loneliness within the framework of attribution theories (attribution theories are discussed in Chapter 8).[9] Their goal has been to learn how people's explanations of their loneliness are related to their views about how loneliness can be overcome. The explanations fall into one of the following three categories: (1) *internality,* (2) *stability,* and (3) *control.*[10] Loneliness may also be a matter of perceptions and social skills.

Internality. Which of the following statements better describes your experiences of loneliness?

1. *I am lonely because I'm not very popular and I don't know how to make friends.*

2. *I am lonely because it's hard to meet people and I haven't been in the right place at the right time.*

If you chose statement 1, you tend to view your loneliness as internal and caused by something about you, such as being shy or not well liked. If you chose statement 2, you see your loneliness as external and caused by something in the environment, such as lack of opportunities or other people not trying.

Stability. People who view their loneliness as stable believe that it is due to some characteristic they possess or to a life circumstance that can't be changed, such as being unappealing or unattractive. A perception of loneliness as unstable implies that the causes of loneliness, either in oneself or in the environment, can be changed, such as by finding new opportunities and learning new social skills.

Control. People differ in the amount of control they feel they have over factors causing loneliness. Some believe that something can be done to change a state of loneliness. Others perceive loneliness as being beyond their personal influence.

Research has shown that feelings of depression, hopelessness, and self-depreciation are most common among people who view their loneliness as internal and stable.[11] These people have little reason to feel a sense of control over their loneliness. People who view their loneliness as external and unstable are more likely to believe they have some control over it and are more active in doing something about it. Fortunately, perceptions of causes for things are learned. Therefore it is possible to teach new ways for coping with loneliness to people who presently view their loneliness as beyond their control. First of all, even though a precipitant of loneliness might be unchangeable (such as losing a spouse, family member, or friend), it is not necessary for the loneliness to last forever. Second, personal traits such as shyness are not permanent. People can learn new social skills and coping strategies. Third, lonely people can change their life-styles and environments. Finally, it is important to realize that loneliness is sometimes a product of unrealistic expectations that can be modified with rational thinking.[12]

Perceptions and Social Skills. In addition to understanding loneliness in terms of attributions about its causes, it is possible to study loneliness from the perspective of interpersonal perceptions and social skills. Lonely people have as many personal interactions as nonlonely people, but the interactions are in less intimate relationships. A study found that lonely people were less able than nonlonely people to communicate interest in another person with whom they were conversing by paying attention to that person's ideas and attitudes and carrying the conversation in that direction.[13] Lonely people disclose less about themselves to others than nonlonely people do. They are harder to know. Lonely people are also less success-ful than nonlonely people in communicating their emotions with facial expres-sions. Although lonely people suffer some deficiencies in social skills, it is impor-tant to realize that they are not necessarily disliked.[14]

Much of the problem suffered by lonely people is due to their *expectations* that they will be rejected. Research suggests that because lonely people have poor self-concepts they are preoccupied with negative feelings about themselves and don't take time to appreciate positive reactions they receive from others. The anticipa-tion of rejection serves as a self-fulfilling prophecy because it discourages lonely people from making social overtures and seeking out personal interactions. It has been demonstrated that lonely people can be trained to increase their conversational skills by learning how to communicate higher amounts of attention to other people's feelings and interests.[15] As a result of this training, lonely people reported feeling less shy and lonely and better about themselves.

Self-Efficacy

There has been a great deal of interest among clinical psychologists in the value of providing clients with coping skills that can be used in everyday life. The goal of these psychologists is to encourage the growth of what Albert Bandura calls *self-efficacy*.[16] Bandura found that self-efficacy plays an important role in determining the likelihood of overcoming an obstacle or undertaking a new challenge. Self-efficacy is built up by teaching new skills that can be practiced in small steps. By learning new coping behaviors in a supportive setting and testing them gradually in the outside world it is possible to experience a reasonable amount of success with minimal anxiety. At first, encouragement and support are provided by a ther-apist, family members, and friends. When a new coping behavior has been mas-tered, it results in experiences of success that reinforce continued feelings of self-competency.

The remainder of this chapter will focus on methods for overcoming shyness and expanding social potentialities. The techniques and strategies that are suggested can be viewed as coping skills for building competence and self-efficacy in social interactions.

Overcoming Shyness

In working to overcome shyness it is useful to understand four problem areas that are often associated with difficulties in meeting people. These problem areas suggest the following goals for people who want to become less shy.[17] You might wish to rate how important each of these goals is for you.

Understanding your shyness

Perfecting social skills

Coping with anxiety

Improving rational thinking

UNDERSTANDING YOUR SHYNESS

All of us have a need to seek explanations for events in our lives. The science of how people go about understanding their experiences is the basis of attribution theories and research, which are described in Chapter 8. An example of the desire for understanding is seen in a study where clients seeking psychological counseling were asked what they wanted to gain from their counseling sessions.[18] Two things that almost all clients wanted were help in talking about what was troubling them and increased understanding about the reasons behind their feelings and behavior.

The value of understanding one's shyness was demonstrated in an experiment in which shy people were assigned to one of three different therapy groups.[19] Shy people in one therapy group were given help in understanding how their shyness could be explained in terms of their developmental history and childhood experiences. Those in a second group received help in understanding their shyness as a product of their thinking styles and self-perceptions. The third group of shy people received counseling that did not focus on finding explanations for shyness. Which counseling approach was most successful? In general, the first two approaches, which helped the shy people find an explanation for their shyness, were more effective than the third approach, which did not. Shy people who received help in understanding their shyness were more actively involved in the counseling sessions and had greater motivation and expectancy for improvement. There were no differences in effectiveness between the approaches that provided either developmental or self-labeling explanations for shyness. It is instructive, however, to consider that a developmental understanding of shyness tends to focus on stable, external causes, which may bias people to say, "Given my history, things couldn't have turned out much differently." A self-labeling understanding of shyness is more amenable to change through rational thinking because it focuses responsibility for overcoming shyness on the person.

Another study found that shy people tend to view social interactions as times when they are being evaluated.[20] Such an attitude toward social encounters is bound to make people feel anxious and defensive about how they will appear to others.

With this orientation toward social interactions it is not surprising that shy people expect the worst and don't enjoy socializing very much. People not suffering from shyness take a very different view. They see social interactions as offering an opportunity for sharing intimacy with others. They are not defensive about how they will appear because they anticipate the positive experiences coming from social encounters. They have learned how to tolerate negative responses and rejections.

PERFECTING SOCIAL SKILLS

Social skills are best perfected in a training group that is designed to provide the following experiences:[21]

1. A description and rationale for new behaviors that are to be learned

2. Demonstration of new behaviors through modeling

3. Practice of new behaviors with feedback about how one is doing

4. Transfer of new behaviors to the natural environment

Participants in training programs in social skills usually sign a contract outlining their goals, the procedures that will be followed in the program, and their own commitment to follow these procedures. Training groups are set up to proceed by gradual steps so that people can learn at their own pace. The trainer usually begins by describing and modeling effective ways of interacting in social situations. He or she models social behaviors in such a way that participants can adapt them to themselves and practice them in the group with the benefit of group feedback. Video recordings are often used. Group participants can also learn to use their imagination to prepare themselves for situations in which effective social skills are required. After sufficient practice and feedback, participants are given homework assignments to gain experience with their new social behaviors in the outside world. Participants receive continued feedback from the group and are encouraged to enlist friends and family members for support. Participants are taught to work gradually from easy to more difficult social interactions, to monitor their progress, and to reward themselves for success. When the training group has ended, participants might agree to meet at a later date for a follow-up or booster session.

COPING WITH ANXIETY

Whether social anxiety is due to actual experiences with rejection or to imagined fears of rejection, it can cause real difficulties in interacting with other people. Reducing anxiety in social situations involves two basic steps. The first step is to develop *self-relaxation* skills. The second is to use these skills during social interactions.

Self-relaxation involves the technique of developing an awareness over the muscles so that they can be systematically relaxed.[22] This is usually accomplished by concentrating on muscles in specific areas of the body, such as the feet, hands, face, or neck, and letting them relax. It is sometimes easier to learn what a relaxed muscle feels like if you first tense it and then release it. When you release the tensed muscles in various parts of your body, you can enhance your feelings of relaxation by thinking relaxing thoughts, such as lying in the sun or floating on a cloud. Deep, slow breaths also aid in self-relaxation.

When the self-relaxation technique has been mastered it can be applied to shyness and social anxiety by means of imagery and in real life. If you place yourself in a relaxed state and then begin thinking about social interactions that make you anxious, you will feel yourself becoming tense. If you counter this tenseness with self-relaxation, you will slowly be able to imagine yourself in more anxiety-provoking situations while retaining a feeling of relaxation. The use of imagery to promote self-relaxation is based on the procedure of *systematic desensitization* developed by Joseph Wolpe.[23] His method is to teach people to think about increasingly anxiety-provoking events while maintaining a state of relaxation. In real life the idea is to use the first signs of anxiety as a cue to tell yourself to relax.[24] It is sometimes helpful to get out of the situation long enough to go through the relaxation exercise and regain your composure. If this is not possible you will have to use your self-relaxation techniques on the spot. This might sound difficult, but if you stop what you are doing right now and take a few deep breaths you will already feel yourself beginning to relax.

Another strategy for coping with anxiety, which can be used in conjunction with self-relaxation, is *adaptive relabeling*.[25] Shy people have a tendency to label their reactions in the following way:

Whenever I'm around people I get tense and anxious.

Shy people then go on to tell themselves:

My tension and anxiety prove that I am a shy person.
Because I am a shy person, I'm bound to feel tense and anxious around other people.

This kind of circular reasoning places shy people in a bind that could be broken if they learned to label their anxiety in an adaptive manner. For example, it would be more adaptive to say:

I get keyed up around strangers because they present a challenge for me to practice my social skills. Being keyed up is sometimes uncomfortable, but it is also a sign that I am doing what I want to do.

The value of positive relabeling was demonstrated in a psychological experiment in which shy people were convinced that their feelings of arousal around a stranger were caused by a loud noise that had been introduced into the experimental set-ting.[26] These people were more successful and comfortable interacting with the stranger than were a second group of shy people, who followed their usual pattern of labeling their arousal in the presence of a stranger as a symptom of shyness. Shy people in this experiment relabeled (or misattributed) their arousal as caused by the noise because they were influenced by the experimenter to do so. It is also possible to use relabeling intentionally and to treat arousal in social situations as a sign of excitement about meeting people, a feeling of challenge, and a chance for practic-ing social skills.

IMPROVING RATIONAL THINKING

Albert Ellis places a good deal of emphasis in his rational-emotive psychotherapy on the relationship between thoughts and emotions. He argues that people often talk themselves into beliefs that are irrational and that cause them to be unneces-sarily unhappy. Do you suffer at times by holding some of these unrealistic expectations?

1. *Everyone must like me.*

2. *I must be perfect.*

3. *It's awful if things don't always go my way.*

4. *I should dwell on the bad things that happen to me.*

5. *Events in my life are beyond my control.*

Consider the thoughts going through the mind of a man who wants to ask a woman for a date. Chances are that he is anxious about it. That's understandable. But he will make things a lot worse for himself if he thinks irrationally and tells himself:

> *I really like her and it would be great to ask her for a date. But if she says no, that would be terrible! I would feel crushed. Since it is such a risk, I feel all upset and nervous and I don't think I can get up the courage to call her.*

Ellis's goal would be to teach the man to talk to himself in a more rational manner.[27] It is likely that the man would have more success (or would at least feel better about himself) if he could say:

> *I really like her and it would be great to ask her for a date. If she says no, that would be unfortunate, but I don't have anything to lose. I feel good about it because if I take a chance and she says yes it will be great. If she doesn't go out with me I won't be any worse off than I am now.*

Because thoughts and self-statements have such an important influence on goals, actions, and reactions to success and failure, it stands to reason that people can

Table 1-1   Adaptive Self-Statements for Approaching Strangers*

Preparing for the challenge

My goal is to become less shy. It will take time. I don't have unrealistic expectations.

I can look at my nervousness as excitement about the challenge.

I know how to relax myself when I get anxious.

No self-defeating thoughts. Think rationally.

Keeping cool during the interaction

Don't think about fear. Just focus on the conversation.

One step at a time. I can handle it.

My nervousness is a perfectly natural response to this challenge.

Relax; I'm in control.

I'm doing fine.

Reinforcing yourself

I did it!

I survived it and that is a success.

It's getting easier each time.

I make more out of my fears than it is worth.

*Adapted with permission from D. Meichenbaum, *Cognitive-Behavior Modification* (New York: Plenum, 1977), p. 155.

benefit by their constructive use. Donald Meichenbaum used Ellis's ideas to develop a therapeutic approach in which people are taught to use self-statements as coping skills.[28] A person who is anxious about approaching strangers might practice the thoughts suggested in Table 1-1. These self-statements can be practiced by imagining the experiences associated with approaching strangers, and they can also be used in real life. It is useful to come up with your own self-statements and to concentrate on the ones that work best for you.

Expanding Your Social Networks

Earlier in the chapter a description was given of arranged marriages as examples of external influences on selection of marriage partners. Even though you are probably not from a culture that practices arranged marriages, numerous external factors determine your access to dating and marriage partners. Research has shown that people usually restrict themselves to marriage partners with similar backgrounds and values. For example, in the United States whites marry other whites 99.8 percent of the time; and blacks marry blacks 99 percent of the time; marriage partners belong to the same religion 93.6 percent of the time.[29] A study of dating couples found that couples who agreed closely on personal values had the highest probability of progressing toward a permanent relationship. Another study found that college students were significantly more attracted toward dates who had similar rather than dissimilar attitudes on issues such as belief in God, birth control, drinking, women's liberation, and preferred entertainment.[30]

Choice of dating and marriage partners is also often limited by the boundaries of social networks. A study conducted in 1931 found that one out of three married couples lived within five city blocks of each other at the time of their marriage application. Although there is much more mobility now than there was at the time of this study, it is still true that people can only date people whom they are able to meet. We generally make acquaintances within our social network of friends, coworkers, or fellow students. This fact has led Alan Kerckhoff to describe personnel directors and college admissions officers as "informal marriage brokers" because they control access to settings in which potential dating and marriage partners are likely to be found.[31] However, it is possible to expand our social marketplace beyond the limits of our social networks to wherever we happen to be at a given time. The challenge for those who want to meet people they pass in everyday life is making social contact. How do you express your desire to meet someone who interests you? How can you tell if that person is interested in you?

Expressing Social Interest without Words

Two behaviors commonly used for communicating social interest are smiling and eye contact. As you will read in Chapter 6, the smile is a universal sign of positive feelings. The function of eye contact in expressing social interest was demonstrated in a research study in which interactions were recorded between unacquainted men and women in a waiting room.[32] When one person entered the waiting room and found a second person already seated, there was an 84 percent chance that they would look at each other. Seventy-eight percent of the people exchanged a verbal greeting. About half of the people looked at each other a second time before the entering person sat down. Interestingly enough, the willingness to exchange a second look was the best predictor of whether the two people would enter into a conversation. It appeared that people used willingness for eye contact to judge the other person's interest in them. Another interesting finding in the study was that men initiated conversations two-and-a-half times more often than women.

People also communicate social interest by placing themselves in each other's proximity. For example, two people at a party, in a museum, or in a bar may "find" themselves standing next to each other. A person working in a store, restaurant, or bank may experience an increase in business from a particular admirer.

Beginning a Conversation

Although people differ in their needs for expressed social interest, they are all faced with the fact that if they want to meet somebody they eventually have to speak. The question to be answered for those wishing to expand their network of

Table 1-2   Most Preferred Opening Lines for Men Meeting Women*

General situations	Type of approach[†]
Hi.	Innocuous
I feel a little embarrassed about this, but I'd like to meet you.	Direct
That's a very pretty (sweater, dress, etc.) you have on.	Direct
You have really nice (hair, eyes, etc.)	Direct
Bars	
Do you want to dance?	Innocuous
What do you think of the band?	Innocuous
Can I have a drink with you?	Innocuous
Can I buy you a drink?	Innocuous
Restaurants	
I haven't been here before. What's good on the menu?	Innocuous
Would you like to have a drink after dinner?	Direct
Can I buy you lunch?	Direct
Since we're both eating alone, would you like to join me?	Direct

acquaintances is, "What do I say when I run across someone I would like to meet?" It is necessary to come up with some kind of opening line. Because opening lines serve such an important function in first meetings, I conducted a series of studies with Frederick Meeker and Richard Staneski to learn how people feel about their use.[33] We studied opening lines used by men for meeting women as well as opening lines used by women for meeting men.

OPENING LINES FOR MEN MEETING WOMEN

We asked more than 500 men and women to list all of the opening lines they

Table 1-2   (continued)

Supermarkets	
Can I help you to the car with those bags?	Direct
Excuse me. Which steak looks better to you?	Direct
Can you help me decide here? I'm a terrible shopper.	Direct
You're buying some interesting things. You must be a gourmet.	Direct
Laundromats	
Would you like to go have a beer or cup of coffee while we're waiting?	Direct
Could you show me how to work this machine?	Innocuous
It's nice to see a person so neat with her clothes. I wish I were that way.	Direct
Would you watch my clothes for a minute?	Innocuous
Beaches	
Want to play frisbee?	Innocuous/direct
Can I bring you anything from the store?	Direct
The water is beautiful today, isn't it?	Innocuous
That's a nice bathing suit.	Direct

*From C. L. Kleinke, F. B. Meeker, and R. A. Staneski, "Opening Lines," unpublished manuscript, 1985.

†Determined by statistical procedure of factor analysis.

Table 1-3 Least Preferred Opening Lines for Men Meeting Women*

General situations	Type of approach†
Is that really your hair?	Cute-flippant
You remind me of a woman I used to date.	Cute-flippant
Your place or mine?	Cute-flippant
Isn't it cold? Let's make some body heat.	Cute-flippant
Bars	
(Looking at woman's jewelry) Wow, it looks like you just robbed Woolworth's.	Cute-flippant
Bet I can outdrink you.	Cute-flippant
I play the field and I think I just hit a home run with you.	Cute-flippant
You're probably wondering what a nice guy like me is doing in a place like this.	Cute-flippant
Restaurants	
Do you think I deserve a break today?	Cute-flippant
I bet the cherry jubilee isn't as sweet as you are.	Cute-flippant
If this food doesn't kill us, the bill will.	Cute-flippant
I just had to come over and see what that was you are eating.	Cute-flippant

could think of that men might use for meeting women. They listed about 250 opening lines for general situations as well as for specific situations such as bars, restaurants, supermarkets, laundromats, and beaches. These lines were then evaluated by more than 1000 men and women between seventeen and thirty-seven years of age. The scale ranged from one (terrible) to seven (excellent).

Preferred Lines. A statistical analysis of the ratings showed that the opening lines fell under one of three different approaches: *cute-flippant*, *direct*, and *innocuous*. As shown in Table 1-2, the most preferred opening lines were those using either a direct approach or an innocuous approach. Table 1-3 shows that the least preferred opening lines were those that were cute-flippant.

Differences between Men and Women. There were some important differences between ratings of opening lines by men and women, which have implications about the kinds of opening lines men should use. Although both sexes agreed that cute-

Table 1–3   (continued)

Supermarkets	
Do you really eat that junk?	Cute-flippant
You shouldn't buy that. It's full of cholesterol.	Cute-flippant
Is your bread fresh?	Cute-flippant
Would you like to trade shopping lists?	Cute-flippant
Laundromats	
A man shouldn't have to wash his own clothes.	Cute-flippant
Those are some nice undies you have there.	Cute-flippant
I'll wash your clothes if you wash mine.	Cute-flippant
I wash my clothes once a month whether they need it or not.	Cute-flippant
Beaches	
Did you notice me throwing that football? Good arm, huh?	Cute-flippant
Let me see your strap marks.	Cute-flippant
Want to stroke with me?	Cute-flippant
You have the most beautiful tan body I've ever seen. Rather than drool all over you let's quench my thirst over a drink at the bar.	Cute-flippant

*From C. L. Kleinke, F. B. Meeker, and R. A. Staneski, "Opening Lines," unpublished manuscript, 1985.

†Determined by statistical procedure of factor analysis.

flippant opening lines were not desirable, men underestimated how much women dislike them. Men also underestimated how much women *like* opening lines that are innocuous. As you might expect, men and women agreed that opening lines using a direct approach are good.

Advice for Men. The results of our study suggest that men are best advised to approach women modestly, to avoid coming on too strong. If women dislike cute-flippant opening lines, why do men persist in using them? One reason is that men's magazines often publish stories about men who see a gorgeous woman, approach her with a cute-flippant opening line, and shortly thereafter ride off into the sunset with her. Men sometimes forget that such stories belong to the realm of fantasy more than to real life. Another reason is that cute-flippant opening lines protect the men from rejection. Because men are often reluctant to admit that they are lonely and in need of companionship, it is easier for them to deny their loneliness by being cute-flippant. Unfortunately, while cute-flippant opening lines may help to protect a man's ego, they are likely to lose the woman. Our recommendation is that innocuous opening lines also offer protection from rejection because they are subtle and do not require the man to "confess" his desire for companionship. Furthermore, they provide the woman an opportunity to reciprocate her interest without being turned off or threatened.

It is true that we found a very small number of women who rated cute-flippant opening lines as "very good" or "excellent." Such women apparently reinforce the magazine myth that men in general can be successful with the "macho" approach. Unfortunately, we have no way of identifying these women. Cute-flippant opening lines are all right for men who are gamblers, but for consistency we recommend the direct or the innocuous approach.

OPENING LINES FOR WOMEN MEETING MEN

To set some groundwork for our study of women's opening lines, we asked 100 men and 100 women which of the following statements matched their beliefs the most:

1. *When trying to meet somebody new, men should approach women, but women should not approach men.*

2. *When trying to meet somebody new, women should approach men, but men should not approach women.*

3. *When trying to meet somebody new, either men or women can approach each other.*

More than 90 percent of the men and women surveyed chose statement 3. Because our respondents (who were university students and employees) felt that men and women are both responsible for initiating social contacts, we extended our study to opening lines used by women. We asked 200 men and women to list all of the opening lines they could think of that women might use for meeting men in a variety of contexts. The fifty-nine most often listed were placed on the same rating scale used in our study of men's opening lines. The opening lines were evaluated by more than 800 men and women between seventeen and forty years of age.

Preferred Lines. A statistical analysis of the ratings showed that the opening lines fell under the same three approaches that men's lines did: cute-flippant, direct, and innocuous. As shown in Table 1–4, the most preferred opening lines were those using either a direct approach or an innocuous approach. Table 1–5 shows that the least preferred opening lines were those that were cute-flippant.

Table 1-4   Most Preferred Opening Lines for Women Meeting Men★

General situations	Type of approach[†]
Since we're both sitting alone, would you care to join me?	Direct
Hi.	Innocuous
I'm having trouble getting my car started. Will you give me a hand?	Innocuous
I don't have anybody to introduce me, but I'd really like to get to know you.	Direct
Can you give me directions to ————?	Innocuous

★From C. L. Kleinke, F. B. Meeker, and R. A. Staneski, "Opening Lines," unpublished manuscript, 1985.

[†]Determined by statistical procedure of factor analysis.

Table 1-5   Least Preferred Opening Lines for Women Meeting Men★

General situations	Type of approach[†]
Didn't we meet in a previous life?	Cute-flippant
It's been a long time since I had a boyfriend.	Cute-flippant
Hey baby, you've got a gorgeous chassis. Mind if I look under the hood?	Cute-flippant
I'm easy. Are you?	Cute-flippant
What's your sign?	Cute-flippant

★From C. L. Kleinke, F. B. Meeker, and R. A. Staneski, "Opening Lines," unpublished manuscript, 1985.

[†]Determined by statistical procedure of factor analysis.

Differences between Men and Women. There were some important differences between ratings of opening lines by men and women, which have implications about the kinds of opening lines women should use. Women underestimated how much men like direct opening lines and overestimated how much they like innocuous lines. Neither men nor women preferred cute-flippant opening lines, but men disliked them less than women.

Advice for Women. Our results suggest that women can afford to use direct opening lines for meeting men. Although men don't necessarily dislike innocuous opening lines, they seem to prefer lines that are clearer in their message. This is probably because men are not used to being approached by women and may not catch on that a woman who uses an innocuous opening line really wants to meet them. We advise women, as we advised men, to use cute-flippant opening lines only if they like to gamble.

Talking as a Sign of Social Interest

When meeting someone for the first time it is not unusual to look for signs of liking and attraction. You read earlier that smiling, eye contact, and physical proximity are used to express social interest. Another way people communicate attraction is by their willingness to carry on a conversation. If you say to a stranger, "Hi, nice day isn't it?" and the stranger says nothing or grunts, you can assume he or she is not enthusiastic about getting to know you. If the stranger responds and goes on to make a new statement, you will probably feel that he or she is willing to make your acquaintance.

Margi Lenga Kahn, Tracy Beach Tully, and I carried out a series of studies to learn whether social perceptions are influenced by how much people talk in a social interaction.[34] We made up tape recordings of conversations between men and women and systematically varied the amount of time each person spoke. In some of the tapes the man talked 80 percent of the time, the woman 20 percent of the time. In other tapes the woman talked 80 percent and the man 20 percent. In a third group of tapes the man and woman each talked 50 percent of the time. Tone of voice, speaking style, and content of the conversations were controlled by using the same men and women for all three levels of talking and by electronically filtering the tapes so that the exact words spoken were unintelligible. Research participants were instructed that they would listen to a taped conversation between a man and woman who had just met and that after hearing the conversation they would rate one of the two speakers on a rating form. The rating form included scales for evaluating how much the speaker was liked and how domineering and outgoing he or she appeared to be. Participants were told that although the tape recordings had been electronically filtered to make the words unintelligible, they could get a reasonable impression of the speakers from their tone and style of expression. We did not tell research participants of our interest in whether their ratings would be influenced by the amount of talking by each speaker.

EVALUATION OF THE SPEAKERS

We conducted the experiment with three different groups of people and obtained the same results each time. Two of our findings were especially interesting. First, people talking 50 percent of the time were liked more than people who talked 20 percent or 80 percent of the time. Second, the 20 percent talkers were evaluated as being exceptionally submissive and introverted. This relatively unfavorable rating was surprising and suggested that people in first meetings are expected to hold up their end of the conversation. It seems that a good listener is not necessarily a person who is quiet but rather one who responds and adds to the other's statements.

We thought that men who talked 80 percent of the time might not be evaluated as unfavorably as women doing so because men are stereotyped as being more domineering than women, and a high amount of talking by men might be expected and taken for granted. This was not so. Both male and female research participants used the same standards in evaluating talking by men and by women.

GEARING TALKING TO THE SITUATION

On the basis of experimental research it seems that if you want to be chosen as a group leader you should talk as much or more than others in your group. If you want to be evaluated favorably as a counselor, you should talk less than your client.[35] If you are meeting strangers, preferably you should talk about half the time. A number of suggestions will be given in Chapter 10 about how to choose conversation topics when you want to make a good impression. At this point the best advice is that when meeting a stranger it is not always important what you say as long as you say something.

Thinking of Things to Say

People who view themselves as being quiet typically complain, "When I meet somebody new, I can't think of anything to say." An alternative assessment is that quiet people have as many ideas and thoughts as anyone else but think of them as "uninteresting," "inappropriate," or "dumb." If you verbalized all of your thoughts, ideas, and associations, you would be talking most of the time. People who can talk a lot have learned not to censor their thoughts so much before they speak. They have also learned to reduce their expectations for "meaningful" conversations and to be satisfied with small talk. We are not born to be good conversationalists. We must learn this skill through practice. Here are some ideas for practicing your talking skills.[36]

USE THE TELEPHONE

The telephone offers an excellent opportunity for practicing conversations. Call the public library and ask the reference librarian for some information you would like to have. Call a theater and ask for show times. See if you can make the person on the telephone laugh. Call a radio talk show. Express an opinion and notice the announcer's reaction.

SAY "HELLO"

Say "Hi" or "Good morning" to people you see at work or school. Smile and say "Hi" to people you pass on the street. Notice their reaction. If they don't respond, that's OK. It's still fun to see that you can do it.

GIVE COMPLIMENTS

Compliment someone standing in line in a bank or grocery store. Maybe the person is wearing some unusual clothing or jewelry. Ask where it came from.

ASK QUESTIONS

Ask questions about a person's dog, running shoes, bicycle, or portable radio. Be open to learning new things. People love to talk about their activities and hobbies. Ask questions that require explanations rather than simple yes or no answers.

SHARE A COMMON EXPERIENCE

Look for something you can share with a person you want to meet, perhaps something unusual about the weather or the experience of standing in a long line or being in a crowd. Maybe something is going on where you both are that you can talk about.

READ, ASK, AND TELL

Read the newspaper, read movie and book reviews, learn about the world political situation and the events in your community. Ask people for their opinions on these issues and share your knowledge with them.

APPRECIATE THE VALUE OF SMALL TALK

Small talk allows strangers to spend time together in a relatively nonthreatening situation. In this way they can communicate their interest in each other. The fact that you are talking and not what you are talking about is important in first meetings. Don't worry if your comments are not brilliant. Make them anyway and keep the conversation going. You'll have plenty of time for "deep and meaningful" talks later.

Environmental Competence

Environmental competence can be defined as the ability to use your environment constructively to achieve particular outcomes or goals.[37] One traditional environmental strategy is to run out of gas on Lovers' Lane. Another is to induce someone you have invited to your house to sit with you on the sofa instead of on a nearby chair. To achieve this you might pile some articles on the chair in the hope that your friend will choose the sofa instead of removing the articles. A second tactic would be for you to sit in the chair, let your friend sit on the sofa, and then later shift yourself to the sofa. To be more direct, you could ask your friend to join you on the sofa. Or, if these tactics seem risky, you could plan ahead and remove the chair from the room.

If you spot someone you would like to meet at a party, concert, or play, your best bet is to take a seat next to that person so you can strike up a conversation. It is a particular challenge when a person who interests you is seated and there are no nearby vacant chairs. With some patience, courage, and creativity you have to maneuver yourself into his or her vicinity. Or you can wait for your chance to approach the person at a later time. If the person is also interested in meeting you, he or she may have the environmental competency to move to a spot that is more accessible.

If you go to a party or bar with friends, it is well to remember that you are much less approachable if you are sitting together talking than if you are sitting quietly by yourself. If you really want to meet people you should spend some time sitting alone. For women, sitting alone is usually sufficient (although there is no law against women starting conversations with men). Men have to be more assertive, but they are also less approachable and less likely to initiate contacts if they stick too closely with their friends.

Negotiating Sexual Relations

One issue that people must negotiate when they are learning to know each other is their willingness to have sexual relations. A study of unmarried college students found that men were most often in the role of initiating such relations while women were most commonly in the role of avoiding them. Once they decided whether they wanted to initiate or avoid sexual relations, men and women used similar strategies.[38] Men said that they were most likely to use seduction as a preliminary. Other strategies included asking the woman, holding hands and touching, and creating a romantic atmosphere. Women also reported using seduction but were more likely than men to use body language, such as sitting close, caressing, and kissing. Men and women reported that they avoided sexual encounters by discussing their relationship, saying they weren't ready because they didn't know each other well enough. They also avoided sex by suggesting activities that were not conducive to a romantic atmosphere. Women, but not men, reported that they used coercive measures, such as leaving the room or asking the man to leave. Because the negotiation of sex is so interwined with people's perceptions of each other's motives, it will be useful for you to read this section again after reading about the attribution theories discussed in Chapter 8.

Learning to Tolerate Rejection

The more you interact with others, the more likely it is that you will be ignored or rejected. By the same token, you will be increasing your chances of having fun and meeting some special people. The lesson here is that your chances of meeting other people will be greatly enhanced if you can teach yourself to tolerate rejection. This is not an impossible task, and many of the coping skills described earlier in the chapter will be useful.

RATIONAL THINKING

What are some of the worst things you can tell yourself about being rejected?

> *If I'm rejected it's just awful.*
>
> *Everyone should love me.*
>
> *If I am rejected it means I am unattractive, unlikable, and no good.*

Weigh these unadaptive thoughts against the following more adaptive self-statements.

> *Even if I'm rejected I can be proud for trying.*
>
> *The more I can tolerate rejection, the more people I can meet.*
>
> *Some people will like me and some people won't like me, but I feel I am accomplishing something when I get out there and try.*

How rational are the following expectations?

> *I can't be happy when I meet a new person unless we both fall in love.*
>
> *If every conversation I attempt doesn't lead to a lasting relationship, it is a failure.*

Can you substitute the following more realistic expectations?

> *If I just say "Hi" to someone, I am achieving a goal.*
>
> *I have to play the odds. The more people I talk to, the more people I will meet.*
>
> *Some conversations go further than others. I must be patient and find satisfaction in making the attempt.*

SELF-RELAXATION

Sit down in a quiet, relaxing place, close your eyes, and imagine that you approach someone you would like to meet and are rejected. What does it feel like? Relax yourself, using the self-relaxation techniques described earlier. Start with mild thoughts of rejection and counteract them with self-relaxation techniques. Work your way up slowly until you can imagine harder rejections while still remaining relaxed. Learn how to relax yourself when you are out trying to meet people. Keep in touch with your feelings of self-doubt and anxiety and use them as cues to put your self-relaxation skills to work.

REWARD YOURSELF

When you succeed in saying "Hi" to somebody, give yourself a pat on the back. Tell yourself you did a good job. You will have rejections. That's part of life and it has nothing to do with your self-worth. Take pride in yourself for making the effort.

BE EASY ON YOURSELF

Go easy on self-punishment. A few setbacks aren't going to add up to much if you keep trying. You are getting to know yourself better. Keep your expectations reasonable so you succeed more often than you fail. Your purpose is not to torture yourself with unrealistic goals. Be reasonable with yourself. Interact with others and have some fun.

Four Tips for Social Interaction

A good way to end this chapter is by considering four tips for better social interaction suggested by research: (1) make a plan, (2) be responsive, (3) look your best, (4) savor your successes.

MAKE A PLAN

One important difference between college students who date a lot and those who don't is that the latter tend to lack confidence about their ability to make a good impression. Lack of confidence can lead to self-doubt and anxiety about seeking new acquaintances. Research suggests that people who don't socialize very much may be hampered as much by their fear of initiating an interaction as they are by any shortcomings in social skills.[39] The solution to this problem is to build up one's self-efficacy. One group of researchers who trained people with various social skills found that the specific plan people followed was not as important as the fact that they had a plan in the first place.[40] A plan or strategy for positive social interactions gives you a feeling of direction and confidence and an opportunity to practice adaptive self-statements.

BE RESPONSIVE

Some college men were introduced to an attractive woman, with whom they chatted for about five minutes.[41] She made an effort to show interest, make eye contact, and hold up her end of the conversation. Another group of men met the same woman but did not have an opportunity to receive her interest and attention. Since the woman was attractive, all of the men liked her. The men who had five minutes of her personal attention, however, were attracted to her more. In fact, five minutes of "positive strokes" were enough to outweigh any disagreements between the men and the woman on personal opinions and attitudes.

College women who were introduced to college men expressed greater liking for men who were physically attractive and who communicated personal attention by saying things such as, "What did you do this week?"; "Sounds like you had a good time."; "Oh, that must have been hard for you!" Women were not attracted toward men who talked a lot about themselves. Men who received training and practice in being attentive were liked more by women than were men who did not have this training and practice. Researchers reported that responsive behaviors such as conversing, smiling, and making eye contact are viewed as positive skills in social interactions as well as in job interviews. People who are attentive and responsive encourage intimacy and closeness from others.[42]

There are two good reasons why we prefer and feel closer to people who are responsive.[43] First of all, responsiveness communicates personal interest and positive feelings. Responsive people are willing to show that they like us, and it's nice to be liked. Second, responsive people give us a feeling of certainty and confidence. We can count on responsive people to listen to us and to respond to what we are saying. They "validate" our existence because they interact with us harmoniously rather than unpredictably. This is probably why people who don't hold up their end of a conversation are not liked as well as people who do. People who are too quiet during initial encounters are unpredictable. We don't know what they are thinking. It is also easy to understand why we prefer people who pay attention to what we are saying. We feel left out when people go off on tangents and talk only about themselves. What does it take to be responsive? Here are some suggestions.[44]

1. Motivation. Be interested enough in the other person to spend time together and put energy into your interaction.

2. Attentiveness. Pay attention to what the other person is saying. What are the issues, feelings, and problems to which he or she desires a response?

3. Empathy. After attending to what the other person is saying, try to understand how he or she is feeling. If you are not sure, ask.

4. Skill. If you have carefully listened to what the other person said and how he or she feels about it, you will be more skillful in making a meaningful

response. You can enhance your responsiveness by using appropriate nonverbal behaviors (smiling, eye contact, body orientation, physical closeness), which will be described in the following chapters.

LOOK YOUR BEST

Research emphasizes that when working to perfect our social skills we should not neglect our appearance.[45] Because physical appearance has an important impact on first impressions it will be discussed more fully in Chapters 3 and 4. For now, your best bet is to dress attractively, or, as my friend Tom Orloff advises, "Put on your Sunday go-to-meeting clothes."

SAVOR YOUR SUCCESSES

A program was set up to help men gain self-confidence and overcome their fears and anxieties in social situations.[46] After the men went through their training they were introduced to a woman for a short conversation. Although the men didn't know it, the woman made a special effort to be cordial and responsive. How did these men compare with men who received the training but did not chat with the woman? All of the men had gained the same knowledge, but men in the first group had seen themselves as engaging in a positive social interaction. The opportunity to experience social success had a significant effect on increasing their self-confidence and reducing their social anxiety. In real life we experience satisfactory and unsatisfactory social interactions. We can reap the benefits of this study, however, by savoring our successes and using the skills suggested earlier for coping with rejections.

Now that you are ready to go out and interact with people, you will experience a growing interest and fascination with first impressions. You will want to learn how first impressions are formed and how they can be enhanced. The following chapters will discuss the results of research studies focusing on first impressions including both nonverbal behaviors (such as facial expressions, tone of voice, eye contact, body language, and use of personal space) and verbal behaviors (such as giving compliments, expressing opinions, and disclosing feelings). The effects of appearance, dress, and physical attractiveness will also be discussed. The information gained will have increased meaning as you experience social interactions throughout your life.

How Moods Affect Liking Other People

Most people would agree that their own moods can color their liking for other people. If you are hot and tired or have a headache, you are a lot less likely to see someone's positive side than if you are comfortable and feeling well and happy. Although you can appreciate how your moods affect your reactions toward others, you may be surprised to learn how pervasive the influence of moods can be. You may also find it interesting to learn how your moods are affected by sources as diverse as the weather, the news, and your own thoughts. Finally, there is the curious experience that occurs when an experience of negative events does not lead to disliking others but actually brings people closer together. Psychologists have conducted research on these questions, which you will read about in this chapter.

The Sunshine Samaritan

If you have ever felt irritable and grouchy on a hot and humid day or withdrawn and noncommunicative on a freezing cold one, you understand from personal experience how the weather can sway your moods. People's shared feelings in different kinds of climate are expressed in sayings such as "winter blues," "spring fever," and "long hot summer."

Psychologist Michael Cunningham satisfied some of his curiosity about the interaction between weather and moods by conducting a scientific investigation of how the climate can affect people's generosity and helpfulness.[1] Researchers asked pedestrians in a city to respond to questions for a survey. In the winter, people were willing to answer more questions when it was sunny, not too windy, and not too cold. In the summer, they answered more questions when it was sunny, mild, and breezy; they didn't want to be bothered if it was cloudy or hot. In another study, researchers went to a moderately expensive restaurant to find out when customers tipped the most. The restaurant had windows to let in the sun and the temperature was controlled. With the amount of the bill and size of party taken into account, it turned out that customers gave larger tips on sunny days. Outside temperature did not affect the size of tips because of the restaurant's controlled climate.

The positive effects of sunshine on generosity can be linked to pleasant associations with the sun—for example, swimming, picnics, and outings. People also feel good on a sunny day because everything looks bright and clear. Some people have suggested that the reputed friendliness of Californians is due to their sunny weather. The next time you wake up on a sunny morning, you might think of Walt Whitman's eulogy, "Give me the splendid sun with all his beams full-dazzling!"

The Warm Glow of a Happy Experience

Positive reactions toward others can be brought about by pleasurable experiences such as success or kindness.

THE GLOW OF SUCCESS

It is a common experience to feel good when you are successful at something. But have you ever noticed how this "glow of success" warms your attitudes toward others? The positive effects of success were demonstrated in a series of research studies in which some people worked on problem-solving tasks and had a chance to experience success. Other people learned how the problem-solving tasks worked but did not have an opportunity to master them and experience success. After their experiences, research participants were confronted by a person (who was part of the experiment) in need of a favor. In one instance the person was collecting for a charity. In another, the person was carrying a stack of books and needed help opening a door. In a third instance, the person carrying an armload of books "accidently" dropped one and needed help picking it up. The group who gave more help was the one who experienced success. Studies with children found similar results.[2] For people of all ages, a successful experience increases one's willingness to help.

One interesting discovery coming from research on success is that successful experiences will often increase our good will toward people who are not necessarily responsible for providing the success. Albert and Bernice Lott explained this phenomenon by describing how positive feelings are associated with, or generalized to, others who are present. A number of studies have shown that children as well as adults feel liking and attraction for people who are with them when they win a prize or reward,[3] even though the people made no direct contribution to the positive outcome.

The warm glow of success is commonly experienced by sports fans who feel friendly and happy toward one another when their team wins. There seems to be some truth to the saying, "Nothing succeeds like success."

COOKIES AND KINDNESS

Positive reactions can be brought about by other favorable experiences besides success. Consider a study in which researchers tended telephone booths so that half of the people using them would find a dime in the coin return slot and the remaining half would not.[4] Immediately after leaving the telephone booths, callers were confronted by an experimenter who "accidently" dropped a manila folder full of papers in their path. Eighty-seven percent of the people who had just found a dime helped the experimenter pick up the papers. Only 4 percent of the people who had not found a dime helped.

Researchers in a second study went to a university library and distributed cookies to a random group of students.[5] Other students in the library did not receive cookies and were not aware that the cookies were being distributed. A short time later, a person who appeared to be unrelated to the researchers approached the students and asked for help with a school project. Students who had received the cookies were more willing than other students to volunteer for a project requiring them to be friendly and helpful. The favorable experience of receiving cookies apparently increased their willingness to volunteer for a task that was consistent with their positive feelings.

The preceding studies show how people's willingness to give favors can be cultivated by an unexpected pleasure as small as finding a dime or receiving a cookie. The fact that the pleasures were unexpected may have a lot to do with their effect. It is also instructive to note that the researchers needing the favors were not suspected as ingratiators because they were not the ones providing the pleasure.

HOW LONG DOES THE WARM GLOW LAST?

Another interesting question about the relation of moods and being helpful is how long the positive effects of a pleasant experience will last. This question was explored in a study where researchers went from door to door in a suburban neighborhood, giving out free samples of stationery.[6] A second group of residents in the same neighborhood did not receive the free samples. Even though the writing paper was not expensive, it was believed that the residents would feel pleased about being given a gift. At various time intervals after the researcher delivered the stationery a second researcher called the residents on the telephone, saying that she was calling from a pay phone and had dialed an incorrect number. After explaining that she had used her last dime, she asked each resident to do the favor of looking up the correct number and making a call to deliver a message for her. Only 10 percent of the residents who did not receive the gift were willing to assist with this request. In contrast, more than 80 percent of the residents who did receive the stationery, within the first five minutes of receipt, agreed to deliver the message. Helping decreased to 50 percent when the call came ten to fifteen minutes after the gift was delivered and dropped to 10 percent if the call was delayed twenty minutes.

So, we see that an unexpected pleasure will enhance the likelihood of our doing someone a favor only for the brief duration of its resulting warm glow.

Movies and the News

After reading about how moods can be changed by the weather and experiences of success and kindness, you won't be surprised to find how moods are influenced by movies and the news. A good example of the effect of movies comes from a study in which some participants watched a happy film, *Good Old Corn,* and others saw a sad film, *John F. Kennedy, 1917–1963.*[7] After viewing their respective films, participants were asked to give their impressions of someone they didn't know. Those who had viewed the happy film gave significantly more favorable evaluations than those who had viewed the unhappy film. It appeared that the moods generated by the films carried over to the participants' feelings toward the stranger.

Another series of studies conducted by Harvey Hornstein and his colleagues shows how feelings toward others can be altered as a result of hearing good and bad news.[8] College students who had signed up to take part in a study of decision making were seated alone in a room to wait until the experimenter was ready for them. While waiting they could hear music coming from a radio. After a few minutes there was a fake news report, designed to be part of the experiment. An announcer reported one of the following two news stories in a trained, professional voice. Half of the students heard a positive news story:

> *A middle-aged man will be saved thanks to a person he has never met. The man, who suffers from a fatal kidney disease, had only a short while to live without an emergency kidney transplant. WWBG had broadcast pleas for help. Late last night a respected clergyman came to the hospital and offered to help. The donor has refused the family's offer to pay his hospital costs. Even in this day and age, some people hear a call for help.*

The remaining students heard a negative news story:

> *A seventy-two-year-old sculptress, beloved by neighborhood children for her statues of Winnie-the-Pooh, was strangled in her apartment last night by what appears to be a self-styled executioner. The murderer, who has been identified as a respected clergyman, was a long-time neighbor of the victim. He had the keys to the apartment because he occasionally baby-sat for the victim's grandchildren and was in the habit of bringing up her mail and packages.*

After the news story the radio continued playing music until it was turned off by the experimenter, who then asked each student a series of questions about his or her views of human nature. Because the students believed the news reports were real, they were influenced to feel quite differently toward humanity. Students who had heard the good news story were more likely than those who heard the bad news to believe that people live clean and decent lives, are basically honest, and try to apply the Golden Rule. Other students who had heard one of the above news stories were given the opportunity to play a game with a stranger in which there was a chance to make money. The students were told that they and the stranger could either compete and try to beat each other or cooperate and share whatever they earned by working together. Students who had heard the good news story expressed more trust and willingness to cooperate than students who had heard the bad news story.

If you paid attention to your feelings as you read the news stories used in these studies, you probably found that they made a similar impression on you.

Whistling a Happy Tune

As the song suggests, if you whistle a happy tune you can often place yourself in a brighter mood. On the other hand, if you persist in thinking unpleasant thoughts, you are likely to end up in a negative mood. The truth of this argument was demonstrated in an experiment in which people were asked to read a series of statements and to experience the feelings in the statements.[9] Some people were given statements that would promote positive feelings, such as, "I'm full of energy," and "I feel great!" Others read statements that would promote negative feelings, such as, "All of the unhappiness of my past life is taking possession of me," and "I want to go to sleep and never wake up." Later, everyone was asked to do a favor for someone who was unrelated to the experiment. People who had placed themselves in a positive mood were more willing to do the favor than people who had placed themselves in a negative mood.

Applying Your Knowledge

Whether or not you have anticipated the results of psychological research on moods and liking from your personal experiences, there are times when you can benefit from reminding yourself about how this knowledge can be applied. For example, if you wished to gain someone's romantic interest, you would want to create an intimate and comfortable atmosphere around a pleasurable activity. You would most likely not choose a noisy and dusty construction site. If you were anxious to close an important business agreement, you would certainly avoid irritating your potential partner at the moment he or she is ready to sign. Although these examples are obvious, you might ask yourself whether you have ever created unpleasant feelings with someone whose approval you really wanted. Research studies on moods and liking reinforce the rule that you will have more success in winning someone's favor if you create a positive and pleasant mood during your interactions. Although unpleasantness and nagging might achieve what you want in the short run, they are not likely to foster feelings of affection and cooperation in the long run.

When people are advised about the value of creating positive moods in others they often ask the following questions.

WHAT ABOUT SHARING UNPLEASANT FEELINGS?

If your goal is to create a pleasant mood with people you value, what should you do with your negative feelings and experiences? Share them. Research on self-disclosure (see Chapter 9) supports your personal experience that it can be boring to be with people who are "always content" or who "never have problems." In order to be close to others you have to open up and share what's inside of you. But remember that those who are *always* complaining and are *consistently* unpleasant can become a drag. Research has shown that chronically depressed people create negative feelings in others and as a consequence they are often rejected.[10] So, if you are feeling depressed, irritable, or angry—share it. But make an effort to counterbalance this negative effect by saying or doing something positive. In other words, be genuine when things are tough, but use your energy and creativity to make things better.

WHAT ABOUT COMPLIMENTS AND FAVORS?

The use of compliments and favors for attracting people has received so much attention from psychologists that it will be discussed more fully in Chapter 10. The question most people ask is, How do we know when a compliment or favor is sincere? When someone's compliment or favor is perceived as insincere, we generally call that person ingratiating. That is why the researchers investigating the effects of "cookies and kindness" arranged that the person who needed the favor was different from the person providing the kindness. It would be suspicious for someone to give cookies and then turn around to ask a favor. The effects of ingratiation present two interesting challenges. The first challenge is to learn how to create a positive atmosphere without relying on compliments and favors. This chapter should provide some useful hints. The second challenge is learning to give compliments and favors judiciously. Advice about how to do this will be found in Chapter 10.

Attraction Resulting from Negative Events

Every year news stories describe how people join together in the face of a flood, fire, earthquake, or other catastrophe. Even though the victims of these disasters had a lot to feel unpleasant about, they were able to put their negative feelings aside and work together in a spirit of closeness and friendship. You might have had a similar kind of experience if you ever felt drawn to someone while sharing a ride on a roller coaster or sitting through a scary movie. The process through which a strong emotional experience can produce feelings of attraction and liking was explained by Stanley Schachter.[11] He proposed that an emotional experience results in a heightened state of physiological arousal for which we are motivated to seek some sort of explanation. Depending on the circumstances and on the motives and actions of others who are present, we may label our feelings as fear, anger, love, or any other emotion that seems appropriate. Schachter believes that the labels we give our arousal have as much to do with our emotional experiences as with the arousal itself. His theory has interesting implications for the study of interpersonal attraction because it implies that emotionally arousing experiences (if appropriately labeled) can result in feelings of attraction, liking, and love.

An Arousal Theory of Love

Ellen Berscheid and Elaine Walster used Schachter's theory to gain a better understanding of romantic attraction and love.[12] These psychologists agree with the conclusion reached so far in this chapter that moods often have a direct affect on people's reactions toward others. They also recognize occasions where interpersonal attraction is heightened as a result of stress, excitement, or arousal. For example, Berscheid and Walster give the example of a man in a national news story who kidnapped a woman friend after she broke off their relationship. Although some people might label the man's emotions in the face of this event as anger or jealousy, he chose to label them as love saying, "The fact that she rejected me only made me want to love her more." Berscheid and Walster adapted Schachter's theory to explain how rejection or other kinds of mistreatment by someone (which ordinarily decrease our liking for that person) can actually cause our attraction toward that person to grow. According to Berscheid and Walster, if we experience heightened physiological arousal in the presence of another person (either as result of something that person does or from external causes), we will follow our natural inclination to label this arousal as representing some kind of feeling or emotion. If the circumstances are right (for example, the person is appealing or the situation is romantic), we are likely to label our arousal as positive attraction or love.

Berscheid and Walster's theory will interest you if you have ever experienced these kinds of romantic feelings. You may also be curious to learn how psychologists have tested the theory in their experimental studies. In order to set up an experimental study of Berscheid and Walster's theory, you first have to find a way to arouse people physiologically. Second, you have to arrange the situation so that they will label this arousal as love. This may sound difficult, but there are enough romantically inclined people in the world that it can be done.

MANIPULATING "AROUSAL" WITH FALSE FEEDBACK

A simple laboratory demonstration of how we label experiences of arousal was conducted by Stuart Valins.[13] He hooked up college men to a machine that would supposedly amplify their heartbeats and then asked them to rate their attraction toward a number of women in *Playboy* photographs. Although the men believed the heartbeats they heard were their own, the "heartbeats" were actually prerecorded to give the impression that some of the women caused them to change while other women did not. The false feedback was believable because the amplifier appeared genuine and the false heartbeats sounded real. As Berscheid and Walster would predict, higher ratings of attraction were given to women who presumably had caused the men's heartbeats to change.

Beliefs about arousal can also work the opposite way if the arousal is given a negative interpretation. Nancy Walsh, Lynn Meister, and I conducted a study in which college women were each interviewed by a college man, who gave the women either a favorable or unfavorable evaluation.[14] Before the interview began the women were attached with electrodes to an instrument that records heart rates. At the end of the interview, half of the women were randomly told that their heart rates were higher than average as a result of their interaction with the man. The remaining women were told that their heart rates were average. Not surprisingly, the women had greater liking for a man who evaluated them favorably rather than unfavorably. In addition, women who received unfavorable evaluations *and* supposedly reacted with increased heart rates were the least willing to meet with the same man for a second interview. It appeared that they interpreted their "arousal" in the face of an unfavorable evaluation as a particularly negative experience. Because the majority of the favorably evaluated women were willing to return for a second interview, the heart-rate feedback they received did not have a noticeable effect.

Studies using false arousal feedback are theoretically important because they show how labeling of "arousal" can be demonstrated in a laboratory setting. However, the technology of false feedback has limited practical application because it is not easy to use in everyday life.[15] For applied purposes, it is necessary to look at psychological studies in which people's experiences of arousal were real.

THE BRIDGE OVER THE CAPILANO RIVER

There is a suspension bridge over the Capilano River in British Columbia that is constructed of wooden boards attached to wire cables. Crossing this bridge is likely to be physiologically arousing because it has a tendency to wobble and sway, and its low handrails permit a clear view of the 230-foot drop to the rapids below. Most of us would label the arousal we felt on a bridge like this as fear or excitement. However, what if we were on the bridge and met an attractive person?

In a study, unaccompanied men aged eighteen to thirty-five were approached by an attractive woman as they stood on this bridge.[16] The woman explained that she was doing a project for a psychology class and asked the men if they would participate by giving their free associations to a series of pictures. The responses of these "aroused" men were compared with the responses of similar men who were asked the same question after they had already crossed the bridge and had some time to relax. After responding to the pictures, all the men were given a telephone number to call if they wanted to learn the results of the study. Which men gave the most sexual associations to the pictures? You can probably guess that the men on the suspension bridge, who were influenced by the presence of an attractive woman, labeled their arousal as sexual attraction. These men were also more likely to call to "find out about the study."

This study provides a good example of what has been defined by psychologists as *misattribution*.[17] Although the men on the suspension bridge were actually aroused by the height and shakiness of the bridge, they presumably labeled, or misattributed, at least some of this arousal as a response to the attractive woman. This might be what happens when we are with someone special on a roller coaster or at a scary movie. In these situations we label the arousal we experience not as fear but rather as romantic attraction or love.

USING MISATTRIBUTION TO INFLUENCE LABELS FOR AROUSAL

One way psychologists have attempted to influence labels for arousal is to threaten men with electric shock while they are in the presence of an attractive woman. The goal in these studies was to induce the men to view (misattribute) their arousal from the shock as a positive reaction to the woman. One group of experimenters accomplished this task. Male research participants expressed increased interest in an attractive woman when they were told that as part of an experiment they would be given an uncomfortable electric shock. Other researchers had less luck convincing men to label their fear of electric shock as romantic attraction.[18] This result is not surprising because when a cause of arousal is very obvious (like an electric shock) we are not so likely to misattribute it to something (or someone) else.

Another team of psychologists increased the physiological arousal of male research participants in a more subtle way by having them run in place for two minutes as part of a study of attitudes toward physical activity.[19] These aroused men expressed more liking for an attractive woman they expected to meet than did less aroused men who only ran in place for fifteen seconds. A second study by these psychologists was similar to research described earlier in this chapter about movies and news stories. College men listened to tape recordings that were designed to be arousing or neutral. The arousing recordings were a story about a grisly killing or a lively comedy. The neutral recording was a description of the circulatory system of a frog taken from a biology text. You might correctly predict that men who heard the comedy recording expressed greater liking for an attractive woman they expected to meet than did men who heard the neutral recording. It might surprise you to learn, however, that men who heard the grisly recording also liked the woman more than did men who heard the neutral recording. (They did not like the woman quite as much as the men who heard the comedy recording.) The experimenters concluded that when the men in their studies were aroused (from running or listening to grisly or comedy recordings) and anticipated meeting an attractive woman, they lost sight of the true source of their arousal and labeled it as a positive reaction to the woman.

It is instructive to point out that aroused men in these studies did not express liking for the woman when she had intentionally dressed and made herself up to appear unattractive. This finding supports Berscheid and Walster's argument that physiological arousal *plus* the appropriate cues for romantic labeling must be present in order to demonstrate an arousal theory of love. Another thing to notice is that all of the research studies on misattribution were conducted with research participants who were men. It would be interesting to know if women also label certain experiences of arousal as romantic attraction. Or are women more objective than men about experiencing romance and love?

How Romantic Are You?

Are you the kind of person who falls in love easily or are you more inclined to hold back and take your time? Psychologists have studied people's propensities for falling in love. One study found that people who are not defensive and who are willing to admit personal shortcomings are more likely to experience romantic love than people who are defensive. This is understandable because falling in love is a risk. Another study found that people who see themselves as having a large amount of control over their fate (internals) are less likely to experience romantic love than people who perceive their fate as influenced by the world around them (externals).[20] This is probably because romantic love is commonly seen as something mysterious that "happens to us" or "engulfs us" rather than as an emotion we "choose to experience."

Cultures have a strong influence on the way people label their feelings of romantic love.[21] Some cultures place a strong value on the experience of love and on the relationship between romantic love and marriage. Other cultures are more pragmatic and base marriage on financial, family, and religious considerations.

It is useful to consider the fact that we can influence the way people label their feelings toward us. Berscheid and Walster give the example of insecure people who habitually complain, "You don't love me, you just think you do; if you loved me, you wouldn't treat me this way."[22] Such people, who then go on to itemize evidence for this conclusion, are helping their partners to label these actions as reflecting indifference or negative feelings. In contrast, people with tact and self-confidence can help their partners label the same actions as a reflection of positive feelings ("I know you had a hard week and weren't always friendly, but you still did something nice for me").

Playing Hard-to-Get

Most people are familiar with the age-old strategy of playing hard-to-get as a way to make someone want you or value you more. It occurred to Elaine Walster that playing hard-to-get might be analyzed in terms of the way people label their feelings when they are rejected. Walster and her colleagues tested the effectiveness of the hard-to-get strategy in the following series of experiments.[23] College men who were participating in a computer dating program were given the name and telephone number of a woman who randomly played easy-to-get or hard-to-get. When the men called the woman in her easy-to-get mood, she immediately accepted their invitation. In her hard-to-get mood she made it more difficult for the men by sounding disinterested and unenthusiastic, but after some hesitation, she also accepted the date. When the men were asked to evaluate their liking for the easy-to-get and hard-to-get woman, there was no difference. In this situation, playing hard-to-get had no effect on attraction.

For a second test of playing hard-to-get, the researchers enlisted the assistance of a prostitute. For half of her clients the prostitute played hard-to-get and said, "Just because I see you this time it doesn't mean that you can have my phone number or see me again. I'm going to start school soon, so I won't have much time, so I'll only be able to see the people that I like the best." She did not communicate this message to her other clients. Results of this experiment showed that playing hard-to-get was not successful in increasing the clients' attraction toward the prostitute. When the prostitute played hard-to-get, her clients were no more likely to call her back, offer her more money, or say they liked her than when she played easy-to-get.

These two failures to show that playing hard-to-get can be a successful strategy prompted Walster and her coworkers to refine their approach. After interviewing a number of men it became clear that although women may appear less desirable when they are easy-to-get, they may also appear too threatening and distant when they are hard-to-get. To test out this possibility, a third study was conducted in which college men were placed in a situation in which they were given the choice of dating one of three women. To control for physical appearance, the men did not actually meet the women but were given the following information about how the women supposedly felt. The first woman was easy-to-get. She made it clear that she was willing to date any of the men. The second woman appeared hard-to-get. She stated that she was not enthusiastic about dating any man in the group. The third woman said that she was interested in dating the man in question but was not interested in dating any of the other men in the study. The third woman who was selectively hard-to-get was overwhelmingly preferred. The men felt the easy-to-get woman was friendly and warm but also unselective and possibly unpopular and overdependent. The hard-to-get woman was seen as a challenge but also as someone who might be picky and hard to get along with. The selectively hard-to-get woman appeared to the men as friendly and warm and also as popular and selective. The men thought she would be easy to get along with, and they liked her because she had chosen them as a date.

The results of research on playing hard-to-get can be analyzed in the following way.[24] First, people prefer someone who likes others over someone who is critical of others. This fact explains why men did not like the woman who was hard-to-get and was not interested in dating any of them. Second, men (and probably women) who are chosen by a selectively hard-to-get person are likely to experience a boost to their self-esteem. While there are circumstances where playing hard-to-get may be a useful strategy, it is usually preferable to take a positive approach and help others feel good in your presence.

Some Conclusions about Arousal and Attraction

Berscheid and Walster's application of Schachter's theory to love and attraction helps to explain how we can experience romantic love and attraction in situations that would ordinarily be negative. Psychologists have demonstrated Berscheid and Walster's theory in research experiments in which people were physiologically aroused (or led to believe they were) and provided with cues (usually the presence of an attractive person) influencing them to label their arousal as positive attraction. Human experience also shows how "arousing" experiences can result in feelings of romance and love. In summing up Berscheid and Walster's theory of romantic attraction, it is important to point out that the occasions under which negative events result in attraction are uncommon. First of all, we are usually conscious of what is arousing us and therefore not likely to misattribute this arousal to love or attraction. Second, in order for arousal to be labeled as love, a "suitable candidate" must be available. Third, unexplained experiences of arousal are generally uncomfortable, and it requires a unique situation to turn feelings of discomfort into attraction and love.[25]

Affiliation and Altruism

Another way to understand why people are drawn together in the face of negative events is in terms of the human need for affiliation. Research studies have shown that people prefer to share negative experiences rather than face them alone. (One exception is when the negative experience is embarrassing.) It is also known that the presence of supportive people during stress can have a calming effect. Therefore, even though negative moods usually stimulate disliking, there are times when the sharing of unpleasant experiences with others can result in positive feelings of relief and support.[26]

Negative moods can also result in kindness from people who have learned to make themselves feel better by helping others. Altruistic responses to negative moods develop as children grow up and are socialized to "fight the blues" by doing something nice for others.[27]

The research results discussed in this chapter can be summarized as follows. First, it is a safe bet that positive moods enhance feelings of cooperation and liking. Good moods help us get in touch with happy experiences. They inspire us to see the positive side of things and to respond to others around us in a favorable way.[28] Therefore, you can't go wrong by creating a pleasant atmosphere in your interactions with others. The only exception might be if as a result of your efforts you came across as ungenuine and ingratiating. More will be said about ingratiation in Chapter 10. When it comes to negative moods the picture is more complex. In most situations, negative moods are likely to result in decreased feelings of liking and attraction. Negative experiences can result in liking, however, if they satisfy the conditions for appropriate labeling of arousal or if they occur within a context of mutual support and sharing. In any event, it is a risky undertaking to create a negative mood for the purpose of getting someone to like you. As a general rule, it is advisable to "accentuate the positive." If you are venturesome, however, and have a special person in mind, you might opt for roller coaster rides, wobbly foot bridges, or scary movies.

Physical Attractiveness:
BIASES AND STEREOTYPES

Although American psychology dates from the turn of the century, physical attractiveness has only recently come under scientific scrutiny. This delay was certainly not due to psychologists' ignorance of the importance attached to beauty in American society. Hollywood and Madison Avenue have been around for a long time. Elliott Aronson explained that psychologists were reluctant to study beauty and attractiveness because it seemed undemocratic to uncover prejudices that favored physically attractive people. Gardner Lindzey pointed out that psychologists have often preferred an environmentalist approach to a genetic approach because the former is more optimistic about possibilities for change.[1] Psychologists may have shyed away from the study of physical attractiveness because it is a trait we are born with rather than an attitude or behavior that is learned. Psychologists have now overcome this barrier to the study of physical attractiveness and have compiled a wealth of data that can increase our understanding of our bias and help us cope with it in a constructive manner.

This chapter will discuss the effects of physical attractiveness on personal relationships. You will read about the pervasive influence of physical attractiveness on the way people are treated and evaluated. You will discover that the bias toward physical attractiveness applies to children as well as adults. This knowledge will enable you to reconsider your prejudices and help you rise above the bias toward beauty in American society.

Physical Attractiveness and Dating

There is considerable disparity between what people say about physical attractiveness and what they do.

WHAT PEOPLE SAY

When men and women are asked what qualities they desire in a dating partner, they tend to underestimate the importance of physical attractiveness. A survey was conducted of people's stated preferences in dating partners during three time periods: 1939, 1956, 1967. Personality characteristics such as dependability, emotional stability, and pleasing disposition were consistently rated as highly important. Physical appearance was never ranked higher than eleventh in importance, and it was sometimes ranked as low as eighteenth. College students in another dating study stated that personality and character were more important than good looks. However, their ratings of how much they like their dates correlated most highly with their date's physical attractiveness. The fact that people downplay the importance of physical appearance when questioned about dating preferences led one group of researchers to conclude that people are either not fully aware of or not fully honest about the value they place on physical attractiveness in their choice of dating partners.[2]

WHAT PEOPLE DO

In actuality, people place high importance on physical attractiveness in their choice of dating partners. Elaine Walster and her colleagues conducted one of the first dating studies at the University of Minnesota.[3] A computer dance was arranged in which men and women who purchased a $1.00 ticket were provided with a blind date. The idea of a computer dance during the school's "welcome week" was very popular and attracted 752 students. When the students arrived to purchase their tickets, they were given a series of intelligence and personality tests and were secretly rated by four judges on their physical attractiveness. Although the participants thought they would be matched with their dates according to the personality tests, they were actually matched randomly, except that the woman was never taller than the man. On the night of the dance, students arrived with their dates and danced or talked until an intermission. At that time they evaluated their dates on a rating form. The results of this study are easy to report. Men and women expressed greatest liking for dates who had been rated by the judges as physically attractive. They expressed least liking for dates who were unattractive. In contrast to the importance of physical attractiveness, students' ratings of their dates were not at all related to the intelligence and personality tests.

A number of other investigators conducted similar dating studies in universities throughout the United States and arrived at the same conclusion.[4] College men and women express greatest liking for physically attractive dates.

DO PEOPLE MATCH UP?

One question of interest among researchers on dating has been whether people choose dates of physical attractiveness comparable to their own. Results from several studies allow us to reach the following conclusions.[5] People will select attractive dates if they are guaranteed that the attractive person is willing to go out with them. When people are asked to choose dates with no guarantee of accept-ance, they tend to be less selective. Attractive people choose attractive dates. Less attractive people choose less attractive dates.

Why do people match up in physical attractiveness with their dating partners? In Chapter 1 it was suggested that dating choices take place within a marketplace. If we view physical attractiveness in terms of costs and benefits, physically attract-ive people have greater value and therefore can set higher expectations for physical attractiveness in a date. Another factor affecting people's sense of value is their self-esteem. We all experience good days when we feel worthy of all relationships and bad days when we feel undesirable to almost everyone. The effect of self-esteem on dating choice was demonstrated in two studies in which college men took an intelligence test and were led to believe that their performance was either excellent or poor.[6] After this experience the men were given a break in a student lounge, where they met a woman who wore makeup and clothing that was sometimes appealing and attractive and sometimes unappealing and unattractive. How did the men react? From what you learned in Chapter 2, you can accurately predict that men whose self-esteem was raised by their positive performance on the test showed more romantic interest in the woman (making small talk, offering to buy her coffee, asking for her telephone number) when she presented an attractive appear-ance. In contrast, the men with lowered self-esteem showed more romantic interest in the woman when she looked unattractive.

In general, attractive people have more dates than unattractive people have.[7] What about exceptionally attractive people? Does their outstanding appearance scare others away? Who invites such people? Is it those who are also handsome? Or is it those who have "guts" or who don't care or realize that their average attractiveness violates the rules of equity in the dating marketplace? At this point we don't have research to answer these questions. By the time you finish this chapter, however, you should have some interesting hunches.

Physical Attractiveness and Marriage

How important is physical attractiveness in choice of marriage partners? On the one hand, it can be argued that physical attractiveness has less influence on mar-riage than on dating because so many other factors must be weighed before one decides whom to marry. When asked for their opinions, college students stated that physical attractiveness played a greater role in dating than in marriage.[8] On the other hand, physical attractiveness can be viewed as more important in marriage because marriage involves greater feelings of permanence and commitment. One way to explore the importance of physical attractiveness in marriage is to test whether married partners match each other in appearance. Consider these research findings. Men and women who are engaged or going steady are more similar in physical attractiveness than would be expected by chance. Those who are married or in serious relationships are more similar in physical attractiveness than those in casual relationships. Dating men and women are more likely to stay together and express love for each other if they are similar rather than dissimilar in physical attractiveness.[9]

Another interesting finding is that men are better adjusted in their marriages when they view their wives as physically attractive and when their wives view them as physically attractive. The correspondence between physical attractiveness and men's marital adjustment can be related to the pressures placed on men by Hollywood movies and men's magazines to have a good-looking wife. Men who adopt these values may feel relieved and gratified when they find an attractive woman to marry. Attractive men also report more satisfaction with romantic relationships.[10] This may be because attractive men get more attention or because they can command more attractive partners. Thus it is easy to conclude that physical attractiveness is a valuable commodity in the marriage marketplace.

Physical Attractiveness and Friendship

After reading about how people match up in physical attractiveness in dating and marriage, you might wonder if physical attractiveness also influences choices of friends. Evidence indicates it does. A study comparing physical attractiveness of friends of the same sex determined that men and women were more comparable in physical attractiveness to their close friends than would be expected by chance.[11] The matching of physical attractiveness among close friends is probably due to the fact that people with similar physical attractiveness share common social skills, self-perceptions, and reactions from others.

The Pervasive Bias Toward Physical Attractiveness

Novels, plays, and fairy tales have expounded the virtues of beauty throughout human history. Heros and heroines are almost always handsome and pretty. When they are not, they vindicate themselves by winning an attractive romantic partner. Throughout our lives the media relentlessly communicate to us: "What is beautiful is good." The research studies summarized in the following section demonstrate how this message has rubbed off.

BEAUTY AS GOOD PERSONALITY

The "what is beautiful is good" stereotype was illustrated in a number of studies in which people gave their first impressions of men and women in photographs. The results were clear. Physically attractive men and women were rated more favorably than less attractive men and women on traits such as being likable, amiable, competent, exciting, appealing, confident, humorous, flexible; possessing appropriate sex-roles; and having favorable attitudes. Similar results have come from studies in which people evaluated women who wore clothing and makeup to appear attractive or unattractive as well as women who were naturally high or low in attractiveness.[12] Physically attractive women were perceived as more popular, likable, calm, warm, friendly, and attentive.

GOOD AS BEAUTIFUL

Research studies have been quite clear in showing how people's physical attractiveness can influence evaluations of their personalities. There is also evidence that people's admirable characteristics can affect ratings of their physical attractiveness. The "what is good is beautiful" stereotype was tested by asking people to evaluate a woman after reading a description of her personality.[13] Various personality descriptions were intentionally written to make the woman appear as a desirable person, an average person, or an undesirable person. Along with the description there was a photograph of the woman, which made her appear high, average, or low in physical attractiveness. The authors of this experiment were not trying to influence ratings of the woman by manipulating the attractiveness of the photograph. They wanted to see if the written description would influence ratings of her attractiveness. Results of this experiment supported the "what is good is beautiful" stereotype in the following way. Ratings of the woman's physical attractiveness depended on her natural attractiveness, but they were also influenced by the descriptions of her personality. More-desirable personality descriptions resulted in higher ratings of physical attractiveness. The authors concluded that people who are troubled by the unfairness of the "beautiful is good" stereotype can take some consolation in the fact that "good is also beautiful."

More recent research found that the "good is beautiful" stereotype held up for evaluations of women but not those of men.[14] It is possible that personality descriptions have less influence on ratings of a man's physical attractiveness because positive characteristics of men are not linked to their appearance as much as are positive characteristics of women.

BEAUTY AS TALENT

Let's face it. Handsome people have an advantage on the job market. Male and female employment consultants from sixty private and public businesses were offered a fee for assessing the performance potential of a job applicant.[15] Each consultant was provided with the applicant's résumé folder, which included a personal history, a summary of academic grades and test scores, letters of recommendation, a personal statement by the job applicant, and a photograph. The consultants did not know it, but the folders were identical in all respects except for the applicant's sex and physical attractiveness. The consultants displayed a strong tendency to recommend male applicants for masculine jobs and female applicants for feminine jobs. The consultants also evaluated attractive applicants as being more qualified than unattractive applicants for the recommended jobs. In general, the consultants felt that attractive applicants had greater employment potential than unattractive applicants. The consultants did not predict different rates of job success for attractive and unattractive applicants once they were hired.

Three other studies found similar results.[16] Attractive job applicants received more favorable ratings on job qualifications and higher recommended salaries than unattractive applicants. Although bias in favor of attractive applicants is real, it may be overemphasized in studies such as those cited in which attractiveness of applicants was the only factor under consideration. When physical attractiveness is balanced against other job qualifications its effects are not as important.[17] However, the influence that physical attractiveness does have on ratings of job qualifications is probably due to perceptions of the job applicant's competency rather than the simple notion that "it would be nice to have an attractive person around the office." Consider the following studies.

College men were given an essay to judge, which was of either high or low quality. Along with the essay was a photograph implying that it had been written by an attractive or unattractive woman. How did the men judge the essays? Not surprisingly, the high-quality essay was evaluated more favorably than the low-quality essay. In addition, essays identified with an attractive woman were considered significantly better than essays identified with an unattractive woman. In fact, the low-quality essay when written by an attractive woman was judged almost as positively as the high-quality essay when written by an unattractive woman. A similar study found that women as well as men judged an essay better written when it was identified with an attractive woman. Participants in a third study evaluated essays supposedly written by men and women of high, medium, or low physical attractiveness. Essays identified with an unattractive writer were rated lowest in quality, regardless of the writer's sex. Essays identified with a highly attractive writer of the opposite sex were rated highest in quality. Essays identified with a writer of the same sex were evaluated more favorably when the writer's physical attractiveness was medium rather than high. This was probably because judges found it easier to identify with (or not be jealous of) a same-sex person of medium rather than high attractiveness.[18]

BEAUTY AS RADIATING

It is apparent that attractive people are often valued as having more admirable traits than unattractive people. The bias in favor of good looks can also be contagious.

College students were asked to give their first impressions of a man who was in the company of a woman. For half the students the woman was dressed and made up to be attractive, and for the other half she had made herself unattractive. Students who thought the woman was the man's particular friend had a more favorable impression of him when the woman was attractive. Ratings of the man were not affected by the woman's attractiveness when she was thought to be a stranger. Research has also demonstrated that women are more favorably evaluated when they are identified with an attractive man and that men and women receive more positive ratings when they are seen with attractive friends.[19]

If beauty radiates from friends and dating partners, does it also radiate from spouses? For men, the answer appears to be yes. Men were judged more positively when they were identified with attractive wives. For women, the answer is more complex. An attractive woman with an unattractive husband is not viewed unfavorably, possibly because she comes across as modest and not "hung up on her looks." Also, while unattractive men gain prestige when they have an attractive wife, unattractive women are not given credit for having an attractive husband.[20] This double standard apparently occurs because people assume that an unattractive husband with an attractive wife must have other desirable qualities to compensate for his bad appearance. Since women are valued from traditional (sexist) viewpoints primarily for their beauty, it may appear unequitable for an unattractive woman to be married to an attractive man.

BEAUTY AS INNOCENCE

If you have any familiarity with jury trials you are aware that the jury decision is partly subjective. Defense and prosecuting attorneys attempt to base their cases on objective evidence, but they are also sensitive to the personal feelings and perceptions of the jurors. Most people know that it is worth the extra effort to look neat and dress formally for a day in court. To what extent are jurors biased by a defendant's physical attractiveness? It is difficult to study the effects of physical attractiveness on jury decisions in actual court cases because the nature of the offense being tried and the strength of evidence produced by both sides cannot be equally balanced among attractive and unattractive defendants. Simulated jury decisions are suitably controlled because participants can be given exactly the same case material, which is attached to a photograph of a defendant who is attractive or unattractive.

More than 100 college students were questioned in a survey asking whether or not jurors should be influenced by a defendant's physical attractiveness. Ninety-three percent of the students said no. However, when a similar group of students were asked to read a case about a male or female student accused of cheating, they were less likely to assign guilt and recommend punishment when the defendant was identified in a photograph as being attractive. Participants in another study were asked to take the role of jurors in a trial in which a male plaintiff was suing a male defendant for damages in an automobile accident. Half of the simulating jurors were asked to make decisions about a trial in which the plaintiff was attractive and the defendant was unattractive. For the remaining jurors the plaintiff was unattractive and the defendant was attractive. Simulating jurors ruled in favor of the plaintiff 49 percent of the time when he was attractive and only 17 percent of the time when he was unattractive. In addition, they awarded more money to attractive plaintiffs than to unattractive plaintiffs. Simulating jurors were also more likely to convict a defendant of car theft when the car was locked and belonged to an attractive rather than unattractive woman.[21] The car owner's attractiveness did not make a difference if she had been careless and left the car unlocked.

Although attractive defendants may be given the benefit of the doubt on many charges, it is possible that attractive people will evoke negative reactions if they use their attractiveness to unfair advantage. Research participants were asked to recommend a jail sentence for a woman who had been found guilty of either a burglary or a swindle.[22] A photograph identified the guilty woman as attractive or unattractive. In the burglary case the results were clear. The attractive woman was given an average sentence of 2.80 years while the unattractive one was sentenced to an average 5.20 years. The swindle case was described as an incident in which the woman had ingratiated herself with a man and induced him to invest money in a nonexistent corporation. In this case, the attractive and unattractive women were both sentenced to 5 years. The foregoing results and a similar follow-up study suggest that physical attractiveness in a jury case is often an asset and rarely a liability. Unattractiveness, however, is a liability. Research participants in two studies were less sympathetic to unattractive rape victims, especially when they were "unfeminine" by resisting their assailant and being aggressive.[23] Unattractive women were also suspected more than attractive women of having provoked the attack.

The frame of mind of jurors can also be an important factor in the judgment of attractive and unattractive defendants. In a simulated jury study one group of participants was specifically instructed to be impartial in making their judgments about an attractive or unattractive female defendant.[24] Participants in a second group, who received no instructions, demonstrated the typical bias, recommending a lighter sentence for the attractive defendant. People in the first group, who had committed themselves to avoid bias, actually leaned over backwards and prescribed a more severe sentence for the attractive defendant. They were probably under some pressure to make a good impression. It would take an exceptional judge or attorney to influence a jury to lean over backwards in favor of an unattractive defendant in an actual trial.

BEAUTY AS GOOD POLITICS

You can probably think of many examples in which good looks have enhanced the popularity of a political candidate. A study of the 1972 Canadian federal election found a significant correlation between objective ratings of political candidates' physical attractiveness and their final votes.[25] This study also indicated that unattractive candidates were put forward more often by unpopular political parties. Major political parties tended to stick with attractive candidates.

Another example of beauty and politics comes from a study comparing photographs of women who support the women's liberation movement with photographs of women who oppose it.[26] When the photographs were rated for attractiveness (and the women's views were not identified) no differences were found. In other words, women supporting women's liberation are equal in attractiveness to those opposing it. However, when college students were asked to choose from the photographs those women they *thought* were in support of women's liberation, they tended to choose photographs of unattractive women. This stereotyped relationship between unattractiveness and support of women's liberation was interpreted by the authors of this study as another "put down" of women in American society.

BEAUTY AS MENTAL HEALTH

Research has shown that attractive people are perceived as being better adjusted psychologically than unattractive people. Research participants listened to a taped interview in which a woman discussed various personal problems. Those who saw a photograph implying the woman was unattractive gave more negative ratings on psychological adjustment. The unattractive woman was also seen as having greater need for psychotherapy or psychiatric hospitalization. Participants in a similar study were asked to determine which people in a series of photographs were psychologically disturbed. Significantly more psychological disturbance was attributed to unattractive people. When participants were asked how they arrived at their judgments, they mentioned characteristics of the people in the photographs such as appearing "hostile" or "withdrawn" or as having a "vacant smile" or "distant eyes." None of the participants was aware (or willing to admit) that judgments of psychological disturbance were actually made on the basis of physical attractiveness.[27]

Other studies have shown that unattractive people are more likely than attractive people to be judged as having unfavorable self-concepts, epilepsy, poor chances for improvement in psychotherapy, and mental illness. In addition to being judged as less mentally healthy, unattractive people view themselves as more susceptible to mental illness. Unattractive people evidently receive enough negative feedback from others to question their self-esteem and ability to cope with life stress.[28]

BEAUTY AS THERAPEUTIC

The bias toward physical attractiveness in relation to mental health is not one-sided. Not only is beauty considered healthy, it is also considered therapeutic.

Videotaped interviews were prepared of a male clinical psychologist with a client in a counseling session.[29] The psychologist was actually an actor made up to be physically attractive or unattractive. In the attractive condition the actor was well dressed and his hair was nicely styled with the "dry look." In the unattractive condition he wore unstylish clothing and padding to make him appear overweight, and he was made up with shadows under the eyes, a mole on the side of his nose, and unstyled hair with the "wet look." The words spoken in the counseling sessions were identical. College students who viewed the videotapes rated the attractive counselor as more competent, friendly, trustworthy, intelligent, warm, assertive, and likable than the unattractive counselor. Students also felt that the attractive counselor would be more successful in helping people with problems such as anxiety, conflicts with parents, dating difficulties, feelings of inferiority, and drugs.

The above study was replicated with a female counselor, who was made up to be attractive or unattractive. Women rated the attractive counselor as more competent, professional, relaxed, likable, and interesting than the unattractive counselor. They also viewed the attractive counselor as more capable in helping people with problems including anxiety, shyness, sexual functioning, career choice, and feelings of inferiority. In this study, the attractive female counselor was not favored by men. The authors concluded that men might have felt hesitant to give unfavorable ratings to the unattractive counselor because of strong negative publicity about male chauvinism and because the experimenter conducting the study was a woman. In a similar study conducted at a different university by a male experimenter, men gave more favorable evaluations to a female counselor when she was made up to be attractive rather than unattractive. College students in two other studies listened to tape-recorded counseling sessions and were given a photograph that made the counselor appear attractive or unattractive. Both studies uncovered a bias in favor of the attractive counselor.[30]

What can be concluded from this research on evaluation of counselors? First of all, the importance of physical attractiveness was probably overemphasized in these studies because the experimenters were investigating the counselors' appearance at its extremes. At moderate levels of physical attractiveness it doesn't matter so much whether one counselor is slightly more attractive than another.[31] When bias toward attractiveness of counselors does exist, however, it has important implications. Successful psychotherapy depends on trust and positive regard for one's therapist. If clients place greater value on attractive therapists, they may generalize from this bias to the expectations they hold for a successful therapeutic outcome.

Behaviors toward Attractive and Unattractive People

In addition to evaluating attractive people more favorably than unattractive people, we are also more positive toward attractive people in our actions. Research has demonstrated that people are more likely to give assistance to someone who is attractive and to exert effort to win an attractive person's approval. There is also evidence that people are warmer and more sociable when interacting with attractive people.

GIVING ASSISTANCE

Willingness to help attractive and unattractive people was tested by placing graduate school applications with a stamped envelope in the telephone booths of a large airport.[32] The applications had photographs of men or women who were either attractive or unattractive. An experimenter watched people as they found the "lost" applications and recorded whether or not they took the trouble to mail them. Significantly more help was given to attractive applicants. Why? The authors of the study thought that people were more willing to mail applications for attractive students because attractive students are better liked and viewed as more qualified for graduate school.

Bias toward assisting attractive people was also demonstrated in two studies in which dimes were placed on the shelves of public telephone booths. A female experimenter who was made up to appear either attractive or unattractive approached people who found the dime and said, "Excuse me. I think I might have left a dime in this booth. Did you find it?" More people returned the dime when the experimenter was attractive. People were also more willing to mail a letter for a woman who was made up to be attractive rather than unattractive. Female experimenters in another study approached men and asked for money to pay for a tetanus shot. The experimenters were made up to be attractive or unattractive. Men gave more money to the attractive woman when she appeared to be bleeding and her need for the money was readily apparent. When there was no sign of injury (and the woman's need for money was questionable), men gave little money regardless of her attractiveness.[33]

WINNING APPROVAL

Several studies have shown that people will go to greater lengths to win approval from an attractive person by sharing more self-disclosure, being more open to the person's influence, and working harder on an assignment. In a study in which men and women were asked to describe themselves to a person of the opposite sex, who was made up to be attractive or unattractive, both men and women disclosed more about themselves to the attractive person. In another study, women volunteered to meet a man and engage in conversation. Before their meeting, the women saw a photograph that pictured the man as attractive or unattractive. They also wrote a brief self-description so the man could gain an idea of their interests. Women revealed more personal information about themselves to men who were attractive. In a third study, college men and women said they would prefer to disclose more personal information to a male counselor who was attractive. However, they did not desire to disclose much about themselves to a female counselor who was attractive. The reason for their reluctance was not clear, though it is possible that attractiveness in a female counselor is threatening because it doesn't fit the stereotype of what a counselor should look like.[34]

Evidence that people are more willing to be influenced by the opinions of an attractive communicator comes from a study in which research participants heard a tape recording of a news commentator arguing in favor of lower speed limits. A photograph identified the commentator as attractive or unattractive. It appeared that participants paid the same amount of attention to the person, regardless of his looks, because they were equally aware of the arguments. When asked about their views on speed limits, however, they expressed opinions that were closer to those of the attractive commentator. Other researchers reported that ninth graders were more influenced by the opinions of an attractive adult and that people were more willing to agree with a petition given to them by an attractive man or woman. Recent studies indicate that a communicator's physical attractiveness may have greatest influence on people's opinions when the persuasive message does not involve a great deal of thought. For example, we may be swayed by the physical attractiveness of a politician who is making an emotional appeal or of a television actor delivering a commercial. A communicator's physical attractiveness is less likely to influence us when we are making a careful or thoughtful decision.[35]

Another example of winning an attractive person's approval is seen in a study in which college men were tested for endurance on a hand exerciser. After the first testing session a female experimenter told half of the men that they were doing very well and half that they were doing poorly. The experimenter was dressed and made up to be attractive in some instances and unattractive in others. The men were then given a second testing session. The men who worked hardest were those who had the attractive experimenter and who did not do well the first time. They made the greatest effort to improve their performance so they could win her approval. It appears that men don't care too much whether they receive a positive or negative evaluation from an unattractive woman. On the other hand, positive and negative evaluations have real meaning when they come from an attractive woman. Women also value an attractive man's approval, as indicated by their willingness to cooperate more with an attractive man than with an unattractive man when playing a competitive game.[36]

EXPRESSING WARMTH

College men participated in a study of the "acquaintance process" by engaging in a ten-minute telephone conversation with a woman they had never met.[37] Before the conversation, each man saw a photograph of a woman. The photographs, fakes, were used to imply to some that the woman was attractive, to others that she was unattractive. Each man then talked over the telephone with a woman who knew nothing about the study. Judges who listened to tape recordings of the men's voices rated the men as sounding more sociable, humorous, and warm when they thought the woman was attractive. Judges also rated tape recordings of the women's voices. Ratings of women's voices were especially interesting because they showed that women expressed more confidence, animation, enjoyment, and liking when they talked with a man who believed they were attractive. This study demonstrates that the bias toward physical attractiveness can serve a self-fulfilling function. If we act in a warm and friendly manner toward attractive people, chances are that their responses will be warm and friendly. Such positive behaviors from attractive people then reinforce our perceptions that attractive people are warm and friendly in the first place.

Physical Attractiveness and Perceptions of Children

It is evident that we are socialized to place high values on physical attractiveness, which influence our evaluations and behaviors toward one another. At what age does this socialization begin? Research indicates that children demonstrate preferences for physically attractive peers by the time they are in kindergarten and that adults as well as children show positive bias toward attractive children as they grow up.

CHILDREN'S BIASES TOWARD ONE ANOTHER

Judgments of preschool and kindergarten children toward attractive and unattractive peers have been measured by asking them to evaluate photographs of children they do not know, as well as photographs of their classmates. These studies found that children as young as three express greater liking for children who are physically attractive. Children identify unattractive peers as engaging in undesirable behaviors such as being aggressive and unfriendly and fighting a lot. Favorable bias toward physical attractiveness also exists among adolescents. Adolescent boys in a summer camp judged photographs of black, white, and Puerto Rican boys they had not met. Black adolescents expressed greatest liking for physically attractive peers in the photographs without regard to ethnic background. Puerto Rican adolescents tended to prefer photographs of Puerto Rican peers and therefore did not demonstrate a bias toward physical attractiveness. White adolescents comprised only 10 percent of the camp population and were not tested. A study of white fifth and eleventh graders found greatest liking expressed for attractive peers who were known personally as well as for attractive peers who were not known personally. Adolescents demonstrated the "good is beautiful" principle by giving higher ratings of physical attractiveness to peers who possessed athletic or academic ability.[38]

ADULTS' BIASES TOWARD CHILDREN

Research provides evidence that teachers as well as other adults assume that attractive children are brighter than unattractive children and less responsible for undesirable behaviors. Five hundred and four elementary school principals were asked to provide an evaluation of a fifth grader on the basis of the student's report card and photograph. The principals were not told that the report card of the student was always the same and that the photograph was varied to make the student appear attractive or unattractive. Male and female principals evaluated attractive fifth graders as more intelligent and as having more educational attainment and educational and social potential. Attractive children were also seen as having parents who were more interested in their education. The principals' evaluations were not influenced by the children's sex. A replication of this study found the same results when elementary school principals evaluated report cards of attractive and unattractive first graders. The assumption that attractive children are more intelligent than unattractive children is not limited to principals. Elementary school teachers also gave higher ratings of academic ability and adjustment to their physically attractive pupils.[39]

Earlier in this chapter you read that attractive adults accused of crimes are often viewed as more innocent than unattractive adults. The same bias is present in judgments of children. College women read a description about a seven-year-old boy or girl who had intentionally hit another child in the head with a hard snowball, causing a deep cut.[40] A photograph identified the child for some women as attractive, for others as unattractive. Women assigned more blame for the incident to an unattractive child and assumed that such a child would commit similar undesirable acts in the future. Unattractive children were also rated as being more dishonest and unpleasant.

The relationship between adult punitiveness and children's physical attractiveness was investigated in more detail in a study in which college students had to decide how many pennies should be taken away each time an eight-year-old child made a mistake on a learning task.[41] It was explained that the child would start with 100 pennies and would be able to keep all of the pennies that were not lost in penalties. Because students observed the child through a television screen they were not aware that the child had been dressed and made up to appear attractive or unattractive at different times. Students penalized children between twenty and thirty cents but did not show a strong difference in punishment with regard to the child's attractiveness. Women took more pennies from the unattractive boy and from the attractive girl. Men penalized attractive and unattractive boys and girls equally. This experiment was somewhat artificial because students were required to penalize the child by withdrawing at least one penny for each error, and it is possible that, if given the choice, they wouldn't have penalized the child at all. It is also not clear whether students withdrew pennies because they disliked the child or because they wanted to push him or her to improved performance. The experiment does, however, raise some important questions. It would be interesting to know if attractive children (or adults) are blamed more than unattractive children for poor performance. Attractive people are expected to do well, and their failure may be attributed to lack of effort (see Chapter 12). Since unattractive people are not expected to do as well, their failures may be attributed to lack of ability, and their successes may be attributed to luck.

The amount of blame assigned to misbehaviors of attractive and unattractive children also depends on expectations about their motives. Elementary school teachers placed more blame for pushing a boy down the stairs on unattractive boys than on attractive boys.[42] The teachers also blamed attractive girls more than unattractive girls for pushing a girl down the stairs. Since attractive girls are not expected to engage in this type of misbehavior, they are blamed more when they do so. Attractive people may receive more disapproval than unattractive people when they fail to live up to positive expectations placed upon them in American society.

Does Beauty Ever Fail?

You have now surveyed an abundance of research demonstrating the advantages of physical attractiveness in American society. Is physical attractiveness ever a liability? Studies have shown that while attractive people are evaluated favorably on likability, competence, and success, they are sometimes suspected of being vain, selfish, egotistical, and rude. Very attractive people may become isolated because they arouse feelings of insecurity and jealousy. Attractive people can also be passed over for jobs when their appearance violates stereotypic expectations. For example, a very attractive woman might appear too feminine to be a tough business executive, and a dapper man might not fit the image of a comic, poet, or scientist. On the other hand, attractive people are often given the benefit of the doubt. Several studies found that men were willing to accept attractive women who did not look at them very much during a conversation. They viewed unattractive women, in contrast, as particularly inattentive and rude when their eye contact was very low. Attractive people are also given more acceptance than unattractive people when they withhold self-disclosure. When all the evidence is added up, it must be concluded that the benefits of physical attractiveness outweigh its liabilities.[43]

Differences between Attractive and Unattractive People

So far, this analysis of physical attractiveness has been from the point of view of stereotypes and biases. Are any of the stereotypes associated with physical attractiveness real, or do they exist only in the eye of the beholder? We can expect differences to exist between attractive and unattractive people for a number of reasons. First of all, physical attractiveness is relatively consistent throughout one's life. Attractive and unattractive people therefore have a lifelong experience of oeing perceived and treated in different manners. This difference can't help but influence them in some ways.[44] Nevertheless, since so many factors determine a person's capabilities and personality, it is fair to assume that actual differences between attractive and unattractive people are not as large as stereotypes suggest. In general, we can expect the greatest differences on traits such as social skills and personal influence that are developed through relating with others. Personality style and intelligence are affected less by physical attractiveness and more by a person's family history and individual development.

SOCIAL SKILLS

The stereotype that physically attractive people are more socially adept appears to hold some truth. Social skills of attractive and unattractive college students were tested by having them engage in telephone conversations with students of the opposite sex. After the conversation, students evaluated each other on how they came across. Physically attractive students were rated as being more likable and as having more social skills than unattractive students, even though students never saw each other and were not aware of each other's physical appearance. If attractive people possess more social skills than unattractive people, it is no wonder that they are also less shy.[45]

Other researchers found that physically attractive men have more daily social interactions with women. Attractive men have greater confidence than unattractive men that their overtures toward women will be reinforced. Because attractive men have more practice socializing and receive more positive responses, they develop greater social competence and gain more pleasure from their social interactions. Interestingly, there appears to be little relationship between women's physical attractiveness and their degree of social interaction with men. This finding can be related to the discussion about opening lines in Chapter 1. Women are less likely to initiate interactions with men and more likely to wait until a man approaches them. Because men seek out women of comparable physical attractiveness, the number of relatively attractive and unattractive women approached by men is likely to balance out.[46] As long as women are content to sit back and wait for men to approach them, they don't have to develop assertiveness. Attractive women often find more enjoyment in social interactions than unattractive women do because men try harder to win attractive women's approval. For women who want to initiate interactions with men, attractiveness is an asset. Such women will also find it useful to practice and develop their social skills.

ASSERTIVENESS AND SELF-DISCLOSURE

Because attractive people are used to receiving positive evaluations and reactions from others they are more confident and assertive. The assertiveness of attractive and unattractive women was tested in the following way.[47] An experimenter asked the women to complete a survey. Just before the experimenter was ready to hand them the questionnaire, someone came into the room with an interruption. The experimenter, appearing to be distracted, left the questionnaire on a table. Attractive women took an average of 76 seconds to make an assertive response and take the questionnaire from the table. Unattractive women waited an average of 368 seconds before responding. Women also waited longer to take the questionnaire when the experimenter was a man rather than a woman.

Another group of researchers reported that men who viewed themselves as attractive were more willing than men who felt unattractive to disclose information about themselves to someone they didn't know.[48] In contrast, women who viewed themselves as attractive were less willing than women who felt unattractive to disclose themselves to a stranger. The researchers concluded that less attractive women use verbal communication for facilitating personal interactions. Attractive women are more content to "let their looks speak for them."

INTERPERSONAL INFLUENCE

Earlier in this chapter you read that people are more willing to be influenced by opinions that are expressed by attractive communicators. Are there differences between behaviors of attractive and unattractive people when they are trying to influence others? Fifth and sixth graders who had been judged by their peers as attractive or unattractive were given the task of inducing another child to eat some bitter tasting crackers.[49] A record of the types of arguments and influence strategies used by the children was obtained with a hidden tape recorder. Unattractive boys were very successful in making other boys eat the crackers by behaving in an aggressive, commanding, and threatening manner. They did not have much luck with girls. Attractive boys were not aggressive but instead used such tactics as coaxing, reassuring, and pleading. This approach was successful with girls but did not work well with boys. Attractive girls were more successful than unattractive girls in persuading boys to eat the crackers. Attractive girls used very little coaxing and pleading. Their good looks and "soft sell" approach worked on boys but not on girls. Unattractive girls had more success in inducing girls to eat the crackers by being directive and assertive.

Another study found that physically attractive college students spoke more fluently than unattractive students when delivering a persuasive message.[50] Attractive and unattractive students did not differ on measures of vocal confidence, gaze, or smiling. Physically attractive students rated themselves as being more persuasive, attractive, interesting, and likely to find a good job than unattractive students. In a field setting, attractive students were able to influence opinions of other people more successfully than unattractive students.

One reason why attractive people obtain more cooperation from others might be because they are better at communicating positive feelings.[51] They may be more adept than unattractive people in following the advice given in Chapter 2 about creating a pleasant atmosphere around those whose cooperation is desired.

HAPPINESS AND SELF-CONCEPT

One approach toward studying the relationship between physical attractiveness and happiness is to ask whether good-looking people are happier than people of average or unattractive appearance. Attractive women in one study rated themselves more favorably than less attractive women did on attractiveness, femininity, self-confidence, being a good date, being a likable person, and having an engaging personality. Other researchers found a significant relationship between women's physical attractiveness and their scores on measures of happiness and self-esteem. Because this relationship did not exist for men, the researchers concluded that women may gain more from being physically attractive. A longitudinal study of physical attractiveness was conducted by comparing the attractiveness of men and women when they were college students in the 1930s with their self-ratings of happiness forty years later. Correlations between self-rated happiness of middle-aged men and women and their physical attractiveness in college were very low.[52]

The best conclusion from the above research is that there is a small but meaningful relation between physical attractiveness and positive self-concept. This is due to the fact that attractive people often receive more favorable reactions and treatment. Over the course of our lives, physical attractiveness may become less crucial to happiness and self-esteem because we learn to use social skills for gaining positive strokes from others. Good-looking people may suffer more from aging than average-looking people because they have to learn to compensate for the fact that their attractiveness no longer works for them.

MENTAL HEALTH AND ADJUSTMENT

If physically attractive people have better self-concepts, do they also have better mental health? A study of women patients in a psychiatric hospital found that less attractive patients were less well adjusted, had fewer social skills, and were hospitalized longer than more attractive patients.[53] Less attractive patients also had poorer adjustment before they were hospitalized. One reason attractive and unattractive psychiatric patients differ in adjustment is because of differences in how they are treated. Compared with more attractive patients, less attractive patients have received less positive attention, they are less well liked, and they have fewer visitors.

Because unattractive people have fewer rewarding interactions than attractive people, it can be expected that the former suffer greater levels of stress. This appears to be especially true for unattractive women, who tend to have higher blood pressure than attractive women.[54] Since physical attractiveness is not quite as important for men in American society as it is for women, unattractive men don't appear to suffer increased stress. Their blood pressure is no higher than that of attractive men.

The fact that unattractive people have less satisfactory social relationships than attractive people might explain why unattractive children tend to be aggressive and why juvenile delinquents are often less attractive than their nondelinquent peers.[55]

PERSONALITY TRAITS

On the whole, differences between attractive and unattractive people on personality traits are hard to find. There is some evidence that attractive people have greater feelings of internal control and less anxiety and depression. Physical attractiveness in college men is correlated with personality characteristics of cognitive inquisitiveness, achievement, and individuality. Physical attractiveness in college women is correlated with being less self-protective and having fewer needs for structure and order. Physically attractive children have higher self-esteem and lower social anxiety.[56]

INTELLIGENCE

Because attractive and unattractive people are not always treated in the same ways, as has been shown, it is understandable that they might differ in some of their behaviors, social skills, and personality orientations. There is less reason to predict that attractive and unattractive people will differ in intelligence, and it appears that they do not. Even though attractive children are perceived as more intelligent than unattractive children, there is little relationship between children's attractiveness and their scores on intelligence and achievement tests. There is also little correlation between physical attractiveness and grade point averages of college students.[57]

Current Questions in Research on Physical Attractiveness

During the past ten years the psychological effects of physical attractiveness have gained increased scientific attention. Results from research studies on physical attractiveness have answered some important questions about dating, marriage, and friendship choices; the bias toward physical attractiveness; and differences between more and less attractive people. We know that the bias toward physical attractiveness is pervasive in American society. We are also aware that some people are more biased toward physical attractiveness than others. What makes the difference? People generally agree about who is more or less physically attractive. But how are judgments of whether people are more or less attractive moderated by the perceiver's self-esteem, experience, and expectations? Although attractive people are usually favored over unattractive people, how do we take into consideration their individual needs or motives? These questions are currently being explored. Researchers are also studying specific characteristics that people use in judging another person's attractiveness. In addition, they are collecting data on people's perceptions of their own physical attractiveness. These issues will be discussed in Chapter 4.

WHO ENGAGES IN THE BIAS TOWARD PHYSICAL ATTRACTIVENESS?

In general, it is accurate to say that all of us, in one way or another, share the bias toward physical attractiveness. However, since everyone has different needs, motives, and styles, it is fair to assume that some people are more biased than others. For example, people who hold traditional attitudes toward masculine and feminine sex typing are more prone to favor attractive people than are those who believe in sexual equality. Such a bias is also more common among men and women with a "macho" attitude toward interpersonal relationships.[58]

Looking at attitudes toward physical attractiveness from an historical perspective, we can see that ideas about what looks and styles are considered attractive have changed, but preference for attractiveness has always been present in American society. It remains to be seen whether psychological research on the bias toward physical attractiveness will have any effect on public attitudes.[59] It is also worthwhile to consider the bias toward physical attractiveness from a cross-cultural perspective. As you will read in Chapter 4, people from different cultures have different ways of defining physical attractiveness. Do other cultures also have a bias toward those who are viewed as attractive?

THE EYE OF THE BEHOLDER

We all learn standards for judging physical attractiveness as we grow up, and our agreement with other members of American society about who is and who is not attractive is far greater than chance. Judgments of physical attractiveness are also in the eye of the beholder. Three particularly important factors influencing people's perceptions of physical attractiveness are self-esteem, experience, and expectations. Those with high self-esteem are more willing than those with low self-esteem to acknowledge that people of the opposite sex are physically attractive. The effect of experience was demonstrated in a study showing that people are more stringent in judging their own and other people's physical attractiveness if they have just watched a television show whose primary characters are very good-looking.[60] These results suggest that a preoccupation with appearance can have adverse effects by promoting self-doubts and unrealistic expectations. Most of us would have problems if we demanded to be as attractive (or to be married to someone as attractive) as the paragons of beauty paraded before us by the media. It might be more realistic to accept the dictum that "beggars can't be choosers" and remind ourselves about the research on matching discussed earlier in this chapter.

In equity terms, expectations about physical attractiveness are governed by costs, benefits, and availability in the social marketplace. As an example of costs, people who view themselves as physically attractive are more optimistic than others about their chances of finding romance. As far as availability goes, men and women in a number of Virginia taverns gave each other more favorable ratings on physical attractiveness as the evening hours wore on. The researchers who conducted this study thought that men and women become less picky about physical attractiveness as time wore on and they came to the realization that their social marketplace for the evening has reached its limits. As singer Mickey Gilley pointed out, "Don't the girls [and presumably the boys] all get prettier at closing time?" A replication of this study in Wisconsin bars found that men rated a woman as prettier toward closing time. Women, however, did not view men as more attractive during late hours. Women's ratings of men's attractiveness were determined primarily by their social interest. Women who were open to meeting men viewed the men as more attractive than women who were not interested in making a male acquaintance. A study in Georgia found that men in a country and western bar rated women as more attractive toward closing time, but that men in a college bar did not. In this study, women were not questioned. Because many factors affect the way people rate each other's attractiveness in bars, these studies may not provide the best test for availability and judgments of physical attractiveness. Although men and women might not always seem prettier at closing time, it remains to be seen if people change their standards for physical attractiveness as the "pickings become slimmer."[61]

INTENTIONS AND MOTIVES

Earlier in the chapter you read that physically attractive people may be frowned upon if they come across as conceited about their looks. The question of how our perceptions of attractive and unattractive people are colored by their apparent motives is relevant to discussions in Chapters 8, 9, and 10 about the ways we explain behaviors. These chapters will help you understand how physical attractiveness influences our judgments about reasons for people's actions. For example, do we feel special gratitude when attractive people do nice things for us because we view them as having power and prestige? Men expressed greater liking for an attractive woman when she openly admitted her desire to change their attitudes. Because the woman's attractiveness gave her power, the men appreciated her willingness to disclose her motives. A similar admission did not influence men's evaluations of an unattractive woman. Since she did not have the power of attractiveness as an advantage, it was less relevant for her to disclose her motives. If we perceive attractive people as having power, we may attribute their actions to inner choice rather than to external demands (see Chapter 8). We may desire to ingratiate ourselves more with attractive people (see Chapter 10). We may view an attractive person's successes as coming from ability while viewing an unattractive person's successes as due to luck (see Chapter 12). We may also do extra favors for unattractive people because we feel sorry for them and think they have unhappy lives.[62]

Physical Attractiveness:
SPECIFICS

The research studies summarized in Chapter 3 showed quite clearly that physically attractive and unattractive people are perceived and treated differently in many facets of their lives. These studies measured evaluations of and behaviors toward people who had been classified as high, medium, or low in physical attractiveness. You may have noticed that the term *physical attractiveness* was always used in a general sense and was never specifically defined. The definition of what makes people attractive provides several interesting directions for research. It is important, first of all, to know how closely people agree in their judgments about who is attractive and who is not. Second, it is important to know whether people's perceptions of their own physical attractiveness accurately reflect ratings of their attractiveness by others. A third research challenge is to identify physical traits or characteristics that differentiate attractive and unattractive people.

This chapter will begin with a discussion about consensus and reliability in judgments of physical attractiveness. A summary will then be given of research that measures preferences and perceptions about different aspects of appearance. The chapter will conclude with a survey of research on people's perceptions of their own physical attractiveness and the effects of these perceptions on their lives.

Judging Physical Attractiveness

To determine reliability in judging physical attractiveness, researchers consider both the opinions people have of others and the opinions they have of themselves.

RELIABILITY OF JUDGES

There is no doubt that people have individual preferences in what they see as attractive and unattractive in others. It is very likely that when judging two people of comparable attractiveness some people will prefer person A and others will prefer person B. Several people judging the same person on a scale of physical attractiveness will probably not assign identical ratings. Research studies measuring people's individual preferences for facial features, body builds, and other physical characteristics will be analyzed later in this chapter. Even though people may have individual preferences about specifics of physical attractiveness, it has been determined that they agree fairly well when making overall judgments about who has a high, medium, and low degree of physical attractiveness. A review of research literature indicates that such agreement is generally quite high for both adults and children.[1]

RELIABILITY OF SELF-RATINGS

The correlation between people's ratings of their own physical attractiveness and judgments made about it by others is moderate to low.[2] In other words, self-ratings of physical attractiveness and judgments by others are in the same ball park but not close. Within this ball park, self-ratings may be raised or lowered by one's mood, self-esteem, personal experiences, and motives.

How do people regard their own physical attractiveness in relation to that of others? I asked two hundred college men and women to estimate their physical attractiveness.[3] On one scale, they rated their attractiveness by choosing a number from 0, or least attractive, to 100, or most attractive. The majority of students rated their attractiveness between 50 and 80. Twenty-one percent rated their attractiveness as lower than 50, 12 percent as 50, and 67 percent as greater than 50. On a second scale they filled in the blank in the following sentence: "I am more attractive than ____ percent of other people of my age and sex." The majority of students rated themselves as being more attractive than 50 to 80 percent of others. Thirteen percent rated their attractiveness in the fortieth percentile or lower, 18 percent placed themselves in the fiftieth percentile, and 69 percent felt their attractiveness was in the sixtieth percentile or above. The major conclusion from this study is that college students lean toward giving themselves high rather than low ratings of physical attractiveness. The study also raises several important questions. Are there measurable differences between people who underestimate or overestimate their physical attractiveness? What sorts of situations or demands influence people's ratings of their own attractiveness? What are the consequences of underestimating or overestimating one's physical attractiveness?

STANDARDS OF JUDGMENT

More than sixty years ago, college students were asked to describe fellow students who had been identified as physically attractive or unattractive.[4] The traits most often associated with attractive women were clean hair, clean teeth, care to avoid unpleasant breath, care when coughing, care of eyes, hair in prevalent fashion, aristocratic bearing, and general care of body. Unattractive women were identified by unfeminine shape of chin; ungainly proportions of bust, shoulders, and hips;

unpleasant expressions of eyes and mouth; lack of care of hair; lack of taste and neatness in dress; absence of aristocratic bearing, and poor physical care. Attractive men were described as avoiding unpleasant breath and taking care of their bodies. Unattractive men were judged according to displeasing shape of eyes, ears, mouth, and lips; lack of care of hands and nails; general lack of care of body; and absence of aristocratic bearing.

In the 1970s, young adults ranked the following characteristics as being most important for their own physical attractiveness and for that of a person of the opposite sex: general appearance, face, weight distribution, facial complexion, and body build.[5] They listed as least important neck, hair color, chin, ears, and ankles.

Psychologists have reflected these judgments about what is important in physical attractiveness by focusing much of their research on studies of the face and body. There has also been considerable research on perceptions of clothing and dress and on perceptions of personal details such as beards, eyeglasses, and body odor.

Attractive Faces and Facial Expressions

Faces may be considered from the point of view of their physical attractiveness and from that of the emotions they express.

STANDARDS OF ATTRACTIVENESS

Researchers who have studied facial features related to attractiveness have arrived at the following conclusions. A survey of American and British college students found that men were regarded as attractive when they had a firm jaw and wide chin, large or "strong" mouth, clear eyes, facial hair, and a large or strong face. Facial features seen as attractive in women included large eyes, smooth skin, full mouth, and delicate features such as small nose, chin, and ears. College women in another study regarded dark hair, square face, Roman nose, and tan skin as being important for attractiveness in men.[6] Small noses, full lips, and fair skin were judged important for attractiveness in women.

In another investigation men and women were asked to state their preferences for eye color, hair color, and complexion in a person of the opposite sex. Women tended to dislike light blue eyes, and men tended to dislike black eyes. Men preferred blond hair, and women preferred black hair. Women expressed more dislike than men for very light and freckled skin. Preferences for facial features were studied by asking college students to draw pictures of attractive and unattractive faces. The attractive faces they drew had fine features such as thin mouths and noses and small ears. Unattractive faces had coarse features such as thick lips, large and flat noses, and large ears. The fact that attractiveness is associated with fine facial features explains why faces of young women are generally viewed as more attractive than those of men and older women. Because stereotypically attractive faces are finely molded, they don't stick in our memories as much as faces with "character."[7] This may be why the fashion and entertainment businesses turn over so many good-looking people. We need variety in pretty faces to make up for their typicality.

Obviously conclusions from research studies about attractive features of the face are influenced by the culture and historical period in which the study was conducted. American women of Asian descent, for example, assign more importance than those of European descent to straight dark hair, small noses, and fair skin in judging female attractiveness. In his book *The Human Face,* John Liggett gives a fascinating account of different perceptions of facial beauty in different cultures over various periods of history.[8] Americans and Europeans prefer women with thin lips, while women in various parts of South America and Africa "improve" their beauty by inserting large discs into their lips. Australian aborigines regard sharp European noses as unattractive and deliberately flatten the noses of their babies. Other examples of "beautification" in various cultures include deforming the shape of the skull, distending ear lobes, filing teeth, and scarring or tattooing the face.

JUDGING FACIAL EXPRESSIONS

In evaluating a person's facial expression we may react according to the expression itself or according to our own bias.

Reactions to Smiling. One facial expression that has received much attention in psychological research is smiling. Your experience will testify that smiling is generally viewed as a positive expression. Children laugh and smile more when they interact with friends than with strangers. College students evaluated each other as being warmer and more empathetic and understanding when they occasionally smiled while listening to someone who was giving a personal disclosure. College women estimated that time passed more quickly when they engaged in eye contact with a person who was smiling rather than frowning. Research participants smiled more at another person when they were trying to induce that person to like them. People smile more when playing positive roles than negative ones. College students were more willing to return a smile to a smiling person who wore a campaign button or T-shirt expressing views that were popular rather than unpopular on the college campus. Smiles are used by a listener to enhance a conversation by communicating that he or she is interested in what the speaker is saying.[9]

One good suggestion for brightening the image you project is to smile. Smiling faces seem more attractive. Smiling not only warms the mood of the recipient, it also arouses positive feelings in the person who is smiling.[10] Try it and see.

Although smiles are usually interpreted as a positive expression of warmth, they can also appear to be a sign of insincerity. Videotapes were made in which a newscaster ended a brief news report with a slight smile or no smile or with raised or normal eyebrows. People who viewed these videotapes evaluated the newscaster as appearing slightly more pleased and dominant when he or she smiled. Raised eyebrows had a stronger effect, making the newscaster appear less sincere and more biased. As another example of negative reactions to smiles, research participants gave more electric shocks to a person in a learning experiment if he or she smiled when the shocks were delivered.[11] It is not clear whether the participants assumed that the smiling person did not mind the shocks or whether the participants interpreted the smiles as a gesture of mockery.

In some situations, smiling may serve to communicate submissiveness, nervousness, or appeasement. Unassertive people smile more when interacting with others than assertive people do. The fact that women smile more than men has been used as an example of submissiveness associated with women's traditional role in American society. College students smiled most in an interview while discussing issues that made them feel uncomfortable. Psychiatric patients smiled less in an interview with a psychiatrist than with nonpatient volunteers.[12] Psychiatrists smiled less when interviewing psychiatric inpatients than when interviewing nonpatient volunteers.

Personal Biases. Our moods and expectations determine the way we interpret people's facial expressions. If we're feeling good we may react differently to a person's smiling or frowning than if we're feeling poorly. The moods of research participants were altered by exposing them to loud noise or to tape recordings designed to elicit feelings of humor or disgust. When these participants were then asked to judge the emotions being expressed by people in a series of photographs, they leaned toward their own moods in making their judgments. The influence of expectations was demonstrated in studies showing that people see more emotion in facial expressions of other people who are typically nonexpressive (who rarely show facial expressions) than in those of typically expressive people (who frequently express themselves in their faces.)[13]

Perceptions of facial expressions are also affected by sex stereotypes. Men and women judged the emotions in the faces of infants who were randomly designated as boys or girls.[14] Judges interpreted a "girl's" facial expressions as showing joy and interest, those of "boys" as showing distress, fear, and anger. These biased interpretations had nothing to do with the infant's actual sex.

FACIAL EXPRESSIONS OF EMOTION

Much of the research on the human face has focused on the communication of emotions. A number of studies have measured people's accuracy in judging emotions from facial expressions. Others have investigated whether facial expressions of emotion are different in various cultures throughout the world or are similar for human beings in general. Research has also been conducted to discover the ways children learn to recognize facial expressions of emotion and the effects on children when adults' facial expressions of emotion are inconsistent with other messages in the situation.

Recognizing Emotions. Judgments of emotions from facial expressions have been studied by measuring how accurately people can label emotions that are portrayed by trained experimenters in live interactions, in photographs, and in films. Paul Ekman and his colleagues analyzed nine studies of accuracy in interpreting emotions from facial expressions that were conducted in the United States over a period of thirty years.[15] Accuracy varied according to procedures used in the different studies, but it was always greater than would be expected by chance. For facial expressions of happiness, accuracy ranged from 55 to 100 percent. For surprise, it ranged from 38 to 86 percent; for fear, 16 to 93 percent; anger, 31 to 92 percent; sadness, 19 to 88 percent; disgust or contempt, 41 to 91 percent. Recognition of emotions was less accurate in studies using live facial expressions than in studies using photographs and films, possibly because other behaviors such as body movement and posture were not as well controlled.

Research with people in other countries (Mexico, England, Germany, France, Brazil, Chile, Sweden, Greece, Japan, Switzerland, and Argentina) found similar results.[16] In all countries, judgments about the emotions of happiness, fear, surprise, anger, disgust or contempt, and sadness were far more accurate than would be expected by chance. Agreement on happiness was highest, averaging over 95 percent. Agreement on sadness was lowest, ranging from 51 to 90 percent. From these studies it appears that facial expressions for emotions are shared among many cultures.

To investigate still further the universality of human facial expressions, Ekman and his colleagues studied people in two preliterate cultures: Borneo and New Guinea.[17] These people had experienced little or no previous contact with Western culture. They were asked to listen to stories in their language and then choose from pictures of Americans with various facial expressions the one that corresponded with the emotion in the story. For both adults and children the recognition of emotions was far better than chance, ranging from 70 to 90 percent. The easiest facial expression to judge was happiness. Most errors came in trying to distinguish expressions of fear from expressions of surprise. In a second series of studies, people in New Guinea listened to stories with various emotions and then showed how their own faces would appear if they were in the story. These posed facial expressions were videotaped and later shown to people in the United States. Americans were able to judge the emotions in the videotapes with an accuracy well above chance. The easiest emotions to identify were happiness and sadness, the most difficult were surprise and fear.

The above studies suggest that there is a universal language of facial expressions. Although people in various cultures are similar in recognizing facial expressions of emotion, nevertheless, there are some interesting differences in their willingness to express emotions. Facial expressions of people in the United States and Japan were videotaped without their knowledge while they were watching an emotional movie.[18] Inspection of the videotapes showed that they reacted with basically the same kinds of facial expressions. When they were interviewed about their reactions by a person from their own culture, however, the Japanese were more likely than the Americans to show happy faces and to hide negative facial expressions. Americans in the interviews showed negative as well as positive facial expressions.

Communicating Emotions. A somewhat different approach toward measuring facial communication of emotions has been to determine if people can accurately recognize facial expressions of others who are undergoing a positive or negative experience. Participants in an experiment learned to avoid an electric shock by pressing a certain button whenever they heard a buzzer and to earn a score on a counter by pressing a different button whenever they heard a bell.[19] After practicing with the buttons, they were divided into pairs. One person could still hear the buzzer and the bell but no longer had buttons to postpone the shock and win the score. The second person, who observed his or her partner through a one-way mirror, could not hear the buzzer and the bell but had buttons to press. Whatever happened to the first person would also happen to the second person. The observing person, therefore, had to judge from his or her partner's facial expressions when it was time to press either the shock-avoidance button or the scoring button. It turned out that observers could do this with an accuracy better than chance. The first person was not told anything about the experimental setup and did not know that the observer was behind the one-way mirror. It was thus concluded that whatever information the observer gained about which button to press was due to the first person's natural facial expressions. A second part of the experiment showed that observers were accurate in judging another person's facial expressions only when they themselves had previous experience with the buzzer and the bell. It was necessary to have empathy in order to read correctly another's facial expressions.

A similar study showed that people could accurately judge whether or not someone in a videotape was about to receive an electric shock. Interestingly, there was more difficulty in judging facial expressions of people who reacted to the electric shock with high physiological arousal. One reason for this is that people who are easily aroused may have learned to hide facial expressions associated with this arousal because negative emotional reactions are not often accepted by others around them. This conclusion was supported in a study showing that people who react to electric shock with physiological arousal tend to control their facial expressions.[20] Those who respond more calmly express themselves in their faces more openly.

Investigators found that people can also correctly judge from facial expressions when someone playing a slot machine has won a penny, a quarter, or a jackpot. Other investigators found that people can accurately judge from facial expressions whether someone is looking at pleasant or unpleasant slides and television scenes.[21]

Conflicting Facial Expressions. Daphne Bugental and her colleagues conducted a series of studies investigating reactions of adults and children to facial expressions that were inconsistent with other emotional messages in an interaction. In one study, analysis of videotapes of discussions between eight-to-twelve-year-old children and their parents showed that fathers' facial expressions and verbal statements were consistent. Fathers tended to smile when they made positive statements and tended not to smile when they made negative statements. Mothers' facial expressions and verbal statements were not consistent. They smiled as often when they made negative statements as when they made positive statements. It was suggested that women may be conditioned to smile in negative as well as positive situations in order to present the submissive feminine appearance that is favored in American society. The study implies that children may be confused about whether a woman's facial expressions reflect her actual mood. To test this idea, an experiment was conducted in which children and adults judged the feelings being expressed by an adult in a videotape.[22] When a man made a negative statement and also smiled, children and adults saw his smile as a sign that he didn't mean his negative remark seriously and was probably joking. When a woman made a negative statement and smiled, adults also took the statement as a joke or remark that wasn't meant seriously. Children, on the other hand, interpreted her statement very literally and did not view the smile as softening or qualifying her remark. This finding is important because it suggests that women may not be successful when they try to lighten the impact of a critical remark to a child with a smile.

When the tendency of mothers to hide their negative feelings by smiling becomes too extreme it can cause conflicts in their children. Research has determined that mothers with disturbed children give more contradictory messages than mothers with normal children.[23] The messages typically contain a critical statement accompanied with a smile or with a syrupy voice. Such messages place the child in a double bind because they say, "I'm mad at you, but since I'm acting nice you aren't allowed to hold me responsible for my anger."

High school students' reactions to contradictory facial expressions were studied by asking them to evaluate photographs of a teacher whose facial expression was either happy or angry.[24] Included with the photograph was a written statement of what the teacher was supposedly saying at the time the photograph was taken. Half the time the teacher's statement was positive and complimentary and half the time it was negative and critical. Not surprisingly, happy faces paired with a positive statement were evaluated as being positive and sincere. Angry faces associated with a critical statement were evaluated as being negative and sincere. Happy faces associated with a negative statement were evaluated as being negative, insincere, and submissive. Descriptions of insincerity ranged from joking and kidding to sarcasm. It appeared as if the teacher delivering a negative message while looking happy were making a gesture of appeasement. Angry faces associated with a positive statement were evaluated as being insincere, negative, and dominant. The teacher speaking positively but wearing an angry face was described by students as being sarcastic and mean.

Evidence that American women learn to conceal their emotions comes from a study comparing the amount of truth or deception revealed in facial expressions of boys and girls at four age levels: five to six years, seven to eight years, nine to ten years, and eleven to twelve years.[25] Girls revealed consistently less in their facial expressions as they grew older, but boys as they increased in age tended to reveal more.

Deception. Do you smile more or less when you are lying? In actuality, there seems to be little or no difference in how much people smile when they are lying or being truthful. Most of us, however, believe that pleasant facial expressions indicate truthfulness while nonexpressive faces signify deception. What are the implications of these research findings for understanding facial expressions of deception? First of all, our ability to discriminate truth from falseness in facial expressions is not as good as we might think. Research participants were videotaped while they expressed their honest opinions on some issues and gave false opinions on other issues. People watching these videotapes could judge with low but better than chance accuracy when participants were lying but could not accurately judge when they were telling the truth. Participants in another study were videotaped while claiming to like someone they actually disliked and to dislike someone they actually liked.[26] People could detect from these videotapes when the participants were deceiving them but could not tell when the participants were expressing the truth.

Paul Ekman and his colleagues concluded that facial expressions are difficult to read for honesty because we are very adept at controlling them to serve our needs. As we grow up, we develop the propensity to use facial expressions selectively. One study found that first-grade children could not falsely convince others that they liked or disliked a particular drink. Their facial expressions betrayed their true feelings. Seventh-grade children were able to make their preferences difficult to figure out. College students were skilled enough to use their facial expressions to give the opposite impression about which drink they preferred. One way to conceal the fact that you are lying is to show expressive facial behavior. If you want to convince others that you are innocent of a transgression or that you like something or someone more than you really do, it doesn't hurt to smile and overdo it a bit. When people are trying too hard to lie, they tend to be overly cautious and self-controlled in their expressions.[27]

Because facial expressions are deceptive, people who suspect someone's truthfulness often discount his or her facial expressions and pay more attention to body language or tone of voice. Even if we learn to suspect the face, however, it is difficult to be a good lie detector. The detection of deception does not appear to be a consistent ability or skill. With practice and feedback, we can greatly improve our accuracy in judging when a particular person is lying. Unfortunately, this training does not increase our ability to judge when other people are lying. People who are good liars are not necessarily good lie detectors. Success in detecting deception in men is not related to success in detecting it in women. Skill in recognizing emotions is not correlated with skill in identifying honesty. Detection of lies is also biased by our expectations. We are more likely to "discover" lies when we think we should find them.[28]

Understanding Smiles. One reason why smiles are hard to interpret is because they can stand for different things in different situations. Paul Ekman and Wallace Friesen defined three different kinds of smiles: *felt smiles, false smiles,* and *miserable smiles.* Felt smiles are those that accompany pleasurable emotions. They communicate genuine positive feelings. False smiles are used to convince others that a positive emotion is felt when it isn't. Miserable smiles occur when a person acknowledges feeling unhappy. We can often distinguish between these types of smiles by knowing the person, his or her motives, and what is happening in the situation. The smiles also differ qualitatively. Felt smiles are the strongest, and their timing is appropriate. They begin and end in a sequence that appears natural. False smiles are often weaker, and they tend to be asymmetrical. They also appear off in timing, coming too early or too late, and they seem to end irregularly or abruptly. Miserable smiles are weak, asymmetrical, and brief. They look unhappy. Ekman and Friesen developed a scoring system for helping researchers measure facial expressions in movements of specific facial muscles.[29] It appears from what has been discussed up to this point that a smile is not always a smile.

Perceptions of the Body

Next to the face, the body is the most important aspect of the person used in judging physical attractiveness.[30] Researchers have studied popular stereotypes about various types of body builds. They have also measured preferences for body builds and physiques and shed light on the negative prejudice in American society against people who are obese.

STEREOTYPES ABOUT BODY BUILDS

American children grow up learning to assign stereotypes to various body builds. Such stereotypes range from being slightly accurate to unfounded. When people come to accept such stereotypes, however, their actions toward others will be biased. The following research studies indicate that stereotypes about people with various body builds are firmly and widely held.

Men and women were asked to look at silhouette drawings or read descriptions of men with three different body builds: (1) soft, fat, round; (2) muscular, athletic; and (3) tall, thin, fragile.[31] Men with the three body builds were characterized as having the following traits:

1. *Soft, fat, round:* old-fashioned, short, physically weak, ugly, talkative, warm-hearted, sympathetic, good-natured, agreeable, dependent on others, trusting, greedy for affection, loving physical comfort, loving eating

2. *Muscular, athletic:* strong, masculine, good-looking, adventurous, tall, self-reliant, energetic, youthful, competitive, bold

3. *Tall, thin, fragile:* thin, young, ambitious, tall, suspicious, tense, nervous, stubborn, pessimistic, quiet, sensitive to pain, private, inhibited, secretive

Elementary school boys showed similar stereotypes in ratings of male body builds. They gave most favorable ratings to a man with a muscular body build. A man with a round fat body was characterized as cheating, argumentative, being teased a lot, forgetful, lazy, unhealthy, lying, sloppy, naughty, ugly, mean, dumb, and dirty. A man with a very thin body was characterized as being weak, quiet, lonely, sneaky, afraid, and sad. Males ranging in age from ten to twenty years rated photographs of men with three different body builds: obese, muscular, thin.[32] Obese men were characterized as being the poorest athletes, drinking and eating the most, and having fewest friends. Muscular men were described as being the best leaders, having the most friends, being most aggressive, having greatest endurance for pain, and being least likely to have a nervous breakdown. Thin men were characterized as eating the least, having least endurance for pain, and being most likely to have a nervous breakdown.

High school students were asked to describe themselves with a series of adjectives.[33] Thin students tended to characterize themselves as being detached, tense, shy, and reserved. Students with a medium body build rated themselves as confident, energetic, adventurous, and enterprising. Chubby students evaluated themselves as kind, relaxed, warm, and softhearted. It isn't known whether the students' self-ratings were accurate or whether they reflected an awareness (or acceptance) of body stereotypes.

PREFERENCES FOR BODY BUILD IN MEN

Women's preferences for male physiques were measured with ratings of silhouette figures that varied on four characteristics: arms, upper trunk, lower trunk, legs.[34] The silhouette figures were drawn so that these parts of the body were thin, medium thin, medium, medium wide, or wide. Women gave greatest preference to male figures with medium wide arms, medium wide upper trunk, medium thin lower trunk, and medium thin legs, that is, they liked tapering V-shaped physiques the most. They liked a pear-shaped physique the least. The V-shaped physique women preferred was that of a man with a moderate build. They were not particularly crazy about a "muscle-man" build with very large arms and muscular chest.

A study with American and Israeli college students found that students from both countries preferred a male physique with a flat rather than protruding stomach and with straight rather than slouched posture.[35] Evidently there is some point to the command: "Stomach in, chest out, head up!"

PREFERENCES FOR BODY BUILD IN WOMEN

College men rated photographs of women who were overweight, underweight, or of average weight.[36] Regardless of their own weight, men rated the underweight women as most desirable for a dating or marriage partner and the overweight women as least desirable. The women's weights did not influence the way they were evaluated on personal characteristics such as warmth, friendliness, competence, and intelligence.

Men's preferences for female physiques were also measured by means of ratings of silhouette figures that varied on three characteristics: bust, buttocks, and legs. The silhouette figures were drawn so that these characteristics were large, moderately large, medium, moderately small, or small. Men had greatest preference for a female figure with a moderately large bust, moderately small buttocks, and moderately large legs. Men who preferred large busts tended to be outgoing people, frequent daters, cigarette smokers, and readers of sports magazines and *Playboy* magazine. Men who preferred small busts were religious, mildly depressed, unambitious, and nurturant toward others. When women rated the same female figures they tended to prefer a somewhat smaller and thinner figure with moderately small bust, small buttocks, and thin legs.[37]

A study with American and Israeli college students found that in both countries they preferred a female physique with a flat rather than protruding stomach and with an hourglass figure. Men expressed greater preference for large busts than women did. When American women were asked to specify their ideal personal physique they stated that they would like to have smaller waists and hips, lighter weight, larger busts, and the same height.[38]

First impressions of female bust size were measured in three studies in which college students evaluated women in photographs.[39] One series of photographs was taken of women with their natural bust size. A second series of photographs was taken after the women had made their busts larger by stuffing cotton in the appropriate places. A third series of photographs was taken after the women had increased their bust size even more. Students estimated that the average bust sizes in the three series of photographs, ranging from small to large, were 34.2 inches, 35.4 inches, and 36.8 inches. Bust size did not affect how the women were rated on characteristics such as being likable, appealing, domineering, or independent. Women with a large bust, however, were consistently evaluated as being more immodest, immoral, incompetent, and unintelligent. It is not known whether these ratings were given because of stereotypes associated with large busts or because the large bust sizes in the photographs were furthest removed from the women's natural bust size. It is fair to conclude from this study that there is no advantage (and possibly a disadvantage) for women who wish to enlarge their busts.

THE STIGMA OF OBESITY

Daily ads in newspapers for weight-reducing programs constantly remind us about the American prejudice against obesity.[40] People who have been physically disabled sometimes suffer because others feel uncomfortable around them, but their physical disabilities are usually attributed to factors beyond their control. Obesity, on the other hand, is often associated with laziness and lack of will power. When we discriminate against obese people it is usually with the feeling that they could lose weight if they tried. The bias against obese people is held by persons of all ages.

Elementary school children were shown drawings of a normal child, a child with the left hand missing, a child with facial disfigurement, a child sitting in a wheelchair, a child with crutches and a brace on one leg, and an obese child. When asked to rank the drawings in order of preference, children consistently rated the obese child as least liked. These results were similar for boys and girls from a wide range of ethnic and social backgrounds. A group of professional adults who were given the same test also ranked the obese child as least liked. Children from seven grade levels (kindergarten through sixth grade) were asked to play a game in which they placed themselves in relation to cut out figures representing thin, medium, or chubby children.[41] Children at all ages placed themselves closest to the figure of the child with the medium body build and farthest from the figure of the child with the chubby build.

Children also learn from an early age that chubbiness is not desirable for themselves. Kindergarten children looked at photographs of chubby, average, and thin children of similar age and specified which children they would prefer to look like. Preference was somewhat greater for the average body build than for the thin body build. Children expressed a consistent aversion toward being chubby. Elementary school and junior high school boys and college men were asked to choose which body build they would prefer from drawings of males who were chubby, muscular, or thin.[42] A majority of respondents preferred the muscular body build, and a small minority preferred the thin body build. Virtually no one wanted to be chubby.

Perceptions of Height

Researchers have approached the question of how perceptions of people are influenced by their height from two directions. One approach is to ascribe positive or negative traits to a person and then have research participants estimate that person's height. A second approach is to measure evaluations given to people who are described as short, medium, or tall in height.

ESTIMATING PEOPLE'S HEIGHTS

There is evidence that men with high status are perceived as taller than men with low status. College students in Australia were introduced to a man who was supposedly either a student, a teacher of low rank, or a professor of high rank. Students were later asked to estimate the man's height. The "professor" was judged as tallest and the "student" was judged as shortest. A similar study was conducted in which student nurses estimated the heights of a fellow student, an instructor in their school, and the school's assistant director.[43] The heights of the instructor and assistant director were overestimated, especially that of the latter.

The relationship between judgments of height and political preference is seen in a study of voters during the 1960 Kennedy-Nixon election. Voters who preferred Nixon perceived him as taller than Kennedy; those who preferred Kennedy perceived him as taller than Nixon. Another study showed that people who expressed liking for Lyndon Johnson when he was president estimated that he was taller than did people who disliked him.[44]

Estimates of height are also affected by personal relations. Men and women feel that others are taller when they hold similar rather than dissimilar attitudes on political and social issues. People view others from preferred ethnic groups as taller than those from less preferred ethnic groups.[45]

These studies demonstrate that we have a tendency to judge people of high status and people we like as taller than people of low status and people we dislike. It has been suggested that we may perceive a person of high status as being taller because we pay closer attention when he or she is introduced. One group of researchers did not find differences in height estimates given to a man or woman who was introduced to college students as an undergraduate student, a graduate student, or a Ph.D.[46] The students probably did not feel the roles of undergraduate and Ph.D. differed very much in terms of desirability and status.

INFLUENCE OF HEIGHT ON EVALUATIONS

Some people have argued that tall men have an advantage over short men in American society. A survey of professional men showed that those who were taller (six feet two inches and over) received average starting salaries 12.4 percent higher than men who were shorter (under six feet). Another survey asked corporate recruiters to choose between two job applicants after reading their applications.[47] The qualifications of the applicants were identical, except that one applicant was listed as being six feet one inch and the other was listed as being five feet five inches. The short man was favored by only 1 percent of the recruiters. Seventy-two percent said they would rather hire the tall man, and 27 percent had no preference.

Women's preferences for men of different heights were measured by having them judge photographs of men's faces who were randomly identified as short (five feet five inches to five feet seven inches), medium (five feet nine inches to five feet eleven inches), or tall (six feet two inches to six feet four inches). Regardless of their own height, women said they liked men of medium height best and felt that such men were most preferable as dates. When men rated the photographs they did not believe that a man's height had an important bearing on his desirability as a date. There appears to be no relationship between men's self-esteem and their actual height.[48] There is a small correlation, however, indicating that men who perceive themselves as tall have higher self-esteem than men who perceive themselves as short.

Two hundred college students listed their ideal height for a dating partner.[49] The majority of women preferred a man to be between five feet ten inches and six feet three inches. The majority of men preferred a woman to be between five feet five inches and five feet eight inches. All but two students said that the man should be taller than the woman. The majority of women preferred a man who was from five to nine inches taller than they were. The majority of men preferred a woman who was from two to seven inches shorter than themselves. Apparently one unwritten rule in American society is that the male member of a couple should not be shorter than the female. It will be interesting to see if couples composed of short men and tall women are more accepted as attitudes toward sex roles become more liberated.

Perceptions of Clothing

We communicate a good deal about ourselves in our choice of dress. Sometimes our clothing reflects our true personalities. On other occasions we may intentionally dress to make a particular impression on others. Either way, people's impressions and reactions toward us are influenced by what we wear. The following research studies demonstrate that there is truth in the old saying, "Clothes make the man."

CLOTHING AS COMMUNICATION

Check whether you agree with the following statements:

1. *I like to dress up and usually spend a lot of time doing so.*

2. *The people whom I know always notice what I wear.*

3. *I approve of skimpy bathing suits and wouldn't mind wearing one myself.*

4. *I like clothes with bold designs.*

5. *When buying clothes, I am more interested in practicality than beauty.*

6. *I buy clothes for comfort rather than appearance.*

These statements come from a clothing questionnaire designed to measure people's feelings about their choice of dress.[50] People's responses on the questionnaire were compared with their scores on a series of personality tests. Items 1 and 2 measure *clothes consciousness*. Clothes consciousness is found in those who are compliant and conforming and anxious to make a good impression. Items 3 and 4 measure *exhibitionism*. Exhibitionism is common in people who are self-confident, outgoing, and somewhat detached from others. Items 5 and 6 measure *practicality*. Characteristics associated with practicality were different for men and women. Men who choose practicality in dress tend to be nonleaders, inhibited, withdrawn, and nonsociable. Women who choose practicality in dress are also nonleaders, but they are clever and enthusiastic.

CLOTHING AND JUDGMENTS OF PERSONALITY

Do you ever wear special clothing to put yourself in a certain mood? It appears that the mood of one's clothing affects the perceptions of others. College students in New Zealand rated photographs of high school students in four different kinds of dress: school uniform, casual clothes, working clothes, and evening clothes. The high school students came across as pleasant when they were in evening dress, youthful when they wore school uniform, relaxed and happy in casual dress, and active when they wore work clothes. In another study, college instructors wore the black suit and Roman collar of the Catholic priest for one of their courses and a conventional coat and tie for another.[51] When they wore priestly dress, they were rated by students as moral, reputable, unusual, and withdrawn. To see if the effects of clothing on students' ratings would wear off over time, one of the instructors was evaluated nine weeks later. Students in the course to which he wore priestly dress still felt that he was more introverted, solitary, unscientific, self-contained, and discouraging. One unanswered question from this study is whether the instructors were evaluated differently because of their appearance or because they acted differently in priestly and secular dress.

CLOTHING AND EVALUATION OF COUNSELORS

Researchers have conducted many studies to determine whether perceptions of counselors are influenced by their dress.[52] These studies suggest conclusions similar to those reached in Chapter 3 regarding counselor attractiveness. Clothing may affect people's judgments of counselors if it is considered in isolation or if it is extreme. If counselors dress with reasonable taste and fashion, their clothing is not likely to make much difference. In general, people prefer counselors who dress formally enough to maintain an image of expertise but not so formally as to appear stuffy and unapproachable. Not surprisingly, counselors come across as more competent when their clothing is in style rather than out of date.

CLOTHING AND RESPONSIVENESS TO REQUESTS

A number of studies have shown that people receive more help and compliance with requests when they are dressed formally or neatly rather than casually or carelessly. Pedestrians were more likely to follow a male experimenter who walked through a red light when he was wearing a coat and tie rather than work clothes. People in train stations and airports were more willing to return a dime that had been left in a phone booth by men and women who were neatly rather than carelessly dressed. People were also more willing to comply with requests for directions and for a dime when the person making the request wore neat rather than sloppy clothing. People were also more willing to sign petitions, give change for a dime, take leaflets, answer questions, and return questionnaires when experimenters making these requests were carefully rather than carelessly dressed. No difference was found in help given by public librarians to a college woman in neat or careless clothing.[53] It is possible that the women were acceptable in both kinds of dress, or maybe librarians are open to helping people regardless of their clothes.

Several explanations have been given for this preference for formality and neatness in dress. Some researchers have found that people in business suits have more status than people in work clothes. Others have suggested that requests for money by a neatly dressed person will seem more legitimate because the person is less likely to be suspected as a panhandler. Still other researchers concluded that people give more help to someone whose clothing indicates attitudes, tastes, and beliefs similar to their own. For example, participants in a peace demonstration dressed as "hippies" were more agreeable about signing a petition when the person carrying the petition was similarly dressed rather than in "straight" clothes. People in straight dress were more willing to give dimes to experimenters wearing straight dress, while people in hippie dress gave more willingly to experimenters in hippie dress. People in an airport gave more money for a phone call to female experimenters when they were neatly dressed rather than carelessly dressed. People in a bus station gave more money to carelessly dressed experimenters. Members of a conservative club were more willing to participate in a survey when a male experimenter making the request was wearing a tie.[54] Working-class people complied equally with the experimenter regardless of whether he was wearing a tie.

The tendency to favor people who communicate similarity of outlook through their dress was demonstrated in a series of studies measuring reactions of middle-class people toward shoplifters (actually experimenters with the stores' permission) who were dressed in straight or hippie clothing.[55] Hippie shoplifters were reported more often than straight shoplifters, and they were evaluated as having lower morality and less admirable personalities.

It can be concluded that clothing influences our perceptions of other people because it tells us something about their intentions and motives and whether they are similar to or different from us. Uniforms represent a special kind of clothing because they create expectations about behavior appropriate in certain situations. Male experimenters who gave a variety of orders to pedestrians in New York City received more compliance when they were wearing the uniform of a security guard rather than ordinary business dress.[56]

Perceptions of Personal Details

Personal details that have received attention from researchers include facial hair, eyeglasses, lipstick, and body odor. Needless to say, the results of these studies depended very much on the age, background, and culture of the people tested. Many of the researchers' conclusions are interesting, however, and should stimulate awareness, curiosity, and further research.

FACIAL HAIR

The popularity of facial hair on men has been cyclical throughout history. The ancient Egyptians regarded beards as a sign of high social rank and the divinity of the ruler.[57] To the early Greeks the beard was a mark of wisdom. In the United States in the 1800s most men wore mustaches or beards. By the 1900s the fashion for facial hair on men declined, and during the 1950s the clean-shaven, short-haired look was in style. During the 1960s men began again to grow their hair, mustaches, and beards.

The following studies of men's facial hair were conducted in the 1970s. Eight men between twenty-two and twenty-five years old were paid to have a barber shave off their beards. Photographs were taken at four stages: full beard, goatee, mustache, and clean-shaven. College students in California who saw the photographs gave most favorable ratings to men with facial hair. They evaluated men with full beards as more masculine, mature, good-looking, dominant, self-confident, courageous, liberal, nonconformist, and industrious than clean-shaven men. Men with mustaches and goatees fell in between. Facial hair had no effect on ratings of the men's intelligence, strength, health, and likability. College students in Tennessee evaluated a man when he had a beard and when he was clean-shaven. When bearded he was rated more enthusiastic, sincere, generous, extroverted, masculine, inquisitive, and strong. There were no differences on ratings given to the bearded and clean-shaven man on eighteen other characteristics including friendliness, dependability, honesty, handsomeness, and popularity. The bearded man was considered more dirty. College women in Wyoming were asked whether they preferred a man with a beard, a mustache, or no facial hair.[58] Their choices were evenly divided between no facial hair and a mustache, with only a small percentage preferring a man with a beard.

EYEGLASSES

In a study in the 1940s, American college students judged men and women to be more intelligent and industrious when they were wearing glasses than when they were not. Judgments of honesty, kindness, dependability, and sense of humor were not influnced by the presence or absence of glasses. This study was repeated in the 1960s in Germany. In a series of drawings, men wearing glasses were evaluated as more intelligent, industrious, dependable, and honest than men without glasses. The presence or absence of glasses did not influence ratings of friendliness and humor. College students in England judged a woman with glasses as more intelligent when they saw her in a photograph but not when they watched her during a fifteen-minute live interview. More recent studies in the 1970s have indicated that American college students view others as less attractive when they are wearing glasses. Students also feel less attractive themselves when they are wearing glasses.[59] Perceptions of people with glasses may continue to change for the worse as glasses become more and more displaced by contact lenses.

LIPSTICK

In a study conducted in the 1930s, college men interviewed college women while they were wearing or not wearing lipstick.[60] The men evaluated women wearing lipstick as more frivolous, placid, introspective, and conscientious than women without lipstick. It would be interesting to repeat this study today in the light of women's liberation, the hippie revolt, and the punk rock movement.

BODY ODOR

In one study, eleven men were paid to wear a cotton T-shirt for forty-eight hours without bathing.[61] These T-shirts were then rated by college students for relative unpleasantness of odor and on a series of descriptive adjectives. Students agreed fairly closely about which T-shirts smelled worst. They characterized these most unpleasant garments as coming from men who were unsociable, dirty, unfriendly, unintelligent, nervous, unsophisticated, unpopular, bad-looking, unhealthy, fat, poor, and unattractive to the opposite sex. In addition they judged these shirts as coming from men who were active, strong, industrious, and athletic. This study also found that the men who donated the T-shirts judged their own body odors as much less unpleasant than those of others.

A second study of body odor investigated reactions to colognes and perfumes.[62] Research participants interviewed a man and a woman who played the role of job applicants. For half of the interviews, the applicants wore a popular fragrance. For the remaining interviews they wore no scent. Results of this study indicated that perfume and cologne had opposite effects on men and women interviewers. Sweet-smelling job applicants were evaluated more favorably on intelligence, friendliness, and liking by women interviewers and less favorably on these traits by men interviewers. The author of this study suggested that while it is advisable to be well groomed for a job interview, perfume and cologne must be used with discretion.

Physical Attractiveness and Self-Image

It might be worthwhile to conclude this discussion of physical attractiveness by taking a look at how our self-images of attractiveness affect our lives. What is the relationship between self-perceived physical attractiveness and feelings of confidence and self-esteem? How does our self-image of attractiveness influence the ways we interact with others? What motivates people to change their appearance with cosmetics and cosmetic surgery? What are the results of these changes?

CONFIDENCE AND SELF-ESTEEM

The influence of self-perceived physical attractiveness on confidence and self-esteem was demonstrated in a study in which research participants were made up cosmetically to have a large scar on their face and then introduced to a stranger for an informal conversation.[63] After the facial scar was applied and inspected by research participants with a mirror, the experimenter pretended to make a final cosmetic adjustment but in fact removed the scar. As a result, one group of research participants talked to the stranger thinking they had a disfiguring facial scar when they actually did not. How did the self-image of having a scarred face affect their feelings about the other person's attitudes toward them? Research participants felt that their "facial scar" caused the other person to feel tense, to look at them more than usual, and to view them as unattractive. The interesting thing about this study is that the "strangers" who spoke to the research participants knew nothing about the falsely perceived scar. The self-image of having a facial disfigurement was enough to color the participants' perceptions of how another person was acting toward them.

Other studies have also demonstrated the negative consequences of feeling unattractive. People who view themselves as unattractive believe they have less chance of finding romance than people who view themselves as attractive. Unattractive people are less inclined to check their appearance while walking past a reflecting window. College women's self-images of physical attractiveness were increased or decreased by having them compare themselves with women who were either less attractive or more attractive than they were.[64] The experimenters were curious to see how these women would react when they received praise from a man. Women who felt attractive appreciated the praise most when they believed it came from men who didn't know what they looked like. They suspected men who might be praising them only because they were good-looking. Women who felt unattractive were more appreciative of praise coming from men who were familiar with their looks. These women seemed grateful that a man would praise them in spite of their unattractiveness. It appears that people who feel attractive have a more positive outlook on themselves and others around them.

COSMETICS

Consumers in the United States spend more than $4 billion a year on cosmetic products. What are the consequences of this investment? Research shows that women are more favorably evaluated when they use cosmetics to present a well-groomed appearance. The prevalence of male beauty products suggests that a similar stereotype exists for men. Women also feel more confident in their social interactions when they are wearing their customary cosmetics. These findings help explain why people use cosmetics. Understandably women who are preoccupied and anxious about making a good impression or who are dissatisfied or insecure about their appearance tend to use cosmetics more than others do.[65] The use of cosmetics is taken for granted in many work and social situations. When cosmetics become an expected part of people's appearance, they feel naked without them.

COSMETIC SURGERY

Cosmetic surgery is being used more often these days for helping people improve their appearance. Cosmetic surgery has obvious benefits. By increasing people's self-esteem and confidence, it can help them be more productive in their social and business life. Research studies have demonstrated that people who have had minor facial surgery usually gain in physical attractiveness. As a result, they are evaluated more favorably on personal traits and abilities. Inmates of New York City prisons were given cosmetic surgery to correct disfigurements ranging from knife and burn scars to lop-ears and tattoos. Compared with a similar group of prisoners who did not receive cosmetic surgery, the "beautified" prisoners who were not addicted to drugs or alcohol had a significantly lower rate of recidivism. The cosmetic surgery did not, however, reduce the recidivism of addicts. It was concluded that although the cost of plastic surgery is relatively high, "it can be considered negligible if the offender is helped to remain out of prison for even one year."[66]

Cosmetic surgery can be detrimental if it causes people to base their self-worth too much on their appearance. It is a bad risk to rely on looks to get through life while neglecting the development of social skills that can provide a sense of internal control and competence.

The Challenge of Feeling Satisfied

You have read a lot in the last two chapters about how physical attractiveness is perceived, judged, and valued in American society. How can you use this knowledge in your everyday life? First of all, an awareness of the bias toward physical attractiveness should encourage you to reconsider your prejudices toward others who are more or less physically attractive. Second, knowing something about how people judge each other will help you when you desire to make a good first impression. There are times when it is in our best interest to groom and dress ourselves according to social demands and expectations. Even nonconformists feel better about themselves when they are looking good. It is also important to remember that physical attractiveness is a mental as well as physical state. As you will read in the following chapters, the image we present to others depends as much on how we act as it does on how we look. You already know that an important part of our self-image hinges on how we feel. Our challenge is to make the most of our physical appearance and then to be satisfied with these efforts. Don't waste time feeling depressed because you are not the most beautiful person in the world. Concentrate instead on developing your social skills (Chapter 1), creating a positive atmosphere (Chapter 2), attending to your self-presentation (Chapter 9), and employing tactics for winning good will (Chapter 10). Keep up your curiosity and have some fun as you experience your interactions with others.

FIVE

Body Language
and
the Human Voice

How do we size up strangers at first meeting? As you are discovering in this book, we form first impressions on the basis of how people look, what they tell us, and how they act. To put it another way, we learn about others from their appearance and their verbal and nonverbal behaviors. Chapters 5, 6, and 7 are about nonverbal behaviors. This chapter will focus on how impressions are affected by body language, speaking style, and tone of voice. Chapter 6 will discuss the influence of physical closeness and crowding. Research and theories on gaze and touch are the topic of Chapter 7.

The Richness of Nonverbal Behavior

We have all known people who are particularly astute in their observations of others. How are they able to reach such accurate conclusions? What clues do they use? Since we all hear the same words when someone speaks, there must be nonverbal messages communicating extra information about what he or she is like. Although we are not always aware of it, we all use nonverbal behaviors to enhance our understanding of others. Consider the following study. Research participants observed videotapes of personal interactions that were between twenty and sixty seconds in length.[1] They were then asked questions about the people in the interactions. The videotapes had been carefully edited so that the answers were not given away. The only way participants could reply correctly was to use whatever information they could gather from nonverbal behaviors. One videotape showed three men talking. Two were married and one was single. Participants were asked to judge who was single. They did so with an accuracy better than chance. Another videotape was of a woman speaking on the telephone. Participants were quite accurate in judging whether she was speaking to a man or woman. A third videotape showed two couples. Participants judged more accurately than by chance which couple was in love. Participants were also able to judge from videotapes which of three women had no children; whether a man and woman were friends, acquaintances, or strangers; and which of two men shown from the waist up was not wearing pants. Although this study does not tell how participants came up with their correct answers, it demonstrates that they could use people's appearance and nonverbal behaviors to do so.

Body Language

You are probably familiar with the term *body language* and know that it has something to do with the ways people stand, sit, or express themselves with gestures. You may be aware of occasions where body language has influenced your perceptions and reactions to others. The first half of this chapter will look at a number of studies investigating the relation between body language and first impressions. A good place to start is by dividing the study of body language into four categories of behaviors: *emblems, illustrators, regulators,* and *adaptors.*[2]

EMBLEMS

Emblems are nonverbal acts or gestures that communicate a specific message. Simple examples are gestures people use for "OK" and "victory." In one of the earliest studies of hand gestures, photographs were taken of an actor's hands as he portrayed thirty-five different emotions. These photographs were shown to people who judged which emotion was being portrayed. Seventy-five percent of the judges agreed on the photograph in which the actor was expressing worship (clasped hands), and 55 percent agreed on the actor's portrayal of pleading or begging (open hands with palms up). About 33 percent of the judges agreed when the actor was portraying thoughtfulness (one hand held loosely over the other), determination (one hand in a fist, the other covering it), and bewilderment (hands held with palms facing straight out and fingers spread). Twenty-five percent correctly perceived the actor's attempts to express threat, humility, surprise, sympathy, distrust, and anger. Only five percent agreed on the hand expressions for admiration, scorn, defiance, and disgust. This study demonstrates that we have a language of hand gestures for communicating emotions in general but not for expressing specific feelings. Participants in a more recent study perceived hands in a gripping or groping posture as active and intentional. Hands in a cupped position were viewed as begging or passive. Hands held so that they hung down in a drooping position were evaluated as weak, submissive, and shy. Hands held so that they pushed or faced outward from the body were rated as immature, uncontrolled, and impulsive.[3]

Even though gestures do not always communicate specific emotions, they are useful for expressing messages and commands. One group of investigators identified more than sixty well-known emblems in American society.[4] Some emblems on which every adult in their sample could agree were those for "be silent," "I warn you," "woman with nice figure," "shame on you," "that was a close call," "it's cold."

American children by the time they are three years old have a good understanding of emblems for the following messages: "yes," "no," "quiet," "going to sleep," "hello," "good-bye," "blowing kisses," and "I'm tired." Most three-year-olds do not correctly understand emblems for "what time is it," "crazy," and "who me?" Nursery school children were asked to tell something to another person without talking.[5] The messages they tried to communicate were "go away," "come here," "yes," "no," "good-bye," "hi," "I want attention." Two adult observers scored the children on how accurately they transmitted the messages. Seven-year-olds were able to transmit more accurately than four-year-olds.

The study of emblems offers an interesting approach toward understanding people from different cultures. Some common emblems for southern Italians are kissing the fingers ("delicious"), scissorlike movements of fingers ("gossip"), pressing the hands flatly together from opposite directions ("jackass"), pulling one's collar or shaking one's tie ("you can't fool me"), and rubbing the thumb and index finger ("money"). Americans and Colombians share the following emblems in common: nodding the head for agreement, clapping the hands for approval, yawning for boredom, shaking one's fist for anger, raising the hand for attention, rubbing hands to indicate feeling cold, waving good-bye, and turning thumbs down for disapproval. More than 1000 people in twenty-five European countries were interviewed about various gestures they use and their meanings.[6] Most people use the emblem of crossed fingers as a sign of protection, but in Turkey, they cross their fingers as a sign of a broken friendship. Southern Italians rotate their forefinger on their cheek as an emblem for something good. In Germany this emblem signifies that someone is crazy, and in Spain it signifies that a person is effeminate. Pulling the eyelid down with the forefinger is a common sign in many European countries for alertness. The vertical horn emblem (extending the forefinger and little finger while holding the two middle fingers down with the thumb) is commonly recognized by Europeans as indicating a cuckhold. Thumbing the nose is almost universally recognized as mockery, and holding the thumb up is widely recognized as an emblem for OK. For most Europeans, a forearm jerk with a closed fist represents the same emblem as the middle finger represents for Americans.

Weston La Barre described the following emblems used by people in various cultures:

> The Semang, pygmy Negroes of interior Malaya, thrust the head sharply forward for "yes" and cast the eyes down for "no." The Abyssinians say "no" by jerking the head to the right shoulder, and "yes" by throwing the head back and raising the eyebrows. The Dyaks of Borneo raise their eyebrows to mean

"yes" and contract them slightly to mean "no." The Maori say "yes" by raising the head and chin; the Sicilians say "no" in exactly the same manner.

Western man stands up in the presence of a superior; the Fijians and Tongans sit down. In some contexts we put on clothes as a sign of respect; the Friendly Islanders take them off. The Toda of South India raise the open right hand to the face, with the thumb on the bridge of the nose, to express respect; a gesture almost identical among Europeans is an obscene expression of extreme disrespect.[7]

ILLUSTRATORS

Illustrators are gestures and movements that people make when they speak. Unlike emblems, illustrators don't usually communicate a specific meaning. Their main function is to enrich or enhance face-to-face communication by embellishing and accentuating particular portions of a verbal statement. People use illustrators to clarify a point by drawing a picture or pointing with their hands. Illustrators also serve to communicate strong (active gestures) or weak (shrugging) emotional involvement in an interaction. Young children use pointing as an illustrator. Older children begin to picture or mimic objects and events with their hands. Adults use illustrators to modify or add new information to a point they are trying to make. The communicative value of illustrators is demonstrated by the fact that people use them more often when they are speaking face-to-face rather than over the telephone. Illustrators serve to make a communication more vivid and to hold the listener's attention by signaling the occurrence of pauses, long discourses, and major points.[8]

Illustrators are an integral part of a conversation. Research indicates that there is a systematic pattern between head nodding and speaking patterns.[9] Listeners nod their heads when they are ready to talk, and speakers nod when they are ready to listen. Speakers engage in most body movements when beginning a sentence and when pausing after a statement. These body movements correspond with the increased involvement they experience when they are trying to formulate their thoughts or emphasize a certain point.

We are all aware of differences in the use of illustrators by people from various cultures and ethnic groups. People from some cultures are reknowned for speaking with their hands. Humorous stories are told about the person who could not talk on the telephone because holding the receiver prevented necessary hand gestures, the orator who could not speak because his rheumatism made him "hoarse," and the person who complained, "you don't let me speak," after someone in an argument grabbed both of his hands.[10]

REGULATORS

Regulators are actions that coordinate the flow of communication between two or more people. They are used to initiate and terminate conversations and to signal when a listener is ready to speak and a speaker is ready to listen. The most common regulator for initiating an interaction is the handshake, which is usually accompanied with gazing and smiling. The traditional handshake has been modified by people from various groups and cultures to include different variations of handclasps and hand signs. Leave-taking also involves a handshake, along with decreased eye contact and turning away from the other person. More extreme regulators for leave-taking are looking at one's watch, rising to one's feet, and moving toward an exit.[11]

Speakers indicate that they are ready to listen by pausing, asking a question, and focusing their eyes on the other person.[12] Listeners communicate their desire to speak by intensifying their gaze toward the speaker, nodding their heads, making an audible intake of breath, and gesticulating. Speakers who are not ready to listen will speak louder, continue gesturing, and possibly touch the other person as a signal to "hold on." Listeners who are not ready to speak will keep the speaker going by remaining attentive, asking questions, restating the speaker's point, or uttering "mm-hmms."

ADAPTORS

Adaptors are movements we make when we find ourselves in a particular mood or situation. Adaptors include things we do with our own bodies (scratching, picking, grooming) and things we do with other objects (doodling, fiddling with a pencil or pen). One series of studies measured adaptors corresponding with various moods. A second group of studies focused on adaptors that occur when people are trying to engage in deception. A third group of studies compared adaptors that are demonstrated most commonly by men and women.

Adaptors Accompanying Moods and Emotions. One approach toward relating adaptors to moods has been to correlate the moods of people in various situations with their body movements. In psychiatric interviews patients' hand movements were correlated with the feelings they were expressing.[13] Throwing the hands in the air and flailing the arms occurred primarily during periods of frustration and anger. These adaptors were often present when the patient expressed feelings of ambivalence about family members. A hand-shrugging movement was associated with expressions of uncertainty, confusion, and inability to cope. Using the hands to cover the eyes occurred primarily during crying and expressions of shame. Rubbing the arms of the chair seemed to show restlessness and agitation. Gesturing with the hand out toward the interviewer occurred mainly in conjunction with an attempt to answer a direct question, often with verbal expressions of "I don't know," "probably," "I mean," or "I suppose." Hand movements of patients changed between the time they were admitted to hospitalization for psychotherapy and the time they were discharged. Acts of rubbing the chair arms and shrugging with the hands or throwing the hands in the air decreased markedly. Instead, a greater diversity of hand movements was developed that was less marked by repetitiveness and agitation.

Studies of interviews have found that people who are angry engage in many head and leg movements but few body movements. People who are depressed show many leg movements and few head movements. Psychiatric patients engaged in more body movements and gestures when they were under stress and talking about disturbing topics than when they were not stressed and were talking about neutral topics. College men were asked questions in a simulated police interview.[14] The interviewer crowded the men by standing very close, and the men's adaptors in the face of this crowding were recorded. Men reacted by turning their head and body away from the interviewer, averting their gaze, and crossing their arms in a self-protective posture.

The responses of college students to interview questions were coded into categories of overt hostility, covert hostility, and other feelings.[15] Overt hostility included statements in which students admitted and expressed hostile feelings in themselves. Covert hostility was defined by statements in which students talked about hostility in other persons and in situations that did not directly involve themselves. Careful scoring of students' body postures during the interview showed that when they were expressing overt hostility they tended to engage in movements focused on objects. Such movements are small gestures that punctuate and emphasize verbal statements. They don't usually involve touching one's body. When students were expressing covert hostility, their movements were generally focused on their own bodies. These movements include touching the hands together and touching or rubbing other parts of the body.

A second approach toward the study of adaptors and moods has been to instruct research participants to enact various moods and to measure the body movements they are making. A series of studies was conducted in which different emotional states were aroused in research participants by confronting them with questions and asking them actively to imagine themselves in various emotional situations.[16] The participants' judgments of their feelings during the experiments were correlated with the gestures and movements they were making. Attitudes of affection coincided with holding one or two fingers on one hand with the opposite hand. Attitudes of shame correlated with hand-to-nose or hand-to-lips gestures; aggression was related to fist gestures, frustration to an open hand dangling between the legs, and suspicion to two hands folded at the fingertips or one hand placed over the other.

Research participants were given the task of approaching another person while they themselves were either in a neutral state or attempting to portray the emotions of fear, anger, and sorrow.[17] Participants came fairly close to the other person when portraying anger and stayed far away when portraying fear. Most eye contact was given in the condition of fear and least in the condition of sorrow. Also when portraying sorrow, participants walked toward the other person fairly quickly. When acting angry, participants approached the other person slowly.

It can be concluded from these studies that agitated body movements often accompany feelings of anxiety and anger. When people are trying to hide or control their anger they fiddle more with their bodies and avoid making hostile gestures. Approaching others slowly and closely is a way of communicating anger. People protect themselves from too much intimacy by turning away and crossing their hands or arms as a barrier.

Adaptors Accompanying Deception. The most common method for studying deception is to compare body movements of research participants when they have been instructed to lie with their body movements when they are telling the truth. Participants who were arguing in favor of an issue in which they did not believe made fewer body movements and leaned or turned away from the person they were trying to deceive. When people are lying, they engage in a higher than usual number of self-manipulations, such as touching themselves, scratching, and tapping their fingers or feet. People also tend to shrug their shoulders and rub or scratch their faces when they are lying. Participants were instructed to give a short speech that was either very persuasive or neutral and objective.[18] When trying to be persuasive, they engaged in higher rates of head nodding and gesticulations and made more facial expressions.

In Chapter 4 you read that people are good at hiding deception in their facial expressions. Because we are less aware of our body language, we sometimes "leak" our attempts to lie through nervous gestures. Since we have better self-awareness of facial expressions, we can communicate specific feelings and emotions more accurately with our faces than with our bodies.[19]

Comparing Men and Women. Observations of men and women in therapeutic interviews found that men pointed more frequently than women and that women shrugged their shoulders, shook their heads, and turned their palms up and out more frequently than men. Women folded their arms across their waist more often than men and kept their legs crossed at their knees throughout a large portion of the interview. Men did not use the closed-leg knee cross. They sat either in an open-leg cross with one ankle on the knee of the other leg or with both feet on the floor. It appeared that the men's pointing and open-leg behaviors represented an active and assertive response to the interview. Women, with their folded-arm posture and predominantly closed-leg cross, came across as more inhibited and inclusive. Body behaviors of men and women were also compared when they were introduced to a stranger in a less threatening situation.[20] Women were more affiliative and intimate than men. Women talked more, nodded their heads more, made more pleasant facial expressions, gestured more, and turned their bodies more directly toward the stranger. Men tended to walk around and not sit still, especially when the stranger acted somewhat negatively toward them. It appears that men respond with more assertive adaptors than women in threatening interactions and that women engage in more affiliative adaptors in friendly interactions.

Body Language in Personal Relationships

Having considered the categories of body language, you are now ready to explore the way body behaviors operate in personal relationships. One way to study this aspect of body language is to place research participants in situations that elicit different kinds of attitudes and to correlate these attitudes with their body movements. Studies using this methodology are called *encoding studies*. In them, attitudes and feelings are manipulated as independent variables, and body movements are measured as dependent variables. In some encoding studies, participants are not aware of the experimental manipulation of their attitudes. In other encoding studies, participants role-play various kinds of interactions with other people. A second approach toward studying body language in personal relationships is to ask research participants to evaluate other people who are engaging in different kinds of body movements. Studies using this methodology are called *decoding studies*.[21] In them, the independent variables are the person's body movements, and the dependent variables are the judgments of the research participants.

ENCODING STUDIES

The studies summarized earlier on adaptors used an encoding methodology by eliciting various moods and motives in research participants and measuring their resulting body movements. Another series of experiments was conducted in which body movements were measured as participants role-played various attitudes. College students in three studies were asked to approach an imaginary person whom they liked very much, moderately, or not at all. Their body behaviors during the role plays were carefully recorded. Students gave lower amounts of eye contact, leaned backward, and stood farther away when approaching an imaginary person whom they disliked. College students in another series of studies were introduced to a stranger.[22] Half of the students were instructed to feel positively toward the stranger and to strike up a friendship. The remaining students were told to feel negatively toward the stranger and to avoid a friendship. When trying to feel positively, men smiled and nodded their heads, and women smiled and used hand gestures. When attempting to feel negatively, students tended not to smile, and they shook their heads.

Similar experiments were conducted in which college students approached an imaginary person who was of high status for some of them, of low status for others.[23] Students raised their heads more, gave more eye contact, and faced more directly when approaching a person of high status.

Encoding studies indicate that we smile, give eye contact, come close, lean forward, and make gestures when interacting with people we like. When interacting with people of high status, we are more straightforward and direct in body language than when interacting with people of low status.

DECODING STUDIES

Some decoding studies have focused on body movements that are related to perceptions of warmth, liking, and positive or negative affection. Other decoding studies have investigated body movements that influence perceptions of credibility and competence. Decoding research can be categorized into studies in which research participants made judgments of people in paintings, photographs, or videotapes and studies in which they interacted with people in real life.

Liking and Affection. Pavel Machotka described how his psychological interest in art was stimulated by the negative feelings expressed by many of his students toward Botticelli's *Birth of Venus*.[24] Venus is an attractive woman in the painting, but she stands in such a way as to close off her body from approach. It occurred to Machotka that the way Venus is standing might make her appear distant and inaccessible. To test this idea, he caused to be drawn a series of figures of a nude woman standing in several positions. In one drawing the woman covered her body with her arms, as in the painting of Venus. In another, the woman held her arms in an open, embracing position. In a third, she stood with her arms at her sides. When people rated these drawings they described the first woman as being self-centered, cold, rejecting, and unyielding. The second woman, with her arms outstretched, was perceived as immodest, dramatic, and exhibitionistic. The woman with her arms at her sides was admired most and judged as being natural, calm, and approachable. It is clear that the nude woman with her arms outstretched seemed too open; but with clothes on, she was judged as perfectly natural. The dress gave her enough of a body boundary to compensate for her open body posture.

A second series of studies demonstrated that perceptions of a person's body posture are influenced by the reactions of other people with whom he or she is interacting.[25] Three pictures were drawn of a man and a woman. In one picture the man and woman reached out toward each other. In a second, the man reached out toward the woman, who leaned away. In a third, the woman reached out toward the man, who leaned away. When they reached out toward each other, the man and woman were both seen as warm, sincere, erotic, active, and aggressive. A man who reached out toward a woman who leaned away was judged as aggressive, active, and evil. A woman who reached out toward a man who leaned away was judged as aggressive and action-oriented. Men and women who leaned away were judged as cold, calculating, nonerotic, passive, and constrained.

College students rated more than 100 nonverbal behaviors in terms of how much liking or disliking they communicated. Nonverbal behaviors that seemed to communicate liking included touching or moving closer, making eye contact, smiling, nodding one's head, using expressive hand gestures, opening the eyes or raising the eyebrows, and orienting one's body toward the other person. Nonverbal behaviors that seemed to communicate disliking included frowning, making little eye contact, moving away, yawning, sneering, picking one's teeth, shaking one's head, and cleaning one's fingernails. To test the effects of these nonverbal behaviors on interpersonal evaluations, videotapes were made of a woman engaging in various combinations of the behaviors as she conversed with a man. People who observed the videotapes evaluated her as less nervous and more socially competent, sincere, warm, and discerning when she engaged in nonverbal behaviors that communicated liking. They also viewed her more favorably when her nonverbal behaviors toward the man were consistently positive rather than unpredictable.[26] They liked her least when her nonverbal behaviors started off positively and later became negative.

Research participants rated videotapes of married couples who were discussing various problems and difficulties.[27] Couples were perceived as having greater marital satisfaction when their interactions included laughter, humor, compromise, mutual attention, and positive physical contact. The actual marital satisfaction of the couples was also positively correlated with these behaviors.

Videotapes were prepared of counseling interviews in which a male counselor sat with different arm and leg positions.[28] College students who viewed the videotapes evaluated the counselor as being warmest and most empathetic when he sat with his arms on the arms of the chair or with his hands in his lap and as coldest and least empathetic when his arms were crossed over his chest. He also seemed warmest and most empathetic with both feet on the floor or with his legs crossed at the knees or ankles. He was considered coldest and least empathetic in an informal, open-leg posture with the ankle of one leg resting on the knee of the other or with one foot propped on a chair and the other on the floor.

Two studies of body language in personal interactions found that leaning or orienting one's body toward another person is perceived as communicating more positive feelings than leaning or turning away. In one study college women came into a room in pairs and received a short lecture by a female experimenter. During the lecture the experimenter turned her body toward one of the students 90 percent of the time and toward the other student 10 percent of the time. Both students later judged that the experimenter had preferred the student toward whom she had turned most often. Participants in a second study were more verbally expressive to a "warm" interviewer, who leaned forward and engaged in eye contact and smiling, than they were to a "cold" interviewer, who leaned away and did not give much eye contact or smile.[29]

The influence of body language on feelings of liking and affection is far reaching. Body language has been shown to affect personal perceptions in pictures, social interactions, marital relationships, and counseling sessions. Positive feelings are communicated by a body language of openness, accessibility, and respect. Nonverbal behaviors of liking and affection should remind you about the suggestions for responsiveness in Chapter 1. A course on body language would be valuable in training in social skills.

Credibility and Competence. Two kinds of body language affecting judgments of credibility and competence are openness and immediacy. College women were more willing to be influenced by the attitudes of another woman when she was seated in an open rather than a closed body posture. An open body posture was defined as leaning back in the chair with outstretched legs and arms and hands away from the body. A closed body posture consisted of sitting with knees pressed together or with crossed legs and with arms crossed or pressed against the body. In another study college students made judgments of an interviewee who had been trained to engage in immediate or nonimmediate body behaviors during a placement interview.[30] When being immediate, the interviewee sat in an attentive posture, oriented her body toward the interviewer, smiled, and made eye contact. When being nonimmediate she smiled little, rarely made eye contact, slouched in her chair, and turned away from the interviewer. She was rated more favorably on a variety of positive traits including liking, competence, motivation, and recommendation for hiring when she was immediate.

Two teams of researchers made videotapes in which a counselor was either immediate or nonimmediate during a counseling session.[31] The immediate counselor leaned forward, turned and gestured toward the client, and made eye contact. The nonimmediate counselor leaned backward, turned away from the client, sat with folded arms, and looked away. College students who viewed the videotapes felt that the immediate counselor was significantly more expert, helpful, and competent than the nonimmediate counselor.

Research on body language and perceptions of credibility and competence indicates that it is advisable to be direct and immediate when we desire to convey our capabilities. It also brings us back to responsiveness. We feel most respect for others who use body language to express interest, attention, and immediacy. More will be said about communicating immediacy in Chapter 9.

The Voice

Messages communicated by tone of voice and speaking patterns are defined as *paralanguage.* They are messages "beyond" or "above" the words being spoken. Four components of human speech that communicate information about a person are *voice qualities* (resonance and articulation), *vocal characterizers* (laughing, crying, coughing, belching), *vocal qualifiers* (intensity and accent), and *vocal segregates* ("uh-huh," "um," "ah").[32] These categories of paralanguage are more specific than many of the variables measured in research on the voice. For this reason, the following discussion will be organized under somewhat broader headings. The first concerns the kinds of impressions we form of people from their voice and whether these impressions are accurate. The second considers characteristics of the voice that are related to expressions of emotion. At the end of the chapter is a section on speaking behaviors in personal relations. It will analyze studies that measured patterns of speech related to a speaker's feelings and motives and speaking behaviors that influence judgments about a speaker's ability, credibility, and likability.

IMPRESSIONS OF THE VOICE

Most research studies measuring impressions of people from their speech have not separated the information that comes from voice tones from the information derived from speaking patterns. The general procedure was to have research participants listen to samples of speech and make judgments and ratings about the speaker on various traits and characteristics. In the majority of examples the vocal cues used by research participants in making their judgments were not specifically defined. Some researchers focused on the accuracy of judgments made on the basis of the speaker's voice. Other researchers measured stereotypes associated with the voice.

Accuracy. How accurate are judgments we make about people from their speech? A speaker's sex can be accurately identified more than 90 percent of the time in normal speech and about 75 percent of the time in whispered speech. People can also identify a speaker's age, height and weight, social class, and photograph with an accuracy better than chance. A series of studies in which research participants judged people they heard but did not see found that people cannot accurately use someone's voice to evaluate his or her intelligence, leadership ability, sociability, occupation, tiredness, and veracity. Apparently people's voices are more useful for predicting their physical characteristics than for judging their personalities.[33]

Studies attempting to measure accuracy of judgments about a speaker suffer from two problems. First, there is usually no control for base rates (see Chapter 11). Research participants could be fairly accurate in judging an adult speaker's height or weight by guessing the average for an adult of the same sex. A speaker's personality traits could be predicted fairly accurately by choosing traits that are typical of the type of speakers included in most research studies. A second problem is that research participants may agree among themselves on how to rate a speaker, but the ratings may have little to do with what the speaker is really like.[34] Interestingly enough, this type of finding is not completely meaningless because it shows that we are taught (rightly or wrongly) to associate certain kinds of stereotypes with various kinds of voices.

Stereotypes. Here are some results from a study of voice stereotypes.[35] Men with breathiness in their voice are seen as young and artistic. Women with breathiness give the impression of being pretty, feminine, petite, high-strung, and shallow. Flatness in the voice is associated with masculinity, sluggishness, and coldness. Nasality is viewed as undesirable. Men with tense voices are evaluated as older, unyielding, and cantankerous. Women with tense voices come across as young, emotional, high-strung, and less intelligent. Increased rate of speaking makes both men and women appear animated and extroverted. Increased variety of pitch tends to identify men as dynamic, feminine, and aesthetically inclined. Women with a wide variety of pitch appear dynamic and extroverted.

Another series of studies investigated stereotypes associated with a speaker's ethnic or cultural identification. These studies found that we identify with people who speak with dialects and accents similar to our own. Speaking patterns of a majority group, however, are more generally accepted than those of a minority group. For example, French and English Canadians prefer speakers with English-Canadian accents over speakers with French-Canadian accents. Jewish and gentile students tended to devalue a speaker when he spoke English with a Jewish accent. American college students give relatively negative evaluations to speakers with a Mexican American accent, a European accent, and a black American accent. White preschool and primary-grade teachers evaluated the spoken responses of black children less favorably than those of white children.[36] These results are especially instructive because the content and verbal sophistication of the children's answers were equal for white and black. The prejudices shown by the teachers against the black children, therefore, were due strictly to the children's accents. The most common differences in the speech of black children from that of white children were the black use of *f* instead of *th* at the end of a word (*mouf* for *mouth*), the use of *d* instead of *th* at the beginning of a word (*dis* for *this*), omission of a postvocalic *r* (*caterpilla* for *caterpillar*), and the omission of a plural *s* (*leg* for *legs*).

Perceptions of Mexican American-accented English were measured in a study that looked at the context and ethnic background of research participants.[37] Overall, white, black, and Mexican American high school students evaluated a speaker with a Mexican American accent less favorably than a speaker with a standard American accent. Within this general prejudice, students evaluated the Mexican American accent more favorably when it was used in a home or family setting and less favorably when it was used in a school setting. Evaluations of a speaker with a Mexican American accent were also more favorable on traits related to personal qualities (good, trustworthy, kind) than on traits related to status (educated, wealthy, successful). Of the three dimensions on which human speech is commonly judged—sociointellectual status, esthetic quality, and dynamism[38]—research has demonstrated that minority accents are judged less favorably on sociointellectual status. It is not yet known how they are evaluated in regard to esthetics and dynamism.

Several issues can be suggested for future research on voice stereotypes. Members of a minority group are evaluated in a better light when they adopt the accent of a majority group. Therefore, training minority people to use "accepted" styles of speech may prove advantageous. This training must be balanced, however, against the importance of maintaining ethnic identity and cultural pride.[39]

COMMUNICATING EMOTIONS WITH THE VOICE

In order to study the way emotions are communicated by the voice it is necessary to separate the words a person is speaking from his or her tone of voice. One method for controlling the content of a spoken message is to employ *standardized speech* by having people communicate different emotions with their voice tones while they are speaking the same words or sentences. A second way to control verbal content is to use *electronic filtering,* which makes spoken words somewhat fuzzy so they cannot be understood but leaves the speaker's tone of expression intact. A third technique is *randomized splicing,* in which an audio tape is cut into short segments and pasted back together in random order.[40]

One series of studies of emotion in the voice used a decoding methodology in which research participants made judgments about the emotions they perceived in a spoken message. The purpose of these studies was to see how accurately people could communicate emotions with their voices and to measure characteristics of people who are relatively skillful and unskillful at recognizing emotions in speech. A second series of studies used an encoding methodology to define specific characteristics of the voice that are associated with different emotions. A third group of studies compared the expression of emotions in speech by people from various cultures. A fourth group of studies compared the amount of information about emotions that is conveyed through the voice and by means of facial expressions.

Decoding Studies. Emotional communication in the voice was studied by having men and women recite the alphabet ten times, each time trying to convey a different emotion.[41] Various speakers portrayed anger, fear, happiness, jealousy, love, nervousness, pride, sadness, satisfaction, and sympathy in different orders to control for the effects of practice. When judges listened to tape recordings of the speakers, they were able to guess all ten emotions with an accuracy better than chance. Anger was the easiest emotion to identify, and pride was the most difficult. Tones of voice for similar feelings (anger-jealousy, fear-nervousness) were more difficult to discriminate than tones for dissimilar feelings. Negative and positive feelings were equally easy to judge. People varied fairly widely in how accurately the judges could identify the emotions and the speakers could convey them.

Several investigators explored individual differences between people in their sensitivity to emotional communication in speech. People who are skillful in judging emotions in spoken messages can also make accurate judgments of emotions that are portrayed by artists and musicians. People who are skillful in portraying emotions with facial expressions are also skillful in communicating emotions with their voices. People who are skillful in communicating emotions in speech are also accurate in judging emotions in the speech of others. There is little correlation between a person's scores on personality tests and his or her accuracy in judging emotions in speech. There are significant correlations between accuracy in judging spoken emotions and scores on tests of auditory discrimination, ability to deal with abstract symbols, verbal intelligence, and knowledge of vocal characteristics.[42]

Experience is also an important influence on people's sensitivity to emotions in speech. Children become consistently better at judging emotions in speech from age five to age twelve. Blind adolescents are very attentive to textures and sounds in speech, but they are less accurate than sighted adolescents in judging emotions. This is probably due to the fact that blind people have less opportunity than sighted people to receive feedback from others about how emotional feelings are labeled and expressed. Schizophrenics are generally less accurate than others in judging emotions in speech,[43] probably because they have a limited and maladaptive emotional learning experience.

Encoding Studies. Emotional expressions in speech can be defined according to the following voice qualities and vocal qualifiers: loudness, pitch, timbre, rate, inflection, rhythm, and enunciation.[44] According to this scheme, soft speech, low pitch, resonant timbre, and slow rate are associated with emotions of affection and sadness. Loud speech, high pitch, blaring timbre, and fast rate correlate with emotions of anger and joy. Sadness is characterized by downward inflection, irregular pauses, and slurred enunciation. Affection and joy have upward inflection and rhythm and clipped enunciation.

Two studies were conducted in which actors read passages that had been written to communicate specific emotions.[45] Analysis of voice patterns indicated that they expressed anger and fear in a higher-pitched voice than that used for contempt and grief. They expressed indifference in the lowest-pitched voice. Voices expressing contempt were characterized by a very slow but steady rate of speech. Voices of grief had an especially large number of pauses, both within phrases and between phrases.

Comparing Cultures. You read in Chapter 4 that people from different cultures agree fairly widely about communication of emotions through facial expressions. Such diverse people have also been compared on their perceptions of emotions in speech. Tape recordings were prepared in which Americans spoke words or read sentences with neutral content while expressing different moods in their voices.[46] The expressed moods were anger, sadness, happiness, flirtatiousness, fear, and indifference. The tapes were played to college students in the United States, Japan, and Poland. As might be expected, Americans recognized the emotions more accurately than did students in Poland and Japan. The foreign students, however, could identify the emotions with an accuracy better than chance. The most difficult emotions for them to identify were flirtatiousness and happiness, perhaps because the voice tone used for expressing flirtatiousness is culturally specific. It is also possible that the ways of flirting in the United States are difficult to translate into other languages.

A similar study was conducted in which students from America, Israel, and Japan recited the alphabet in their own language while expressing emotions of anger, jealousy, love, nervousness, pride, and sadness.[47] People from the same as well as different cultures could judge which emotions were being expressed with an accuracy better than chance. The easiest emotions to recognize were anger and sadness. The most difficult to identify were nervousness and jealousy.

It can be concluded from this research that there is a culturally shared expression of emotions in the voice. Cross-cultural agreement is greatest for vocal expressions of anger, sadness, and fear. Emotions such as jealousy, attraction, and pride are more difficult to convey with one's voice and may be communicated more easily through gestures and facial expressions.

Comparing the Voice and Face. Are emotions expressed more accurately by the face or voice? It depends on how the question is approached. Several studies were conducted in which people communicated different emotions on videotape.[48] Research participants who only saw faces could judge the emotions more accurately than participants who only heard voices. These studies suggest that the face communicates emotions more accurately than the voice.

Another way to compare information from the face and voice is to measure how closely they correspond with judgments made from exposure to the whole person. In studies using this approach, research participants rated emotions either from a person's face, voice, or body. These ratings were compared with judgments based on all three pieces of information. When studied this way, the face, voice, and body were found to be "specialized" for different emotions. When people are being honest, the face is most prominent in communicating sociability, trust, dominance, and likability. The body stands out in communicating awkwardness, tenseness, and honesty. The voice communicates expressiveness and positive rather than negative feelings. When people are being dishonest, the voice takes on a greater role in determining how they are judged on tenseness, trust, honesty, dominance, and likability. The fact that the voice communicates more about people when they are lying can be explained by research showing that facial expressions are under our greatest conscious control. We often choose what we want to show in our faces while "leaking" our true feelings with our body and voice.[49]

A final point to consider is that people differ in their modes of expression. Some people express themselves with their faces, some rely on their voice, and others convey their feelings with their body. Therefore, it is probably not so important to ask how the face, voice, and body compare in accuracy.[50] A better direction for research is to learn more about how people choose to express various feelings in different kinds of situations.

The Voice in Personal Relationships

The voice has been studied in many different kinds of interactions. One series of studies measured people's speech in situations in which they were instructed to lie, were inclined to disinclined to be assertive, and were confronted with discomfort and anxiety. Another group of studies investigated how speech influences judgments about a person's confidence, ability as a counselor or psychotherapist, leadership ability, and likability.

One method for studying speaking behavior is to have an observer press a button whenever a particular person talks.[51] The button is connected to clocks and counters to provide information about amount of talking as well as length and number of statements made. Information can also be recorded about the number of times a person breaks a silence, how much a person talks relative to how much he or she listens, how often one person interrupts another, how often an interrupted person yields, and how often one person responds or fails to respond to someone's statement. Other voice characteristics that have been measured in personal interactions include intensity, pitch, rate of speech, and number of speech disruptions.

DECEPTION

Two questions will be addressed in this section. Do people speak differently when they are lying? Can we accurately recognize in a person's speech when he or she is being truthful or lying? The answer to the first question is yes. When lying, people talk more slowly and with more hesitations, they make more speech errors, and they speak in a higher-pitched voice. People's voices also seem weaker and more tentative when they are lying. Even though there are measurable differences in people's voices when they are truthful rather than lying, detecting lies from speech is not easy. Research studies by a number of different investigators lead us to conclude that we can detect lying in the voice with an accuracy that is often better than chance but rarely impressive.[52]

ASSERTIVENESS

When you wish to be assertive, it stands to reason that you talk in a forceful tone, especially when you feel confident that your words will be heeded. Internally oriented people (people who feel control over their lives) use more vocal intonation to convey a message than do externally oriented people (people who feel controlled by the environment).[53] The latter are more likely to choose assertive-sounding words than to express themselves with an assertive-sounding voice.

Even though we may use a more assertive voice when we feel confident, we can also bolster our confidence by using an assertive voice. Mothers of normal children use appropriate intonation and assertiveness in their voices when they express approval and disapproval to their children.[54] Mothers of disturbed children, in contrast, speak with little intonation and assertiveness when expressing approval and disapproval. They teach their children to ignore them because they are inconsistent in providing emotional feedback. Such inconsistency causes a vicious cycle because when disturbed children don't respond, their mothers begin to feel loss of control as parents.

An assertive voice is confident and consistent but not necessarily loud. Loud speech communicates aggressiveness but also insecurity. A loud voice might be useful for intimidation but it can result in a shouting match if the other person decides to meet your decibel level.[55]

DISCOMFORT AND ANXIETY

Measures of speech that have most often been correlated with discomfort and anxiety are speech disruptions, heightened pitch, and faster rate of speaking. Speech disruptions are measured by the number of times a speaker vacillates on words for the same meaning, repeats the same word twice, stutters, omits part of a word, doesn't complete a sentence, and makes slips of the tongue. These measures of speech have been studied in situations in which discomfort was instilled by means of uncomfortable interview topics, difficult or stressful tasks, and uncomfortable personal interactions.

Uncomfortable Interview Topics. Clients in psychotherapy and people in interviews talk with more speech disruptions when they are discussing issues that make them anxious or angry. People also talk faster when they are interviewed on topics that are uncomfortable.[56]

Difficult Tasks. Difficult tasks result in higher-pitched speech and faster speaking rates. Participants in one study spoke with higher-pitched voices when a perceptual task requiring verbal reporting became increasingly difficult. Another study found higher pitches in the voices of airline pilots who were experiencing flight difficulties. Research participants spoke in higher-pitched voices when they described a gory movie, and they talked faster when they were expecting to receive an electric shock.[57]

Personal Interactions. Research indicates that people change their speaking patterns when they feel uncomfortable interacting with someone of another race. One study found that white college students gave favorable evaluations to a black student after they were introduced. Their voice tones, however, contained signs of discomfort and negativity. White college students in another study gave shorter instructions and spoke with more speech disruptions when they were interviewing a black student than when they were interviewing a white student.[58] This study is important because it showed that the interviewer's nonverbal behaviors rubbed off on the interviewees. Interviewees with comfortable interviewers were also comfortable. Those with uncomfortable interviewers gave responses with speech disruptions and feelings of discomfort.

Speaking behaviors of people have also been measured when they are involved in positive interactions. People speak with lower volume and with fewer periods of silence when playing positive rather than negative roles. Interviewees give longer answers to interview questions when the interviewer is warm, attentive, and someone with status. An interviewer's warmth and attentiveness is contagious because when people find themselves giving longer answers in interviews they enjoy the interview more.[59]

COUNSELING AND PSYCHOTHERAPY

The relationship between psychotherapists and clients is unique. They meet in a structured setting to work on particular problems. Within this structured relationship they experience a whole range of feelings and interpersonal struggles. The richness of the therapeutic relationship has stimulated research into both the spoken and unspoken communication taking place in counseling and psychotherapy.[60]

One group of researchers evaluated tape recordings of therapeutic interviews that had been judged by psychotherapists as successful and unsuccessful.[61] During successful interviews the voices of psychotherapists had a medium or normal amount of intensity and stress and a soft, warm, relaxed tone. In the unsuccessful sessions the therapists more often sounded flat or monotonous, and they paused more and uttered more "uhs" and "uhms."

Another group of investigators prepared videotapes of counseling sessions in which the counselor intentionally spoke with a vocal intonation of concern or of indifference.[62] Vocal concern was characterized by soft, low voice tones and slow speech rhythm. Vocal indifference was expressed with harsh, high-pitched voice tones and rapid speech. Counselors who viewed the videotapes evaluated the counselor who spoke with vocal concern as communicating more empathy, respect, and genuineness than the counselor who spoke with vocal indifference.

Perceptions of counselors are also affected by the amount of time they talk during a counseling session. People generally feel that therapists should talk less than their clients. Research studies indicate that therapists who listen more than they speak are evaluated as being more attentive, helpful, empathetic, and competent. The fact that experienced counselors talk less in counseling sessions than inexperienced counselors indicates that the counseling profession is aware of this advice.[63]

LEADERSHIP

It was suggested in Chapter 1 that if you want to be chosen as a group leader you should talk a lot. This conclusion is basically correct. After all, people choose leaders who are visible and prominent. By talking a lot, potential leaders express their commitment to a group and their interest in keeping a group discussion going. People are generally chosen as group leaders when their participation is task-oriented and focused on moving the group to achieve its goals. This is especially true when the goals or purposes are unclear or ambiguous. Task-oriented statements are forceful and persuasive. They are directed toward achieving agreement and commitment. By behaving in a task-oriented manner, leaders clarify their roles as initiators and their subordinates' roles as performers. This role clarification is useful in corporations, agencies, and businesses whose focus is on production. Leaders of social and therapy groups are more likely to direct themselves toward maintaining group cohesiveness. They take on the role of facilitators to help group members experience meaningful personal relationships.[64]

LIKING

To gain insight into the relationship between liking and talking it is useful to refer back to the discussion about responsiveness in Chapter 1. Particular voice characteristics do not appear to be as important for reinforcing feelings of attraction as what people say and how they say it. You read in Chapter 1 that people prefer others who hold up their end of the conversation. People also like others who show interest in them and who make appropriate self-disclosures, compliments, and agreements. You will read more about this subject in Chapters 9 and 10.

CONFIDENCE AND CREDIBILITY

How do you express confidence and credibility with your voice? How do you communicate that you know what you're talking about? Research studies have provided the following answers to these questions.

Use an Expressive Tone. When delivering arguments with confidence we speak with an animated and expressive tone. People perceive energetic voices as communicating credibility. The only exception might be if we become so excited that we speak in a high-pitched voice and undermine our confident self-presentation by appearing nervous and shallow.[65]

Speak Fluently. Speech disruptions are associated with nervousness and incompetency. Don't break up your speech with pauses, stammers, and repeated words. Avoid "ahs," "uhms," and "you knows." Try to formulate your thoughts so you can convey your points in full sentences. You don't need to beat an issue to death. The idea is to express yourself completely and concisely.[66]

Speak Faster. It is better to increase your rate of speaking than to slow it down. People talk faster when they are feeling confident. They are also viewed as more extroverted, competent, persuasive, enthusiastic, and forceful when they don't talk too slowly. Because a rapid rate of speech communicates competence, it is often easier to persuade others when you present your argument briskly.[67]

Use Powerful Speech. The following tips for using powerful speech come from researchers who have studied speaking styles in courts of law.[68] Assume that a witness is asked the following question: Are you familiar with Park Square? Which answer should the witness give in order to come across as competent and credible?

    1. *Well, yes. I'd say I am.*

    2. *Yes. I know this area of town very well.*

You probably agree that answer 2 is more powerful than answer 1. Which of the statements below would you rate as powerful? Which ones sound powerless?

    1a. *Well, it seems like I've known him really long. I know him pretty well.*

    1b. *I've known him for three years and in that time I've gotten to know him well.*

    2a. *It was very dark that night.*

    2b. *Let's see. I'd have to say it was fairly dark that night.*

    3a. *Well sir. He seemed, you know, kind of angry.*

    3b. *He started yelling and acted as if he was very angry.*

The more powerful statements are 1b, 2a, and 3b. Here are some suggestions to help you learn to speak in a more powerful style.[69]

    1. Avoid the use of *hedges.* Hedges are prefatory remarks, such as "I think," "I guess," "I mean," "kinda," "sort of," "you know," "OK."

    2. Avoid *hesitations,* such as pauses and disruptions like "uh," "um," and "well."

    3. Don't be *overly polite.* Don't overdo the use of "sir," "madam," "if you please," "if you say so."

4. Avoid expressing *uncertainty* by making statements that sound like questions.

5. Don't overuse *intensifiers,* such as "very," "really," "for sure." Intensifiers are meant to be used sparingly to increase the force of a statement. If you use them all the time they lose their effectiveness.

6. Speak in *sentences.* There are times when a question is best answered with a simple yes or no. There are also occasions where it is more fruitful to respond with a full statement. Try to tell the difference. Remember the advice about responsiveness in Chapter 1.

7. Don't overuse *big words.* Use correct terms and jargon when it is appropriate. But don't throw in big words when it is not necessary. You'll just rub people the wrong way.

Remember these suggestions for powerful speech when you read about verbal immediacy in Chapter 10. You will find some interesting connections.

SIX

Personal Space and Crowding

This chapter is about physical closeness, personal space, and crowding. Personal space is a fascinating phenomenon for researchers because it is subtle and yet pervasive. Every time we interact with others we are subject to the influences of proximity and moods reinforced by the environment. Many of the research conclusions presented in this chapter will doubtless match your personal experiences. At the same time, you may be curious to discover how consistently you are affected by your environment of space and people and how you can moderate these forces by exercising environmental competency.

Seating Arrangements

In Chapter 1 you were introduced to the concept of environmental competence, which was defined as the ability to make changes in the environment to satisfy personal needs. The example presented there involved the challenge of maneuvering yourself within the conversational space of someone you wish to meet. Seating arrangements and environmental design provide two avenues for exercising environmental competence.

LEADERSHIP

Where would you sit if you wanted to lead a group seated around a table? Chances are that you would choose a seat at the head of the table. Leaders usually sit at the head of the table, and people who sit at the head of the table are usually chosen as leaders.[1] There are several reasons why leadership is given to the person placed at the head of a group. First of all, people who are leadership oriented tend to sit at the head of the group in the first place. People sitting at the focal point of a group talk more and receive more communication from others. Also other people expect the person at the head of a group to be the leader. Group members make a practice of reserving the head of the table for a person of high status or leader. When we observe people sitting at a table we assume that the person at the head of the table is the leader.[2]

SOCIAL INTERACTIONS

Where should you sit if you want to meet someone at an informal dinner? It depends on how brave you are. If you want to go along with the dinner conversation you should sit facing the person because informal conversations usually flow between people who are seated facing each other rather than side by side. College students in the United States and Britain usually choose to sit facing each other for a casual conversation. On the other hand, if you are feeling brave enough to slip out of the dinner conversation and engage this person privately, you should sit beside him or her. American and British college students generally choose to sit side by side or across the corner of a table for intimate conversations.[3]

COOPERATION AND COMPETITION

What are the best seating choices for cooperating and competing? American and British college students prefer sitting side by side for a cooperative interaction and facing each other for a competitive interaction. Close seating appears to be more conducive to cooperation than to competition. One group of research participants was encouraged to cooperate on a task and to work for the highest possible joint score.[4] They did better on the task when they were seated close together rather than far apart. Participants in a second group, who were instructed to be competitive and to try to earn the highest possible individual score, did better on the task when they were seated far apart.

Architecture and the Environment

Psychologists and architects have shared a growing interest in the relationship between human behavior and architecture and environmental design.[5] Although you might agree that social interactions can be influenced by the environment, you are probably not aware of the consistent effect of environmental settings on your everyday behavior. The design of an environment has been found to influence choice of friends, social communication, and moods.

CHOICE OF FRIENDS

If you have ever lived in a dormitory or apartment building you have experienced the influence of proximity on choosing your friends. Our circle of friends is determined by many factors, some intentional and others unintentional. But you can't meet people with whom you don't interact, and the more contact you share with someone the greater the chances you'll come to know each other. A study was conducted of choices of friends at a police academy where trainees were assigned to dormitory rooms and seats in classes in alphabetical order. Social factors such as religion, marital status, parents' education, and ethnic background had some effect on choice of friends, but propinquity was by far the most important influence. Another study reported a direct relationship between proximity and choices of friends for people living in housing projects. Similar effects of proximity were found in college dormitories.[6] Students had a greater proportion of friends living next door or two doors away rather than down the hall or on a different floor.

SOCIAL INTERACTIONS

How would you design a cocktail lounge if you wanted to facilitate social interactions between people? Most likely you would arrange tables and counters so that people could sit facing each other. How would you design an airport waiting room to inhibit social interactions? Although you might not be sympathetic to this goal, it can be accomplished (as it is in most airports) by arranging all of the seating side by side and by keeping any rows of seats facing each other at a distance too great for comfortable conversation.

The effects of seating arrangements on social interactions were demonstrated by introducing college students in pairs and seating them in chairs that were placed in one of three positions: directly facing, at right angles, or side by side.[7] Students were most sociable and affiliative when they were facing each other. Their social interaction was lowest when they sat side by side.

Researchers have used knowledge of the effects of environmental design on human behavior to modify social interactions. One group of researchers increased the social communication between residents of a home for the elderly by placing chairs that normally stood against the walls around small tables. The staff of the home complained that the chairs and tables cluttered the room, but, as a result of this simple change in room design, conversations and social interchanges between the residents nearly doubled. The effects of modified seating arrangements were also studied in the dayroom of a psychiatric hospital. When the chairs were arranged around tables there was more social interaction between patients and greater patient satisfaction and rapport than when the chairs were placed against the walls. An environmental psychologist supervised the remodeling of a dining room for 800 college students by partitioning the one large hall into a number of attractive smaller eating areas.[8] This change in room design resulted in a significant increase in social interactions and student satisfaction. These studies are instructive because they show how environmental factors are often neglected as important forces on behavior.

CLASSES AND INTERVIEWS

Observations of student participation in college classrooms have determined that most participation comes from students sitting in the front rows and least from those sitting at the rear or sides of the room. Students in seminars talk most when they are facing their instructor. Students generally avoid sitting next to the instructor, and if they are caught in such a position they are usually quiet. Students in college courses are commonly allowed to choose their own seats. Students in high schools and elementary schools are usually assigned to seats by the teacher. The use of assigned seats can have the effect of self-fulfilling prophecy by encouraging participation by good students and discouraging participation by poor students. A study of seating patterns in elementary schools found that teachers often seated the students they liked most in the front rows and those they liked least in the back rows.[9]

How are you affected by the furniture arrangement in the office of a business person, doctor, or professor? One study found that senior faculty members were more likely than junior faculty to sit with a desk between themselves and visitors. Another investigator concluded that medical patients are often more at ease when there is no desk separating them from their doctor. College students who were anxious about an interview felt that the interviewer was less competent when he sat behind a desk.[10] The anxiety of these students apparently caused them to experience the barrier of the desk in a negative manner. Students who were not anxious about the interview were not adversely affected when the interviewer sat behind a desk.

POSITIVE AND NEGATIVE MOODS

You have seen that the design of an environment can have a dramatic influence on interactions between people. The environment can also affect our positive and negative moods. College students were asked to rate other people in photographs.[11] Students who were seated in an attractive room with comfortable furniture, carpeting, and curtains gave more favorable evaluations than students who were seated in an unattractive storage room. Students also rated their own moods more positively when they worked in the attractive room.

People associate moods with different colors.[12] Red suggests excitement, stimulation, defiance, and hostility. Blue is associated with security, comfort, calmness, and serenity. Black is associated with power, strength, despondence, and dejection. Purple implies dignity and status, and yellow is identified with cheerfulness. Research has not yet determined the degree to which people's interpersonal behavior is affected by colors in their environment.

The relationship between moods and room temperature has been more closely investigated. Research participants were seated in rooms that were either uncomfortably hot or comfortable and mild. Participants in the hot room experienced more negative moods and gave less favorable personal evaluations to a stranger. Although they had negative moods, they did not express their discomfort by delivering an extra high number of electric shocks to another person when given that opportunity. It appeared that their primary goal was to get out of the room rather than to punish a stranger. Participants in the hot room did deliver fewer shocks when they were given a cooling glass of lemonade. These studies may remind you of the research on moods and weather summarized in Chapter 2. Researchers have determined that riots and collective violence occur more often in hot weather.[13] Relatively few riots take place when it is cooler than seventy degrees Fahrenheit and virtually none when the temperature is below freezing.

HUMANIZING ARCHITECTURE AND THE ENVIRONMENT

Psychologists are becoming more outspoken about suiting architectural and environmental design to human behaviors and needs. Many buildings that are attractive and impressive from the outside have not been designed to satisfy the psychological requirements of people on the inside. College students are less cooperative and socially responsible when they are assigned to high-rise rather than low-rise student housing.[14] Public housing projects are often so alienating to inhabitants that they end up being abandoned and torn down. Other examples of alienating environments include airports, hospitals, and many schools. You might find it instructive to pay attention to your environment and to notice the effects it has on people's moods and social behaviors.

Reactions to Physical Closeness

When people come close to us, they affect us in many ways. Physical closeness to someone often contributes to our judgments about what that person is like. Physical closeness can also influence feelings of comfort and anxiety as well as willingness to comply or agree with the other person's opinions and requests. In any relationship or interaction there is a range of interpersonal distances from too close to appropriate to too far. Anthropologist Edward T. Hall arrived at the following classification of "appropriate" distances for people in the northeastern United States: *intimate relationships* (one foot and less); *casual personal relationships* (one to four feet); *social-consultative relationships* (four to twelve feet); *public relationships* (twelve feet and over).[15] By analyzing studies of people's reactions to physical closeness we can increase our understanding of interpersonal distances that are viewed as most appropriate and comfortable for different kinds of interactions.

JUDGMENTS OF OTHERS

With everything else equal, we assume that people who are sitting or standing close to each other like each other better than people who are sitting or standing far apart. The effects of physical closeness on the formation of impressions were studied by having research participants interview a person who intentionally sat at a distance of two, four, six, or eight feet.[16] After the interview, participants evaluated the interviewee. Those who sat four feet away received the most favorable ratings, those who sat eight feet away the least favorable. In this interview situation, a seating distance of eight feet was too far, causing the interviewer to seem impersonal and withdrawn. Two feet was too close, which made both the interviewer and interviewee anxious and uncomfortable.

Men and women were introduced in pairs and left in a room for fifteen minutes to get to know each other. The original distance between participants was four feet. After five minutes, the woman moved her chair closer to a distance of two-and-a-half feet or farther to a distance of six feet. When questioned later most of the men stated that they had noticed the woman's movement. Their feelings toward her, however, depended primarily on her physical attractiveness. Participants in a similar study were introduced to two strangers.[17] One stranger sat close (one-and-a-half feet away), and the other sat at a distance (eight feet away). Participants liked strangers of the opposite sex better when they sat close. When strangers were of the same sex, their distance didn't matter. The seating distances in this study were more extreme than those in the previous study and noticeable enough to make a difference.

ANXIETY AND DISCOMFORT

A number of studies have been conducted to determine optimal sitting distances for different kinds of interactions. People don't want to be "too close for comfort," but they do want to be close enough to communicate as much intimacy as they feel like sharing.

Reactions of psychiatric patients were compared when they were seated three, six, or nine feet from a therapist during a psychiatric interview. Patients demonstrated most speech disruptions and reported having greatest problems in communicating their feelings when they were seated at a distance of nine feet. In general, both patients and therapists preferred the seating distance of six feet. Similar conclusions were reached in a study showing that college students spent more time talking about personal issues when they were seated five feet from an interviewer than when they were seated two feet or nine feet away. College students stated that they would be least anxious in a counseling interview if they sat at a distance of four feet from the counselor. They felt they would be more anxious sitting seven feet away and most anxious at a distance of two-and-a-half feet. Reactions of college students were studied during an interview that included questions about their backgrounds, interests, and future goals.[18] Students expressed greater comfort about the interview when they were seated two-and-a-half feet from the interviewer than when they sat one-and-a-half feet away.

It can be concluded from the research cited that people prefer to sit four to six feet away from an interviewer during a serious interview. They can tolerate somewhat closer distances for a casual interview.

PERSUASION AND CONFORMITY

When we want to persuade someone to agree with an argument or to do us a favor we find ourselves coming close enough to the person to make our presence influential but not overbearing. The effects of physical closeness on change of attitude were studied by exposing research participants to an experimenter who delivered a persuasive message from a distance of two feet, six feet, or fifteen feet. The optimal distance for changing someone's attitude was fifteen feet. At the closer distances, participants seemed to be distracted by the experimenter's presence, probably because they felt unduly pressured. Research participants in a similar study listened to the opinions of an experimenter who was seated at a distance of four feet or ten feet.[19] Distance did not affect how much participants changed their opinions, but they did express more nonverbal agreement with head nods and more arousal with gestures when the experimenter was seated at a distance of four feet.

The amount of weight lost by clients in a weight reduction clinic was compared after they worked with a counselor who sat at a distance of two or five feet.[20] If the counselor was accepting and approving, clients lost more weight when they consulted at a distance of two feet. If the counselor was neutral and somewhat impersonal in manner, clients lost more when they consulted at a distance of five feet. It seems that a close interaction distance for persuasion can be overbearing unless it is moderated with acceptance and approval.

Even though people don't like to be persuaded by others who come too close, it is necessary for persuaders to make their presence felt. Research participants were three times as likely to obey the orders of an experimenter to give electric shocks to another person when the experimenter sat next to them than when he or she talked to them from an adjoining room.[21]

INVASIONS OF PERSONAL SPACE

Up to this point you have considered studies of physical closeness from the viewpoint of asking which interpersonal distances are too close, appropriate, or too far for different kinds of interactions. Studies of invasions of personal space have measured people's reactions to interpersonal distances that were intentionally designed to be too close. Not surprisingly, people become uncomfortable when a stranger comes inappropriately close, and they attempt to compensate by reducing the intimacy of this physical closeness in one way or another. One way is to move away. A series of studies was conducted in which experimenters invaded people's personal space by sitting very close to them on park benches or in libraries. People reacted by "freezing" and becoming "vigilant" and finally by getting up and walking away. They were usually too anxious or puzzled by the invader's inappropriate closeness to hold their ground or to say something. Other researchers invaded the personal space of pedestrians waiting at the corner for a red light.[22] These pedestrians crossed the street faster than other pedestrians and made negative comments when they were asked how they felt about the person who had invaded their space.

Reactions to invasions of personal space depend on the status, age, and sex of the invader and on perceptions of the invader's motives. Students in a college library were more likely to escape from an invader who was dressed like a professor rather than like a fellow student. Adults reacted positively to invasion of their personal space by a five-year-old and negatively to invasion by a ten-year-old. People are less comfortable when men invade their space than when women do so. Women escape invasions of personal space more often than men.[23]

If you want to introduce yourself to a stranger, you have to avoid invading his or her personal space. Women often prefer the safety of a barrier like a table or counter between them and an unknown person.[24] Men don't like face-to-face seating that demands too much eye contact with people they don't know.

Crowding

On the surface, crowding might appear as an example of a prolonged invasion of personal space. Two factors qualify this definition, however. First, unlike invasions of personal space, crowding is generally not viewed as intentional. Second, crowding takes place over relatively longer periods of time and gives people the capacity to develop adaptive responses.

The issue of crowding was first brought to public attention by animal researchers who found social pathology in colonies of mice that had become overcrowded to the point that adequate nesting space was no longer available. Similar pathology would undoubtedly also occur in humans if they were crowded to the point that they could no longer carry on their daily self-care activities. Outside of such extreme crowding, it appears that people can adapt remarkably well to high population densities. Humans have language and the ability to think. These capacities can make life harder during times when we have unrealistic expectations or tell ourselves things that make us unhappy. They can also give us more options for adjusting to crowding in the ways we anticipate, interpret, and react to crowded situations.[25]

Jonathan Freedman has argued that population density in large cities is not necessarily bad and indeed has many virtues. He points out that cities provide an efficient means of housing large numbers of people and that city streets, parks, and neighborhoods are safer and more desirable when they are filled with people than when they are deserted. Freedman outlined a theoretical model treating population density as an intensifier of whatever positive or negative feelings are present in a given situation. This model was supported in a series of experiments in which research participants were placed in crowded or uncrowded rooms in contexts that were either pleasant or unpleasant. When people experienced the pleasure of receiving praise or succeeding at a task, they experienced more positive feelings in the crowded room. People who had an unpleasant experience of receiving criticism or failing at a task felt better in the uncrowded room. Other models of crowding have also suggested that reactions to population density are moderated by positive or negative interpretations of the situation.[26] People's reactions to crowding depend on how much the crowding interferes with their needs, goals, and feelings of control. They also react differently to crowding according to their individual preferences for personal space.

NEEDS AND GOALS

A number of researchers have determined that crowding is particularly detrimental when it interferes with people's needs and goals. Although a crowded situation is not desirable for studying or going home during rush hour, it is preferable for a party or outdoor concert when a "critical mass" is necessary if people are to interact and have a good time.[27]

People can work quite well in a crowded room as long as they don't have to move around so others get in their way. People working in a crowded room can adapt when others are close enough to infringe on their personal space, but they reach their limits when they are interrupted and distracted from what they are trying to do.[28]

PERSONAL CONTROL

Crowding is also detrimental when it threatens our feelings of control. The relationship between crowding and personal control was tested experimentally by crowding unsuspecting people in a college library elevator. Half of the elevator riders were crowded by a group of researchers toward the control buttons. The remaining riders were crowded away from the control buttons. What effect did the opportunity to press the button for one's own floor have on these people? Young adults felt more negatively about the crowding experience when they were pushed away from the buttons. They didn't mind the crowding as much when they could personally press the button for their floor. Older adults didn't mind being crowded away from the buttons. They either reached over to the buttons or simply asked one of the crowders to press their floor. Participants in another experiment felt more comfortable in a crowded group when they were given a chance to play a useful leadership role.[29] Constructive input on the group process permitted them to maintain a sense of personal control.

The relationship between crowding and personal control has also been studied in living situations. A study was conducted to compare reactions of college students who lived in crowded or uncrowded dormitory rooms.[30] Owing to a shortage of space, some students found themselves living with two other students in a room designed for two. Other students were lucky enough to live with one other student in a double room. Not surprisingly, students who were crowded three to a room were less satisfied and more uncomfortable. One of the major factors contributing to their discomfort was lack of personal control. With an extra person in the room it was much harder to regulate study time, sleeping, and privacy.

Personal control is often limited in dormitory living because residents can't choose whom they pass in the hallway, bump into in the bathroom, and meet in the lounge. This problem is greatest in large dormitories with long open corridors where residents face many unwanted encounters. Students living in such dormitories are generally less satisfied with their living situation and less positive about their social interactions than students living in dormitories where rooms are arranged in short corridors or suites.[31]

After reading about the detrimental effects of crowding in college dormitories, you won't be surprised to learn how crowding impinges on the lives of people confined to psychiatric hospitals and prisons. Not only do patients and prisoners have fewer opportunities to modify their environment, they also have weaker coping skills. Residents in crowded hospitals and prisons face many frustrations in meeting their needs because of scarce resources. They also suffer from lack of control over unwanted interactions and from the strain of having to be on guard against unstable people with whom they are obliged to live. Research has implicated crowding in psychiatric hospitals and prisons with higher than average rates of stress, illness, antisocial behavior, emotional problems, suicide, and death.[32]

PREFERENCES FOR SPACE

People have individual preferences for personal space. Some people like to stand or sit close. Others prefer to keep their distance. How do preferences for closeness and space influence reactions to crowding? Not surprisingly, people who like closeness don't mind crowds as much as do people who like space, and they do not suffer so much physiological stress when they are in a crowded situation. On an individual level, those who like closeness are more outgoing, leadership oriented, and self-confident. These traits allow them to exercise control in crowded situations. On a cultural level, some societies teach children from a young age to adapt to a high population density.[33] People from congested cities often feel lonely and isolated when they move to the country. On the other hand, imagine the discomfort of a farmer or rancher riding a subway during rush hour.

Coping with Crowding

It is clear that crowding can be detrimental when it prevents us from regulating our lives and achieving our needs and goals. How can we learn to cope? Research studies provide the following suggestions.

MODIFY YOUR ENVIRONMENT

One imporant question raised by researchers who studied crowding in dormitories is whether the negative effects of crowding can be reduced by altering the environment. Residents of large dormitories achieved greater feelings of control over their interactions when the long corridors in which they lived were divided into two short corridors separated by a lounge.[34] As a result of this simple environmental change, residents were more sociable and more at home in their living situation. Although it might not be possible for you to make architectural changes when you are crowded, there are other ways to exercise environmental competence. People working in large offices often put up decorations or erect "barriers" around their desks to gain privacy and to personalize their space. Campers in crowded parks hang blankets to define their territory. Apartment dwellers partition balconies and terraces with plants and furniture. With these thoughts in mind, it is useful to make the distinction between controlling one's space and being antisocial. It is important to be aware of our tolerances for crowding and to feel we can modify our environment when it is getting the better of us. We can also profit by developing our coping skills so we don't always need to withdraw or seek physical changes when faced with a crowding experience.

CONTROL YOUR ANXIETY

One way to control your anxiety in crowded situations is to anticipate the crowding so you can prepare for it. On the other hand, when anticipation makes you anxious and you expect the worst, your stressful experiences become more difficult than they need to be. One group of research participants was told that they would be interacting with others in a crowded room.[35] Participants in a second group expected to meet others in an uncrowded room. In fact, neither group was ever crowded. However, because participants in the first group let their anticipation of crowding get the better of them, they were much less positive toward one another and more negative about being in the experiment.

You can control your anxiety in crowds by following the relaxation exercises outlined in Chapter 1. You can also be easy on yourself. If you are trying to accomplish something in a crowded situation, you should set realistic goals. People who are determined to maintain high productivity while being hindered by others can do so, but they pay a price in stress.[36]

USE COPING STRATEGIES

Here are three strategies for coping with crowding: (1) set priorities, (2) think adaptively, (3) take action.

Set Priorities. How do you react when faced with a million things to do at one time? Do you try to accomplish them all at once and end up being overwhelmed? Or do you make a list of priorities and work on them one at a time? Residents of large dormitories adapt much better when they set priorities for social interactions.[37] By making friends selectively and reserving time for themselves they maintain a greater sense of control over their living situation than residents who are caught up following the crowd and trying to make friends with everybody.

Think Adaptively. What can you tell yourself in a crowded situation that will help you function at a reasonable level? People who were going to shop in crowded stores were provided with several different strategies to prepare themselves for the crowded situation.[38] Shoppers who anticipated the crowd and the fact that it would be a hindrance suffered less discomfort and interference than shoppers who did not anticipate the crowd. Shoppers had greatest success coping with the crowd when their mental preparation was geared toward experiences (such as encountering many people, feeling anxious or frustrated) that were personally relevant. A more general mental preparation, such as positive thinking, was not as useful. When we prepare mentally for a crowding experience, we anticipate the crowding and think adaptively about how we can maintain our sense of control. You might find it useful to make a list of adaptive self-statements for crowding similar to those suggested for shyness in Chapter 1 (Table 1-1).

Take Action. Two action-oriented strategies are to escape the crowd and to modify the environment. If these responses are not feasible, you might wish to exert a leadership role to help the group achieve a structure. People feel less discomfort in a crowded group when the group has an operating procedure or a leader.[39] By taking an active role you can help yourself as well as others around you.

Factors Influencing Closeness

You would undoubtedly agree that the space you put between yourself and another person depends on how well you know that person and how you feel toward each other. You might be surprised to learn, however, about the number and variety of factors influencing your interaction distances. Interpersonal distances are related to individual characteristics such as culture, age, and sex. They are also associated with people's relationships, motives, and feelings.

CULTURE AND ETHNIC BACKGROUND

Our preferences for the physical distance we maintain from others are a product of experience and culture. Anthropologists have reported that Arabs, Latin Americans, and southern Europeans generally prefer closer interaction distances than Americans, Japanese, and northern Europeans.[40] The story is often told how Americans at international conventions appear to prefer holding conversations near walls and in corners. The reason is that the foreign participants often like to stand closer to other people than Americans do. When they are talking to Americans they come to the distance most comfortable to them. The Americans then back away to their preferred distance. The foreigners again come closer, and the Americans again back away until both parties have waltzed themselves to the edge of the room.

Interpersonal distances were recorded between Mexican American, black, and white visitors at a public zoo. Mexican Americans stood closest and blacks stood farthest apart. When college students kept records of how close other people came to them, it turned out that white students came closer on the average than black students. Two observational studies of interaction distances between elementary school children in New York City determined that black and Puerto Rican children interacted at closer distances than white children.[41] These differences in interpersonal distance were especially prevalent for children in the first and second grades.

These studies are interesting because they used natural rather than contrived methods for observing relatively large groups of people, but their conclusions show discrepancy. The first studies concluded that whites have closer interaction distances than blacks, and the second studies concluded that blacks have closer interaction distances than whites. The reason for this discrepancy is that in large-scale observational studies it is difficult to control extraneous variables. The first studies focused on adults, and the second studies focused on children. In addition, the black and Puerto Rican children in the second studies came from lower socioeconomic backgrounds. It is therefore not known whether the observed differences in interpersonal distance were due to age, ethnic background, or social class. On the basis of additional observational data it was concluded that, regardless of race, lower-class children maintain closer interaction distances than middle-class children.[42]

Another variable influencing interpersonal distances is the nature of the interaction. With regard to the discrepancy in the studies cited, it is likely that the relationships of people visiting a public zoo are different from those of children in school and of college students interacting with people in their everyday lives.

AGE AND SEX

Two studies comparing interaction distances of children of different ages found that younger children (first through fifth grades) come closer to one another than older children (seventh through twelfth grades). By the time they are twelve, children use interaction distances similar to those of adults. It has been concluded by a number of researchers that women generally prefer closer distances than men.[43]

STATUS

People often maintain greater distance from someone who has power or status. This increased distance is motivated by respect for the territory of the person of higher status and the desire to avoid appearing inappropriately intimate. One group of investigators observed interaction distances of U.S. naval personnel and found that low-ranking personnel stood farther away when they initiated an interaction with a higher-ranking officer than when they initiated an interaction with a person of their own rank. Higher-ranking officers felt equally free to come close to fellow officers and people of lower rank. Other researchers demonstrated that physical attractiveness can communicate power by showing that pedestrians kept greater distances when walking past a woman who was dressed and made up to be attractive rather than unattractive. College students did not maintain greater distances from someone who was introduced as a research professor, but it is likely that research professors don't hold as much status for students as high-ranking officers hold for military personnel. Male employees in a utility firm maintained similar distances from other employees of equal or different status, but they oriented their bodies more directly toward other employees of equal status.[44]

There are also occasions when people use physical closeness to identify with a person of high status. College students in a psychology experiment came closer to a male professor than to a male student.[45] However, they stayed farther away from a female professor than from a female student, perhaps because they were not comfortable with a woman in the role of professor. It is also possible that the two professors gave out different feelings of approachability.

FAMILIARITY AND LIKING

Physical closeness is related to how well people know each other and how much they like each other. Participants in several studies came closer when they approached an imaginary person they liked rather than disliked. College students sat closer to another person when they were trying to develop a friendship than when they wanted to avoid it. Observations of interaction distances between people have indicated that friends and acquaintances stand closer together than strangers. This finding is especially true of women friends and friends of the opposite sex. College students reported that they maintain closer interaction distances with close friends than with acquaintances.[46] Interaction distances with parents were similar to distances with strangers.

Two observational studies determined that junior high school and college students sit closer to classmates they like and farther from classmates they dislike. Couples who liked each other after a blind date stood closer together than couples who did not like each other. Research participants sat closer to someone with whom they shared similar rather than dissimilar attitudes. Kindergarten children play at a closer distance when they are friendly rather than unfriendly. Experimenters approached pedestrians in politically conservative and politically liberal neighborhoods.[47] People in the conservative neighborhood came closer to experimenters who were wearing a "flag" button rather than a "peace" button. People in the liberal neighborhood came closer to experimenters who wore the peace button.

DISCOMFORT AND NEGATIVE MOODS

When we feel uncomfortable in an interaction with another person we usually increase the distance between us. Studies of interaction distances and discomfort have focused on the effects of anxiety about being evaluated, experiences of failure, reactions to competitiveness, and proximity to people who are disabled.

Research participants stayed farther away from an experimenter when they were told that the experimenter was going to judge their sex appeal and physical attractiveness. College students sat farther away from an instructor when they were expecting to be reprimanded than when they were expecting to be praised. College men were interviewed by a woman student who gave them eye contact or who did not look at them during the interview.[48] Men who received no eye contact felt that she was inattentive, and they sat farther away from her after the interview.

An experiment was conducted in which participants experienced success or failure. Those who experienced failure kept a greater distance from others than those who experienced success. Participants in another study played a game with someone who was either cooperative or competitive.[49] Participants later avoided sitting next to the person who was competitive.

Research has shown that people with physical disabilities suffer not only the disability, but also the avoidance of others with whom they come in contact. Participants in one study stayed farther away from a man when he was made up to look as if his leg had been amputated. Participants in other studies kept greater distances from a person who was introduced as being either an epileptic or a bisexual.[50]

DOMINANCE AND AGGRESSION

Invading someone's personal space is a good way to express dominance and aggression. Research participants were intentionally insulted by an experimenter while they were working on some tests. Later, when the insulted participants were given the task to walk toward the experimenter as a test of the "orienting reflex," they came much closer than participants who had not been insulted. Participants in another study approached an experimenter while simulating the following emotions: neutrality, fear, anger, and sorrow. They came closest to the experimenter when they were simulating anger, and they stayed farthest away when they were simulating fear.

Invasions of personal space are sometimes used by police interrogators to intimidate suspects into confessing.[51] Military officers invade the personal space of enlisted men to maintain discipline and exert their authority.

It is interesting to reflect on the fact that physical closeness can be associated with such a variety of feelings, ranging from love and friendship, anxiety and discomfort, to threat and dominance. You read in this chapter how preferences for personal space and reactions to physical closeness are determined by the following factors:

1. Background and culture

2. Sex and personality

3. Environment

4. Nature of interaction

5. Relationship with person(s) involved

6. Personal motives

7. Perceptions of other person's motives

In Chapter 7 you will discover that these factors also affect interpersonal behaviors of gaze and touch.

You are also beginning to understand that personal interactions are affected not only by ongoing behaviors but also by perceptions, judgments, and interpretations about the meaning and causes of these behaviors. The process through which people explain one another's actions is of major importance in the perception of people and it will be analyzed from many directions in the last five chapters of this book.

SEVEN

Touch and Gaze

The focus in this chapter is on touch and gaze. These nonverbal behaviors are important because they are so closely linked with the concepts of responsiveness and immediacy that are discussed throughout this book. Touch and gaze communicate intimacy and closeness. They intensify whatever feelings are present in an interaction. For this reason, the effects of touch and gaze depend very much on the personalities, motives, and perceptions of givers and receivers. The complexity of these nonverbal behaviors has stimulated an active effort by researchers to figure out how they work. This chapter will bring you up to date on what has been discovered about the giving and receiving of touch and gaze.

Touch

Touch represents the most intimate form of physical closeness and has been viewed by psychologists as an essential means of communication in human development. Lawrence K. Frank begins his essay on the importance of touch for the developing child with the following description:

> The skin is the outer boundary, the envelope which contains the human organism and provides its earliest and most elemental mode of communication.[1]

Ashley Montagu refers to touch as follows:

> . . . a sensation to which basic human meanings become attached almost from the moment of birth [touch] is fundamental in the development of human behavior. The raw sensation of touch as stimulus is vitally necessary for the physical survival of the organism. In that sense it may be postulated that the need for tactile stimulation must be added to the repertoire of basic needs in all vertebrates, if not in all invertebrates as well.[2]

Sidney Jourard provides the following observations about touch:

> I watched pairs of people engaged in conversation in coffee shops in San Juan (Puerto Rico), London, Paris, and Gainesville (Florida), counting the

number of times that one person touched another at one table during a one-hour sitting. The "scores" were, for San Juan, 180; for Paris, 110; for London, 0; and for Gainesville, 2. On another occasion I spent two hours walking around the Teaching Hospital at the University of Florida, seeking episodes of body-contact. I watched nurses and physicians tending to patients, I observed relatives in conversation with patients, and I patrolled corridors, watching interchanges between nurses and nurses, physicians and nurses, and physicians with each other. During this time, two nurses' hands touched those of patients to whom they were giving pills; one physician held a patient's wrist as he was taking a pulse; and one intern placed his arm around the waist of a student nurse to whom he was engaged. Clearly, not much physical contact was in evidence. By contrast, I have seen happily married spouses touch one another dozens of times before others—a kiss, a handclasp, a hug. And miserably married persons whom I have seen in psychotherapy have often complained of too little, or too much physical contact. Finally, I have encountered individuals who become furious, and jump as if stung if they are brushed against, or touched on the shoulder or chest during a conversation.[3]

Research on touch has been directed toward investigating differences between people in how much they touch, what touch means to them, and their reactions to being touched.

How Much Do People Touch?

One way to determine how much people touch one another is to ask them. Two studies were conducted in which college students indicated where and how often they were touched by their mother, father, friend of the same sex, and friend of the opposite sex. Women appeared to be more accessible to touch than men. This finding might be a carry-over from the fact that girls are touched more by mothers and female teachers than boys are. Students reported that friends of the opposite sex touched them most often and their fathers touched them least often. There was more touching between friends of the opposite sex in 1976 than in 1966. A similar survey conducted in Japan found that Japanese college students touch each other only half as much as do American college students.[4]

Men in American society don't mind being touched by women they don't know, but they are uncomfortable about being touched by other men, whether they are friends or strangers.[5] Women don't mind being touched by men and women with whom they are well acquainted. They are most troubled by touch from men they don't know.

Another way to study how much people touch is to observe them. Observations of elementary school and junior high school children resulted in the following conclusions. There is more touching between children of the same sex than between children of the opposite sex, and overall amounts of touching decrease as children grow older. Observations of pairs of people who were saying goodbye or greeting each other in an airport indicated that some sort of physical contact was present in 85 percent of the interactions. Men were more likely to shake hands with each other, and women were more likely to hug. Lovers held hands and kissed. Observations of touching among nursing home residents found that elderly women engaged in more touching than elderly men.[6]

The Meanings of Touch

Touch seems to have different meanings for people in different situations, but it intensifies whatever interaction is taking place. Two studies were conducted in which married and unmarried college students described how they felt about being touched by their spouse or closest friend of the opposite sex.[7] One interesting finding was that unmarried men were more inclined than unmarried women to equate sexual touching with warmth and love. The implication of this result is that men who are trying to be friendly and playful by means of sexual touching may come across to women as unpleasant and annoying. A second important finding was that married men were less likely than their wives to equate sexual touching with warmth and love. Wives viewed sexual touching as communicating emotional states. Husbands, in contrast, interpreted sexual touching (especially when initiated by their wives) less as a sign of affection and more as an attempt by the wife to assert power. Obvious problems can arise when a woman touches her husband sexually to express warmth and the husband perceives his wife as trying to dominate him.

The meaning of touch has also been studied by asking people to give their impressions of others who touch or do not touch in various situations. Research participants evaluated engaged couples in a videotaped interview. In half of the interviews the couples held hands, and in half they did not touch each other. The observers liked the couples better when they touched. They also viewed the touching couples as closer, more attentive toward each other, and more nervous than nontouching couples. Participants in a similar study rated a male interviewer and a male job applicant in a videotaped job interview.[8] In half of the interviews the interviewer shook the applicant's hand before and after the interview, and in half of the interviews the interviewer did not shake hands. Hand shaking did not influence ratings of the interviewer. Job applicants, however, were evaluated as more sincere and as liking the interviewer more when the interviewer shook their hand. It appeared that the interviewer's willingness to shake hands influenced judgments about what the applicant was like.

A more direct form of touching than a handshake is placing one's hand on someone's shoulder. When one person is touching another person on the shoulder (and nothing is known about their relationship), the toucher is viewed as assertive, warm, expressive, and dominant. The person being touched comes across as submissive and introverted. Interestingly enough, these perceptions of initiated and received touch match our experiences. Research participants who were given a role in which they touched another person felt a greater sense of enjoyment and contribution to the experiment than participants who were assigned to the role of being touched.[9]

Reactions to Touch

How do you feel about being touched? Your answer to this question naturally depends on what is going on and who is doing the touching. Researchers have examined reactions to touch in many contexts and situations.

STRUCTURED INTERACTIONS

Participants in one study responded more favorably to a series of slides they were viewing when they were lightly touched by an experimenter of the opposite sex. Men in another study performed more poorly on a problem-solving task when they were unexpectedly touched by the experimenter during the testing period. The touching did not hinder their performance if it was justified by their being told that touching was the easiest way for the experimenter to signal the time. Women performed equally well on the tasks whether the touch by the experimenter was justified or unjustified. In general, women liked him better when they were touched, and men liked him better when they were not touched. Participants in a third study were introduced to a person who either initiated or did not initiate a handshake.[10] They felt more favorably toward men when they shook hands. Women participants liked women who shook hands but men participants did not. Men seemed to feel that a woman who offered a handshake was too assertive and unfeminine.

COUNSELING INTERVIEWS

Touch is a positive and acceptable experience in counseling situations. College students evaluated a male interviewer more favorably and disclosed more about themselves when he touched them lightly as they came into the room. Responses of female clients in counseling interviews were compared when they were touched or not touched by the counselor. Touching involved shaking the client's hand and touching the client four times during the fifty-minute interview. Clients who were touched by the counselor engaged in more self-exploration than clients who were not touched. Such touching did not influence ratings made by the clients about their feelings toward the counselor and the interview. College men and women rated their experiences in a twenty-five-minute counseling interview as more posi-tive when the interviewer shook hands before and after the interview and touched them five times during it. The positive effects of touch were strongest for students who were touched by interviewers of the opposite sex. Students were not affected by a counselor's touch when it was given in a rehearsed and controlled manner during a fifty-minute interview. Touch appears to have positive effects primarily when it is accompanied by expressions of warmth. Reactions of encounter group members were compared in groups that did exercises involving interpersonal touching and groups that did not involve touching.[11] Participants who had the ex-perience of touching rated one another more favorably and expressed greater will-ingness to share closeness and express personal feelings.

HOSPITALS

Sidney Jourard argued that nurses and other people in helping relationships can exert a positive influence on their clients by touching them more often. Although touch can often provide a positive experience, it must be guided by the context and situation. Female hospital patients awaiting surgery reacted favorably to the experi-ence of being touched by a nurse, saying that they felt better and were less anx-ious.[12] They also showed more interest in reading about their surgery and demon-strated greater physiological signs of relaxation after their operation. Male patients who were touched by nurses reacted very differently. They demonstrated more negative responses than men who were not touched. Men seemed to react nega-tively to touch in the hospital because it exaggerated their feelings of helplessness and dependency.

LIBRARIES

Students' reactions were compared after they were touched or not touched by the library clerk who checked out their books in a college library.[13] Students who were touched said they felt better, and they rated the library clerk more favorably than students who were not touched. Positive reactions to touch were stronger for women than for men.

Other Meanings of Touch

A particular aspect of the intensifying function of touch is its positive effect on compliance. Touch may also be considered in its relation to power.

TOUCH AND COMPLIANCE

A number of studies have found that people are more likely to agree with requests if the person making the request lightly touches them. Dimes were left in telephone booths, and a female experimenter approached people who found the dime with the following request: "Excuse me. I think I might have left a dime in this phone booth a few minutes ago. Did you find it?" She touched half of the people lightly on the arm or shoulder but not the other half. Sixty-three percent of the people who were not touched returned the dime, and 96 percent of those who were touched returned it. Female experimenters in a second study approached people in a shopping mall and said: "Excuse me. Could you lend me a dime?"[14] Again, the experimenters touched half of the people but not the other half. The experimenters received dimes from 29 percent of the people who were not touched and from 51 percent of those who were.

Because these studies only used female experimenters, two additional studies were conducted in which male and female experimenters asked people to answer a questionnaire or sign a petition. Regardless of the experimenter's sex, people who were touched lightly on the arm agreed more often with the request. In some situations touch might be useful for salespeople. Shoppers in a supermarket were more willing to sample and buy a new brand of pizza when the salesperson offering the pizza touched them.[15]

Studies of touch and compliance are similar to the research discussed earlier on distance and persuasion because they show that when we want to influence others it helps to reinforce our presence. Of course, you will notice that the touching in the above experiments was subtle and not overbearing. Touching will surely have negative effects if it is indiscreet. Since touch is an intensifier, its favorable effects depend on a positive and appropriate interaction. Physical closeness and touch that is inappropriate or associated with negative feelings will result in decreased cooperation and compliance.[16]

TOUCH AND POWER

In addition to serving as an intensifier of social interactions, touch can function as a gesture of dominance and power. Nancy Henley has argued that touch can be related to the amount of intimacy that is shared between two people when it is reciprocal. She views instances of asymmetrical touch (where one person touches another and it is not appropriate for the other person to touch back) as an expression of personal power. Observations of people in various situations confirmed Henley's hypothesis that persons of higher status (such as bosses, doctors, and teachers) more frequently touch persons of lower status (workers, nurses, students) than vice versa.[17] Henley thinks that men are generally given more status than women in American society and exert this status through the use of unreciprocated touch. She encourages men to refrain from using touch as power and women to resist what she calls "the male skin privilege" when it is used to exert control.

Advice on Touching

You have discovered that there are interesting differences between men and women in how they initiate and react toward touch.[18] Even though women often suffer more than men from unwanted touch, they like to touch and to be touched by the right people. Men tend to be more instrumental than women in their use of touch. American men are particularly uncomfortable about being touched by other men. Women don't react as negatively about being touched by other women.

A good suggestion for men is to use a gentle touch with women that expresses warmth and caring rather than dominance and control. Women are advised to be sensitive to men's fickleness about being touched. Women usually view sexual touching as the most intimate kind of touch. Men, on the other hand, may tolerate sexual touching and feel threatened by touching that communicates more intimacy and caring than they are ready to reciprocate.

Gaze and Eye Contact

People have always been fascinated by the nonverbal messages that are communicated through the eyes. The direction of gaze from one person to another can be related to feelings as diverse as love and affection and hostility, threat, and dominance. Gaze has been described as a means of monitoring other people's behaviors, as a system for regulating conversations, and as a channel for expressing feelings. Gaze can communicate a desire for affiliation, and it can serve as a signal of threat and dominance.[19] The following discussion of gaze will address three major issues. It will begin with a summary of research studies measuring people's interpretations of the meaning of gaze as well as their reactions to the gaze of others. An analysis will then be presented of studies measuring how much people gaze at each other in various situations. The chapter will conclude with a discussion of current theories relating gaze with other nonverbal behaviors of closeness and intimacy.

This chapter is particularly concerned with the process of people looking at each other. The terms *gaze* and *looking* are used to describe the process of focusing one's eyes on another person. The terms *eye contact* and *mutual gaze* are used when two people are simultaneously focusing their eyes on each other. *Staring* refers to "a gaze or look which persists regardless of the behavior of the other person."[20]

The Meanings of Gaze

The various meanings of gaze have been studied in surveys and by asking people to give their impressions of others who are gazing or not gazing in various situations such as social interactions, counseling sessions, and courtrooms.

SURVEYS

American college students stated that they would be most comfortable interacting with a person who gazed at them 50 percent of the time. They said they would be less comfortable with someone who gazed 100 percent of the time, but that 100 percent gaze was preferable to no gaze, except when they and the other person were silent. Students did not like the idea of receiving constant gaze from another person when it was not accompanied with talking. They said that they would usually feel more comfortable receiving constant gaze from a person of the opposite sex and from someone their own age or younger. College students in Britain associated intermittent gaze more closely with liking than continuous gaze or no gaze.[21] Continuous gaze was associated with the potency and power of the person gazing.

SOCIAL INTERACTIONS

A number of studies have been conducted in which people gave their impressions of a man and woman talking to each other. Half of the people saw the man and woman actively gazing at each other. The remaining people saw them look at each other very little. Not surprisingly, the man and woman were perceived as being closer, more attracted toward each other, and liking each other more when they were gazing at each other more.

The association between gaze and liking is not limited to social interactions between men and women. People generally give the impression of liking each other more when they look at each other a fair amount during casual interactions.[22]

COUNSELING SESSIONS AND INTERVIEWS

Gaze is an important way for counselors to communicate interest and attentiveness to their clients. Research indicates that counselors are more favorably evaluated when they look at their clients very often rather than very seldom during a counseling interview. Interviewers as well as interviewees are perceived as being more intelligent and competent when they give a reasonable amount of eye contact during an interview.[23] It does not make a good impression to gaze down or off to the side too much during an interview.

COURTROOMS

In Chapter 5 you read about the virtues of powerful speech for affirming your credibility. Eye contact is also important for communicating self-confidence. Research participants judged the credibility of a witness in a videotaped courtroom trial.[24] In half the videotapes the witness looked at the attorney who was questioning him, and in the other half he avoided gazing at the attorney. The witness was judged as being more credible when he gazed at the attorney.

Reactions to Gaze

Like our response to touch, our response to gaze depends on the situation and on who is gazing. As with touch, studies of reactions to gaze can be understood by defining gaze as a behavior that intensifies whatever feelings are being shared between two people. In general, we can expect positive responses to gaze in cordial and friendly interactions and negative responses to gaze in hostile and threatening interactions.

SOCIAL INTERACTIONS

Several studies have shown that gaze is interpreted favorably when people are first introduced to each other in a social interaction. We usually prefer people who look at us over those who look away. Our reactions to other people's gaze at first meeting also depend on their physical attractiveness and intimacy and on our moods. Two studies demonstrated that men did not react unfavorably to attractive women who did not look at them very much.[25] It appeared that attractive women were given the benefit of the doubt when they withheld their gaze. Less attractive women were not excused by the men when they were unwilling to share eye contact.

Although we like people to be attentive by looking at us, we feel uncomfortable if they are too intimate. Research participants who received very personal and complimentary statements from a stranger preferred it when the stranger didn't gaze very much. When the stranger gave mixed or negative evaluations, higher amounts of gaze were acceptable. We are more likely to appreciate a person's gaze when we are anxious and looking for support.[26] We would just as soon not have others look at us when we are feeling embarrassed and on the spot.

INTERVIEWS

Interviewers are evaluated as being more attentive when they gaze at the interviewee relatively often during an interview. Interviewees give longer answers to questions when the interviewer is gazing at them. Assuming that interviewers who withhold gaze are not interested in them, the interviewees keep their responses brief. Gazing interviewers are most preferred during a positive and supportive interview.[27] Interviewers who have to give negative or critical feedback are often appreciated more if they reduce the impact of their statements by keeping their gaze to a minimum.

GAZE AND COMPLIANCE

The effects of gaze on compliance are similar to those for touch. Gaze tends to increase compliance with requests that are legitimate and appropriate. For example, people were more willing to lend dimes, make change, take leaflets, and offer rides to experimenters who gazed at them while asking for their assistance. On the other hand, gaze intensifies negative feelings and leads to decreased compliance with illegitimate and inappropriate requests. Researchers either stared or did not stare at passengers during a four-minute ride between two stops on a New York subway.[28] When the train came to the second stop, the researcher stood up to get off and "accidently" dropped a bundle of papers at the passenger's feet. Significantly fewer passengers helped to pick up the papers when the researcher had stared at them.

Another experiment testing the relationship between gaze and legitimacy of request found that people in an airport were more willing to give dimes to an experimenter who gazed at them and said the dime was needed for a telephone call.[29] People were less cooperative about giving dimes when the experimenter gazed and said the dime was wanted to buy candy. Experimenters probably came across as tactless when they gave steady gaze while making this kind of inappropriate request.

People in a shopping center were asked to attend to a woman who needed help.[30] Half the time the woman gazed at them and half the time she did not. When it was clear what kind of assistance she needed (locating a contact lense), people helped her more often when she gazed at them. When her need was ambiguous, she received more help when she was not gazing. It appeared that gaze from a woman with an unknown problem caused others to be wary and to avoid being involved.

AVOIDANCE AND ESCAPE

As a rule, we feel uncomfortable when someone is staring at us, and we attempt to reduce the impact of the stare by confronting the person or by withdrawing from the situation. Experimenters stood on street corners and gazed constantly or not at all at pedestrians and automobile drivers who were waiting for a red light.[31] When the light changed to green, pedestrians and motorists crossed the intersection significantly faster when they had received constant gaze from the experimenter. Students in a college library remained in their seats for shorter periods of time than usual when they were confronted by a person who sat down at their table and stared at them.

Staring can be defined as a behavior that "demands a response." We are usually motivated to move away from a stranger who is staring at us because we feel ambivalent about what kinds of responses we should make. If a staring stranger is sexually appealing, however, or has other favorable attributes, we may react in a more positive manner. For example, people are less likely to avoid a staring person who is smiling. Pedestrians did not cross the street as fast to avoid a staring experimenter who was made up to be physically attractive as they did to avoid one who appeared very unattractive.[32]

Avoidance of staring has also been studied in children. Adult experimenters stared at children in a shopping center and recorded whether the children averted their gaze or engaged in eye contact.[33] Compared with five-to-nine-year-old children, children between eighteen months and four years old were less likely to avert their gaze and more inclined to give eye contact to the staring adult. It appears that children do not learn to avoid gaze from others until after they are four or five. Very young children are curious and responsive to adults who stare at them.

GAZE AND DOMINANCE

Gaze has been related to expressions of threat and dominance in animals and humans. Men were introduced to a male experimenter who gazed at them almost constantly or very little during a three-minute interaction. The experimenter was evaluated as being more dominant when his gaze was frequent rather than infrequent. Men in another study were less likely to deliver electric shocks to another man who had angered them when he gazed at them constantly rather than not at all.[34] Constant gaze made the disliked man's presence very salient, and it inhibited aggressive responses by the angered recipients. In contrast, they delivered more shocks to another man when his gaze was not consistent and when it appeared that the shocks would cause him to gaze less.

Men and women were less likely to violate the personal space of a man who was standing in front of the buttons in an elevator when the man was staring at them. Men, but not women, were also more reluctant to violate the space of a staring woman. When given the choice, men were equally likely to violate the space of gazing men and gazing women. Women preferred to violate the space of gazing women. Research participants averted their gaze when following instructions to invade the space of two people who were standing and conversing, apparently as a gesture of appeasement.[35]

Men were not any more or less competitive when playing a two-person game with another man who gazed at them constantly or not at all.[36] However, they evaluated a very competitive man as being most friendly and cooperative when he gazed. It is possible that they preferred the competitive man when he gazed because he appeared more open and candid. The constantly gazing and competitive man might also have intimidated others into giving ratings that were desirable. Interestingly enough, a very cooperative man was evaluated as being most friendly and cooperative when he did not gaze. He probably appeared inappropriately intimate when he consistently cooperated and continuously gazed.

DIFFERENCES BETWEEN MEN AND WOMEN

Women are often more open than men about sharing intimacy, in relation to gaze as well as touch. In one study men and women were introduced in couples and left in a room for ten minutes to come to know each other. After ten minutes the experimenter came into the room, pointed to a one-way mirror, and said that he had recorded the amount of time the person facing the mirror had gazed at the person facing away from the mirror. For half the couples the gazing person was the woman, and for half it was the man. The experimenter randomly told participants that the gaze was either more frequent than the gaze of most other participants, as frequent as, or less frequent. Although the experimenter's feedback was purely random, it was believable because people have very little awareness of their gaze, and the men and women had no way to compare their gaze with that of other participants. After this false feedback about gaze, participants were asked to rate how much they liked each other on a questionnaire. Women were most favorable toward men whose gaze had supposedly been frequent. They were also more positive toward men when they believed that their own gaze had been frequent. Men's reactions were exactly opposite. They were most favorable toward women when they were told that the woman's gaze or their own gaze had been infrequent. The differences between men and women were interpreted as a function of sex-role stereotypes. Males in American society are socialized to be more reticent than females about expressing feelings and emotional closeness. Other researchers have also found that women are more inclined than men to perceive gaze as communicating friendship and to view their own and other's gazing with positive feelings.[37]

The tendency for females to prefer greater amounts of gaze than males appears at an early age. Preschool boys and girls played a game with a woman who gazed at them either 20 percent or 80 percent of the time. After the game the children showed how much they liked the woman by placing cardboard figures representing the woman and other familiar people on five steps ranging from liking to disliking. Girls liked the woman more when she gazed 80 percent of the time. Boys showed a strong preference for the woman when she gazed 20 percent of the time. Boys probably interpreted the woman's gaze as a sign that they were doing something wrong because boys, in general, experience more punishment and negative sanctions from teachers in school. By the age of six, girls are more sensitive than boys in perceiving gaze and physical closeness as communicating friendship and liking.[38]

Factors Influencing Gaze

Our inclinations about how much to gaze at others are influenced by our motives and personalities as well as by a variety of factors related to the person and the situation. A summary of research literature has determined that people are most likely to gaze at each other when they are discussing nonthreatening topics, when they share mutual feelings of attraction, and when they are attempting to dominate or threaten each other. Mutual gaze is also likely when their personalities are characterized by extraversion and need for affiliation, and when they are from cultures that emphasize and encourage visual interaction.[39]

PERSONAL FEELINGS AND MOTIVES

Our personal feelings and motives also influence the frequency of our gaze.

Affiliation and Friendship. Gaze is more frequent between friends and people who are emotionally close to one another. Dating couples who expressed strong love for each other on a love scale engaged in more mutual gazing than dating couples with low scores on the love scale. Children as well as adults share greater amounts of eye contact with friends than with nonfriends. People gaze more when they like others than when they dislike them. Gaze is more frequent between people who are motivated to win each other's friendship and approval.[40]

Dependency. We generally gaze at people when we are dependent upon them in one way or another. Research participants increased their gaze toward an experimenter when they were made to feel dependent on him for assistance with a difficult task. Younger preschool girls gazed more at a female adult while being tested than did older preschool girls, probably because younger girls are more dependent on a female teacher's attention and approval. Preschool boys are not as dependent on attention and approval as preschool girls, and they gaze at female adults significantly less.[41]

Persuasion and Deception. Earlier in this chapter you read that gazing behavior by a witness in a courtroom is viewed as a sign of credibility. Most people gaze relatively frequently when they are trying to be persuasive and relatively infrequently when they are lying (unless they are being bold).[42] Our eyes often express the guilt and nervousness resulting from not being truthful.

Communicating Emotions. Research participants communicated positive and negative emotions toward a video camera in different ways so that they would be interpreted as weak or strong personalities.[43] Participants gazed more at the camera when communicating strong emotions than when communicating weak emotions. The amount of gazing was not affected by whether the emotion was positive or negative.

Anxiety. White college students gazed less when they were interviewing black students than when interviewing white students, apparently because the white students felt anxious in a formal interaction with someone of a different race. Research participants gazed less at an interviewer when they believed they were responding poorly and felt anxious about it.[44]

Elation and Depression. A number of research studies have indicated that people gaze more when they are feeling elated and less when they are feeling depressed.[45]

Threat and Dominance. When we are cooperating with others we generally prefer to have the possibility of mutual gaze.[46] During a competitive interaction, we may prefer seeing our adversary without allowing our adversary to see us.

Embarrassment. We tend to avoid gazing at others when we are feeling anxious or embarrassed. People gaze less at interviewers when the interviewer asks personal and embarrassing questions rather than nonpersonal ; nd neutral questions. Research participants gazed less at other participants in an experiment after experiencing failure than after experiencing succcess.[47]

BEHAVIORS AND CHARACTERISTICS OF OTHERS

We are more inclined to gaze at people when they are behaving positively toward us and when they are giving approval. We also like to gaze at others who are physically attractive.

College men were introduced to a male interviewer who gave some a personal evaluation that was positive and complimentary and others one that was negative and critical. Not surprisingly, men who received a negative evaluation gazed less at the interviewer than men who were given a positive evaluation. College women were introduced to a college man who gave personal evaluations that were positive for some, neutral or negative for others.[48] Women expressed greatest liking for the man who evaluated them positively, and they gazed at him most. They expressed least liking for the man who evaluated them negatively, but they gazed at him more than they gazed at the man who was neutral. Probably the negatively evaluated women were trying to figure out the reason for the man's unfavorable evaluation.

People gaze more at others who have high status, particularly when their status places them in a position to give reinforcement and approval. College men gazed more at a woman who was interviewing them when the woman was dressed and made up to be very attractive rather than very unattractive.[49]

PERSONALITY

Are there individual differences among people in how much they gaze at others? In order to answer this question, we must first determine that gazing is a consistent and stable behavior. Research indicates it is. High consistencies have been observed in individuals' gazing behavior in different situations over different periods of time.[50]

Some relationship has been found between people's gazing behaviors and their scores on personality tests. Willingness to gaze at others is positively related to measures of nurturance, affection, dependency, affiliation, feminine sex-role orientation, extraversion, and manipulativeness. There are inconsistent conclusions about whether willingness to gaze is correlated with measures of internal control and social desirability.[51]

RACE AND CULTURE

Just as there are differences among people from various cultures and ethnic groups in their use of personal space, there are also cultural differences in how people use and react to gaze. For example, people from "contact cultures" (Arabs, Latin Americans, southern Europeans) gaze more at each other than people from "noncontact" cultures (Asians and northern Europeans). Michael Argyle and Mark Cook described a number of fascinating cultural rules for defining appropriate and inappropriate gazing. Navaho Indians are taught that it is impolite to gaze directly at another person during a conversation. Japanese people look more at the neck than at the eyes. Among the Luo of Kenya, a man and his mother-in-law turn their backs on each other while speaking. Too little gaze in some cultures is interpreted as a sign of dishonesty and insincerity. In other cultures, turning the eyes downward is viewed as a gesture of respect. A study of gazing by white and black American adults suggested that whites gaze more while listening while blacks gaze more while speaking.[52] If this is true, some discomfort can arise between whites and blacks in social interactions because they have different expectations about how to signal attentiveness and taking turns in a conversation.

SEX DIFFERENCES

A review of research literature indicates that women and girls generally gaze more at others than men and boys do. The difference between males' and females' gazing has been explained in terms of sex roles, which influence women to be more emotionally warm and affiliative and more attentive and sensitive to what is going on in an interaction. It has been suggested that men gaze more than women during interactions that are uncomfortable and threatening.[53] More research is needed on this question.

Theories of Gaze and Intimacy

A good way to wrap up this chapter is by analyzing theories developed by psychologists for understanding the relationship between nonverbal behaviors of intimacy. It will also be instructive to look at questions and issues that are in the forefront of nonverbal behavioral research.

THE INTIMACY-EQUILIBRIUM MODEL

Michael Argyle and his colleagues formulated an intimacy-equilibrium model to explain the relationship between gaze, touch, physical closeness, and other behaviors in intimacy, such as body orientation and forward lean, openness of posture, and self-disclosure. The equilibrium model is based on the assumption that people prefer to maintain a balanced amount of intimacy in their interactions with each other. If one person sits too close, for example, the second person is likely to restore equilibrium by gazing or smiling less, by leaning or turning away, or by reducing the intimacy of the conversation. Because the intimacy-equilibrium model cannot specify exactly which behaviors people will choose for maintaining equilibrium, it is most useful for providing an overview of the dynamics of approach and withdrawal in human interactions.[54] Even though the intimacy-equilibrium model does not usually generate specific behavioral predictions, it has been exemplified in a number of research studies.

The intimacy-equilibrium model has been supported most consistently in studies showing that people increase their gaze when seated far from another and decrease it when sitting close. The fact that an inverse relationship was not found between gaze and seating distance by some researchers may be due to the operation of reciprocation discussed later. The maintenance of equilibrium between gaze and distance is also different for men and women. Women research participants gazed most at a stranger who sat at a distance of six feet because this distance provided the greatest sense of comfort for women.[55] Men gazed most at a stranger who sat at a distance of ten to fifteen feet because this distance gave them the greatest sense of comfort.

The intimacy-equilibrium model has also been useful for explaining the results of studies showing that people engage in less self-disclosure when they are seated very close rather than at a distance. Other studies have demonstrated that people compensate for close seating distances, direct gaze, and intimate interviews by turning their bodies away, gazing and smiling less, and reacting with signs of nervousness and discomfort.[56]

Compensatory reactions to greater and lesser amounts of intimacy are most apparent when intimacy is altered during the course of an interaction. The intimacy-equilibrium model is therefore best demonstrated in studies measuring people's responses when they experience both much and little intimacy during the same interaction. Although we are likely to compensate for too much intimacy from a stranger by withdrawing, we may feel rewarded by intimacy from people we like and respond to them with reciprocation. We are inclined to reciprocate with intimacy toward others when we want to be close to them and when we feel their intimacy toward us is positive and appropriate.[57] We are inclined to compensate by withdrawing our intimacy from others when we don't wish to be close and when we perceive their intimacy toward us as ingratiating and inappropriate. You will gain more insight into how we judge people's motives and ingratiation in Chapter 8 and Chapter 10.

THE INTIMACY-AROUSAL AND SEQUENTIAL MODELS

In Chapter 2 you were introduced to a theory outlining the conditions under which we interpret physiological arousal as an experience of romantic love. Because gaze, touch, and physical closeness can elicit physiological arousal, it occurred to Miles Patterson that reactions to these indications of intimacy might be understood in terms of a self-labeling of arousal model. Gaze, touch, closeness, and other intimacy behavior can serve as additional sources of arousal to the roller coaster rides, threat of electric shock, and scary movies mentioned in Chapter 2. The arousal theory is useful for explaining people's responses when they experience intimacy and physiological arousal for which there is no immediate explanation. One problem with the theory is that such occasions don't happen very often. First of all, another person's intimacy does not always elicit physiological arousal.[58] It is usually inappropriate or unexpected gaze, touch, or closeness that is arousing. Second, when someone's intimacy causes physiological responses, we are usually aware of the reason for these responses. We are therefore not as interested in seeking the reason for our physiological arousal as we are in understanding the reasons or motives for the person's intimacy.

With these thoughts in mind, Patterson formulated a sequential functional model for explaining responses to another person's intimacy.[59] This model takes into account a number of important issues. You have already read how reactions to gaze depend on the recipient's sex, personality, culture, and motives in addition to the behavior and characteristics of the gazing person. Reactions to gaze (and other indications of intimacy) are also affected by the function served by the behavior in a particular interaction. Different functions include providing information, regulating interchanges, expressing closeness, exercising social control, and facilitating communication. Finally, as you will read in the following chapters, our reactions to others are influenced by our perceptions and interpretations of their personalities and motives. When people express (or withdraw) intimacy, we ask ourselves what this means and how we feel about it.

GAZE, TOUCH, AND AWARENESS

In Chapter 8 you will be introduced to attribution theories, which explain how we go about understanding the reasons for other people's actions. Sometimes we pay close attention to other people's behavior and are very aware of our responses. On other occasions, our interactions with others are automatic and outside of our immediate awareness. Our awareness of how much people gaze at us depends on the situation. You have probably experienced discomfort at being stared at during various times in your life. Have you ever felt rejected when someone did not look at you enough? We are most conscious of another person's gaze when it is unusually frequent or unusually infrequent and when we are feeling insecure, dependent, or threatened. Otherwise, most of us go through our day paying little attention to how much people look at us. Research indicates that people are not very accurate in reporting how much others gazed at them in various kinds of interactions. How aware are we of our own gaze? In most situations, people are not very accurate in reporting how much they gazed at others.[60] It is possible that we are more aware of when we give or receive touch because it is a stronger stimulus. On the other hand, we probably pay little attention to how much we give or receive direct body orientation, head nodding, forward lean, or self-disclosure. Maybe after reading this chapter you will pay more attention to your own and others' indications of intimacy.

How We Explain Behaviors:

AN INTRODUCTION TO
ATTRIBUTION THEORIES

Check the following statements with which you agree:

1. *I prefer complex to simple things.*

2. *I prefer my life to be filled with puzzles that I must solve.*

3. *I prefer a task that is intellectual, difficult, and important to one that does not require much thought.*

4. *I prefer just to let things happen rather than try to understand why they turned out that way.*

5. *I only think as hard as I have to.*

6. *Thinking is not my idea of fun.*

These statements are taken from a need for cognition scale, which was developed to measure how much people like to spend their time in thought.[1] If you agreed with the first three statements and disagreed with the last three, chances are that you enjoy analyzing problems and finding solutions. If you disagreed with the first three statements and agreed with the last, you probably prefer other kinds of activities. Either way, no matter how much you like to analyze things, this chapter is relevant because we all need at times to understand the reasons for one another's actions.

This chapter is about how we explain one another's behaviors. The theories you will encounter here are called *attribution theories* because they were formulated to describe how we understand, interpret, and make attributions about behaviors. A behavioral attribution is an explanation for why the behavior occurred. It is an assignment of responsibility or cause. Behavioral attributions are important because our reactions toward others are often affected by our perceptions of their motives. We want to know what they did but also why they did it.

Two questions we commonly ask when trying to understand someone's behavior are: (1) What caused the behavior? and (2) What does the behavior reveal about this person's motives and personality?[2] Imagine that you received a gift. If the gift were given by a family member or friend, you would probably know the gift's reason or meaning. If it came from an acquaintance or stranger, you would be quite curious about the cause and meaning behind it.

Fritz Heider provided the groundwork for attribution theories by describing how people are predisposed to seek causes for each other's actions.[3] He pointed out that we want to find reasons for behaviors because we feel most comfortable in a predictable world. According to Heider, we explain another person's behaviors by weighing how much the behavior was caused by forces in the situation or environment (*situational causes*) and how much by motives, choices, and personality (*dispositional causes*). Behaviors that occur primarily because of situational causes are predictable because they can be expected again in similar situations. Behaviors that occur primarily because of dispositional causes can be predicted in similar and possibly different situations. Behaviors that are not clearly a function of either the environment or personality are ambiguous because they are apparently due to chance. They offer no predictability about their future occurrence.

Edward E. Jones, Keith Davis, and Harold Kelley elaborated Heider's ideas by developing theories to explain how we make attributions about the relative influence of dispositional and situational causes on people's behaviors.

Jones and Davis's Correspondent Inference Theory

The attribution theory developed by Jones and Davis is called correspondent inference theory.[4] Jones and Davis attempted to define the conditions under which we can learn something about a person by observing that person's behavior. When behavior tells us something about a person, there is *high correspondence* between the behavior and our judgments about that person. When behavior does not tell us anything about a person, there is *low correspondence* between the behavior and our judgments about the person. Imagine that you are at a dinner party with people you have never met. When the salad is served, the person next to you picks up her fork. This behavior doesn't tell you much about the person because most people eat salad with a fork. But what if someone else at the table ate his salad with his fingers? Such behavior would probably influence your opinion about that person. Jones and Davis pointed out that uncommon behavior tells us more about a person than common behavior and that behavior with relatively low social desirability tells us more about a person than behavior with high social desirability. They also suggested that we make more definitive judgments about people when their behavior is relevant to our lives and directed toward us personally.

UNCOMMON BEHAVIOR

We are likely to learn less about a person who acts like everyone else than about a person whose actions are different and unique. This principle was demonstrated by college students when they made judgments about an unacquainted student who engaged in activities that were common (like going to a movie on Friday night) or uncommon (like inspecting a stamp collection on Friday night). Students felt they knew more about the stranger whose activities were uncommon than they knew about the stranger whose activities were common. Participants in a similar experiment felt more confidence in their knowledge about someone who chose responses on a questionnaire that were not chosen by others.[5] It is hard to learn anything about someone who answers questions like everyone else.

UNEXPECTED BEHAVIORS

We generally learn more about a person whose behavior is inconsistent with our expectations. Expected behavior serves mainly to confirm things about someone we already know. Unexpected behavior is more likely to catch our attention because it suggests something about the person that is unique or new. We expect people will behave in certain ways on the basis of their social groups, personalities, and previous actions.[6]

As a simple example of expectancies, how would you judge the motivation of a college student with a high grade point average and a low college aptitude score? If you are like most research participants you would view this student as having greater motivation (because the high grade average is unexpected) than a student with a high grade average and high aptitude score (whose high grades can be taken for granted).[7]

Participants in another study of expectancies judged the attitudes of a person who wrote an essay that was in some instances in favor of and in others opposed to the legalization of marijuana.[8] Participants were led to believe that the essay writer held either liberal or conservative attitudes on other social issues. Results of the study demonstrated the importance of expectancies on judgments of attitudes. Raters were more certain about the essay writer's beliefs when the argument in the essay was unexpected. The liberal person who wrote an antimarijuana essay was judged as being particularly unfavorable toward marijuana. The conservative person who wrote a promarijuana essay came across as particularly favorable toward marijuana.

The studies cited suggest what you should do if you plan to express an opinion or argument people don't expect to hear. If you want them to take you seriously, it is best to prepare them ahead of time by explaining "where you are coming from."[9] If you wish to make your true opinion ambiguous, you can express the argument without giving your reasons for it.

Although behavior usually tells more about a person when it is unexpected, we may have reduced confidence about the meaning of extreme behavior. For example, we are likely to view a person's inappropriate friendliness or unexpected silliness or anger as a response to the situation or as motivated by some idiosyncrasy or ulterior motive.[10]

UNDESIRABLE BEHAVIOR

You have now seen how unusual behavior reveals more about a person than usual behavior. The same line of reasoning holds for behavior that is socially desirable. If a person engages in socially desirable behavior, we don't know whether to attribute it to personal traits or to the rewards of acceptance and approval that typically follow desirable behavior. When a person engages in undesirable behavior, we assume the person wouldn't have acted that way unless he or she really wanted to. One example of this principle can be seen in a study in which speakers were judged as more honest when they expressed views that opposed rather than supported the views of their audience.[11] We are not sure whether a speaker who supports the opinions of an audience is doing so out of personal belief or merely to please the audience. A speaker who disagrees with an audience is presumably expressing personal beliefs because there is little chance in this instance of receiving acceptance and approval.

A second example of the effects of social desirability on explanations for behavior comes from a study in which raters heard an interviewer describe to a job applicant the traits he was looking for.[12] When the applicant described himself as possessing these traits, raters had little confidence in their judgments about the applicant's qualifications. It wasn't clear if the applicant really possessed the desired traits or if he claimed them only to please the interviewer. When the applicant described himself as having somewhat different traits than those desired, raters were much more confident that his claims accurately represented his qualifications.

BEHAVIORS THAT AFFECT US PERSONALLY

We tend to take a person's actions most seriously when they affect us personally.[13] Personally relevant behavior is judged by determining whether it was intentional or caused by forces in the environment or situation.

One kind of behavior that often affects us personally is aggression. Jones and Davis used their theory to explain the conditions under which we hold someone responsible for aggressive behavior. A person who is provoked is less likely to be blamed for aggression than a person who behaves aggressively without provocation. Someone who is chronically aggressive is also viewed differently from someone whose aggressiveness is unexpected. We don't necessarily like a chronically aggressive person, but an aggressive act by that person has a smaller effect on our judgments because it is expected. We are also less likely to blame a person for negative acts if the person is "mentally ill" or maladjusted. Research shows that people can tolerate a maladjusted person's negative behaviors when they are predictable.[14]

Unpredictable negative behaviors by a maladjusted person result in our feeling frustrated and rejected.

RULING OUT ALTERNATIVE EXPLANATIONS

We have greatest confidence about the reasons for someone's behavior when we can narrow down the number of competing explanations. Research has found that the number of explanations ruled out is less important than having only a few plausible causes remaining.[15] For example, suppose that a man chooses to date a woman who is attractive, intelligent, wealthy, and red-haired. Since there are many possible reasons for dating the woman, we aren't sure which of them caused the man to make his decision. On the other hand, if the man chose a red-headed woman of mediocre attractiveness, low intelligence, and no wealth, we would be more confident in attributing his choice to her red hair.

An interesting demonstration of ruling out alternative explanations for an action is seen in an experiment in which college students were given the choice of sitting next to a handicapped or a nonhandicapped person while watching a film.[16] When these two persons were watching the same film, students showed no sign of avoiding the handicapped one. When the two persons were watching different films, most students chose to sit next to the nonhandicapped one. These actions can be understood in the following way. When the handicapped and the nonhandicapped persons were watching the same film, students could not avoid the handicapped person without making their motives obvious. When the two were watching different films, students could avoid the handicapped person by making it look as if their seating choice were motivated by preference for the other film.

Another example of alternative explanations comes from a study in which people attributed helpful behavior from a stranger to external causes (rewards and approval) while attributing unhelpful behavior from a stranger to internal causes (mood and personality).[17] The reasons for the stranger's helpful actions were ambiguous because the actions could be motivated by either external gains or a helpful personality. Because of the strong possibility of external gains, the stranger's helpful behavior was explained in this manner. Unhelpful actions are less ambiguous because they are not likely to result in external gains (except in competitive circumstances). By ruling out the possibility of external motivation, people settled on personality factors as a reasonable explanation for the other stranger's unhelpful behavior.

SUMMARY OF CORRESPONDENT INFERENCE THEORY

In their correspondent inference theory, Jones and Davis describe when behavior provides information about a person's traits and personality (high correspondence) and when it does not (low correspondence). We are likely to learn more about a person whose behavior is uncommon, unexpected, socially undesirable, and personally relevant. We are less certain in our judgments about people whose behavior is taken for granted, motivated by obvious external causes, idiosyncratic or suspicious, and not personally relevant.

Kelley's Covariation Model

Harold Kelley derived two models describing how people explain one another's behavior. His covariation model is based on situations in which people observe behavior over a certain period of time. His causal schemata model applies to situations in which people attempt to explain behavior they have observed on a single occasion.[18]

In his covariation model Kelley proposed that we seek explanations for behavior by asking the following questions:

1. *Is the behavior* distinctive? *Was the behavior chosen for a special purpose or reason or is it something the person does regardless of the situation?*

2. *Is the behavior* consistent? *Does the person engage in this behavior regularly or is it sporadic?*

3. *Is there* consensus? *Do others respond in the same way or is the behavior unique to this person?*

To have an idea of how the covariation model works, consider how we would explain Bill's warmth and attentiveness toward Mary. We would first determine whether or not Bill's behavior is distinctive. Is his attentiveness directed toward Mary as a special person (high distinctiveness) or does he give warmth and attention to many people (low distinctiveness)? Next, we would ask whether Bill is attentive to Mary fairly consistently or only on certain occasions. Finally, we would want to know if Mary receives a lot of attentiveness from other people (high consensus) or if Bill's attentiveness is unusual or special (low consensus).

The covariation model outlines the conditions under which we attribute behavior to the acting person (Bill), to the person acted upon (Mary), or to the context or situation in which the behavior is shown (see Table 8-1). We would most likely attribute Bill's warmth and attentiveness to Bill (he likes Mary) under conditions of high distinctiveness, high consistency, and low consensus (attribution A). In other words, we are most confident that Bill really likes Mary when he is especially attentive toward her, when he is consistently attentive, and when his attentiveness is special because Mary does not receive the same amount of attentiveness from others. Under conditions of low distinctiveness, high consistency, and low consensus we would conclude that Bill likes to give warmth and attentiveness to many people, not only to Mary (attribution B). We would attribute his attentiveness to some quality possessed by Mary when distinctiveness, consistency, and consensus are all high (attribution C). In this situation we can see that Bill likes Mary, but that other people also like her. Finally, we would conclude that Bill's attentiveness is due to the situation when consistency is low (attribution D). If Bill is only warm and attentive toward Mary in certain situations, there must be something about the situation that causes this behavior. In attribution D, consensus influences our judgments about whether the situation specifically affects Bill (low consensus) or also affects others (high consensus). Distinctiveness influences our judgment about whether the situation leads to warmth specifically toward Mary (high distinctiveness) or whether the situation results in warmth and attentiveness toward people in general (low distinctiveness).

Table 8-1   Attributions from Kelley's Covariation Model*

Attribution for behavior	Available information		
	Distinctiveness	Consistency	Consensus
A. Attribution to Bill (Bill really likes Mary.)	High	High	Low
B. Attribution to Bill (Bill likes to give warmth and attention.)	Low	High	Low
C. Attribution to Mary (People like to give Mary warmth and attention.)	High	High	High
D. Attribution to situation (Bill's warmth and attention are caused by the situation.)	—	Low	—

*Adapted with permission from B. R. Orvis, J. D. Cunningham, and H. H. Kelley, "A Closer Examination of Causal Inference: The Roles of Consensus, Distinctiveness, and Consistency Information," *Journal of Personality and Social Psychology,* 1975, *32,* 605–616.

TESTING THE COVARIATION MODEL

Kelley's covariation model has been tested by measuring how people's behaviors are explained when distinctiveness, consistency, and consensus are systematically varied. Research has shown that the predicted attributions in Table 8-1 are generally supported. All things being equal, explanations for behavior are influenced more by the behavior's distinctiveness than by its consensus. However, consensus does influence explanations for behavior when it is brought to an observer's attention. Information about consensus is less important for explaining action-oriented behavior than for explaining passive behavior. This is probably because action-oriented behavior (such as stating an opinion or making a decision) appears to be intentional and freely chosen. We can gain some idea of a person's motives for action-oriented behavior without comparing him or her with others. Passive behavior described as having "occurred" or "taken place" is more difficult to explain because it gives little information about the person's intentions. By taking into consideration the actions of others we gain a better idea of whether the behavior is unique or something anyone else would do. Consensus also has greater influence on explanations for behavior that is socially desirable rather than undesirable.[19] When explaining desirable behavior we need to look at consensus to discover if the action was personally chosen or if it is a common reaction shared by others. Because undesirable behavior is uncommon, we can usually assume it was intentional without considering the reactions of others.

EXPLAINING THE PERFORMANCE OF RACE HORSES

In the following experiment, people observing horse races judged whether a particular horse's performance was due to the horse, to the other horses in the race, or to external circumstances having to do with the race track.[20] It turned out that consistency was the most important factor influencing explanations for a race horse's performance. Horses who consistently won were given credit, and those who consistently lost were blamed. When horses were inconsistent by sometimes winning and sometimes losing, credit or blame was difficult to assign. The performance of inconsistent horses was most often attributed to external circumstances or to the competition.

WHEN INFORMATION IS INCOMPLETE

How do we explain behavior when information about distinctiveness, consistency, and consensus is incomplete? Research has shown that we assume the missing information is consistent with predictions in Table 8-1.[21] For example, when explaining a behavior with low distinctiveness (attribution B), research participants "filled in" the missing information about consistency and consensus and attributed the behavior to the behaving person. When explaining a behavior with high consensus (attribution C), they assumed that distinctiveness and consistency were high and attributed the behavior to the person toward whom it was directed. When explaining a behavior that was ambiguous, research participants tended to assume high consistency and low distinctiveness and they attributed the behavior to the behaving person.

ADDITIONS TO THE COVARIATION MODEL

The covariation model can be elaborated by adding a fourth piece of information (a comparison person) to the factors of distinctiveness, consistency, and consensus.[22] In Table 8–1, for example, assume that Bill has chosen to be warm and attentive toward Mary instead of Sue. Sue is then a *comparison person*, who influences our explanation for Bill's behavior. If Bill's friends agree that Mary is a better choice for Bill than Sue, we can say there is high consensus on the comparison person and we attribute Bill's choice of Mary to some quality possessed by Mary. If Bill's friends feel that Sue is a better choice than Mary, there would be low consensus on the comparison person, and we would attribute Bill's choice to something particular about Bill.

SUMMARY OF KELLEY'S COVARIATION MODEL

Kelley's covariation model describes how people explain behavior on the basis of distinctiveness, consistency, consensus (and, where relevant, comparison person). In its simplest terms the model suggests that behavior will be attributed to the behaving person under conditions of low distinctiveness, high consistency, and low consensus.[23] When distinctiveness, consistency, and consensus are all high, the covariation model predicts that behavior will be attributed to the person or object toward whom the behavior is directed. Behavior is attributed to the situation when distinctiveness is high and consistency and consensus are low. When information about distinctiveness, consistency, and consensus is incomplete, people assume the missing information is consistent with the predictions in Table 8–1. When explaining ambiguous behavior, there is a tendency to assume high consistency and low distinctiveness and to attribute the behavior to the behaving person.

Kelley's Causal Schemata Model

Unlike the covariation model, which requires that people observe one another's behavior over a certain period of time, the causal schemata model describes how people make attributions about the causes of behavior they have observed on a single occasion. According to the causal schemata model, we explain behavior from a single observation by determining which possible causes for the behavior are present. We then weigh the relative influence of these potential causes by subtracting out the ones that are least relevant.[24]

In Chapter 10, calling people by name will be discussed as a strategy for winning good will and cooperation. Consider how we would use the causal schemata model to explain the behavior of a job applicant calling a job interviewer by name. Broadly speaking, there are two possible explanations for this behavior (see Table 8–2). The applicant may be using the interviewer's name because of personal warmth and friendliness or because of external gains associated with making a good impression. Because of the strong possibility of external gains, we would probably conclude that the applicant's behavior is motivated by the desire to make a good impression rather than by warmth and friendliness. What if we turned the example around so the job interviewer calls the job applicant by name? Since an interviewer is not dependent on an applicant's approval, the motivation for external gains can be ruled out. We can be more certain that the interviewer called the applicant by name because of warmth and friendliness.

Table 8–2   Attributions from Kelley's Causal Schemata Model*

DISCOUNTING PRINCIPLE

Behavior	Possible causes	Probable explanation
Job applicant uses interviewer's name	a. Warmth and friendliness b. External gain	External gain
Interviewer uses job applicant's name	a. Warmth and friendliness	Warmth and friendliness

AUGMENTATION PRINCIPLE

Behavior	Possible causes	Probable explanation
Beating unskilled tennis opponent	a. Ability b. Easy opponent	Easy opponent
Beating skilled tennis opponent	a. Ability	Ability
Boss polite in a group	a. Social norms b. Sincerity	Social norms
Boss polite in private	a. Sincerity	Sincerity

*Adapted with permission from H. H. Kelley, "The Process of Causal Attribution," *American Psychologist*, 1973, *28*, 107–128.

DISCOUNTING PRINCIPLE

The above analysis of how we explain use of people's names can be related to what Kelley calls the *discounting principle*.[25] It proposes that we discount (or are less certain about) the role of a given cause in producing behavior when other plausible causes for the behavior are present. Because it is very probable that a job applicant may call a job interviewer by name for external gains, we would be inclined to discount the importance of warmth and friendliness. The discounting principle is relevant to strategies for winning good will and cooperation, which are discussed in Chapter 10. For example, when someone does something nice for us, we must decide whether we should discount this favor because the person may have ulterior motives.

AUGMENTATION PRINCIPLE

Kelley defined an *augmentation principle,* which proposes that our certainty about a cause for behavior will be greater when the behavior occurs in spite of factors that normally stand in its way. For example, if a tennis player beats an unskilled opponent, we don't know whether to attribute the victory to the tennis player's ability or to the weakness of the opponent (see Table 8–2). A victory against a strong opponent is more easily attributed to the winner's ability.

For another example of the augmentation principle, imagine that you and your boss have a disagreement. If your boss responds politely in the presence of other people, you don't know whether this politeness is sincere or should be discounted as "public behavior." If your boss responds politely in private, you can probably view the politeness as sincere because your boss is passing up the opportunity to impress you with his or her authority and status.

MULTIPLE SUFFICIENT AND MULTIPLE NECESSARY CAUSES

The use of people's names, a tennis victory, and a boss's politeness are examples of what Kelley describes as behavior with *multiple sufficient causes.*[26] In situations involving multiple sufficient causes there are several possible causes for behavior, each of which is sufficient to make the behavior occur. Using a person's name could be caused either by personal friendliness or by the desire to make a good impression. A tennis victory could be caused either by a tennis player's ability or by a weak opponent. A boss's politeness could be caused either by sincerity or by social norms.

An example of how people interpret multiple sufficient causes is seen in a study in which research participants gave explanations for other people's successes and failures. The experiment was set up so that success could have been due to either high effort or high ability, and failure could have been caused by either low effort or low ability. How did participants arrive at their explanations? When they could observe a direct connection between a person's persistence and the resulting success or failure, they tended to attribute the result to effort (or lack of effort). In other words, when the effects of effort were very obvious the possible influence of ability was discounted. When there was no apparent correlation between effort and outcome, success and failure were attributed more to ability. The message from this study is that if you want to appear to have high ability, you should downplay the exertion and effort you put into your successes. If you are bound to fail, you can emphasize your efforts so people will think you really tried. Or you can show minimal exertion and attempt to convince others that you could have succeeded if you "felt like it."[27]

The main focus in explaining behavior with multiple sufficient causes is to determine which of the possible causes provides the best explanation for the behavior.[28] In situations involving *multiple necessary causes,* several causes must be present before the behavior will occur. In order to have a date with a particular person, for example, it might be necessary for the interested person to be intelligent, attractive, charming, and wealthy, *as well as* being a good disco dancer. Behavior with multiple necessary causes is generally behavior that is extreme or difficult. What would it take for you to give up your belongings and move to Tahiti? Probably more than one cause.

The main focus in explaining behavior with multiple necessary causes is to determine which of many causes were necessarily present to account for the behavior.[29] In explaining why a particular couple broke up, for example, we would have to determine the existence of a number of causes, such as incompatible goals, physical separation, family interference, and involvement with another person. When the multiple necessary causes are present but weak, the resulting action will be weak. As multiple necessary causes become stronger, the behavior will become stronger.

SUMMARY OF KELLEY'S CAUSAL SCHEMATA MODEL

Kelley's causal schemata model describes how we explain behavior we have observed on a single occasion by considering all possible causes. For behavior with multiple sufficient causes, our object is to decide which of these causes provides the best explanation for the behavior. We discount or subtract out the least plausible explanations and pay particular attention to causes that appear to outweigh social and personal inhibitions. For behavior with multiple necessary causes, our goal is to determine how many necessary causes were present to account for the behavior. Behavior with multiple necessary causes becomes stronger as the strength and number of causes is increased. We can predict behavior with multiple necessary causes by weighing present causes against absent ones.

Combining Attribution Theories

Attribution theories describe the way we act like detectives in seeking explanations for behavior. We are motivated to understand one another's behaviors because we feel most comfortable in a predictable world and because we want to know the answers to the following questions:[30]

1. *Why did a person choose a particular behavior? (Is there a simple explanation or are many causes involved?)*

2. *Does the behavior reveal something about the person? (Was the behavior personally motivated or due to the situation? Did the person have positive or negative intentions?)*

3. *Can we predict whether the person will act the same way in the future? (Is this something the person does regularly or sporadically?)*

By combining attribution theories in Table 8-3 we can gain an overview of the kinds of behaviors that tell us something about a person and help answer these questions.

Attribution theories are particularly relevant in situations in which we are paying close attention to one another's motives. This happens most often when we are making new acquaintances, negotiating important decisions, and personally involved because we feel attraction or threat. Attribution theories can also shed light on the strategies we use for winning other people's good will and cooperation, as will be discussed in Chapter 10.

Table 8-3   Behaviors That Tell Something about a Person

Behaviors	Attribution theory
Uncommon behaviors	Correspondent inference theory
Unexpected behaviors	Correspondent inference theory
Undesirable behaviors	Correspondent inference theory
Behaviors that affect us personally	Correspondent inference theory
Behaviors with no obvious external gain	Correspondent inference theory
Behaviors with high distinctiveness and low consensus	Kelley's covariation model
Behaviors that occur despite external inhibitions	Kelley's causal schemata model

When We Don't Make Attributions

Attribution theories are based on situations in which we take account of other people's behavior. Under these circumstances we have a natural tendency to figure out explanations for their actions.[31] As you have read, we pay particular attention to another person's behavior when it has an impact on our lives. During impersonal or routine interactions with others, we are less likely to pay attention or seek explanations for their behavior. This is a good thing because it would be exhausting if we attempted to understand everyone's actions at all times.

Ellen Langer conducted a series of studies to shed light on how we "rest our brains" and act "mindlessly" in situations that are not relevant to our interests or well being.[32] For example, how do you respond when someone asks, "How are you?" In most situations, it is doubtful whether you exert your mind to come up with anything more than, "Fine."

RESEARCH ON MINDLESSNESS

Studies of mindlessness are designed to compare people's responses in situations that are personally relevant with their responses in situations that are not. Mindful behaviors are expected in the former situations, and mindless behaviors in the latter.

In one experiment, a researcher approached people using a copying machine and asked permission to interrupt their work in order to make some copies.[33] Half the time the researcher had five pages to copy and half the time twenty pages. He made the request in one of three ways. Request 1 consisted of simply asking to use the machine: "Excuse me, I have five (twenty) pages. May I use the machine?" Request 2 included the above question plus the explanation, ". . . because I have to make copies." Request 3 included the explanation, ". . . because I'm in a rush." It is clear that there was no essential difference in the meanings of request 1 and request 2. Request 3 differed because it gave a justification for interrupting the person already at the machine. How did people respond to these requests?

More than 90 percent of the people were willing to relinquish the machine to a researcher who had five pages and made either request 2 or request 3. Only 60 percent of the people gave up the machine for request 1. These results provide an example of mindlessness because if people had listened closely to request 2 they would have noticed that it was no more legitimate than request 1. Apparently people mindlessly assumed that request 2 contained a good reason for interrupting them to use the machine.

When the researcher had twenty pages to copy, the results were different. Forty-two percent of the people gave up the machine for request 3, but only 24 percent of them relinquished it for request 1 and request 2. The inconvenience of waiting for the researcher to make twenty copies was enough to make people pay attention and realize that request 2 was not legitimate.

A second example of mindlessness was demonstrated in a study in which secretaries were sent a memo with a message that was worded for some as a request and for others as a demand.[34] The request read, "I would appreciate it if you would return this paper immediately to room 238." The demand read, "This paper is to be returned immediately to room 238." Half the memos were signed and half were not. It is clear that the memos made no sense and that any amount of thought would prompt a person to throw them away. That is not, however, how the secretaries responded. More than 90 percent mindlessly returned the memos to room 238 when they were written in the form the secretaries were used to seeing (request and signature). When the memos were unusual (demand and no signature), 40 percent of the secretaries looked closely enough to realize they had no meaning and did not return them.

WHEN ARE PEOPLE MINDLESS?

There are many occasions when our responses to others are mindless. People living in cities pass thousands of persons each day without paying any attention to what they are doing. When we bump into somebody we automatically say, "Oops, excuse me." How often do you neglect to count your change when you are making a small purchase? Do you remember when you last said "Thank you" to a salesperson?

Ellen Langer concluded that people are not mindless when they are in situations that are unusual or novel, when more than a usual amount of effort or energy is being demanded of them, and when they have unexpected positive or negative experiences. Other researchers have determined that we are mindful of another person's actions under the following circumstances:[35]

1. When we are instructed to be empathic or to pay attention to the person.

2. When we expect to meet the person.

3. When the person is unusual or novel.

4. When we observe the person undergo a serious experience.

5. When we receive privileged information about the person.

6. When the person acts in a way that is unexpected or surprising.

Research also indicates that we are mindful of another's behavior when we are emotionally aroused, personally involved, and threatened by loss of control over our environment.[36]

Applying Your Knowledge about Attribution Theories

This chapter gave you a background in attribution theories and an understanding of how we go about explaining one another's actions. A summary of the process of making behavioral attributions can be outlined in three basic steps:[37]

1. We weigh the importance of the following explanations:
   (a) The behavior reflects a choice, motive, or decision on the part of the behaving person.
   (b) The behavior occurred because of the person toward whom it was directed.
   (c) The behavior is a response to the situation or environment.
2. We form a hypothesis about which of the above explanations is correct.
3. We test our hypothesis by evaluating the nature of the behavior (Jones and Davis) and its distinctiveness, consistency, and consensus (Kelley).

Because our search for behavioral explanations is based on preconceived hypotheses, this attributional process is open to subjectivity and bias. The issue of accuracy and biases in perception of persons has received much attention in psychological research and will be discussed later in this book.

The following chapters will show you how to apply your knowledge of attribution theories in ways that are both practical and interesting. Chapter 9 applies attribution theories to self-presentations and attempts to make good impressions. Chapter 10 presents an attributional analysis of strategies for winning good will and cooperation. Chapters 11 and 12 describe how attribution theories have contributed to the study of accuracy, bias, and subjectivity in judging others.

NINE

Presenting Yourself to Others

The popular singer, Sammy Davis, Jr., summed up the topic of this chapter when he said, "As soon as I go out of the front door of my house in the morning, I'm on, Daddy, I'm on." This approach toward life echoes Shakespeare's observation that "All the world's a stage" in which we play many parts. Although you might not be as conscious of being "on" as Sammy Davis, Jr., the fact is that you are communicating something about yourself whenever you interact with other people. In some situations, for example, social occasions or at work, you may intentionally try to project a particular image. This is called *impression management*. In other situations you may not consciously choose to control the image you are projecting. This is called *self-presentation*.[1] Often it is difficult to know how much of what we are communicating about ourselves is conscious and how much is unconscious, and the distinction between impression management and self-presentation becomes blurred. It is certain, however, that in all interactions, whether we are talkative or silent, reserved or energetic, outspoken or tactful, we are providing information that influences other people's perceptions of us. In this chapter you will read how people form impressions of one another from their self-presentations and styles of interaction.

Self-Disclosure

How much do you reveal about yourself when you meet other people for the first time? Do you express your thoughts and feelings without hesitation or are you more inclined to be cautious and size up the situation before disclosing yourself?

Self-disclosure is defined as "any information exchange that refers to the self, including personal states, dispositions, events in the past, and plans for the future." It is usually assumed that self-disclosure is communicated verbally and that it is intentional and voluntary. We know from personal experience that different situations call for different amounts of self-disclosure and that personal openness that is viewed as appropriate in one setting might be seen as inappropriate in another setting. Consider the results of a study in which researchers approached people in a large metropolitan airport and asked them for a handwriting sample.[2] To provide an example of what they were asking for, the researchers first wrote a brief "handwriting sample" of their own. It was planned ahead that the researchers' samples would express a statement that was either low, medium, or high in self-disclosure. The low-disclosure statement read:

> *Right now I'm in the process of collecting handwriting samples for a school project. I think I will stay here for a while longer and then call it a day.*

The medium-disclosure statement read:

> *Lately I've been thinking about my relationships with other people. I've made several good friends during the past couple of years, but I still feel lonely a lot of the time.*

The high-disclosure statement read:

> *Lately I've been thinking about how I really feel about myself. I think that I'm pretty well adjusted, but I occasionally have some questions about my sexual adequacy.*

If you were in the airport at the time of the study, which researcher would you like best? People in the airport gave highest preference to researchers when their self-disclosure was low. This result is not surprising when you think about the impersonal nature of most interactions in a large airport. Because people are not accustomed to personal closeness in such a setting, any amount of self-disclosure by the researchers seemed inappropriate and out of place.

Now look at a study in which previously unacquainted college women were introduced in pairs and given a chance to chat with each other.[3] It was secretly arranged that one of the women was a research volunteer while the other woman was a researcher who was trained to disclose herself either personally or superficially. When being personal, the researcher revealed, among other things, that her mother had caught her having sexual relations with a male friend. When being superficial, the researcher talked about plans for her summer vacation and gave a brief sketch of her family. Whom did the research volunteers like better? In this situation the personal self-discloser was liked somewhat more than the superficial self-discloser. College women apparently felt that it was appropriate for a woman they didn't know to share an embarrassing experience in the context of a psychology experiment. A third group of women chatted with a researcher who engaged in high self-disclosure by revealing that her mother had caught her having sexual relations with a woman friend. This researcher was not liked. For college women participating in this study, at least, self-disclosure about a woman's sexual relationship with another woman was more than they wanted to hear.

COMPARING REACTIONS TO SELF-DISCLOSING MEN AND WOMEN

After reading about people's responses to self-disclosure by women, you might be curious to know how people react to self-disclosure by men. Researchers have concluded that personal self-disclosure is generally more acceptable when it comes from a woman than from a man. In one study, for example, men and women felt it was quite appropriate for a woman to reveal to a stranger that she had been in a car accident in which her brother was killed or that she was upset because her mother recently entered a psychiatric hospital for a nervous breakdown. This kind of personal disclosure was not acceptable when it came from a man. Research participants in another study preferred women who shared a lot about themselves during an interview.[4] They preferred men when the men shared only a moderate amount of information about themselves.

After reading these studies showing different reactions to self-disclosure by men and women, Margi Lenga Kahn and I were curious about whether there is *any* topic on which self-disclosure is acceptable from men. We conducted a series of experiments in which research participants evaluated men and women who engaged in personal self-disclosure on one of three issues: suicide, sex, or competitiveness.[5] Research participants were told that college men and women had been introduced in a study of first impressions. Before their introduction, the men and women were given a chance to send each other a brief introductory message. In one instance, the message included a description of a recent suicide by the self-discloser's mother or father. You can guess that a man who disclosed this kind of information to a woman he had never met was not liked very much. It might surprise you, however, that this self-disclosure was quite acceptable when it came from a woman. Men were also not liked when they revealed personal preferences about sex. In contrast, self-disclosure about sexual preferences was quite acceptable when it came from a woman. We thought that a man's self-disclosure of personal feelings of competitiveness might be accepted because of the competitive stereotype associated with men in American society. This was not true, however. Neither men nor women were liked when they revealed strong feelings of competitiveness.

Our research found that men were not liked when they didn't disclose anything about themselves, and they were particularly disliked when their self-disclosure was very high. Men were liked best when they disclosed something, but not too much. Women were liked when their self-disclosure was about suicide or sex, but they were not liked when they admitted to feelings of competitiveness. To summarize our results another way, neither men nor women were liked when they shared nothing about themselves, but women were given more acceptance than men when engaging in self-disclosure that was very high.

WHEN IS SELF-DISCLOSURE APPROPRIATE?

As well as being more acceptable from women than from men, self-disclosure is also more acceptable in certain situations. As you might expect, it is judged as more appropriate when it is given to a friend rather than to a stranger and when it is directed to someone similar in age. People prefer others who disclose at about the same level of intimacy as they do. Those who respond with unexpectedly high self-disclosure are viewed as maladjusted, while those who respond with unexpectedly low self-disclosure seem cold and withdrawn.[6]

JUDGMENTS ABOUT A DISCLOSER'S MOTIVES

Our reactions to self-disclosure depend on judgments we make about the discloser's motives. For example, we are likely to favor someone who gives us high self-disclosure when we feel he or she has chosen us because of respect and trust. A person who discloses himself or herself indiscriminately we do not value as much.[7]

Irwin Altman and Dalmas Taylor described how personal closeness increases slowly over a period of time. Research on self-disclosure has supported this analysis of friendship development. We generally feel more comfortable when strangers don't present us with a personal self-disclosure right away but hold back until we know them better. One occasion when it might be advisable to come out with a personal disclosure early in a relationship is when we might be suspected of being deceptive and of putting up a false front. If people are certain to find out something negative about us anyway, we are better off volunteering the information than holding back and appearing that we have something to hide. Another occasion where early self-disclosure might be valued is when it helps to engender a feeling of openness and trust. For this reason, counselors and therapists are often valued when they open a therapy session by sharing something personal about themselves.[8]

SUGGESTIONS

We can derive a number of suggestions from self-disclosure research. First, when deciding how much to disclose about yourself to others, it is important to find the happy medium.[9] Self-disclosure helps to establish a feeling of closeness and trust and is the avenue through which friendships grow. If you hold back all your thoughts and feelings, you are likely to seem disinterested and withdrawn. People won't come to know you very well. On the other hand, if you reveal too much too soon, you may appear inappropriately intimate and make others around you uncomfortable. Second, people are generally open to hearing more self-disclosure from women than from men. Third, those who disclose a lot about themselves are more comfortable receiving self-disclosure from others than are those who don't disclose much about themselves. Our goal with people we want to know is to disclose enough about ourselves to build intimacy but not so much as to cause discomfort. Over time, the amount of self-disclosure we can comfortably communicate will grow.

Immediacy in Communication

If you ask a friend to go to a movie, which of the following replies would make you happier?

1. *I'd like to go with you.*

2. *I guess I'll go if you want me to.*

Chances are that you'd feel better if your friend responded with reply 1. Imagine that someone you really care about makes one of the two following comments:

1. *I like you.*

2. *There's something about people like you that I like.*

Again, you would probably prefer comment 1. The first statements in the above examples are more meaningful than the second statements because the first are more personal, more direct, and more immediate. *Immediacy* is defined as the directness and intensity of a verbal communication.[10] Immediate communication gives a feeling of greater intimacy and closeness than nonimmediate communication.

HOW IMMEDIACY IS MEASURED

Immediacy is measured according to three scoring categories: spatio-temporal, denotative specificity, and agent-action-object.[11] A statement can be scored to determine which of these categories apply. A total score for the least degree of immediacy is derived by adding up the number of categories applicable. The terms used to define categories of immediacy may sound complicated, but the examples given below should make them easy to understand.

Spatio-Temporal Category. A statement is less immediate if it includes words that separate the speaker in space or time from the object of the verb in the statement or the person to whom the statement is addressed. It is scored as spatially less immediate (S) when it contains demonstratives such as "that" or "those" rather than "the," "this," or "these." It is scored as temporally less immediate (T) if the object or recipient of it is separated from the speaker in time. The following statements are less immediate:

> *I like those shoes. (S)*
>
> *You've been a good friend. (T)*
>
> *I've liked that smile. (S, T)*

More immediate forms of the previous statements are these:

> *I like your shoes.*
>
> *You are a good friend.*
>
> *I like your smile.*

Denotative Specificity Category. A statement is less immediate if it focuses only on part of the issue (P), depersonalizes the issue from individuality to a general class (C), and treats the subject, object, or recipient implicitly rather than explicitly (I). Some examples of statements with low denotative specificity follow:

> *My hand touched him. (P)*
>
> *Everybody liked the movie. (C)*
>
> *One would say the book is dull. (C)*
>
> *Connie is attractive. (I)*
>
> *Richard is friendly. (I)*

More immediate forms of the previous statements are these:

> *I touched him.*
>
> *I liked the movie.*
>
> *I think the book is dull.*
>
> *I think Connie is attractive.*
>
> *Richard is friendly to me.*

Agent-Action-Object Category. Statements are less immediate if they contain a separation between the speaker and an action, between another person and an action, or between the speaker and another person. An occurrence that is described as unilateral (U) is less immediate than an occurrence that is mutual. The statement, "Jeff kissed Mindy" is less immediate than "Jeff and Mindy kissed each other." "Zoe drove me to school" is less immediate than "Zoe and I drove to school together." Another example of a lesser degree of immediacy in agent-action-object relationships is the inclusion of passivity (P). The statement, "I have to go to a movie with Patricia tonight" is less immediate than "Patricia and I are going to a movie tonight." "The fear of failing overcame me" is less immediate than" I was scared I might fail." "I was met by Gerry yesterday" is less immediate than "Gerry and I met each other yesterday." A third kind of a lesser degree of immediacy is the introduction of a qualification or modification (M). "I sort of feel angry" is less immediate than "I am angry." "It seems to be a good play" is less immediate than "It is a good play." "I guess we like each other" is less immediate than "We like each other." Another kind of qualification or modification has to do with the intensity, extensity, or frequency of a statement. "I like some things about her" is less immediate than "I like her." "We generally go out together" is less immediate than "We go out together."

LIKING AND POSITIVE EXPERIENCES

People are more immediate when communicating about positive experiences and people whom they like. One series of studies found that people write more-immediate descriptions about a person they like than about someone they dislike. Research has also shown that people make statements with more immediacy when talking to an interviewer about someone they like than when talking about someone they dislike. Studies of immediacy in letters of recommendation indicate that people write longer recommendation letters for someone they like and shorter letters for someone they dislike.[12]

A second series of studies demonstrated that people use more immediacy when describing experiences of success than when describing experiences of failure. People are also more immediate when expressing firm convictions than apprehensions. There is evidence that people are more immediate when they are being truthful than when they are being deceptive.[13] Nonimmediacy is sometimes used as a strategy to disclaim or discount one's responsibility for a negative statement. It is less immediate to say, "Some people have felt you could change," than to say, "I feel you should change."

RESPONSES TO IMMEDIACY AND NONIMMEDIACY

Although some of the differences between immediate and nonimmediate communications are subtle, people are sensitive to them in how they respond. Research participants in one experiment evaluated the amount of liking in statements made by two different speakers about another person. One speaker made immediate statements such as, "I know Fran," "I visited Art," "I saw Paula." The second speaker expressed nonimmediate statements such as, "Our friends know Fran," "I visited Art's house," "I saw Paula's car." The immediate speaker was seen as liking the person more than was the nonimmediate speaker. Participants in a second experiment judged statements that varied in amount of nonimmediacy separating the speaker and person spoken about in distance or time, activity-passivity, or reciprocity.[14] Examples of immediate statements were, "Ted is showing me his house," "I'm going to write a letter to Gene," "Carl and I go for rides." Nonimmediate statements were, "Ted showed me his house," "I have to write a letter to Gene," "I have gone for rides with Carl." Participants felt that the immediate speaker liked the person who was being talked about more than the nonimmediate speaker did.

Responses to immediacy in letters of recommendation were measured by asking people to evaluate letters that were relatively short, medium, or long.[15] The letters were objective and described the education and employment experiences of a job applicant. Even though they did not differ in quality, they were rated differently on the basis of their length. Long letters were considered most favorable toward the job applicant and short letters least favorable.

BEING MORE IMMEDIATE

You can practice being more immediate with people who are important to you by paying attention to your communications with them. For example, instead of waiting for a loved one to ask, volunteer the statement, "I love you." When interviewing for a job, don't say, "I've sort of been interested in that job." Say, "I'm very interested in this job." If a friend makes you angry, don't say, "I was kind of upset." Say, "What you did makes me angry." If you tell someone about a book you have enjoyed, don't say, "Some people would think it's OK." Say, "I think it's great!"

Presenting Your Strengths and Weaknesses

What is the best strategy for presenting your strengths and weaknesses? When should you be modest? Under what conditions is it advantageous to emphasize your positive strengths? Psychologists who have studied self-presentation strategies within various contexts make the following recommendations.

EMPHASIZING POSITIVE ASSETS

The values placed by American society on modesty and achievement are not in contradiction if we define modesty as not overstating one's assets. There is nothing in the definition of modesty that requires us to understate them. The best advice for presenting yourself to people who can verify your claims is to be accurate. If you overstate your accomplishments, they will find out about it and think you were bragging. If you understate your accomplishments, they will question your self-confidence. If you have to predict your performance for people who will learn about it later, it is safest to be moderate. If you succeed, you will appear modest, and if you fail, you won't appear as boastful as if your prediction had been exaggerated. There is no advantage to predicting an inferior performance unless you are certain that you will fail. Then at least you will appear to be accurate. If people know of your success, you can gain credit by saying, "I did pretty well," instead of, "I was great!" People will not particularly like it, however, if you devalue the importance of your success by saying, "I did well, but it's no big deal." When people have no way of verifying your claims, there is no reason not to amplify your success (within reason, of course). Modesty has little advantage in this situation, and self-depreciation is defeating. Research studies have shown that people generally follow this advice.[16] Participants in these studies gave accurate self-assessments when their claims could be verified and somewhat enhanced self-assessments when their claims could not be verified.

When presenting positive assets to someone of higher status, it is necessary to minimize possible suspicion resulting from your dependence on that person's approval. In such a situation it may be more credible to focus your self-presentation on objective assets such as competence and performance rather than on subjective assets such as personality traits. It has been suggested that people of high status have more latitude than people of low status in communicating positive assets because the credibility of the former is less suspect when they emphasize personal strengths and they can afford a bit more modesty in admitting personal weaknesses. Self-presentation strategies of students of high and low status in a naval officers' training program were compared in an experiment in which they were motivated to win another person's approval.[17] Those of high status were more likely than those of low status to emphasize their positive qualities on important traits. In addition, high-status students were more modest in communicating unimportant traits. Low-status students could not afford the strategy of being modest by deemphasizing their strengths on less important traits. Their concern was to minimize their weaknesses on important traits and to emphasize their strengths on unimportant traits. They attempted to avoid "coming on too strongly" by not emphasizing their strengths on important traits.

BASKING IN REFLECTED GLORY

Another method for emphasizing positive assets is to call attention to one's association with respected groups or people. This self-presentation strategy, called *basking in reflected glory,* was demonstrated in a study showing that undergraduates were more likely to wear clothing like sweatshirts and hats that announced their university affiliation when their football team had recently been victorious.[18] Undergraduates also used the pronoun *we* more often to describe their team's victories than to describe their team's losses. This finding can be related to the previous discussion on immediacy.

The basking-in-reflected-glory strategy is most likely to be effective if the association with respected others is communicated subtly. We have all experienced occasions where people came across as phony by dropping names and overplaying their association with respected groups or famous personalities.

Positive assets can also be communicated by playing up the quality of one's own affiliations and playing down the quality of other people's affiliations. The strategy of enhancing oneself while demeaning others was investigated in studies in which undergraduate students took a creativity test and received feedback that their performance was either average or very poor.[19] After the test, students evaluated their university and a rival university. Those who performed "poorly" were more likely to overrate their university and underrate the rival university than those whose performance was "average." Although it is understandable that people might react to failure by enhancing themselves and derogating others, it is not clear how they will be evaluated when they do so. Additional research is needed to study perceptions of people whose self-presentation strategies involve basking, self-enhancing, and making scapegoats of others.

Just as people try to play up affiliations that reflect on them favorably, they often downplay affiliations that discredit them. Most people have experienced the embarrassment of being associated with others who were behaving inappropriately even though they themselves were behaving correctly. The strategy of maintaining a good image by dissociating oneself from others was tested in an experiment in which research participants interacted with an obnoxious researcher who presumably was very similar to them in opinions and beliefs.[20] In order to dissociate themselves from this obnoxious person, participants began to express opinions that were discrepant with their true beliefs.

MINIMIZING FAULTS

In general, it seems sensible not to advertise your faults. One exception to this rule might occur if someone is already aware of your faults and you are likely to be suspected of hiding them. Dale Carnegie suggested that admitting one's faults can work successfully to allay suspicion as well as to win sympathy:

> Say about yourself all the derogatory things you know the other person intends to say—and say them before he has the chance to say them—and you take the wind out of his sails. The chances are a hundred to one that he will then take a generous, forgiving attitude and minimize your mistakes.[21]

Research has shown that it is advantageous to admit a negative experience in the early stages of a relationship if it was caused by your fault and if it is certain to become known at a later time.[22] By admitting your fault early, you may or may not win the other person's sympathy, but you will at least show that you have nothing to hide. A negative experience that was not a result of your fault is best withheld until later because admitting that experience too soon may be suspected as a sympathy-arousing ploy.

MAKING BLUNDERS

People sometimes try to make themselves open and approachable by appearing humble and admitting or showing a fault or weakness. How effective is this strategy? The theory that extremely able people will appear more human and likable if they commit a small blunder was tested in the following experiment.[23] Research participants listened to a tape recording in which a college student was being interviewed as a candidate for the college quiz bowl. Half the participants heard a candidate who had a superior academic record and seemed nearly perfect. The remaining participants heard a candidate who was quite ordinary. The tape recording was set up so that at the end of the interview half the participants heard the candidate commit a blunder by spilling coffee all over himself. The taped interviews for the remainder did not contain this blunder. What effect did the fuss over the spilled coffee have on evaluations of the candidates? Research participants expressed greater liking for the superior candidate when he spilled the coffee and less liking for the ordinary candidate when he spilled it. It was concluded that the blunder increased the attractiveness of the superior candidate because it made him appear more human and more approachable. It was detrimental to the ordinary candidate because it only emphasized his shortcomings.

A replication of this experiment showed that it was primarily people with average self-esteem who liked a competent student better after a blunder. The explanation was that people with high self-esteem felt personally threatened by a very competent student and therefore used his blunder as an excuse for finding fault with and derogating him. The researchers concluded that people with low self-esteem liked less the competent student who blundered because they were disillusioned about someone who had been a potential person to admire. A third experiment demonstrated that we tend to find fault with people of similar ability when they blunder because we gauge our own value against them.[24]

All in all, it appears that attempting to make a good impression by committing a blunder is a risky strategy because the conditions under which it might be effective are so limited.

PLAYING DUMB

Another way to show weakness is to play dumb. Who plays dumb more often, men or women? The results of an interview study with men and women in forty-eight states might surprise you because 30 percent of the men and only 23 percent of the women admitted to playing dumb at some point in their lives.[25] The study found that people are particularly motivated to play dumb when they are in a relationship in which they are *supposed* to be of equal or inferior capability but are in reality of superior capability. This explains why people are more likely to play dumb when they are well educated and work in high-status occupations and why women sometimes feel obliged to play dumb with their spouse. When people feel required to play dumb because of social expectations it can be a frustrating and demeaning experience. Respondents in the interviews who said they played dumb very often were characterized as having low self-esteem, being unhappy, and feeling alienated. Although playing dumb is not recommended, it appears to be expected in some social relationships and job situations for maintaining stability and getting ahead.

Conforming to Social Stereotypes

It is a common experience to present a favorable image by conforming to social roles and stereotypes. Conformity can be communicated by the way you dress and the ideas you express. For example, a study of conformity to sex-role stereotypes found that people preferred men and women who acted according to their ideals of "appropriate" male and female behavior. In a similar vein, women participating in a dating study described themselves in ways that would match the stereotype of the "ideal" woman held by a man they wanted to date.[26] Men's self-descriptions were not measured, but it seems fair to assume they would present the image for the "ideal" man held by a woman they wished to date.

We all know of the pressures placed on us by jobs and social conventions to act and dress in prescribed ways. Although conformity may sometimes be necessary, it is also important to appreciate the value of treating others as people who are unique. Check whether you agree with the following statements:

1. *I tend to express my opinions publicly, regardless of what others say.*

2. *It is better to break the rules than always to conform to an impersonal society.*

3. *As a rule, I strongly defend my opinion.*

4. *I do not like to go my own way.*

5. *I tend to keep quiet in the presence of persons of higher rank, experience, etc.*

6. *Feeling "different" in a crowd of people makes me uncomfortable.*

These statements come from a need-for-uniqueness scale.[27] If you agreed with the first three statements and disagreed with the last three, you place a relatively high value on being unique. It is useful to be sensitive to other people's need for uniqueness so that you can treat them as individuals without making them feel deviant or out of place.

Self-Handicapping

Every time you set your goals a little lower than your abilities you are engaging in a *self-handicapping* strategy. Underachievers are self-handicappers because they keep their aspirations at a moderate level in order to avoid failure. People sometimes use drugs and alcohol to handicap themselves by relying on drug and alcohol symptoms as an excuse for inadequate behavior. The self-handicapping strategy appears to be used most often by people who are uncertain about their competence.[28] People who know they will succeed have no need to handicap themselves, and people who are sure to fail avoid even the small challenge of a handicap by sticking with attainable objectives.

This explanation of self-handicapping was tested in an experiment in which research participants worked on an intellectual task.[29] Some participants experienced expected success and others experienced unexpected success. Before working on a second test the participants were asked to choose between one of two drugs that were supposedly being investigated in the study. One drug was expected to enhance intellectual performance, and the other was expected to inhibit it. Which drug did participants choose? The majority of those who had experienced expected success chose the performance-enhancing drug. They apparently wanted to see if the drug would help them do better. In contrast, the majority of participants who experienced unexpected success chose the performance-inhibiting drug. It appeared that they were not confident that they could succeed on the second test because they were uncertain about why they had succeeded on the first. By choosing the performance-inhibiting drug they could feel safer on the second test because failure could be blamed on the drug. Another interesting finding in this study was that men engaged in self-handicapping more often than women. The reason was not clear. It is possible that women felt less need to handicap themselves because they viewed their intellectual performance less as an indication of skill and more as a result of luck (see Chapter 12).

Another self-handicapping strategy is the exaggeration of psychological or physical symptoms. Studies of psychiatric patients have shown how they use psychotic symptoms to obtain privileges and to maintain control over their protected environment. An example of symptom exaggeration in college students is seen in a study in which students took a test of intellectual ability and then rated themselves on feelings of anxiety.[30] Students who generally feared taking tests said they were more anxious than students who did not fear tests. This difference in self-reported anxiety was most pronounced when the experiment was set up so that anxiety could be used as a reasonable excuse for poor performance. When anxiety was no excuse, students who feared tests handicapped themselves by reporting that they hadn't given their full effort.

Most of us have used self-handicapping at one time or another when we faced a difficult challenge and were doubtful about success. Life would be unnecessarily harsh if people couldn't give themselves a break by lowering their expectations when facing questionable odds. Self-handicapping only becomes a problem when it turns into a habit rather than a skill for coping with life's harshest demands.[31] People who use self-handicapping to excuse all their failures, bad habits, and lack of initiative are likely to lead unproductive lives.

Directions for Future Research

The process of self-presentation involves three basic components: (1) the situation, people, or demands that elicit self-presentation; (2) the self-presentation; (3) the reactions, responses, and outcome of the self-presentation. This chapter focused on self-presentation strategies and the conditions under which they may or may not be effective. It will now be useful for researchers to relate these self-presentation strategies to the following five factors that are likely to bring them about.

1. type of situation (social, work, school, public, private)

2. self-presenter's goals (enhance credibility, win approval, avoid disapproval, gain control)

3. social norms (fairness, modesty, reciprocity, altruism)

4. self-presenter's personality (need for approval, anxiety, social skills)

5. audience (attractiveness, sex, status, familiarity, power)

Can an understanding of these factors help us recommend particular self-presentation strategies? Some answers to this question have already been provided in this chapter. Another useful research direction is to learn more about the outcome of self-presentations. The primary focus has been on how self-presentations influence other people's evaluations of the self-presenter. Another focus is to explore the effects of self-presentations on the self-presenter's perceptions of people's reactions and on the effects of these perceptions on his or her concept of self.[32]

If you had been asked before reading this chapter whether you ever engaged in impression management you might have responded in an indignant tone (which is a self-presentation) that you always attempt to project an honest image of yourself. Now you can understand that even when we are honest, we have to gauge our actions to suit particular situations and individuals with whom we are involved. Getting along with others requires us to respond with sensitivity to their preferences and expectations. We can learn about other people as well as ourselves by observing one another's self-presentations as we go through our lives.

Winning Good Will and Cooperation

One of life's most consistent challenges is gaining cooperation and good will from other people. Whether we are interviewing for a job, discussing a grade with a teacher, asking for a raise, seeking affection from a friend or family member, negotiating a business transaction, or requesting service from a salesperson, our desire is to influence someone else to meet our needs. Since most of us depend on other people for some kind of favor every day, it is small wonder that Dale Carnegie's book *How to Win Friends and Influence People* was a record best seller. Since Carnegie's book was first published in 1936, psychologists have produced a wealth of research on methods for winning good will and cooperation. Many of his observations and recommendations have been borne out in psychological research. Other tactics have been refined and modified. In this chapter it is possible with the advantage of hindsight to filter recommendations for winning friends and influencing people through fifty years of psychological research to arrive at a number of useful formulations and conclusions.

Avoiding Flattery and Ingratiation

It is perhaps ironic that while suggesting a compendium of techniques for winning people's good will, Dale Carnegie rejected the use of flattery.

> No! No! No! I am not suggesting flattery! Far from it. . . . The difference between appreciation and flattery? That is simple. One is sincere and the other insincere. One comes from the heart out; the other from the teeth out. One is unselfish; the other is universally condemned.[1]

Carnegie's admonition against flattery presents us with an interesting challenge. Our desire is to gain other people's favor, but we want to use approaches that are sincere. A good place to start is with the realization that flattery and sincerity are in the ear of the listener. A compliment or favor that appears insincere and inappropriate to some people in some situations may be graciously accepted by other people in other situations. The goal is to match the way we seek favors to people's preferences and to the norms of the situation.

A discussion of tactful approaches toward gaining favor may begin by considering the insights of the psychologists Edward E. Jones and Camille Wortman, who analyzed the problem of winning cooperation and good will with their pioneering research on ingratiation. *Ingratiation* is defined as "a class of strategic behaviors illicitly designed to influence a particular other person concerning the attractiveness of one's personal qualities."[2] Flattery is one kind of ingratiating strategy. Giving favors and presenting a false image are other ingratiating strategies. Like flattery, judgments about when someone is being ingratiating are in the ear of the listener. The challenge is to learn how to seek favor from particular people in particular situations by using an approach that will be viewed as acceptable, appropriate, and noningratiating.

This chapter will first analyze methods for winning cooperation and good will that are relatively transparent and obvious, such as giving compliments and praise and rendering favors. Later the chapter will consider more subtle approaches toward gaining favor, such as emphasizing our similarity with others and using methods of intimacy like calling people by name.

Compliments and Praise

In his book, Dale Carnegie described the "gnawing and unfaltering human hunger" for appreciation. Abraham Lincoln recognized this need when he said, "Everybody likes a compliment." A good example of appreciation of positive evaluations is seen in experiments in which people received evaluations that were either positive, neutral, or negative. Results clearly showed that people liked most someone who evaluated them positively and liked least someone who evaluated them negatively. Research studies have also found that people prefer other people who give favorable evaluations about their personalities and their performance on different kinds of tasks. David Mettee and Elliot Aronson concluded from a review of research literature that we reach to the furthest reasonable extremes to accept compliments and praise.[3] They pointed out that even though we may not *personally* believe we possess a particular quality, we are quite willing to allow others to perceive that quality in us. It is only when compliments are too extreme for us to convince ourselves of their validity or when their validity is called into question by other people or sources of information that we are likely to view a complimenting person as ingratiating.

JUDGING COMPLIMENTS BY ATTRIBUTION THEORIES

The attribution theories described in Chapter 8 can help us understand how we decide which compliments are suspect and which are sincere. For example, employees who compliment their boss, students who compliment their teachers, and athletes who compliment their coach are particularly suspect because they are dependent on the good graces of the person they are complimenting. In terms of Kelley's causal schemata model, it is difficult in these instances to know whether the compliment was motivated by sincerity or by desire for external gain. People who are in a dependent relationship with another person face what has been called the *ingratiator's dilemma* because it is very difficult in such a situation to present a compliment that will be interpreted as sincere.[4]

Kelley's covariation model can help us understand that compliments are most likely to be interpreted as honest when they reflect qualities actually possessed by the recipient. This would occur when distinctiveness, consistency, and consensus are all high (attribution C and attribution F in Table 8-1). Compliments that can fit almost anybody (low distinctiveness) do not appear as valid as compliments that make the recipient unique (high distinctiveness). Compliments usually appear more truthful when they are reinforced by other people (high consensus) than when they are only a possible idiosyncrasy of the complimenter (low consensus). In general, compliments have greater validity when they are reinforced with high consistency than when they are sporadic. An exception might occur if a compliment was given so "consistently" that it became boring or taken for granted. In terms of correspondent inference theory, the compliment would have low correspondence because it was no longer uncommon or unexpected. This example is related to the gain-loss principle discussed later in this chapter.

The insights from attribution theories have guided psychologists in studying how people evaluate compliments by judging their validity and by considering the existence of ulterior motives. These studies can now be reviewed and conclusions about the conditions under which compliments are perceived as legitimate or illegitimate may be derived.

JUDGING THE VALIDITY OF PRAISE

An example of an "invalid" compliment is seen in a study in which employees at a telephone company were divided into teams and presented with problems to solve.[5] Team members worked individually on the problems with the understanding that their individual scores would be combined into a total score to determine which team would win. Some employees were led to believe that they had done very well on the problems and had helped their team win. Other employees were told that they had done poorly and had caused their team to lose. After the contest the group members read a note that had supposedly been sent to them by one of their teammates. Half of the participants received positive notes stating that the teammate would like to have them on the same team in the future. The remaining participants received negative notes in which the teammate expressed the desire not to be on the same team again. It is not surprising that participants who had done well and helped their team win preferred teammembers who were positive. It is also understandable that participants who had done poorly and caused their team to lose reacted unfavorably toward positive teammembers. It was a bit far-fetched for teammembers to tell someone who had caused their team to lose that they would still like to be on the same team in the future.

Another study testing the plausibility of praise had college students perform a simulated game in which they acted as air controllers and made a series of critical decisions.[6] Four other students observed the participants as they played the game and evaluated their competence. One evaluator gave a very positive evaluation, and the others gave average ratings. Even though approval is usually appreciated, the positive evaluator in this situation was not liked. A single positive evaluation was apparently too far from the participants' sense of reality to be taken seriously.

Participants in a third study were given the task of arguing in favor of a particular issue.[7] Half the participants were told that their performance had been very good. The remainder were led to believe that they had done poorly. Then the participants received positive or negative evaluations from people who had observed them arguing. Again, it is not surprising that participants who felt they had performed well were favorable toward people who evaluated them positively. Participants were especially negative in their feelings when they had done poorly and an evaluator who did not agree with the topic of their argument gave them a positive evaluation. It is unpleasantly condescending when someone who disagrees with you gives a positive evaluation for poor performance.

LOOKING FOR ULTERIOR MOTIVES

Attribution theories predict that we are likely to view praise and compliments as illicit when there is a strong possibility that they are motivated by the desire for personal gain. This prediction was supported in a study in which participants received positive, neutral, or negative evaluations about their performance. When they believed that the evaluator was motivated to be accurate and objective, they preferred the positive evaluator. When they were told that the evaluator would probably ask them for a favor after the study, they preferred the neutral evaluator. Research participants in a similar study received either favorable or unfavorable evaluations by someone who had observed their performance in an interview.[8] Half the participants thought the observer had no ulterior motives and was being objective. The remainder were under the impression that the observer was trying to win their approval. When the evaluations were favorable, participants liked the observer with no ulterior motives more than the one with such motives. When the evaluations were unfavorable, participants preferred the observer who had ulterior motives. This second finding is interesting because it involved a situation in which the observer was apparently trying to win a participant's favor by being derogatory.

If we receive negative evaluations from someone who is trying to win our approval, we can ignore the evaluations and save our self-esteem much more easily than if we are evaluated negatively by someone who is being objective.

Another example of reactions to unfavorable evaluations is seen in a study in which research participants were negatively rated by an evaluator who was either dependent or not dependent on their approval.[9] Not surprisingly, participants did not like the negative evaluator who was not dependent. However, it is intriguing that they liked the negative evaluator who was dependent. Apparently they gave him "extra credit" for being honest and resisting the temptation to give a positive evaluation for the sake of ingratiation.

Strategies for Giving Compliments

Edward E. Jones and Camille Wortman analyzed strategies for giving compliments from the vantage point of attribution theories.[10] You may find it useful to relate these strategies to your experiences and the knowledge you have gained about perceiving people and forming impressions.

MINIMIZING ULTERIOR MOTIVES

Compliments are most effective when we can play down any possible dependence we have on the person we wish to compliment. One way to do this is to call attention to the investment we have made in our relationship with that person. Another way is to minimize the perception of ulterior motives by arranging it so that our compliment is "overheard" by the recipient or delivered by a "disinterested" third party.[11] Under these circumstances the person we wish to compliment is less likely to question our motives because it appears that the compliment reached him or her without our knowledge.

MAXIMIZING CREDIBILITY

We are likely to view a compliment as more credible when we perceive the complimenting person as someone who is discerning rather than indiscriminate. The influence of discernment was tested in an experiment in which college women received favorable or unfavorable ratings from a male evaluator. Half the women were given the impression that he was discerning. They watched him judge paintings and saw that he was confident and discerning enough to use both positive and negative sides of the rating scale. The remaining women were led to believe that he was not discerning and somewhat wishy-washy because he always stuck to the middle of the rating scale. You can guess that women liked the man better when he gave favorable evaluations. In addition, whether the evaluations were favorable or unfavorable, they liked him much more when he was discerning. People like to be praised, but they especially like praise from someone who is discriminating. Jones and Wortman suggested that compliments will appear more discerning if the complimenter does not praise other people in the recipient's presence and if he or she describes positive traits about the recipient that are not too exaggerated to be true. Compliments also appear more credible if they agree with the self-perceptions of the recipient.[12]

Another strategy for making credible compliments is to include a few neutral or mildly negative evaluations along with the positive ones. Jones described this approach as concocting "a judicious blend of the bitter and the sweet." Consistently positive evaluations have potential problems because they can cause the complimenter to appear nondiscriminating and because the recipient might come to take them for granted. Elliot Aronson called this problem the *law of marital infidelity*. He pointed out that two people who have been pleasantly attached for many years can become bored and lose their appreciation for each other's praise. A compliment from a stranger might therefore have a stronger impact than the same compliment from one's partner because it is new and unexpected. In the same vein, two people accustomed to a positive relationship may be more adversely affected by the contrast of negative exchanges with each other than by an isolated negative communication from a stranger. An analysis of the possible satiating effects of consistent praise led to the formulation of a *gain-loss* model, which suggests that it may be more effective to give another person negative evaluations followed by positive ones than to give all positive ones.[13] This approach can be called a "gain" strategy because it implies that people who receive initial negative evaluations will be motivated to gain subsequent positive evaluations. The gain-loss model also suggests that people will like an evaluator who is first positive and then negative less than an evaluator who is consistently negative.

THE "GAIN" STRATEGY

Research leads to the conclusion that the "gain" strategy for giving compliments can be effective if it makes the recipient feel satisfied or relieved that he or she has overcome the originally negative evaluation. To ensure such satisfaction, the original negative evaluation has to be on the same issues as the subsequent positive evaluation. In addition, the original evaluation cannot be too negative lest it outweigh any possible feelings of relief from the subsequent positive evaluation. Jones and Wortman recommend that the negative evaluation should be restricted to a minor fault that the recipient is willing to admit. It is also important that the evaluator's shift from a negative to a positive evaluation be credible and tactful. Credibility and tact can be enhanced by shifting from negative to positive evaluations gradually and by having the evaluations "overheard" by the recipient or delivered by a "disinterested" third party.[14]

The "gain" strategy for giving compliments is risky. In one experiment research participants reacted favorably when they met a single evaluator who switched from negative to positive evaluations, but when they were exposed to two evaluators, they preferred the one who was consistently positive over the one who was first negative and then positive.[15]

MINIMIZING THE COST OF PRAISE

Praise will be most effective if it is given in such a way as to minimize its potential cost to the recipient. Compliments given to a person in a group are more likely to make the recipient feel awkward by not knowing how to respond than compliments given privately. Praise given for small accomplishments might make the recipient feel underrated, while praise for large accomplishments can make him or her feel obliged to repeat the same performance in the future. Whenever there is the possibility of ulterior motives on the part of the complimenting person, praise can make the recipient feel obligated to reciprocate. The costs of praise can be minimized by delivering compliments privately, by telling the recipient that his or her performance was "better than you expected," and by focusing compliments on accomplishments that don't demand a repeat performance.[16] The cost or praise can also be minimized (with a risk) by using "negative compliments" such as those described below.

"SPONTANEOUS" AND "NEGATIVE" COMPLIMENTS

Sometimes there are situations in which a compliment is expected. Imagine that you are with a group of people and someone has cooked a good dinner, received an award, bought a new shirt, or had his hair cut. Because it is socially appropriate to deliver a compliment on these occasions, the motives of people who give them are not known. While it may be socially important to deliver a compliment when it is expected, it is also useful to consider making it again "spontaneously" at a later time.[17]

A "negative" compliment, given in the form of a mild insult, can serve to play down any dependence the complimenter may have on the recipient. If you tell people their performance was terrible or that they look awful, they aren't likely to suspect you of being ingratiating. And if you have the right kind of relationship they will receive this "negative compliment" in a positive way. Research participants approved of someone who had insulted a fellow student when the insult was based on the good intention of shaming the student into studying.[18] They did not approve when the insult was exploitative and used to impress a professor. It must be remembered that "negative" compliments are risky in the same way as the "gain" strategy because they can backfire if they are taken the wrong way.

MAKING COMPLIMENTS MORE EFFECTIVE

Compliments are often more effective when they are specific rather than general.[19] For example, instead of telling someone, "You look nice," it is more specific to say, "That sweater looks good on you," or "Your hair looks great." If a student writes a good paper, a professor could give a general compliment like "You are a good writer," or a specific compliment like "You gave some well organized arguments in this paper." Specific compliments are preferable first of all because the recipient can learn from them. General compliments don't teach us what we did well and what we should change. Specific compliments are also more credible because they are based on objective facts. To give a specific compliment the complimenter has to know what he or she is talking about. Another advantage of specific compliments is that they are easier to accept because they don't leave room for doubt. It might sound nice to be told you are beautiful, a genius, or a great athlete. But think about how easy it is to find exceptions to these statements. Unless you know the complimenter very well, such sweeping compliments will probably result in negative feelings after you have looked at yourself and decided the compliments are not always true.

Another way to make a compliment more effective is by focusing it on a person's accomplishments rather than on his or her abilities. If you are complimented for writing a good book or cooking a good meal you can take pride in this particular achievement. On the other hand, being complimented on being a great writer or an excellent cook has problems because you may feel obligated always to be a greater writer or an excellent cook. Praise for accomplishments is more credible than praise for abilities. It is also less likely to make the recipient feel anxious and self-critical.

A third suggestion for making a compliment more effective is to focus on feelings rather than evaluation. Consider the following compliments: "I love the way you dance," "Your singing really turns me on," "Being around you makes me feel good." These compliments communicate appreciation, and they don't require verification because they are not based on comparisons or standards. As long as they are sincere, the recipient doesn't have to weigh the evidence for their accuracy. Compliments based on feeling provide a good way for being responsive and generating positive affection (see Chapter 1 and Chapter 2).

Rendering Favors

The rules for using favors to win cooperation and good will are similar to those for delivering praise and compliments. People who do favors face the same challenge as people who give compliments because their goal is to render a favor in a way that will seem sincere. Favors are most effective when the doer is of equal or higher status than the recipient, when the favor is perceived as appropriate, when it does not subject the recipient to high costs, and when it is attributed to the doer's generosity. Favors will not be taken as a sign of generosity and will be discounted if the doer is suspected as motivated by the desire for personal gain.

Kelley's covariation model suggests that favors can be used to convey two different kinds of impressions.[20] A person who wishes to come across as a kind and considerate individual who does favors for everyone should do favors with high consistency and low distinctiveness (attributions B and D in Table 8-1). A person who desires to win the approval of a specific recipient should render favors with high consistency and high distinctiveness (attribution A in Table 8-1).

APPROPRIATENESS AND ULTERIOR MOTIVES

People who wish to do a favor for someone are especially vulnerable to the ingratiator's dilemma if the recipient of the favor has higher status or power. This dilemma can be appreciated by considering a study in which college students were less favorably evaluated (because of suspected ulterior motives) when they did a favor for one of their professors than when they did the same favor for a maintenance man in their building. A similar study showed that a person was more positively evaluated when he did a favor for someone whose status he did not know than when he did a favor for someone he knew was of higher status. In a third study of the ingratiator's dilemma research participants judged a favor given to them by a person of higher status as motivated by generosity.[21] However, when the same favor came from a person of lower status, they perceived it as a response to their influence and power.

People wishing to render favors must be certain that the favor will be viewed as appropriate. In one experiment people were more favorable toward others who shared their earned scores on a task that had previously been designated as "cooperative" rather than "competitive." In another study women were told that they would be interviewed by a marketing representative in a context that for some of them should be considered formal, for others informal.[22] Half the women were given a flower by the interviewer and half were not. It was expected that women would find the gift of a flower appropriate in the informal interview and inappropriate in the formal one. Results of the study supported this prediction. When the interview was informal, the interviewer's gift led to increased cooperation and willingness to carry out a marketing test. When the interview was formal, the gift significantly decreased the women's cooperativeness and willingness.

INTENTIONALITY AND GENEROSITY

Favors are most effective when they are attributed to the generosity of the person granting them. Favors that appear unintentional or accidental are more likely to be discounted and attributed to impersonal factors such as chance. For example, participants in a research study were positive and helpful to a person who intentionally gave them some useful information but were not particularly helpful when the information was provided accidently. People participating in another study liked better a person who did them a favor voluntarily rather than at the bidding of the experimenter.[23]

COSTS

One of the most serious challenges for a person doing a favor is to minimize the costs of the favor to the recipient. Favors are not likely to be effective if the recipient feels obliged to reciprocate. The costs of reciprocation were demonstrated in an experiment showing that research participants would not return a favor to someone they were required to evaluate accurately.[24] Apparently they wanted to avoid a conflict of interest and remain independent of the person doing the favor in order to give an unbiased evaluation. When told that the accuracy of their evaluation was not important, they were less reluctant to acknowledge the favor and more willing to give something in return.

The Foot-in-the-Door Approach

An interesting way to overcome the ingratiator's dilemma associated with doing favors is to request a favor. Such advice might sound strange at first. But consider Ben Franklin's account of how this can be done:

> I therefore did not like the opposition of this new member who was a gentleman of fortune and education with talents that were likely to give him great influence in the House which indeed, afterward, happened. I did not, however, aim at gaining his favor by paying any servile respect to him, but, after some time, took this other method.
>
> Having heard that he had in his library a certain very scarce and curious book, I wrote a note to him, expressing my desire of perusing that book and requesting that he would do me the favor of lending it to me for a few days.
>
> He sent it immediately . . . and I returned it in about a week with another note expressing my sense of the favor.
>
> When we next met in the House, he spoke to me (which he had never done before) and with great civility; and he ever afterward manifested a readiness to serve me on all occasions, so that we became great friends and our friendship continued to his death.[25]

Psychologists have called Ben Franklin's strategy the *foot-in-the-door* approach because it implies that if you can persuade someone to do a small favor for you, he or she will later be more willing to do a larger favor. The success of the foot-in-the-door approach was demonstrated by showing that neighborhood residents were more willing to agree to having a large campaign sign in their front yard if they were first asked to display a small campaign sticker on their car. Other researchers found similar results. For example, pedestrians were more willing to give dimes to panhandlers who had first asked them for the time. People were more willing to donate money to the Cancer Society if they had been asked earlier to wear a Cancer Society pin. College students were more likely to volunteer to work on a university publicity campaign if they had first been asked to write letters encouraging high school students to attend college. Neighborhood residents participated more fully in a trash recycling program when they had previously been approached for their cooperation on an opinion survey. A request for a small favor has also been suggested as a way of establishing a friendly relationship following an argument.[26]

Why should performance of a small favor increase people's willingness to agree to do a larger favor? Psychologists explain that such agreement reinforces the self-image of being a helpful person. By causing people to feel "helpful" with a small request, you can often increase their willingness to agree to a larger request.

If this explanation is correct, people who refuse a favor should be *less* willing to do a second favor. Researchers found this is true.[27] When people were asked to do a favor that would cause considerable inconvenience, they tended to refuse. Having the self-image of being "refusers," they were less willing to agree with a later, more reasonable request.

A review of research suggests that the foot-in-the-door approach is most effective when the following conditions are met.[28]

1. The initial request must be moderate enough that people will agree to it. If people refuse, the whole strategy can backfire because refusal may influence them to perceive themselves as people who refuse.

2. People have to believe they are consenting to the initial request out of their own choice, not because of external pressures or rewards. However, it helps if consent gives them a feeling of satisfaction.

3. The second request can be larger than the first request, but it has to be kept within reasonable limits.

Tact and diplomacy are often demanded when negotiating for a favor because of the human tendency to resist when there is a feeling of pressure.[29] The foot-in-the-door approach is a useful strategy to consider when dealing with others of higher status or power or with a strong bargaining position.

Arousing Guilt

Research studies have shown that people can be induced to comply with requests if they are made to feel guilty. In one study of guilt arousal, a researcher approached women in a shopping center, handed them a camera, and asked them to take his picture. For half the women the camera was rigged to make them think they had broken it. The remaining women also found that the camera was broken but were not led to believe that it was their fault. Shortly after this incident the women met a second researcher, who was carrying a broken grocery bag from which a few items had "accidently" fallen. Results of this study showed that 54 percent of the women who were "guilty" of breaking the camera informed the researcher that she was losing her groceries. In contrast, only 15 percent of the "nonguilty" women called the broken bag to the researcher's attention. In another study participants were given the task of monitoring a voltage meter that was supposedly an important part of an experiment. Half the participants were led to believe that they had ruined the experiment when the meter was secretly switched to a higher reading. These participants were later more willing to donate money to a summer research fund than participants who had not "ruined" the experiment. In a third study college students were made to feel guilty when they thought they had upset a pile of computer cards and ruined someone's thesis.[30] They were later more willing to assist with another experiment than students who had not knocked over the cards.

Participants in three other experiments were made to feel guilty because they had supposedly harmed another person by giving electric shocks or by failing at their half of a cooperative task.[31] These guilty participants were later more willing to volunteer to help with a different experiment, to take shock for another person, or to donate blood.

Guilt can also be aroused by a mild insult. Residents in a neighborhood were called on the telephone by a researcher who identified himself as a member of a national polling organization.[32] One group of residents were mildly insulted by the researcher's telling them that they were generally unconcerned and unhelpful about the welfare of the other members of their community. A second group of residents was complimented by the researcher for being helpful and concerned. Residents in a third group were not evaluated by the researcher. Two days after the initial phone call, all the residents were called by a woman who identified herself as a member of a neighborhood food cooperative and asked if they would be willing to cooperate with a neighborhood project by making a list of all the household goods in their house. Residents who had previously received the complimentary phone call were more willing to help than those who received the neutral phone call. Residents who received the insulting phone call, and presumably felt guilty about their lack of community concern, expressed the greatest willingness to help.

A mild insult successfully increased helping behavior in this experiment for two reasons. First, the woman asking for help was not the same person who delivered the insult. It is unlikely that people would turn around and help the same person who previously insulted them. Second, the experiment was set up so that residents could vindicate themselves and "prove" they were helpful people by agreeing with the second request. Participants in a related experiment did not offer cooperation when they were insulted because they became defensive and put their efforts into denying the truth of the accusation.[33]

Although research shows that mild insults and guilt arousal can sometimes induce people to agree with requests, there is the danger that people might also react
with denial of responsibility or anger toward the guilt-provoking person.[34] In any
event, it is doubtful that people complying with requests because of guilt will like
the requestor.

Agreeing

You read in Chapter 1 that people often prefer others who are similar to themselves. This preference suggests that favorable responses can be gained by agreeing
with other people's opinions. Agreers are subject to the ingratiator's dilemma in the
same way that people giving compliments and doing favors are. It is therefore advisable to express agreement in such a way as to minimize ulterior motives, maximize credibility, and maximize reinforcement.

MINIMIZING ULTERIOR MOTIVES

Like compliments, agreements will appear less ingratiating if they are "overheard"
or communicated by a "disinterested" third party. The suspicion of ulterior motives can also be minimized by agreeing with other people before they express
their opinions. If we state an opinion and someone agrees with us, we don't know
if that person is sincere or is just agreeing to make a good impression. But if someone else states an opinion similar to ours before we have made our view known, we
would more than likely interpret this agreement as real. When the external pressures for conformity are high, it may be advantageous to gain "extra credit" by *not*
agreeing and waiting to express agreement "spontaneously" at a later time.

MAXIMIZING CREDIBILITY

Research has shown that agreement is most convincing if given judiciously rather
than lavishly. One way to maximize your similarity with another person while
still appearing credible is to agree on important issues and to disagree (at least
mildly) on unimportant ones. Credibility can also be enhanced by showing willingness to disagree with others in the presence of the person whose approval is
desired.[35]

MAXIMIZING REINFORCEMENT

An agreement is most effective when it reinforces a recipient by reducing his or
her feelings of uncertainty. Research has shown that people have greater appreciation for agreement if they have recently been confronted with disagreement. People are also more favorable toward someone who changes from disagreement to
agreement than the reverse.[36]

Agreement can be reinforcing because it provides the recipient with a sense of persuasiveness. The positive experience of persuasiveness was demonstrated in an experiment in which research participants gave a persuasive speech to a listener who (1) showed high agreement from the beginning, (2) switched from low agreement to moderate agreement, or (3) switched from moderate agreement to high agreement.[37] In general, participants liked the listener in condition 3 best because he rewarded them by agreeing and also by making them feel persuasive.

Another example showing how agreement can reinforce feelings of persuasiveness is seen in an experiment in which research participants communicated over an intercom system with a person who either agreed, disagreed, or first disagreed and then agreed (yielded) on a number of selected topics.[38] The yielding person had the highest reinforcement value, demonstrated by the fact that participants pressed their "talk button" fastest when they spoke to him. He was also liked best, while the disagreeing person was liked the least.

"STRATEGIC" AGREEMENT

The research just summarized suggests that agreement can be used to communicate similarity and to reinforce another person's feelings of persuasiveness. However, it is also important to show that you are not wishy-washy and that you have your own opinions. People who yield too easily are likely to appear ingratiating and unintelligent. Therefore, it is recommended that you agree "strategically" while maintaining the image that you can think for yourself.[39]

Using People's Names

Many of the self-presentation strategies summarized in Chapter 9 can be helpful for gaining favor and cooperation. The most direct self-presentation strategies for this purpose are those involving communication of closeness and intimacy, such as self-disclosure and immediacy, already discussed. Another way to communicate intimacy is to call people by name. Dale Carnegie recommended using a person's name as one of his six "rules" for inducing someone to like you (the other rules are to show genuine interest in the person, to smile, to be a good listener, to talk about the person's interests, and to make the person feel important).[40] However, because calling people by name is a rather explicit expression of intimacy, it has to be done with thoughtfulness and tact. Perhaps you can identify with the following experience.

While shopping for a car, I was struck by how many times the salespeople called me by name. Although I was aware of Carnegie's advice, being called by name so often sounded out of place. It occurred to me that salespeople face the ingratiator's dilemma because they are dependent on customers for a sale. To learn more about how people react to being called by name, I conducted a series of research studies with Richard Staneski and Pam Weaver. Our experiences told us that to be called by name by people we like is pleasing, but it is suspect when the name user might want some sort of favor.

Our research yielded the following results. In one study we asked people to listen to tape-recorded job interviews and to give their impressions of job applicants. Some applicants called the interviewer by name several times during the interview. Others used the interviewer's name only at the beginning and end of the interview. Our respondents said they would be more willing to hire applicants who did not overuse the interviewer's name. They also rated these applicants as being more competent and having more favorable personalities. In a second study we introduced college-aged men and women and gave them some time to talk.[41] Before our introductions we secretly asked half of the men to call their partners by name during their conversation. These men were liked less than men who did not make a special effort to use the woman's name.

When does using a person's name result in a favorable reaction? We found positive responses to name use when we had an attractive woman interview two men together about their attitudes on social issues.[42] The interviewer intentionally called one of the men by name more often than the other. When the men were asked to evaluate the interview, they said that the interviewer seemed to like the man whom she had called by name more than the man whose name she had used less often. Men who were called by name liked her better than did men who were not called by name.

We also found positive reactions to interviewers who called job applicants by name.[43] Apparently, it is acceptable for interviewers to use applicants' names because the interviewers are not the ones who are trying to win approval or make a good impression. Interestingly enough, applicants were evaluated more favorably when interviewers called them by name. It appeared that the interviewer's willingness to use an applicant's name increased the applicant's credibility.

Our research found that Dale Carnegie's advice about the positive effects of using people's names is correct, with a qualification. Calling a person by name can make a positive impression, but it must be done judiciously. Like any advice about making a good impression, using a person's name has to be suited to the situation. You should be particularly prudent about calling someone by name when you need that person's favor or approval.

Attribution theories are useful for analyzing favor-winning tactics because they clarify how we come to view each other as being ingratiating or noningratiating. It is hoped that this chapter has heightened your appreciation of the sensitivity and tact required for winning good will and cooperation. Although successful human diplomacy is to some extent an art, the research summarized here demonstrates that it is also a science.

ELEVEN

Accuracy in
Perceiving People

First impressions of people are important regardless of how accurate they are because they often determine whether or not a relationship will be pursued or abandoned. Two people meeting at a social gathering or business conference, for example, sometimes make snap judgments about whether they want to spend time learning to know each other. If they decide not to, a potential friendship is lost. Job interviewers and college admissions personnel often make decisions affecting an interviewee's career on the basis of first impressions in a single interview. Because our lives are affected by our impressions of others as well as by their impressions of us, this book focuses on how first impressions are formed and managed. The accuracy of first impressions, however, is still a relevant concern. Therefore, this chapter will first describe how accuracy in perceiving people has been defined and studied. Some conclusions will support your personal experiences, while others may be unexpected and even surprising.

Accuracy of First Impressions

If you talked with people about their experiences in meeting others, you would obtain reports of first impressions ranging in accuracy from "perfect" to "completely wrong." This discrepancy is due partly to the fact that people differ in how transparent they are in showing themselves and in how perceptive they are in making personal judgments. Discrepancy also occurs because people don't always define accuracy in the same way. In order to study accuracy of perception of people scientifically, it is necessary to agree on a definition of accuracy and a procedure for measuring it.

Henry Clay Smith described four approaches people use to understand one another: rational understanding, artistic understanding, practical understanding, and empirical understanding.[1] *Rational understanding* reflects the degree to which someone feels empathy and identification with another person. It is subjective and is measured by asking people to describe and share their feelings. *Artistic understanding* reflects an awareness of the tangible aspects of a person such as appearance and mannerisms. It is measured by the ability to describe or portray a person's appearance and mannerisms objectively. *Practical understanding* is the degree to which a person can influence another person's behavior. It is measured by its success. It differs from empirical understanding because the former is based on intuition. *Empirical understanding* is a person's accuracy in making predictions about another person's behaviors and actions. It is measured by testing. Writers and actors are recognized for their skills in describing and portraying people's emotions (rational understanding) and expressing the dynamics of interpersonal relationships (practical understanding). Politicians and lawyers are often experts in practical understanding. Experimental psychologists focus their research on empirical understanding. For this reason, accuracy of perceiving people will be defined as a measure of how closely our impressions of another person correspond with objective facts about that person.

PREDICTING PEOPLE'S SELF-RATINGS

Some of the earliest researchers in perceiving people studied how accurately people could predict other people's self-ratings. They thought that accuracy in such predicting could be used as a measure of empathy with others. Rosalind Dymond, who pioneered this investigation, had research participants consider the following traits: superior-inferior, friendly-unfriendly, leading-following, shy-self-assured, sympathetic-unsympathetic, secure-insecure.[2] On each trait they (1) rated themselves, (2) rated another person, (3) predicted the other person's self-rating, and (4) predicted how the other person would rate them. Dymond proposed that two measures of empathy could be derived from these ratings. One measure was defined by the agreement between someone's prediction of another person's self-ratings and the other person's actual self-ratings. A second measure was defined by the agreement between someone's prediction about the ratings he or she would receive from another person and the actual ratings given by the other person. The agreement between someone's ratings of another person and the other person's self-ratings was defined as a measure of accuracy.

Unfortunately, the measures of empathy and accuracy incur problems because they are susceptible to bias from *response styles*. For example, if both you and the person you are judging have a tendency to check rating scales in the same way (such as marking slightly to the right of center), you would accurately "predict" that person's ratings simply because of similar response styles. Lee Cronbach analyzed the ways in which rating form comparisons are biased by response styles and outlined a mathematical method through which this bias might be controlled. Because of the difficulties in distinguishing between real and apparent accuracy in predicting another person's self-ratings, researchers have begun to focus more on predicting people's actions.[3]

PREDICTING PEOPLE'S BEHAVIOR

Another way to measure accuracy in perceiving people is to predict how a person will behave. College aptitude tests, for example, are designed to predict a student's success in college. Personnel directors are trained to predict how a prospective employee will perform on the job. The accuracy of these predictions can be measured by comparing them with the student's or employee's actual performance. In making this comparison, however, it is necessary to account for *base rates*. Base rates are similar to response styles in the sense that you would be accurate more often than not by predicting that a particular college student's grade average is at the average for students in that college or that a worker's performance is at the average for workers in that company. In order for a behavioral prediction to be accurate, it has to be better in the long run than base rates. The improvement of a prediction over a base rate has been defined by Walter Mischel as the prediction's *incremental validity*. The challenge of making behavioral predictions that are more accurate than base rates is sometimes quite difficult. Mischel summarized a number of studies showing that psychological interviews and personality tests were less accurate in predicting people's self-descriptions and scholastic performance than simple base rates consisting of average self-descriptions and average scholastic performance.[4] Look at it this way. What if you wanted to predict the starting income of 100 graduating engineers and you knew that the average starting income for a graduate engineer was $30,000. If you chose $30,000 as your prediction for all 100 engineers, you would be fairly close for the majority and only miss on the high and low extremes. An achievement test, psychologist, or psychic has to be pretty good to do better than that.

Generalized Personality Descriptions and the Barnum Effect

Imagine that after taking a battery of psychological tests you are given the following description of your personality:

> You have a strong need for other people to like you and for them to admire you. You have a tendency to be critical of yourself. You have a great deal of unused capacity which you have not turned to your advantage. Disciplined and controlled on the outside, you tend to be worrisome and insecure inside. You prefer a certain amount of change in your life. You pride yourself as being an independent thinker and do not accept other's opinions without satisfactory proof. At times you are extroverted, affable, sociable, while at other times you are introverted, wary, and reserved. Some of your aspirations tend to be unrealistic.[5]

If you are like most people who have been given this personality description, you will agree that it is "good" or even "excellent." Indeed, the description is "accurate" because it could be true for almost anybody. A review of research on people's willingness to accept this kind of generalized personality description resulted in the following conclusions.[6] Men and women are equally willing to accept such descriptions. So are college students, industrial supervisors, and personnel managers. People are willing to accept generalized personality descriptions even when they are unfavorable. This willingness has been labeled by Paul Meehl as the "Barnum effect" because, like P. T. Barnum's circuses, the descriptions have "a little something for everybody." Because generalized descriptions are as accurate as the base rates on which they are formulated, it is perhaps not surprising that people often judge them as being more accurate than descriptions derived from actual personality tests. One group of psychologists had people take a "personality test" developed by the humorist Art Buchwald, which he called the North Dakota Null Hypothesis Brain Inventory.[7] After answering true-false questions such as "I salivate at the sight of mittens," "I am never startled by a fish," "I think beavers work too hard," the participants were given a generalized personality description. People who took Buchwald's test (believing it was legitimate) found the generalized personality descriptions every bit as accurate as people who received descriptions after taking an actual personality test.

Another demonstration of the Barnum effect was conducted by a psychologist who advertised himself as an astrologer in the newspapers and received hundreds of requests for his services.[8] He sent everyone the same "horoscope" consisting of a generalized personality description. More than 200 grateful clients responded by writing "thank you" letters and praising his ability.

Horoscopes appear to use generalized personality descriptions. I once asked fifty people to look at twelve randomly numbered astrological personality descriptions and to pick the one that belonged to them.[9] Four people chose the description that matched their astrological sign, and forty-six chose a description matching a different sign. The accuracy of people in choosing the "correct" personality description was therefore no greater than guessing or chance.

ENHANCING THE BARNUM EFFECT

People are more likely to accept generalized personality descriptions if the person giving the descriptions acts competently, seems to have high prestige, and uses psychological jargon. People are also more impressed by psychological tests that appear "individualized" and by horoscopes based on the exact day, month, and year of their birth.[10] Acceptance is also more likely if the personality descriptions have *face validity*. A test or measure has face validity when it is plausible and appears to make sense.

If you want to impress people with your ability to analyze their handwriting, act competently, make them think you are attending very personally to them, and give them a generalized personality description. Handwriting analysts have learned to increase their practice by sizing up the person whose handwriting they are judging and giving descriptions that would be most appropriate for that particular person: a casually dressed student, a well-dressed business person, a man or woman with children. It seems reasonable to characterize people with large handwriting as outgoing. It is plausible that people who write sloppily should be "creative" and "individualistic." People with very neat handwriting could be called "thoughtful" and "sensitive." The point is that it doesn't matter whether or not the relationships between specific styles of handwriting and certain personality characteristics are true, so long as people accept their face validity.

A similar demonstration of face validity showed that college students as well as clinical psychologists have stereotypic beliefs about personality traits that are manifested in the draw-a-person test (in which you are asked to draw a person) and in the Rorschach test (in which you are asked to describe what you see in inkblots).[11] This research found that college students and clinical psychologists were inclined to label a man who drew a picture of a man with broad shoulders as being concerned about manliness. People who drew figures with atypical ears were stereotyped as being suspicious, and those who drew figures with large heads were viewed as having high intelligence. The students and psychologists believed that men who reported seeing sex organs, feminine clothing, or buttocks in Rorschach inkblots were homosexuals. In fact, all of these stereotypes are false. Men concerned about their masculinity are no more likely to draw pictures of men with broad shoulders than men not so concerned. Suspicious people don't draw strange ears any more often than nonsuspicious people, and size of a person's head in a drawing has nothing to do with the artist's intelligence. Gay men are no more likely to see sex organs, feminine clothing, and buttocks in inkblots than men who are heterosexual. Since all of the above "diagnostic signs" are plausible, however, people are inclined to believe them.

WHY GENERALIZED PERSONALITY DESCRIPTIONS ARE POPULAR

After reading about the fallacies of face validity and the Barnum effect, you may wonder why people accept generalized personality descriptions without questioning their incremental validity. There are at least two reasons. First, people like explanations for things. The ancient Greeks explained the existence of the sun by inventing the god Apollo, who drove a blazing chariot across the sky. In the Middle Ages doctors often drained blood from patients in the belief that evil humors in it caused their illness. Only 300 years ago, witches were burned in Massachusetts because they were believed to cause otherwise unexplained events in the community. In the twentieth century there is an abundance of conflicting theories about how the universe was formed, numerous hypotheses about who *really* wrote Shakespeare's plays, and heaven knows how many "cures" for the common cold.

Generalized personality descriptions are also popular as a result of what B. F. Skinner has defined as *intermittent reinforcement*.[12] If you have ever played a slot machine it is probably because there is a chance that you might win. The hundreds of times you pull the handle fruitlessly are easy to forget compared with the few times you hit the jackpot. The same principle works in perceiving people. We tend to remember when our judgments and predictions about others are correct, and we find it easy to overlook (or rationalize) our incorrect perceptions.

To put it briefly, generalized personality descriptions are popular because they provide explanations that are plausible and proven correct often enough to reinforce their apparent validity.

TEACHING PEOPLE TO SEEK RELEVANT INFORMATION

A growing understanding of the fallacies of generalized personality descriptions has prompted psychologists to develop programs for training people who make personnel decisions to recognize information about job applicants that is useful, relevant, and valid.[13] Participants in these seminars learn about the Barnum effect and are trained to overcome their reliance on information that has face validity (such as age, sex, and physical attractiveness) but that does not accurately predict an applicant's performance. Participants are taught to use experimental research for determining the most useful facts related to a potential employee's performance.

Attributional Errors

The Barnum effect demonstrates that we are not as accurate in our empirical understanding of others as we sometimes believe. It also presents a good example of how our perceptions of others are influenced by the ways in which we process information. As a result of recent research on the influence of styles of information processing on accuracy in perceptions of others, psychologists have discovered a number of "attributional errors" to help us understand how we sometimes err in forming impressions.

UNDERESTIMATING THE IMPORTANCE OF BASE RATES

The Barnum effect is based on people's willingness to accept generalized personality descriptions without determining their incremental validity over that of stereotypes and base rates. People also underestimate the importance of base rates when predicting the behavior of others. Consider a hypothetical college student who often goes to art museums and spends a good deal of time listening to classical music and reading poetry. You might guess that the student is majoring in art, music, or literature. But what if the student was at a university where only 10 percent of the students are majoring in the arts and the rest are majoring in the sciences? Unless there is evidence that science majors rarely or never go to museums, listen to classical music, or read poetry, there is a nine-to-one chance that you would be better off guessing that the student is majoring in science. However, most people who are given this problem prefer to use their intuition rather than knowledge of base rates in predicting the student's major.[14]

The underutilization of base rates was also demonstrated by asking people to predict how research participants would respond in various psychology experiments.[15] Before making their predictions, the people were provided with personal descriptions of the research participants and with data showing how other participants had responded in the same experiment. Since there is no way to assess the usefulness of the personal descriptions, it would make most sense to assume that a research participant would react like the majority of other participants in the experiment. The prediction makers, however, did not make optimal use of base rates and allowed their predictions to be biased by "clues" they gathered from the personal descriptions.

The fact that intuitions often outweigh the use of base rates is also apparent in a study in which clinical psychologists were provided with different amounts of information about a person's background and asked to make predictions about his or her behavior.[16] It turned out that the amount of background information given to the psychologists had no effect on the accuracy of their predictions. Because of their intuition, however, the psychologists *believed* that the background information made their predictions more accurate.

Our tendency to be overinfluenced by pieces of information that are vivid and salient (at the expense of base rate information) has been defined as the *availability bias*. Imagine that you have been reading *Consumer Reports* to decide upon a car.[17] After analyzing hundreds of repair records the magazine has recommended automobile A. Just when you have decided to buy it, a friend tells you about someone who owned that kind of car and had a great deal of repair trouble. Statistically speaking, you should not weigh one unfavorable report very strongly against hundreds of favorable reports (assuming that *Consumer Reports* and your friend are equally reliable). However, since the unfavorable report is very vivid and salient, you are likely to respond with a bias against automobile A.

Another example of the availability bias comes from a study in which college students were more influenced by course evaluations by two or three unacquainted students who spoke to them face-to-face than by tabulated data on course evaluations by almost everyone who had taken the course. The authors of the study concluded that people tend to view base-rate information as boring and prefer the vividness of "eyewitness" descriptions. The power of vivid "evidence" was demonstrated by showing that exposure to a single welfare recipient or prison guard was enough to influence people's opinions toward all welfare recipients and prison guards.[18]

Because of our preference for vivid evidence, we are most likely to use base-rate information accurately when it is salient and readily available and when the base rates in question are relatively high, easy to understand, and clearly relevant to the issue.[19] Otherwise, we will probably neglect base-rate information and rely on our intuitions.

ACCEPTING PLAUSIBLE CAUSES

Because we overestimate the accuracy of our premises, we often settle on explanations for behavior that seem most sensible or plausible even though they might not be correct. The plausibility error can be understood by considering an experiment in which people read a written description of a woman and evaluated her on four traits: intelligence, likability, sympathy, and flexibility.[20] The descriptions were varied to give different kinds of information about the woman's physical attractiveness, academic record, supposed involvement in an automobile accident, an interview during which she accidently spilled coffee, and the likelihood that evaluators would meet her. After rating the woman on the four traits, people were asked to specify how much each of the five pieces of information had influenced their evaluations. On ratings of intelligence, the reports were accurate. People stated that they were influenced by information about the woman's academic record and this was true. They were not accurate in reporting which information influenced their ratings of the woman's other traits. They *believed* that their ratings of likability were determined by the woman's attractiveness and academic record because these reasons appeared most plausible. However, likability ratings were *actually* influenced (in a positive way) by the coffee-spilling incident and by the expectation of a personal meeting. People *believed* that their ratings of sympathy were determined by the woman's involvement in an automobile accident and that their ratings of flexibility were determined by her academic record, but they were both *actually* influenced by the expectation of a personal meeting. The researchers concluded that people were accurate about the information influencing their ratings of intelligence because the actual reason for their rating (the woman's academic record) was also the most plausible. People did not accurately explain their other ratings because the actual causes of these ratings did not happen to be the most plausible.

Another example of the plausibility error is seen in a study in which college students were asked to evaluate an instructor in a videotaped lecture.[21] Half the students saw the instructor acting in a warm and friendly manner and half saw him acting in a cold and unfriendly manner. Because students only observed the instructor once, they had no way of knowing that his warm and cold behavior was intentionally designed to influence their feelings. Not surprisingly, students liked the instructor when he was friendly and disliked him when he was unfriendly. They also rated the unfriendly instructor as less attractive and as having unappealing mannerisms and speech. When students were asked to explain their ratings, however, they did not believe that their feelings of liking or disliking had any effect. On the contrary, they reported that their liking for the instructor had been influenced by his attractiveness, mannerisms, and speech (which was impossible because these traits were always the same). Because the students were not aware (or willing to admit) that their liking or disliking for the instructor could influence their evaluations about his attractiveness, mannerisms, and speech, it was more plausible for them to assume that the instructor's traits had influenced their liking.

You can see that the researchers went to some lengths in these experiments to contrive situations in which the actual causes for people's behavior would not be obvious or plausible. Our everyday behavior often occurs for reasons that match our intuitions, and our explanations for them are therefore correct.[22] To understand how we are biased when actual causes for behaviors are not plausible, it will be useful to consider a few more research examples. The following studies show how people choose plausible (but incorrect) explanations for their actions when these explanations stand out as making the most sense.

Research participants were asked to volunteer for electric shocks. Some participants were reassured that the shocks would not be harmful, and some participants were not reassured. After stating how much shock they were willing to take, participants were asked whether the reassurance had any effect on their willingness to volunteer. They tended to believe that the reassurance increased their willingness to volunteer (because it seemed quite plausible that it should), but results of the study showed that the reassurance actually had no effect. Participants in a second experiment read a passage from a novel and rated its emotional impact. For some participants, a very emotional series of sentences was omitted. After completing their ratings, participants were asked whether the omission of the sentences had influenced their ratings. They believed that the omission had reduced their ratings of the passage's emotional impact (because it seemed quite plausible that it should), but results of the study showed that it had not. Participants in a third experiment watched a film and rated how much they had enjoyed it. Half the watchers were exposed to some distracting noise in the hallway, and the other half were not. After rating their enjoyment of the film, participants were asked if the noise had influenced their ratings. Those exposed to the noise tended to believe that it had reduced their enjoyment (because it seemed quite plausible that it should), but results of the study showed that the noise had no effect.[23]

A common example of the plausibility error occurs when you are asked to explain the cause for something you did in years past. Since it is difficult to remember (or to know) what influenced you so long ago, your explanation is likely to be biased by the causes that appear most sensible at the present time. For example, I can give many reasons why I enjoy being a psychologist, but few of these reasons were in my consciousness when I chose my college major many years ago.

THE FUNDAMENTAL ATTRIBUTIONAL ERROR

In Chapter 8 you read how attribution theories were derived to define conditions under which behavior is likely to be attributed to dispositional versus situational causes. You may remember that dispositional explanations for behaviors refer to causes within a person, such as personality style, attitudes, or moods. Situational explanations for behavior focus on causes in the environment like rewards, obligations, and social norms. The fundamental attribution error is the tendency to overestimate the role of dispositional factors and to underestimate the role of situational factors when judging the causes of behaviors.[24] Consider some research examples.

If you read an essay that was written out of free choice, it would be reasonable to assume that the essay reflected the beliefs of the writer. However, what if the topic of the essay had been assigned? Could you still conclude that it expressed the writer's true beliefs? It might surprise you to learn that research participants interpreted an essay as reflecting the essay writer's beliefs even when the writer had been instructed to argue for a particular viewpoint. Participants also assumed the preassigned arguments in a speech were caused more by the speaker's beliefs than by the external influence of the assignment.[25]

One reason why people wrongly attribute the arguments in assigned essays and speeches to the writer's and speaker's beliefs is that they usually find some statements in the speech or essay that agree with their own beliefs. Since it makes sense to interpret these agreeing statements as belief statements, it is easy to "generalize" and view the entire essay or speech as a belief statement. Another reason is that when people read essays or hear speeches they think more about the personality of the writer or speaker than about the context in which the essay or speech was produced. This explanation has a lot to do with the phenomenon of salient cues, which is discussed in the following section. The more attention people pay to a writer's or speaker's personality, the more likely they are to lose sight of the external fact that the topic has been assigned.[26]

A third reason for the fundamental attributional error is our habit of using trait words not only to *describe* behavior but also to *explain* behavior. For example, we might describe the behavior of people who work hard as manifesting high ambition. There's no problem with that. But we then turn around and explain the hardworking behavior as caused by high ambition. In a similar vein, we are inclined to describe behavior of social withdrawal as demonstrating shyness or low self-esteem and then use shyness and low self-esteem as an explanation for social withdrawal.

The problem with using trait words to explain behavior is that these explanations are based on a circular argument.[27] It is false to assume that a behavior is dispositionally caused simply because we can give it a trait, or dispositional label.

It is not easy to help people overcome the fundamental attributional error and attribute an externally motivated essay to its true cause. One group of researchers successfully eliminated the fundamental attributional error by telling research participants that a writer had *copied* an essay that was assigned by an experimenter.[28] With this explicit attention to situational causes, participants no longer assumed the essay reflected the writer's beliefs.

The fundamental attributional error is not limited to perceptions of essays and speeches. For example, research participants felt they could judge a woman's personality on the basis of her friendly or unfriendly behavior even when they were told that she had been instructed to act friendly or unfriendly. Examples of the fundamental attributional error on a larger scale can be seen in Milgram's obedience studies, Zimbardo's prison study, and Latané and Darley's bystander intervention studies.[29] These studies showed quite dramatically how psychologists as well as nonpsychologists underestimated the influence of situational factors on people's behavior. The behavior of participants in these studies was not predicted by personality tests (which presumably measure dispositions) and was far more extreme than anyone (who underestimated the influence of situational factors and overestimated people's dispositions to behave in a "reasonable manner") would have predicted.

Additional Attributional Errors

Besides the attributional errors discussed so far there are a number of others involving such factors as salient cues, roles, false consensus, nonoccurrences, and stereotypes. All of these endanger the accuracy of our empirical understanding of others.

SUSCEPTIBILITY TO SALIENT CUES

Not surprisingly we tend to assign causes to one another's actions that are most obvious, apparent, or salient. Research has shown that we lean toward giving dispositional explanations for a person's behavior when the person stands out and gains more of our attention than the context of the behavior or the environment. Participants in one series of studies observed a group discussion and gave judgments about the relative influence of the group members on its progress. The focus of the participants' attention on specific group members was intensified by seating the participants directly facing the group member or by instructing them to pay particular attention to that member. These studies showed that observers attributed the greatest amount of influence to the person whose visibility and salience had been enhanced. Another series of studies found that people attributed more influence on a group discussion to group members whose salience was emphasized by their uniqueness. A black person was evaluated as being most influential in a group that was otherwise all white. Similarly, a woman was evaluated as being most influential in a group of men. The attention of observers was also directed toward particular group members by training these members to engage in noticeable body movements or with the use of special lighting. As a result of this increased visibility, observers gave more dispositional explanations for these group members' behaviors.[30]

On the other hand, when the context of a person's behavior is more conspicuous than the person, we lean toward giving situational explanations for his or her behavior. This principle was demonstrated in an experiment in which environmental salience was emphasized by arranging it so that all group members were of the same sex and similarly dressed. Because the members faded into their environment, observers tended to give situational explanations for their behaviors. Observers in another study gave situational explanations for a person's behavior when the impact of the environment was heightened by placing a slide projector or video camera in the room.[31]

The lesson from this research is that if you want to receive credit or responsibility for your behavior in a group, you should dress or act in a way that will gain attention and make you stand out. If your goal is to avoid responsibility, you are best advised to keep a low profile so that attention is focused on other people or on the environment. The next time you are in a group, observe who is conspicuous and who fades into the background.

UNDERESTIMATING THE POWER OF ROLES

Sometimes we attribute people's actions to their personalities because we underestimate the degree to which they are influenced by social roles. One example of this error comes from an experiment in which research participants were randomly assigned to one of three roles in a quiz game: contestant, questioner, or observer.[32] The questioner was given the task to think of ten challenging but not impossible questions for the contestant. Observers made ratings of the questioners and contestants. It might surprise you to learn that observers evaluated the questioners as being more knowledgeable than the contestants, yet how could that be true if the questioners and contestants were assigned at random? It appeared that observers judged the questioners' and contestants' intelligence on the basis of their assigned roles. This experiment reminds us of the fact that privileged people are often admired for their advantageous position in society when, in fact, it is merely an accident of birth. By the same token, disadvantaged people may underestimate their potentialities by attributing their low position to personal weakness rather than to the social roles created by society.

The power of roles was also demonstrated in studies in which people were recruited to work on various tasks such as word puzzles and math problems[33] in three phases. In phase 1 they worked alone, in phase 2 they worked in pairs, and in phase 3 they again worked alone. During phase 2 the experimenter gave the arbitrary labels of "boss" to one member of the pair and "assistant" to the other member. Interestingly enough, people who were given the label of boss performed better in phase 3, while those given the label of assistant performed more poorly in phase 3. The experience of being assigned to the role of boss or assistant was enough to affect people's self-expectations and consequent performance. These research results show how people in positions of lower status may be reluctant to attempt tasks on which they could succeed because of erroneous expectations of failure on the basis of their social roles. Ask yourself whether the average politician or corporation executive is more intelligent than you are.

THE FALSE CONSENSUS ERROR

An attributional error known as the false-consensus error is the assumption that other people have the same reactions to everyday experiences that we do. It was demonstrated in a series of experiments in which participants predicted the behaviors of others in situations they themselves had experienced.[34] In one experiment, people were asked to volunteer their help for a television commercial. The majority of volunteers believed that other people would also volunteer. People who refused to volunteer, in contrast, assumed that others would refuse. Participants in a second experiment predicted that other people would feel the same way they did about walking around a university campus for thirty minutes wearing a sandwich board sign that read, "EAT AT JOE'S."

One reason for the false-consensus error is that when we have limited information about another person, our inclination is to assume that he or she would respond in the same way to a particular situation as we would. For this reason, we are most likely to predict that another's actions will agree with ours in situations where there are noticeable rewards, pressures, or behavioral norms. We are less likely to assume that someone will respond similarly when we take the time to attend to that person's uniqueness and individuality. Another reason for the false-consensus error is that we usually choose friends and associates who are similar to us. We may therefore falsely assume (or want to believe) that everyone is similar.[35]

OVERLOOKING NONOCCURRENCES

We can sometimes learn about a person by noticing which behavior he or she does *not* choose in a given situation.[36] If a person is friendly in a social interaction, for example, we don't know whether to attribute the friendliness to the person or to the demands of the situation. The absence of friendly behavior, on the other hand, is likely to tell us something about the person. In terms of correspondent inference theory, the presence of common or socially desirable behavior tells us less about a person than the absence of such behavior.

Even though nonoccurrences provide valuable information, most people have not learned to recognize their importance. Consider the following sequence of numbers: 2, 4, 6.[37] Your job is to find out what rule governs the sequence of these numbers by adding numbers to it and receiving feedback about whether they are correct or incorrect. If you are like most people, your first choice would be 8. The answer is correct. Possibly you would try one additional test and choose 10. The answer is again correct. Your conclusion, then, is that the rule for the sequence is to increase each successive number by two. However, this conclusion is wrong. The correct rule is to increase each successive number, but it doesn't matter by how much. You could only discover this rule by attempting to disconfirm your original theory. After choosing 8, you should have chosen 9, 11, or even 100. Any of these choices would have led you to the correct conclusion.

Now that you are aware of the importance of nonoccurrences, consider a hypothetical blood test that can supposedly diagnose schizophrenia. How can you determine if the test is accurate? Say that 90 percent of all schizophrenics are correctly diagnosed (positive hits) and 10 percent are not (false negatives). Ninety-percent accuracy sounds pretty good. But if 80 percent of all nonschizophrenics are *also* diagnosed as schizophrenic (false positives), the value of the test is questionable. You have to consider disconfirmations as well as confirmations in evaluating the accuracy of your test.

What kinds of questions would you ask if you were interviewing people for a job and were looking for a person who was outgoing and sociable? You would probably ask the applicant to talk about his or her activities and social life. That's OK, except that any job applicant could come up with examples of social life. And the more you pursued the issue, the more evidence you would receive to confirm that the applicant can be outgoing. Most interviewers limit their questions to those confirming an applicant's qualifications.[38] It is also important, however, to ask disconfirming questions. It would be useful in the above example to ask the applicant about times when he or she is introverted, retiring, or even grouchy.

STEREOTYPING

Knowledge about attributional errors helps us understand why we stereotype people without paying attention to their individuality. One major attributional error associated with stereotyping is the tendency to categorize others in terms of their group memberships. A number of studies have shown that people perceive group members as being similar, even when they are not. People also usually favor members of their ingroup over equally deserving members of outgroups. A second attributional error influencing stereotyping is our susceptibility toward salient cues. Undesirable behavior, for example, is remembered more when it is identified with political, racial, or cultural groups that stand out. We pay less attention to undesirable behavior of people in groups that are common and familiar. A third attributional error influencing stereotyping is the tendency to see in others what we expect to see. When research participants were asked to recall descriptions they had read about people in various professions, their memories were biased by their expectations. Because doctors are expected to be "thoughtful" and "wealthy," participants falsely remembered that doctors had been described that way. Similarly, respondents reported descriptions of "enthusiastic" and "talkative" for salesmen, "productive" and "serious" for librarians, and "attractive" and "comforting" for stewardesses. These stereotypic descriptions were "recalled" by research participants even though they were not in the original written descriptions.[39]

Research on stereotyping shows that prejudicial behaviors can become self-perpetuating because we have a tendency to see in others what we expect to see. We then act according to these biased perceptions. The way we treat others, in turn, determines how they respond to us. This phenomenon often occurs when people of different races interact. The perpetuation of stereotypes also takes place when interviewers ask leading questions that imply evidence that does not really exist. Research has found that observers often falsely believe leading questions are based on evidence.[40] On top of this, respondents in interviews commonly allow themselves to be led by leading questions and therefore supply a false sense of support for the questions' validity. Because a respondent's cooperation in an interview is more salient to observers than the hidden pressures behind leading questions, observers can find "evidence" not only in the leading questions but also in the respondent's replies.

Perseverance of Attributional Errors

While reading about attributional errors in perceiving people you might have been wondering why people don't seem to figure them out. One reason is that it is easy to find "evidence" for them in everyday life. Attributional errors persevere even in the face of contradictory information. For example, people in an experiment were led to believe that they were very accurate or very inaccurate in discriminating between authentic and fictitious suicide notes.[41] After this successful or unsuccessful experience, the people were told that the feedback about their accuracy had actually been random. They were then asked to rate objectively their ability to discriminate between suicide notes. You would expect that the participants would simply ignore the original false information when making their objective self-ratings, but that is not what happened. Despite the fact that the random feedback about their "success" or "failure" in discrimination had been clearly explained, people were still influenced by their expectations. Those who had experienced a false sense of success rated themselves as having more ability than those who had experienced a false sense of failure. Interestingly enough, observers also evaluated "successful" judges as having more ability than "unsuccessful" judges, even though they too were instructed that the feedback about accuracy had been random.

Another example of the perseverance of attributional errors comes from an experiment in which participants were given the experience of using case history information to explain an event that had presumably occurred in someone's life.[42] They were then told explicitly that the event was hypothetical and had been contrived for the experiment. Even after this debriefing, however, participants continued to hold some belief that the event they "explained" had actually occurred. Apparently, the experience of "finding evidence" for an event in a case history was sufficient to instill a belief about its reality.

The predisposition to perceive events in the world selectively as supporting our viewpoints has been defined as *creeping determinism*. This phenomenon was demonstrated in a study in which research participants predicted outcomes of various events ranging from world affairs to particular people's lives.[43] Participants were given a limited amount of information on which to base their predictions and were randomly informed that the event they were predicting from this information had turned out in a certain way. Selective perception was evident because participants used the information to predict whatever outcome they were told had occurred. In other words, they were able to use the same information as "evidence" for any number of randomly described outcomes.

Another example of creeping determinism is seen in a study in which people were asked to recall predictions they had made about various events that had since come to pass. In general, they believed that their predictions had been more accurate than they actually were. Having learned of the outcome, it was easy for them to remember selectively that it was what they had originally predicted. Our selective memory for facts that confirm our theories supports the adage that hindsight is easier than foresight.[44]

The research summarized in this chapter helps us understand that our perceptions of others are not always as accurate as we might think. Our interpersonal judgments are not objective, and they can be biased by a variety of attributional errors. The knowledge you have gained about attributional errors will be useful when you read Chapter 12 about biases that occur when people make attributional errors in their perceptions of one another.

Biases in
Perceiving People

It is a safe bet that you can relate many of the attributional errors described in Chapter 11 to your own personal experiences. You have probably made attributional errors when judging others. Other people have made attributional errors when forming impressions about you. This chapter will continue with a discussion about how attributional errors lead to stereotypes and biases in perceiving people. It will begin by analyzing research showing how people determine whether behavior is due to situational or dispositional causes. You will learn how explanations you give for your own actions can differ from your explanations of the same actions by others. The remainder of the chapter will describe areas of our lives where interpersonal biases have a significant and sometimes detrimental effect. A summary of research will show how biases and stereotypes can influence interpersonal and international relationships, reactions to undeserved suffering, and responses to successes and failures.

The Actor-Observer Phenomenon

In Chapter 8 you read how attribution theories are used to explain how people seek explanations for one another's behavior. One of the primary questions we try to answer is whether behavior is due to someone's motives, choices, or personality (dispositional causes) or to norms, demands, or forces in the environment (situational causes). As research results on behavioral attributions started to come in, Edward E. Jones and Richard Nisbett noticed that people have a tendency to attribute their own behavior to situational causes while attributing someone else's behavior to dispositional causes. This tendency is called the *actor-observer phenomenon.*[1] Jones and Nisbett explained it in the following way. When we observe other people's behavior, we tend to pay more attention to their expressions and appearance than to the context or situation. This personal focus causes dispositional factors to be more apparent and available than situational factors for explaining their behavior. Our tendency to make dispositional attributions for other people's behavior is reinforced because we often see them in the same roles. When we observe others in only one role, their behavior appears to be more consistent than it actually is. Consider those people you see only at work or in a particular class at school. You might not realize that they act differently in other situations, such as on vacation, at a party, or even at home. Using the concepts described in Chapters 8 and 11, we can say that personal features of others are often more *salient* than their environments. Because we see them in limited roles their behavior appears to be *consistent*. Salience of personal features and high consistency are cues for making dispositional attributions for behavior.

Compare this description of how we see other people's behavior with our perceptions of our own behavior. When we behave we are very aware of our environment and of the norms and rewards affecting us. It is therefore easy to give situational explanations for our actions. Because we are much less aware of our expressions and appearance (unless we are observing ourselves in a mirror), we are not likely to focus on dispositional explanations for what we do. In addition, it is easy for us to be aware that we act differently in different situations. Therefore, when explaining our own behavior, norms and rewards in the environment are more salient than personal factors, and behavioral consistency is low. Salience of environmental forces and low consistency are cues for attributing behavior to situational causes.

Jones and Nisbett formulated their ideas about the actor-observer phenomenon on the basis of research showing how people tend to give situational attributions for their behavior and dispositional attributions for other people's behavior. In this research, people are called *actors* when explaining their behavior and *observers* when explaining the behavior of others. A number of representative studies follow.

PREDICTING FUTURE BEHAVIOR FROM PAST BEHAVIOR

The actor-observer phenomenon was demonstrated in several studies showing that observers used other people's past behavior as a basis for predicting their future behavior. Actors, in contrast, thought that their future behavior depended on the future situation. Apparently observers assume that other people's behavior is dispositional and therefore expect it to be consistent from the past to the future. Actors do not predict their future behavior from past behavior because they view their actions as a function of situational factors, which may vary from one context to another.

Research participants observed people who agreed or refused to volunteer for a cause.[2] When they were asked to predict these people's future behavior, they believed that agreers would volunteer for other causes and that refusers would not. As observers they apparently perceived the agreeing or refusing to volunteer as dispositional and therefore predictive of future actions. When they predicted their own volunteering behavior, the results were very different. As actors they did not use their willingness or unwillingness to volunteer as a basis for predicting their response to future requests. They were more likely to believe that their future volunteering would depend on the particular issue or situation.

Observers in other studies used people's past successes and failures for predicting their future successes and failures, presumably because the observers perceived these results as a stable and consistent indication of the people's abilities.[3] Actors were more likely to view their past and future performances as independent and influenced by the nature and difficulty of the task. They were less inclined to predict their future successes and failures on the basis of past performance. We sometimes suffer when people give dispositional explanations for our failures because we are then denied encouragement that we can do better in the future. We also suffer when our successes are labeled as dispositional because we may be expected to have future successes with no allowance for failure.

Another study demonstrating the actor-observer phenomenon found that observers were more likely than actors to use verbal statements for predicting future actions.[4] Observers apparently felt that other people's statements and actions reflected the same motives and dispositions. Actors were less inclined to see a connection between what they said and what they did. They felt that their statements and actions were independent and determined by the demands of the situation. The implication of this study is that we may hold others more accountable than we hold ourselves for living up to commitments and promises.

EXPLAINING CHOICES AND DECISIONS

The actor-observer phenomenon suggests that people as observers will attribute other people's choices and decisions to dispositions and that as actors they will attribute their own choices and decisions to the situation. This prediction was supported in a study showing that college men were most likely to explain their choice of a woman friend by giving situational explanations having to do with her characteristics or qualities.[5] In explaining why a friend chose a particular woman friend, men were more inclined to rely on dispositional factors such as the friend's need for companionship or desire for certain personal rewards.

An example of the actor-observer phenomenon on a larger scale is seen in a study modeled after the 1972 Watergate burglary.[6] A group of criminology students were approached by an experimenter posing as a private investigator, who asked if they would participate in a special investigation that necessitated the surreptitious entry of an office building. (Of course, an actual burglary was never carried out.) After replying, the students were asked to give reasons for their decision. Most of the reasons were related to situational factors such as the possibility of monetary reward, the quality of the plan, and the probability of avoiding arrest. A second group of students were given a description of the burglary plan and told that another person had either agreed or refused to participate. These observing students tended to give dispositional reasons for the decision, such as enjoyment of adventure, belief in a cause, or willingness to be persuaded. We can see from this study that while people may attribute their own antisocial behaviors to external causes ("I was only following orders"), we, as observers, are more likely to hold them accountable for their actions.

REVERSING THE ACTOR-OBSERVER PHENOMENON

As research on the actor-observer phenomenon gained scientific attention, psychologists began to explore how it could be reversed. Do we ever view our own behaviors as caused by dispositions? When might we give situational explanations for actions by others? During the past ten years, researchers have outlined a number of factors influencing whether we explain behaviors according to dispositions or forces in the situation. These factors will be described in the next part of this chapter. A good place to begin is with a discussion of how explanations for causes of behaviors can be measured.

Measuring Behavioral Attributions

There are two recommended methods for measuring dispositional as distinct from situational explanations for behavior.[7] The *situation questionnaire* asks people to estimate a percentage for the degree to which behavior appears dispositional and the degree to which it appears situational. The *situational-personal questionnaire* asks people to rate the influence of dispositional causes and situational causes on two separate scales whose scores are then combined to arrive at a single figure.

It has been suggested that people should be given the option of specifying when their behavioral explanations are uncertain and when the cause of the behavior they are trying to explain is ambiguous. It has also been pointed out that people might give different explanations for behavior depending on whether it is described as an action or an occurrence. An action is viewed as behavior that someone chooses or initiates, and it is likely to be judged as dispositional. An occurrence is behavior that happens or is caused, and it is likely to be judged as situational. Another issue to consider when measuring behavioral attributions is whether to ask respondents to give reasons for a certain behavior or specific causes that brought it about. People looking for reasons are more likely to focus on dispositions while people looking for causes are more likely to focus on the situation.[8]

We usually know when our actions are determined by forces and pressures in the environment, and we can list these situational causes when explaining our behaviors. The actor-observer phenomenon occurs for situationally caused behaviors because observers cannot appreciate how the situation affects us as much as we can. On the other hand, when our actions are determined by inner motives and feelings, we can list these dispositional causes for why we acted as we did. The actor-observer phenomenon is less likely to occur for dispositionally caused actions because we are more aware of our dispositions than observers are.[9]

To summarize the discussion of reversing the actor-observer phenomenon up to this point, the phenomenon is more likely to occur for situational behaviors than for dispositional behaviors. It is also easier to demonstrate the phenomenon when people are asked to focus on reasons for actions than when people are asked to specify causes for occurrences. In addition to these semantic considerations, the actor-observer phenomenon is influenced by more concrete factors such as actors' and observers' motives and their points of view.

Observers' Motives

The influence of observers' motives on attribution of behavior takes several forms such as liking, expectation, and desire to control.

LIKING

We tend to perceive a positive action by someone we like as dispositional and a positive action by someone we dislike as situational. In a similar vein, we sometimes "excuse" a liked person for an undesirable behavior that we choose to attribute to the situation. We may hold a disliked person responsible for the same behavior because we see it as coming from his or her dispositions. Research has shown that observers are somewhat more cautious about giving dispositional explanations for negative actions by a disliked person when they are required to explain or defend their judgments.[10] There are many occasions, however, when evaluators are not obligated to justify their evaluations. People who are disliked by these evaluators consequently suffer from a negative attributional bias.

EXPECTATIONS AND ROLES

Expectations and roles have a strong influence on attributions given for behaviors of others. The influence of roles was demonstrated in an experiment in which research participants were assigned to one of three roles: counselor, client, or observer.[11] Participants listened to a taped interview between a client and therapist and judged the degree to which the client's problems were due to situational or dispositional causes. It turned out that people in the role of counselor tended to explain the client's problems as caused by dispositions. People in the role of client explained the client's problems as caused by factors in the situation. These differences occurred regardless of whether the client's problems were described as long-standing or recent. People in the role of observer leaned toward dispositional explanations when the client's problems were described as chronic and situational explanations when the problems were described as recent.

Expectations and roles also influence behavioral explanations given by trained clinicians. Professional psychotherapists were asked to watch a fifteen-minute segment of a videotaped interview and to give their evaluations of the man being interviewed. The interview centered around his feelings about his work experiences. Half of the psychotherapists were told that the man was an applicant for a job. The other half were told that he was a psychiatric patient. In reality, all of the videotapes were identical. Psychotherapists who thought the man was interviewing for a job described him as "realistic," "enthusiastic," "pleasant," and "relatively bright." Those who thought the interviewee was a patient and who were oriented toward the use of psychodynamic and trait theories gave the following evaluation: tight defensive person . . . conflict over homosexuality; dependent, passive-aggressive; frightened of his own aggressive impulses . . . impulsivity shows through his own rigidity . . . considerable hostility, repressed or channeled. These psycho-dynamically oriented psychotherapists perceived the "patient's" behavior as caused by dispositions.[12] Psychotherapists who thought the man was a patient and who were behaviorally oriented did not bias their evaluations of the interviewee. This was probably because behavioral psychotherapists are oriented toward describing behaviors as a function of the situation and do not expect that behaviors are caused by underlying dispositions.

MOTIVATION FOR CONTROL

Dispositional attributions provide a sense of understanding about another person because they imply that his or her actions are predictable. The desire for predict-ability was demonstrated in an experiment in which people played a competitive game.[13] They tended to give dispositional explanations for their opponent's actions, especially when they expected to play against the same opponent in the future. The study also found that people with high scores on a need-for-control scale gave more dispositionally oriented descriptions of their opponent than people with low scores on need for control.

Actors' Motives

Two motives influencing whether people give dispositional or situational explanations for their own behaviors are the desire to maintain self-esteem and the need for control.

SELF-ESTEEM

When people selectively explain their actions in ways that maintain or enhance their self-esteem, they are engaging in a *self-serving bias*. Such a bias often occurs when people explain their social behavior and their experiences of success and failure. Research shows that we like to take credit for our positive social interactions, but we attribute our negative social experiences to factors in the situation. We also tend to attribute our successes to dispositions of skill and effort and our failures to situational factors such as task difficulty and bad luck. As with judging others, we are more cautious about using self-serving attributions when we are held accountable for our statements.[14]

The self-esteem motive is apparent in people's use of personality traits for explaining one another's behaviors. You read in Chapter 11 that we tend to ascribe other people's actions to traits while preferring to explain our behaviors as determined by the situation. We are willing, however, to describe ourselves as possessing certain value-laden traits, such as "sentimental," "open-minded," and "light-hearted."[15]

MOTIVATION FOR CONTROL

Dispositional explanations for people's actions sometimes serve to enhance their feelings of control. For example, people tended to interpret their moves in a competitive game as reflecting their personalities. By interpreting their responses as coming from dispositions instead of the situation, they were able to gain a greater sense of control over the game. Participants in another study explained their agreement to take electric shocks as resulting from their personal feelings. Although participants could recognize the external influence of the experimenter's authority, it was desirable for them to perceive their decision to be shocked as a product of their personal choice.[16]

Actors' and Observers' Points of View

People's explanations for their actions are influenced by their visual and psychological points of view. Actors' and observers' visual perspectives were reversed in an experiment in which men were introduced in pairs and given some time to talk and become acquainted.[17] During the conversation each man was watched by an observer. In addition, a television camera mounted directly above each man's head recorded the conversation from his perspective. The first part of this study demonstrated the actor-observer phenomenon. The men gave situational explanations for their own behavior. Observers explained the men's behavior as dispositions. In a second part of the study, the men watched themselves on videotape from the point of view of the person with whom they had been talking. In this way, their visual perspective was altered so they became observers of their own behavior. As a result of this reversed point of view, they evaluated their actions with fewer situational and more dispositional explanations. The visual perspective of the observers was also reversed by allowing them to watch the videotape from the men's point of view. Consequently, the observers gave fewer dispositional and more situational behavioral explanations. This study shows how videotapes can be used to help people experience personal interactions from their own as well as someone else's point of view.

Several researchers altered observers' psychological points of view by encouraging them to be empathic and to consider another person's behavior from that person's perspective. As a result, observers gave more situational explanations for the other person's behavior. The empathy of observers was also heightened by telling them that after viewing a performer's success or failure on a challenging task they themselves would be tested on the same task.[18] Compared with other observers, these empathic observers gave explanations for success or failure that matched the explanation given by the performer. It appears that we are more empathic with others when we share a common challenge and when we make a special effort to understand their actions from their viewpoint.

Actors' viewpoints appear to change over time. Research has found that actors are more likely to give dispositional explanations for their behavior several weeks after it than immediately after it.[19] This "dispositional shift" probably occurs because when recalling a previous act it is easier to remember one's feelings than to remember specifics about the situation. The increased focus on oneself causes behavioral explanations to be more dispositional and offers another reason why it is difficult to give accurate reports about things we did in the past.

An understanding of the actor-observer phenomenon will help you appreciate why people often misunderstand the motives behind other people's behavior. The remainder of this chapter will focus on a number of areas in our lives that can be adversely affected by attributional biases. Since knowledge is power, it is hoped that the following discussion will enable you to constructively readjust your interpretations of other people's actions.

Conflicts in Relationships with the Opposite Sex

Attribution theories have suggested several useful approaches for understanding conflicts that are experienced by men and women who are married, living together, or dating. In keeping with the definition of attribution theories outlined in Chapter 8, these approaches have to do with how couples explain and interpret each other's actions. Two particularly relevant questions in relationships with a person of the opposite sex are (1) Which partner feels greatest responsibility for initiating activities? and (2) How much do partners agree about reasons for conflict in their relationship?

RESPONSIBILITY FOR ACTIVITIES

How do people in relationships with a person of the opposite sex respond when they are asked who contributes the most energy in initiating activities? It might not surprise you to learn that most people feel they take the bulk of this responsibility on themselves. For example, both men and women believe that they do more than their partner to plan leisure activities, that they take more initiative in carrying conversations, and that they spend greater effort on physical appearance. One explanation for this bias is that it is quicker and easier to focus on one's own contributions than it is to weigh them against the contributions made by one's partner. In attributional terms, one's own contributions in a relationship are more salient and available. There are also personal elements to this bias. Happy couples who are getting along well are more likely than unhappy and dissatisfied couples to share credit for initiating positive and constructive activities. Unhappy couples tend to blame each other for negative actions.[20]

AGREEMENT ABOUT CONFLICT

Conflicts in relationships with a person of the opposite sex were explored in an interview study in which couples (either dating, living together, or married) listed their major conflicts.[21] Typical areas of conflict included being too quiet or passive; being rejecting, nonaffectionate, or insensitive; being irresponsible, overemotional, or aggressive; being critical and demanding; and being unwilling to share common interests and activities. Couples were also asked to explain why they thought the conflicts existed. The causes given fell very much into what would be predicted by the actor-observer phenomenon. People tended to explain their own conflict-producing behavior by using situational causes that made the behavior appear reasonable and appropriate. For example, they explained their aggressive and irresponsible actions as caused by something their partner had done. In a similar manner, they explained critical and demanding actions as showing concern and a desire to help their partner. People explained their own lack of affection and sharing by saying that external demands made them too busy or preoccupied. When explaining the causes for their partner's behaviors, people took a dispositional point of view, saying their partners were aggressive and irresponsible because of undesirable personality characteristics and habits. Critical and demanding behavior was attributed to the partner's negative feelings and lack of concern. Lack of affection and sharing were attributed to the partner's laziness and inconsiderateness. This study shows that attributional biases are present even in relationships in which people are well acquainted and emotionally involved.

Another study of conflicts in couples measured how much men and women agreed on the importance of various conflict-producing issues.[22] They agreed on the importance of conflicts about attitudes, values, friends, and parents. On several other issues, interesting differences between men and women emerged. Incompatibility in sexual relations was rated more by men than by women as a significantly important source of conflict. Of even greater interest is the fact that men overestimated the importance assigned by women to sexual incompatibility, falsely assuming that women felt the same way they did. Women made a similar error in underestimating the importance assigned to sexual incompatibility by men, falsely assuming that men felt the same way they did. Conflicts related to financial problems or caused by time spent on work and educational activities were rated as being more important by women than by men. Women overestimated men's ratings of importance on these issues, assuming that men felt the same way they felt. Men underestimated women's ratings of importance on these issues, assuming that women's feelings were similar to theirs.

Disagreement between men and women on the importance of sexual compatibility was also apparent in a study of dating relationships that had recently been dissolved.[23] Men gave the following rankings of issues they felt would have been most important in keeping their relationship together: first sex, then meeting mutual needs, similarity of attitudes and beliefs, helping each other, love. Women ranked love as most important, followed by meeting mutual needs, similarity of attitudes and beliefs, helping each other, and finally sex.

In addition to attributional biases, assignment of responsibility for marital conflict is also influenced by sex roles. In a 1977 survey, men and women both tended to blame wives for conflicts revolving around feminine sex-typed activities such as housekeeping.[24] Husbands were blamed more than wives for conflicts revolving around masculine sex-typed responsibilities such as finances. This sex-role bias may be less prominent in couples who have gained a broader acceptance of roles that are appropriate for men and women.

Attributional studies of conflicts between men and women have important therapeutic implications because they suggest that couples would get along better if they could learn to appreciate each other's viewpoints about the reasons for conflicts and problems. These studies also support the suggestion made earlier in this chapter about using videotapes for helping people to observe their actions from their partner's point of view.[25]

Conflicts between Nations

Urie Bronfenbrenner emphasized the importance of attributional biases in international conflict in his description of the *mirror-image* effect. He pointed out that the

United States views itself as a peace-loving country that requires armaments not as offensive weapons but as defenses against the aggressive intent of the Soviet Union. The Soviet Union takes the same perspective, viewing itself as the peaceful country and the United States as the aggressor. In attributional terms, the United States and the Soviet Union give very different explanations when they engage in a military action than they give when the other country engages in a military action. This apparent double standard was measured by asking American college students to rate their attitudes toward a series of international actions that had in reality been engaged in by both the United States and the Soviet Union. These actions included establishing rocket bases near the other country's borders, sending troops to aid in an independent country's civil war, and giving refuge to political exiles. American students demonstrated a double standard by being more favorable toward an international action when it was identified as a United States action than when it was identified as a Soviet action. It is likely that a parallel double standard favoring Soviet actions would be shown by people in the Soviet Union. It is to be hoped that an understanding of the mirror-image effect will help us rise above the simplistic view of regarding ourselves as the "good guys" and certain other countries as the "bad guys."[26]

Belief in a Just World

One of our greatest attributional challenges is to come to terms with negative events in our lives. Do you accept unhappy experiences stoically, do you blame yourself or others, or do you rely on religious faith for finding an answer to suffering? One factor influencing our explanations of negative events is the degree to which we believe in a *just world* where human beings are rewarded for their good deeds and punished for their bad deeds. Melvin Lerner described this need.[27] We don't usually have trouble accepting situations in which positive behavior results in positive outcome and negative behavior results in negative outcome. We do have difficulty, however, dealing with the fact that many negative experiences in the world are not deserved. How do we reconcile our desire to believe that the world is just with our observations of undeserved suffering, especially when it might happen to us? Researchers have studied people's views of a just world by exposing them to others who are suffering and measuring their rationales for explaining, reconciling, or coming to terms with this suffering. We can understand the conclusions from this research by following the attributional processes outlined in Figure 12-1.

IS THE SUFFERING UNJUST?

The attributional processes in Figure 12-1 begin when we are exposed to a person who is suffering. If the person is suffering as a result of personal choice or fault, or

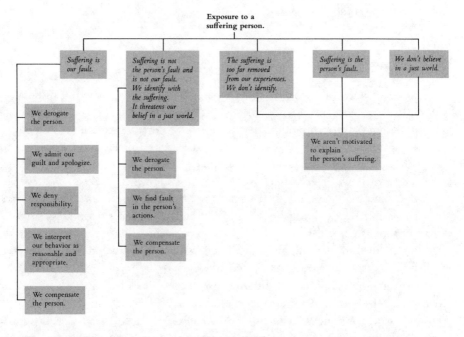

Figure 12–1

if the suffering is too remote to threaten us directly, we are not likely to experience a conflict with our belief in a just world, and we will probably not be motivated to seek an explanation for this negative event. We will also not be motivated to come to terms with the person's suffering if we do not believe in a just world. Check whether you agree with the following statements:

1. *Basically, the world is a just place.*

2. *Students almost always deserve the grades they receive.*

3. *Crime doesn't pay.*

4. *I've found that a person rarely deserves the reputation he has.*

5. *Good deeds often go unnoticed and unrewarded.*

6. *Many people suffer through absolutely no fault of their own.*

These statements come from a scale that measures people's beliefs in a just world.[28] People who believe in a just world tend to agree with the first three statements and to disagree with the last three. They are more motivated than people who don't believe in a just world to seek explanations for negative experiences. Going back to Figure 12–1, if the person's suffering is viewed as being unjust (it is not the person's fault, it is potentially threatening, we believe in a just world), we judge whether or not we are personally responsible.

ARE WE RESPONSIBLE?

If we are not responsible for the suffering and have some means at our disposal to end it or to compensate the person, we will do so. If there is no way to provide compensation we determine whether the person's negative experience could also happen to us. If we are potential victims of the same suffering, we are likely to respond with sympathy and understanding and place our blame on the source of the suffering. If we are not likely to suffer the same negative experience, we are inclined to blame the sufferer. If the person is a stranger or someone we dislike, we can rationalize the suffering by derogating him or her and convincing ourselves that the suffering was deserved. If the person is a friend or someone we respect, we are less inclined to derogate his or her character and more inclined to explain the suffering as a consequence of something the person said or did.

If we are responsible for the suffering, our attempts to alleviate our guilt and to maintain our belief in a just world depend on whatever options are available. If possible, we attempt to make restitution by compensating the person or by admitting our regret and guilt. If methods for restitution are not available (or involve more cost and effort than we are willing to expend) we probably rationalize our harm doing by derogating the victim, by convincing ourselves that the harm was very minor, or by attributing our harmful behavior to circumstances beyond our control ("I couldn't help it") or to external demands ("I was only following orders").[29]

To gain familiarity with research on the just-world phenonemon we can first review studies in which research participants were not responsible for another person's suffering. Under these circumstances, how did they explain the suffering person's negative experience?

College students were given a case report of a woman who was raped and asked to indicate the degree to which they believed she was at fault. The woman was described either as a married woman, a virgin, or a divorcée. Surprisingly, students assigned greater fault to the married woman and the virgin than to the divorcée. The researchers explained this result with the argument that a rape of a married woman or virgin was more threatening to the students' beliefs in a just world and they therefore had greater need to rationalize it by attributing it to the fault of the victim. The results of this study can also be understood as an example of prejudice against divorced women. A similar study found that people blamed a rape victim significantly more when she was unacquainted rather than acquainted with her assailant. Apparently, the rape of a woman by a stranger was a stronger threat to people's beliefs in a just world and increased their motivation to rationalize this event by derogating the victim. Research participants in a third experiment evaluated an unmarried woman less favorably when an unplanned pregnancy turned out badly than when it did not. Why should people be so unsympathetic toward the woman who suffered? Again, it appeared that people making the ratings had a greater need to restore belief in a just world by derogating the woman when her pregnancy had bad effects. The victim was also blamed in a study in which women were held more responsible when they were victims of a completed rape than of an attempted rape.[30]

In his book *Blaming the Victim,* William Ryan described how we often blame socioeconomically disadvantaged people for their plight by self-righteously claiming that they suffer because of "who they are" and by assuming that they could overcome their disadvantages if they "wanted to."[31] Defense attorneys for accused rapists often blame the victim by casting doubt on her character. It is easy to maintain our belief in a just world by blaming other people for their troubles. But how would you feel if others blamed your suffering on you?

Explaining Successes and Failures

The final application of attribution theories in this chapter is to a topic relevant to all of us. How do we explain other people's successes and failures? How do our explanations influence our choices to respond with rewards and punishments? Bernard Weiner and his colleagues outlined four kinds of explanations that are used for understanding successes and failures: *ability, effort, task difficulty,* and *luck.*[32] These explanations are related to correspondent inference theory (see Chapter 8) because the first two are dispositional explanations and the last two are situational explanations. They also make use of judgments about consistency and consensus that are described in Kelley's covariation model.

ABILITY

Ability is judged on the basis of consistency. Consistent success (or failure) on the same or similar tasks is taken as a sign of high (or low) ability. Inconsistent success or failure makes judgments of ability more ambiguous and is more likely to be attributed to luck.

EFFORT

Effort is judged by observing the covariation between exertion or persistence and successful outcome. Success and failure that follow directly from energetic or unenergetic performance are attributed, respectively, to high and low degrees of effort. Success and failure that are independent of exertion and persistence are usually explained as caused by task difficulty or luck.

TASK DIFFICULTY

Task difficulty is inferred from the performance of other people on the task. Success on a task at which most people succeed and failure on a task at which most people fail are attributed to task difficulty (high consensus). Success on a task at which others fail and failure on a task at which others succeed are attributed to ability and effort (low consensus).

LUCK

Success and failure that are inconsistent and not related in a predictable fashion to persistence and exertion are attributed to luck.

These explanations were tested experimentally by presenting research participants with instances of other people's successes and failures in which past performance was sometimes consistent and sometimes inconsistent with present performance. Luck and effort were used to explain successes and failures when there was low consistency between past and present performance. Task difficulty and ability were given as explanations when there was high consistency. The analysis of success and failure on the basis of ability, effort, task difficulty, and luck was derived from the assumptions of attribution theories. Other researchers took a different approach by presenting research participants with instances of success and failure and asking them what information they would need to explain them. People generally requested information about the four factors of ability, effort, task difficulty, and luck. They also asked about the mood and identity of the person who succeeded or failed. Success and failure were explained on the basis of effort. Ability was also used for explaining success and mood was also used for explaining failure.[33]

Helping People Succeed

You might remember from Chapter 1 that people are most likely to suffer from being lonely when they attribute their loneliness to stable and internal causes that they feel are unchangeable and beyond their control. This conclusion is instructive because it suggests ways for helping people experience more success. One group of researchers taught school children to appreciate the fact that their past failures were not always due to lack of ability but were often caused by insufficient effort. This reinterpretation of failure encouraged the children to try harder. As a result of their increased effort they experienced greater success. Another group of researchers helped college freshmen who were worried about their academic performance appreciate the fact that their worries were not uncommon and that many freshmen in the past had been able to improve their grades after their first semester. Freshmen who learned to appreciate that grades are changeable and not stable had significantly more success than other freshmen in improving their grade average, in answering questions from a study book for the Graduate Record Examination, and in staying in college rather than dropping out.[34]

Emotional Reactions to Success and Failure

Bernard Weiner and his colleagues raised two questions about the relation between emotional reactions and experiences of success and failure.[35] Do people feel similar emotions after experiencing success and failure? How much do we use people's feelings for explaining their successes and failures? The first question was explored by asking research participants to recall the emotions they felt when they experienced success or failure that was due to either dispositional causes (ability, effort, personality) or to situational causes (other people, luck). The emotions reported after success from dispositional causes were pride, competence, confidence, and satisfaction. Success from situational causes was associated with emotions of gratitude, thankfulness, surprise, and guilt. Dispositionally caused failure was associated with emotions of guilt, resignation, and regret. Situationally caused failure was associated with anger and surprise.

The second question was answered by asking research participants to read case descriptions in which people who succeeded or failed had different emotions. Research participants used these emotions for reaching conclusions about the causes of the success and failure. When people were described as feeling competence and satisfaction, their successes were attributed to ability and effort. Successes of people who felt surprised and grateful were attributed to luck or ease of the task. Failures of people who felt incompetent, ashamed, and guilty were attributed to lack of ability and effort. Failures of those who felt bitter and displeased were attributed to bad luck and difficulty of the task. The above studies complemented each other by demonstrating that we explain other people's successes and failures on the basis of the same emotions we experience after our own successes and failures. They are also relevant to the self-presentation strategies discussed in Chapter 9. Professional athletes typically react to failure by acting angry and displeased rather than disappointed and ashamed. How do you communicate your successes and failures?

Rewards and Punishments

There are at least two reasons why the rewards and punishments we give to others are influenced by our interpretations of their successes and failures. First, explanations for people's successes and failures affect our perceptions of their emotions. We tend to give more credit to a successful person who feels pride and satisfaction than to a successful person who feels gratitude and guilt. We also react differently to a person's failure when the person is resigned and regretful than when he or she is angry. Resignation and regret imply that the person tried hard but just couldn't do it. Anger implies that the person's effort was not sufficient and that he or she will try harder next time.

Second, attributions about the causes for others' successes and failures influence our use of rewards and punishments because they tell us something about the person's apparent sincerity and effort. Three studies demonstrate this influence. In the first, research participants took the role of grade school teachers and recommended rewards or punishments to students whose performance ranged from very good to very poor.[36] The students were described as having either high or low ability and as having expended high or low amounts of effort. Participants recommended more reward for successful performance. In addition, successful students who expended high amounts of effort were given more rewards than successful students who did not work very hard. Punishment was given more for failure. The greatest punishment for failure was given to students of high ability who did not try. Less able students who expended a good deal of effort were given the least amounts of punishment.

A second experiment measured how much punishment and reward would be given by research participants to "trainees" for correct and incorrect responses on a learning task.[37] Half the participants were told that their trainee was very competent and that they could expect a good performance. The remainder were told that their trainee was not competent and that they should expect a poor performance. The participants reacted to these expectations by giving more punishment for incorrect responses by competent trainees than by incompetent trainees, especially when the task was easy. In this instance they punished the competent trainees for not trying harder. They gave least punishment to noncompetent trainees who had poor performance when the task was difficult because the trainees appeared to be trying as hard as they could. Interestingly, participants gave the highest rewards for correct responses to competent trainees. They gave lower rewards to noncompetent trainees who made correct responses because they saw the trainees as having insufficient ability (even when their responses were correct) to deserve the highest rewards.

A third study investigated the amount of reward that research participants recommended for performance by people on various tests of athletic skill.[38] Not surprisingly, participants recommended more reward for people whose efforts were high rather than low. In addition, they rewarded more highly people who did not have the benefit of training and who lacked physical ability when they "overcame" their limitations and turned in a good performance.

These studies demonstrate how successes and failures are selectively rewarded according to attributions made about their causes. Since rewards and punishments also influence successes and failures, it is easy for a self-fulfilling prophecy to develop between people who are dispensers of rewards and punishments (bosses, parents, teachers) and people who are recipients (workers, children, students). This self-fulfilling prophecy is perpetuated by a feedback system in which the dispenser's preconceptions about the recipient's ability influence the delivery of rewards and punishments. These rewards and punishments in turn produce performance by the recipient that supports or "justifies" the dispenser's preconceptions.

It is also interesting to consider rewards and punishments from the point of view of the values of American society. B. F. Skinner pointed out that we are more inclined to punish undesirable behaviors than to reward desirable behaviors because the use of rewards challenges our belief in free will.[39] In terms of correspondent inference theory and Kelley's causal schemata model, it is acceptable to use rewards so long as they don't undermine dispositional explanations for desirable behaviors. We like to believe that people engage in positive actions because they "choose to," not because they want a reward. Skinner also described the curious fact that punishment is not as likely as reward to undermine our belief in free will because a person who is punished for undesirable behavior did not "have" to engage in it. Punishing such a person is acceptable because it is assumed that people engage in undesirable actions out of free choice.

Interpersonal perceptions are often subjective. I hope that the knowledge you have gained about biases and stereotypes from this book will make your interactions with people more effective and fulfilling.

Notes

CHAPTER 1

1. B. F. Skinner, *Beyond Freedom and Dignity* (New York: Knopf, 1971).

2. Z. Rubin, *Liking and Loving: An Invitation to Social Psychology* (New York: Holt, Rinehart, and Winston, 1973), pp. 188, 189.

3. P. G. Zimbardo, *Shyness* (Reading, Mass.: Addison-Wesley, 1977).

4. D. Riesman, *The Lonely Crowd* (New Haven: Yale University Press, 1953); P. E. Slater, *The Pursuit of Loneliness* (Boston: Beacon Press, 1970).

5. N. Bradburn, *The Structure of Psychological Well-Being* (Chicago: Aldine, 1969); L. A. Peplau, D. Russell, and M. Heim, "The Experience of Loneliness," in I. H. Frieze, D. Bar-Tal, and J. S. Carroll (eds.), *New Approaches to Social Problems: Applications of Attribution Theory* (San Francisco: Jossey-Bass, 1979).

6. P. Shaver and C. Rubenstein, "Childhood Attachment Experience and Adult Loneliness," in L. Wheeler (ed.), *Review of Personality and Social Psychology,* Vol. 1 (Beverly Hills, Calif.: Sage, 1980).

7. L. A. Peplau and D. Perlman, "Blueprint for a Social Psychological Theory of Loneliness," in M. Cook and G. Wilson (eds.), *Love and Attraction* (Elmsford, N.Y.: Pergamon Press, 1979); L. Wheeler, H. Reis, and J. Nezlek, "Loneliness, Social Interaction, and Sex Roles," *Journal of Personality and Social Psychology,* 1983, *45,* 943–953.

8. D. Russell, L. A. Peplau, and C. E. Cutrona, "The Revised UCLA Loneliness Scale: Concurrent and Discriminant Validity Evidence," *Journal of Personality and Social Psychology,* 1980, *39,* 472–480. See also D. Russell, C. E. Cutrona, J. Rose, and K. Yurko, "Social and Emotional Loneliness: An Examination of Weiss's Typology of Loneliness," *Journal of Personality and Social Psychology,* 1984, *46,* 1313–1321. A more specific measure of loneliness in different kinds of relationships was derived by N. Schmidt and V. Sermat, "Measuring Loneliness in Different Relationships," *Journal of Personality and Social Psychology,* 1983, *44,* 1038–1047.

9. L. A. Peplau and D. Perlman (eds.), *Loneliness: A Sourcebook of Current Research, Theory, and Therapy* (New York: Wiley, 1982).

10. J. L. Michela, L. A. Peplau, and D. G. Weeks, "Perceived Dimensions of Attribu-

tions for Loneliness," *Journal of Personality and Social Psychology*, 1982, *43*, 929–936; L. A. Peplau, D. Russell, and M. Heim, *op. cit.*

11. L. A. Peplau, D. Russell, and M. Heim, *op. cit.*

12. *Ibid.*

13. W. H. Jones, "Loneliness and Social Contact," *Journal of Social Psychology*, 1981, *113*, 295–296; W. H. Jones, S. A. Hobbs, and D. Hockenbury, "Loneliness and Social Skills Deficits," *Journal of Personality and Social Psychology*, 1982, *42*, 682–689.

14. On disclosure see J. H. Berg and L. A. Peplau, "Loneliness: The Relationship of Self-Disclosure and Androgyny," *Personality and Social Psychology Bulletin*, 1982, *8*, 624–630; G. J. Chelune, F. E. Sultan, and C. L. Williams, "Loneliness, Self-Disclosure, and Interpersonal Effectiveness," *Journal of Counseling Psychology*, 1980, *27*, 462–468; C. H. Solano, P. G. Batten, and E. A. Parish, "Loneliness and Patterns of Self-Disclosure," *Journal of Personality and Social Psychology*, 1982, *43*, 524–531. On communication see A. C. Gerson and D. Perlman, "Loneliness and Expressive Communication," *Journal of Abnormal Psychology*, 1979, *88*, 258–261. On dislike see W. H. Jones, J. E. Freemon, and R. A. Goswick, "The Persistence of Loneliness," *Journal of Personality*, 1981, *49*, 27–48.

15. R. A. Goswick and W. H. Jones, "Loneliness, Self-Concept, and Adjustment," *Journal of Psychology*, 1981, *107*, 237–240; W. H. Jones, C. Sansone, and B. Helm, "Loneliness and Interpersonal Judgments," *Personality and Social Psychology Bulletin*, 1983, *6*, 437–441; W. H. Jones, S. A. Hobbs, and D. Hockenbury, *op. cit.*

16. M. R. Goldfried and G. C. Davison, *Clinical Behavior Therapy* (New York: Holt, Rinehart, and Winston, 1976); M. J. Mahoney and C. E. Thoresen, *Self-Control: Power to the Person* (Monterey, Calif.: Brooks/Cole, 1974); A. Bandura, "Self-Efficacy: Toward a Unifying Theory of Behavioral Change," *Psychological Review*, 1977, *84*, 191–215; A. Bandura, *Social Learning Theory* (Englewood Cliffs, N. J.: Prentice-Hall, 1980).

17. J. P. Curran and M. Fischetti, "Heterosexual-Social Anxiety," in R. Daitzman (ed.), *Clinical Behavior Therapy and Behavior Modification* (New York: Garland Publishing, 1981).

18. D. P. Saccuzzo, "What Patients Want from Counseling and Psychotherapy," *Journal of Clinical Psychology*, 1975, *37*, 471–475.

19. M. A. Hoffman and H. Teglasi, "The Role of Causal Attributions in Counseling Shy Subjects," *Journal of Counseling Psychology*, 1982, *29*, 132–139.

20. M. R. Goldfried, W. Padawer, and C. Robins, "Social Anxiety and the Semantic Structure of Heterosocial Interactions," *Journal of Abnormal Psychology*, 1984, *93*, 87–97.

21. R. M. Eisler and L. W. Frederiksen, *Perfecting Social Skills: A Guide to Interpersonal Behavior* (New York: Plenum, 1980).

22. H. Benson, *The Relaxation Response* (New York: Avon, 1976).

23. J. Wolpe, *The Practice of Behavior Therapy* (New York: Pergamon, 1974).

24. M. R. Goldfried, "Systematic Desensitization as Training in Self-Control," *Journal of Consulting and Clinical Psychology*, 1971, *37*, 228–234.

25. C. L. Kleinke, *Self-Perception: The Psychology of Personal Awareness* (San Francisco: W. H. Freeman, 1978), chap. 3.

26. S. E. Brodt and P. G. Zimbardo, "Modifying Shyness-Related Social Behavior Through Symptom Misattribution," *Journal of Personality and Social Psychology*, 1981, *41*, 437–449.

27. A. Ellis, *Reason and Emotion in Psychotherapy* (New York: Lyle Stuart, 1962), especially p. 50.

28. D. Meichenbaum, *Cognitive-Behavior Modification* (New York: Plenum, 1977).

29. Z. Rubin, *op. cit.*, pp. 195, 196.

30. On values see A. C. Kerckhoff and K. E. Davis, "Value Consensus and Need Complimentarity in Mate Selection," *American Sociological Review*, 1962, *27*, 295–303. On attitudes see D. Byrne, C. R. Ervin, and J. Lamberth, "Continuity Between the Experimental Study of Attraction and Real-Life Computer Dating," *Journal of Personality and Social Psychology*, 1970, *16*, 157–165.

31. On propinquity see J. H. S. Bossard, "Residential Propinquity as a Factor in Marriage Selection," *American Journal of Sociology*, 1931, *38*, 219–224. See also A. M. Katz and R. Hill, "Residential Propinquity and Marital Selection: A Review of Theory, Method, and Fact," *Marriage and Family Living*, 1958, *20*, 27–34. In addition see A. C. Kerckhoff, "The Social Context of Interpersonal Attraction," in T. L. Huston (ed.), *Foundations of Interpersonal Attraction* (New York: Academic Press, 1974).

32. M. S. Cary, "The Role of Gaze in the Initiation of Conversation," *Social Psychology*, 1978, *41*, 269–271.

33. C. L. Kleinke, F. B. Meeker, and R. A. Staneski, "Opening Lines," unpublished manuscript, 1985.

34. C. L. Kleinke, M. L. Kahn, and T. B. Tully, "First Impressions of Talking Rates in Opposite-Sex and Same-Sex Interactions," *Social Behavior and Personality*, 1979, *7*, 81–91.

35. R. G. Harper, A. N. Wiens, and J. D. Matarazzo, *Nonverbal Communication: The State of the Art* (New York: Wiley, 1978), chap. 2; C. L. Kleinke and T. B. Tully, "Influence of Talking Level on Perceptions of Counselors," *Journal of Counseling Psychology*, 1979, *26*, 23–29.

36. P. G. Zimbardo, *op. cit.*, chap. 10.

37. J. D. Porteous, *Environment and Behavior* (Reading, Mass.: Addison-Wesley, 1977).

38. M. N. LaPlante, N. McCormick, and G. G. Brannigan, "Living the Sexual Script: College Students' Views of Influence in Sexual Encounters," *Journal of Sex Research*, 1980, *16*, 338–355; N. B. McCormick, "Come-Ons and Put-Offs: Unmarried Students' Strategies for Having and Avoiding Sexual Intercourse," *Psychology of Women Quarterly*, 1979, *4*, 194–211.

39. R. E. Glasgow and H. Arkowitz, "The Behavioral Assessment of Male and Female Social Competence in Dyadic Heterosexual Interactions," *Behavior Therapy*, 1975, *6*, 488–498; D. P. Greenwald, "The Behavioral Assessment of Differences in Social Skill and Social Anxiety in Female College Students," *Behavior Therapy*, 1977, *8*, 925–937.

40. W. O. N. Scott and B. A. Edelstein, "The Social Competence of Two Interaction Strategies: An Analog Evaluation," *Behavior Therapy*, 1981, *12*, 482–492.

41. J. A. Gold, R. M. Ryckman, and N. R. Mosley, "Romantic Mood Induction and Attraction to a Dissimilar Other: Is Love Blind?" *Personality and Social Psychology Bulletin*, 1984, *10*, 358–368.

42. T. E. Kupke and S. A. Hobbs, "Selection of Heterosocial Skills I. Criterion-Related Validity," *Behavior Therapy*, 1979, *10*, 327–335; T. E. Kupke, K. S. Calhoun, and S. A. Hobbs, "Selection of Heterosocial Skills II. Experimental Validity," *Behavior Therapy*, 1979, *10*, 336–346. On responsiveness see J. C. Conger and A. D. Farrell, "Behavioral Components of Heterosocial Skills," *Behavior Therapy*, 1981, *12*, 41–55; A. S. Imada and M. D. Hakel, "Influence of Nonverbal Communication and Rater Proximity on Impressions and Decisions in Simulated Employment Interviews," *Journal of Applied Psychology*, 1977, *62*, 295–300; L. C. Miller, J. H. Berg, and R. L. Archer, "Openers: Individuals Who Elicit Intimate Self-Disclosure," *Journal of Personality and Social Psychology*, 1983, *44*, 1234–1244.

43. D. Davis and T. Holtgraves, "Perceptions of Unresponsive Others: Attributions, Attraction, Understandability, and Memory of Their Utterances," *Journal of Experimental Social Psychology*, 1984, *20*, 383–408; D. Davis and W. T. Perkowitz, "Consequences of Responsiveness in Dyadic Interaction: Effects of Probability of Response and Proportion of Content-Related Responses on Interpersonal Attraction," *Journal of Personality and Social Psychology*, 1979, *37*, 534–550.

44. *Ibid.*

45. R. E. Glasgow and H. Arkowitz, *op. cit.;* D. P. Greenwald, *op. cit.;* T. E. Kupke, K. S. Calhoun, and S. A. Hobbs, *op. cit.*

46. F. M. Haemmerlie and R. L. Montgomery, "Purposefully Biased Interactions: Reducing Heterosocial Anxiety Through Self-Perception Theory," *Journal of Personality and Social Psychology*, 1984, *47*, 900–908.

CHAPTER 2

1. M. R. Cunningham, "Weather, Mood, and Helping: Quasi Experiments with the Sunshine Samaritan," *Journal of Personality and Social Psychology*, 1979, *37*, 1947–1956.

2. A. M. Isen, "Success, Failure, and Reaction to Others: The Warm Glow of Success," *Journal of Personality and Social Psychology*, 1970, *15*, 294–301; A. M. Isen, N. Horn, and D. L. Rosenhan, "Effects of Success and Failure on Children's Generosity," *Journal of Personality and Social Psychology*, 1973, *27*, 239–247.

3. A. J. Lott and B. E. Lott, "The Power of Liking: Consequences of Interpersonal Attitudes Derived from a Liberalized View of Secondary Reinforcement," in L. Berkowitz (ed.), *Advances in Experimental Social Psychology*, Vol. 6 (New York: Academic Press, 1972); A. J. Lott and B. E. Lott, "The Role of Reward in the Formation of Positive Interpersonal Attitudes," in T. L. Huston (ed.), *Foundations of Interpersonal Attraction* (New York: Academic Press, 1974). See also G. L. Clore and D. Byrne, "A Reinforcement Model of Attraction," in T. L. Huston (ed.), *Foundations of Interpersonal Attraction* (New York: Academic Press, 1974); W. B. Griffitt, "Attraction Toward a Stranger as a Function of Direct and Associated Reinforcement," *Psychonomic Science*, 1968, *11*, 147–148; W. B. Griffitt and P. Guay, "'Object' Evaluation and Conditioned Affect," *Journal of Experimental Research in Personality*, 1969, *4*, 1–8; A. J. Lott, B. E. Lott, and G. Matthews, "Interpersonal Attraction Among Children as a Function of Vicarious Reward," *Journal of Educational Psychology*, 1969, *60*, 274–282; K. W. Wyant, J. A. Lippert, F. W. Wyant, and D. G. Moring, "The Duration and Generalization of Attraction," *Journal of Research in Personality*, 1977, *11*, 347–355.

4. A. M. Isen and P. F. Levin, "Effects of Feeling Good on Helping: Cookies and Kindness," *Journal of Personality and Social Psychology*, 1972, *21*, 384–388.

5. *Ibid.*

6. A. M. Isen, M. Clark, and M. F. Schwartz, "Duration of the Effects of Good Mood on Helping: Footprints on the Sands of Time," *Journal of Personality and Social Psychology*, 1976, *34*, 385–393.

7. C. Gouaux, "Induced Affective States and Interpersonal Attraction," *Journal of Personality and Social Psychology*, 1971, *20*, 37–43.

8. H. A. Hornstein, *Cruelty and Kindness: A New Look at Aggression and Altruism* (Englewood Cliffs, N. J.: Prentice-Hall, 1976); H. A. Hornstein, E. LaKind, G. Frankel, and S. Manne, "The Effects of Knowledge about Remote Social Events on Prosocial Behavior, Social Conception, and Mood," *Journal of Personality and Social Psychology*, 1975, *32*, 1038–1046.

9. D. Aderman, "Elation, Depression, and Helping Behavior," *Journal of Personality and Social Psychology*, 1972, *24*, 91–101.

10. J. C. Coyne, "Depression and the Response of Others," *Journal of Abnormal Psychology*, 1976, *85*, 186–193.

11. S. Schachter, "The Interaction of Cognitive and Physiological Determinants of Emotional State," in L. Berkowitz (ed.), *Advances in Experimental Social Psychology*, Vol. 1 (New York: Academic Press, 1964); S. Schachter and J. E. Singer, "Cognitive, Social, and Physiological Determinants of Emotional State," *Psychological Review*, 1962, *69*, 379–399.

12. E. Berscheid and E. Walster, "A Little Bit about Love," in T. L. Huston (ed.), *Foundations of Interpersonal Attraction* (New York: Academic Press, 1974); E. Walster, "Passionate Love," in B. I. Murstein (ed.), *Theories of Attraction and Love* (New York: Springer, 1971).

13. S. Valins, "Cognitive Effects of False Heart-Rate Feedback," *Journal of Personality and Social Psychology*, 1966, *4*, 400–408.

14. N. A. Walsh, L. A. Meister, and C. L. Kleinke, "Interpersonal Attraction and Visual Behavior as a Function of Perceived Arousal and Evaluation by an Opposite Sex Person," *Journal of Social Psychology*, 1977, *103*, 65–74.

15. C. L. Kleinke, *Self-Perception: The Psychology of Personal Awareness* (San Francisco: W. H. Freeman, 1978).

16. D. Dutton and A. Aron, "Some Evidence for Heightened Sexual Attraction under Conditions of High Anxiety," *Journal of Personality and Social Psychology*, 1974, *30*, 510–517.

17. C. L. Kleinke, *op. cit.*

18. D. Dutton and A. Aron, *op. cit.*; D. T. Kenrick, R. B. Cialdini, and D. E. Linder, "Misattribution under Fear-Producing Circumstances: Four Failures to Replicate," *Personality and Social Psychology Bulletin*, 1979, *5*, 329–334.

19. G. L. White, S. Fishbein, and J. Rutstein, "Passionate Love and the Misattribution of Arousal," *Journal of Personality and Social Psychology*, 1981, *41*, 56–62.

20. K. K. Dion and K. L. Dion, "Self-Esteem and Romantic Love," *Journal of Personality*, 1975, *43*, 39–57; K. L. Dion and K. K. Dion, "Correlates of Romantic Love," *Journal of Consulting and Clinical Psychology*, 1973, *41*, 51–56.

21. C. L. Kleinke, *op. cit.*, chap. 2; Z. Rubin, *Liking and Loving: An Invitation to Social Psychology* (New York: Holt, Rinehart, and Winston, 1973).

22. E. Berscheid and E. Walster, *op. cit.*

23. E. Walster, G. W. Walster, J. Piliavin, and L. Schmidt, "'Playing Hard-to-Get': Understanding an Elusive Phenomenon," *Journal of Personality and Social Psychology*, 1973, *26*, 113–121.

24. K. A. Matthews, D. Rosenfield, and W. G. Stephan, "Playing Hard-to-Get: A Two-Determinant Model," *Journal of Personality and Social Psychology*, 1979, *13*, 234–244.

25. G. D. Marshall and P. G. Zimbardo, "Affective Consequences of Inadequately Explained Physiological Arousal," *Journal of Personality and Social Psychology*, 1979, *37*, 978–988; C. Maslach, "Negative Emotional Biasing of Unexplained Arousal," *Journal of Personality and Social Psychology*, 1979, *37*, 953–969.

26. S. Schachter, *The Psychology of Affiliation* (Stanford, Calif.: Stanford University Press, 1959); I. Sarnoff and P. G. Zimbardo, "Anxiety, Fear, and Social Affiliation," *Journal of Abnormal and Social Psychology*, 1961, *62*, 356–363; S. Epley, "Reduction of the Behavioral Effects of Aversive Stimulation by the Presence of Companions," *Psychological Bulletin*, 1974, *81*, 271–283; D. T. Kenrick and R. B. Cialdini, "Romantic Attraction: Misattribution versus Reinforcement Explanations," *Journal of Personality and Social Psychology*, 1977, *35*, 381–391; D. T. Kenrick and G. A. Johnson, "Interpersonal Attraction in Aversive En-

vironments: A Problem for the Classical Conditioning Paradigm?" *Journal of Personality and Social Psychology,* 1979, *37,* 572–579.

27. R. B. Cialdini and D. T. Kenrick, "Altruism as Hedonism: A Social Development Perspective on the Relationship of Negative Mood State and Helping," *Journal of Personality and Social Psychology,* 1976, *34,* 907–914.

28. A. M. Isen and T. E. Shalker, "The Effect of Feeling State on Evaluation of Positive, Neutral, and Negative Stimuli: When You 'Accentuate the Positive,' Do You 'Eliminate the Negative'?" *Social Psychology Quarterly,* 1982, *45,* 58–63; A. M. Isen, T. E. Shalker, M. Clark, and L. Karp, "Affect, Accessibility of Material in Memory, and Behavior: A Cognitive Loop?" *Journal of Personality and Social Psychology,* 1978, *36,* 1–12.

CHAPTER 3

1. E. Aronson, "Some Antecedents of Interpersonal Attraction," in W. J. Arnold and D. Levine (eds.), *Nebraska Symposium on Motivation* (Lincoln: University of Nebraska Press, 1969); G. Lindzey, "Morphology and Behavior," in G. Lindzey and C. S. Hall (eds.), *Theories of Personality: Primary Sources and Research* (New York: Wiley, 1965).

2. On preferences see J. W. Hudson and L. Henze, "Campus values in Mate Selection: A Replication," *Journal of Marriage and the Family,* 1969, *31,* 772–778. On college dating see A. Tesser and M. Brodie, "A Note on the Evaluation of a 'Computer Date'," *Psychonomic Science,* 1971, *23,* 300. For conclusions see H. L. Miller and W. H. Rivenbark, "Sexual Differences in Physical Attractiveness as a Determinant of Heterosexual Liking," *Psychological Reports,* 1970, *27,* 701–702.

3. E. Walster, V. Aronson, D. Abrahams, and L. Rottman, "Importance of Physical Attractiveness in Dating Behavior," *Journal of Personality and Social Psychology,* 1966, *5,* 508–516.

4. R. W. Brislin and S. A. Lewis, "Dating and Physical Attractiveness: A Replication," *Psychological Reports,* 1968, *22,* 976; D. Byrne, C. R. Ervin, and J. Lamberth, "Continuity Between the Experimental Study of Attraction and Real-Life Computer Dating," *Journal of Personality and Social Psychology,* 1970, *16,* 157–165; J. P. Curran and S. Lippold, "The Effects of Physical Attraction and Attitude Similarity on Attraction in Dating Dyads," *Journal of Personality,* 1975, *43,* 528–539; A. Tessor and M. Brodie, *op. cit.*

5. E. Berscheid, K. K. Dion, E. Walster, and G. W. Walster, "Physical Attractiveness and Dating Choice: A Test of the Matching Hypothesis," *Journal of Experimental Social Psychology,* 1971, *7,* 173–189; T. L. Huston, "Ambiguity of Acceptance, Social Desirability, and Dating Choice," *Journal of Experimental Social Psychology,* 1973, *9,* 32–42; J. Shanteau and G. F. Nagy, "Probability of Acceptance in Dating Choice," *Journal of Personality and Social Psychology,* 1979, *37,* 522–533; W. Stroebe, C. A. Insko, V. D. Thompson, and B. D. Layton, "Effects of Physical Attractiveness, Attitude Similarity, and Sex on Various Aspects of Interpersonal Attraction," *Journal of Personality and Social Psychology,* 1971, *18,* 79–91.

6. On marketplace value see P. M. Blau, *Exchange and Power in Social Life* (New York: Wiley, 1964); E. Walster, G. W. Walster, and E. Berscheid, *Equity: Theory and Research* (Boston: Allyn and Bacon, 1977). On self-esteem see S. Kiesler and R. Baral, "The Search for a Romantic Partner: The Effects of Self-Esteem and Physical Attractiveness on Romantic Behavior," in K. J. Gergen and D. Marlowe (eds.), *Personality and Social Behavior* (Reading, Mass.: Addison-Wesley, 1970); R. J. Pellegrini, R. A. Hicks, and S. Meyers-Winton, "Situational Affective Arousal and Heterosexual Attraction: Some Effects of Success, Failure, and Physical Attractiveness," *Psychological Record*, 1979, *29*, 453–462.

7. E. Berscheid, K. K. Dion, E. Walster, and G. W. Walster, *op. cit.;* E. Berscheid and E. Walster, "Physical Attractiveness," in L. Berkowitz (ed.), *Advances in Experimental Social Psychology*, Vol. 7 (New York: Academic Press, 1974).

8. W. Stroebe, C. A. Insko, V. D. Thompson, and B. D. Layton, *op. cit.*

9. On those engaged see B. I. Murstein, "Physical Attractiveness and Marital Choice," *Journal of Personality and Social Psychology*, 1972, *22*, 8–12; I. Silverman, "Physical Attractiveness and Courtship," *Sexual Behavior*, 1971, *1*, 22–25. On those married see N. Cavior and P. J. Boblett, "Physical Attractiveness of Dating Versus Married Couples," *Proceedings of the 80th Annual Convention of the American Psychological Association*, 1972, *7*, 175–176; B. I. Murstein and P. Christy, "Physical Attractiveness and Marriage Adjustment in Middle-Aged Couples," *Journal of Personality and Social Psychology*, 1976, *34*, 537–542; R. A. Price and S. G. Vandenberg, "Matching for Physical Attractiveness in Married Couples," *Personality and Social Psychology Bulletin*, 1979, *5*, 398–400; G. L. White, "Physical Attractiveness and Courtship Progress," *Journal of Personality and Social Psychology*, 1980, *39*, 660–668. On those dating see V. S. Folkes, "Forming Relationships and the Matching Hypothesis," *Personality and Social Psychology Bulletin*, 1982, *8*, 631–636; G. L. White, *op. cit.*

10. On adjustment see B. I. Murstein and P. Christy, *op. cit.* On satisfaction see R. J. Sternberg and S. Grajek, "The Nature of Love," *Journal of Personality and Social Psychology*, 1984, *47*, 312–329.

11. T. F. Cash and V. J. Derlega, "The Matching Hypothesis: Physical Attractiveness Among Same-Sexed Friends," *Personality and Social Psychology Bulletin*, 1978, *4*, 240–243.

12. G. R. Adams and T. L. Huston, "Social Perceptions of the Middle-Aged Varying in Physical Attractiveness," *Developmental Psychology*, 1975, *11*, 657–658; J. C. Brigham, "Limiting Conditions of the 'Physical Attractiveness Stereotype': Attributions About Divorce," *Journal of Research in Personality*, 1980, *14*, 365–375; S. R. Deitz, M. Littman, and B. J. Bentley, "Attribution of Responsibility for Rape: The Influence of Observer Empathy, Victim Resistance, and Victim Attractiveness," *Sex Roles*, 1984, *10*, 261–280; K. K. Dion, E. Berscheid, and E. Walster, "What Is Beautiful Is Good," *Journal of Personality and Social Psychology*, 1972, *24*, 285–290; B. Gillen, "Physical Attractiveness: A Determi-

nant of Two Types of Goodness," *Personality and Social Psychology Bulletin,* 1981, 7, 277–281; S. Hagiwara, "Visual Versus Verbal Information in Impression Formation," *Journal of Personality and Social Psychology,* 1975, *32,* 692–698; R. C. Mashman, "The Effect of Physical Attractiveness on the Perception of Attitude Similarity," *Journal of Social Psychology,* 1978, *106,* 103–110; A. G. Miller, "Role of Physical Attractiveness in Impression Formation," *Psychonomic Science,* 1970, *19,* 241–243; J. P. Nielsen and A. Kernaleguen, "Influence of Clothing and Physical Attractiveness in Person Perception," *Perceptual and Motor Skills,* 1976, *42,* 775–780; M. Snyder, E. D. Tanke, and E. Berscheid, "Social Perception and Interpersonal Behavior: On the Self-Fulfilling Nature of Social Stereotypes," *Journal of Personality and Social Psychology,* 1977, *35,* 656–666; W. Stroebe, C. A. Insko, V. D. Thompson, and B. D. Layton, *op. cit.* For additional references relating physical attractiveness and personality ratings see T. F. Cash, "Physical Attractiveness: An Annotated Bibliography of Theory and Research in the Behavioral Sciences," *JSAS Catalog of Selected Documents in Psychology,* 1978, *11,* Ms. 2370. See also R. Barocas and P. Karoly, "Effects of Physical Appearance on Social Responsiveness," *Psychological Reports,* 1972, *31,* 495–500; R. E. Kleck and C. Rubenstein, "Physical Attractiveness, Perceived Attitude Similarity, and Interpersonal Attraction," *Journal of Personality and Social Psychology,* 1975, *31,* 107–114; C. L. Kleinke, R. A. Staneski, and D. E. Berger, "Evaluation of an Interviewer as a Function of Interviewer Gaze, Reinforcement of Subject Gaze, and Interviewer Attractiveness," *Journal of Personality and Social Psychology,* 1975, *31,* 115–122; C. L. Kleinke, R. A. Staneski, and S. L. Pipp, "Effects of Gaze, Distance, and Attractiveness on Males' First Impressions of Females," *Representative Research in Social Psychology,* 1975, *6,* 7–12; R. J. Pellegrini, R. A. Hicks, and S. Meyers-Winton, *op. cit.*

13. A. E. Gross and C. Crofton, "What Is Good Is Beautiful," *Sociometry,* 1977, *40,* 85–90.

14. G. Owens and J. G. Ford, "Further Considerations of the 'What Is Good Is Beautiful' Finding," *Social Psychology,* 1978, *41,* 73–75.

15. T. F. Cash, B. Gillen, and D. S. Burns, "Sexism and 'Beautyism' in Personnel Consultant Decision Making," *Journal of Applied Psychology,* 1977, *62,* 301–310.

16. R. E. Carlson, "The Relative Influence of Appearance and Factual Written Information on an Interviewer's Final Rating," *Journal of Applied Psychology,* 1967, *51,* 461–468; R. L. Dipboye, R. D. Arvey, and D. E. Terpstra, "Sex and Physical Attractiveness of Raters and Applicants as Determinants of Résumé Evaluations," *Journal of Applied Psychology,* 1977, *62,* 288–294; R. L. Dipboye, H. L. Fromkin, and K. Wiback, "Relative Importance of Applicant Sex, Attractiveness and Scholastic Standing in Evaluation of Job Applicant Résumés," *Journal of Applied Psychology,* 1975, *60,* 39–43.

17. R. E. Carlson, *op. cit.;* R. L. Dipboye, H. L. Fromkin, and K. Wiback, *op. cit.*

18. For the first study see D. Landy and H. Sigall, "Beauty Is Talent: Task Evaluation as a Function of the Performer's Physical Attractiveness," *Journal of Personality and Social Psychology,* 1974, *29,* 299–304. For the second study see S. S. Fugita, P. E. Panek, L. L. Balascoe, and I. Newman, "Attractiveness, Level of Accomplishment, Sex of Rater, and the Evaluation of Feminine Competence," *Representative Research in Social Psychology,*

1977, *8*, 1–11. For the third study see R. Anderson and S. A. Nida, "Effect of Physical Attractiveness on Opposite- and Same-Sex Evaluations," *Journal of Personality*, 1978, *26*, 401–413.

19. For a man with a woman see M. L. Meiners and J. P. Sheposh, "Beauty or Brains: Which Image for Your Mate?" *Personality and Social Psychology Bulletin*, 1977, *3*, 262–265; H. Sigall and D. Landy, "Radiating Beauty: Effects of Having a Physically Attractive Partner on Person Perception," *Journal of Personality and Social Psychology*, 1973, *28*, 218–224. For a woman with a man see R. E. Geiselman, N. A. Haight, and L. G. Kimata, "Context Effects on the Perceived Physical Attractiveness of Faces," *Journal of Experimental Social Psychology*, 1984, *20*, 409–424; M. H. Kernis and L. Wheeler, "Beautiful Friends and Ugly Strangers: Radiation and Contrast Effects in Perceptions of Same-Sex Friends," *Personality and Social Psychology Bulletin*, 1981, 7, 617–620; K. Strane and C. Watts, "Female Judged by Attractiveness of Partner," *Perceptual and Motor Skills*, 1977, *45*, 225–226.

20. J. Hartnett and D. Elder, "The Princess and the Nice Frog: Study in Person Perception," *Perceptual and Motor Skills*, 1973, *37*, 863–866; D. Bar-Tal and L. Saxe, "Perceptions of Similarly and Dissimilarly Attractive Couples and Individuals," *Journal of Personality and Social Psychology*, 1976, *33*, 772–781; D. Bar-Tal and L. Saxe, "Physical Attractiveness and Its Relationship to Sex-Role Stereotyping," *Sex Roles*, 1976, *2*, 123–133.

21. For the first survey see M. G. Efran, "The Effect of Physical Appearance on the Judgment of Guilt, Interpersonal Attraction, and Severity of Recommended Punishment," *Journal of Research in Personality*, 1974, *8*, 45–54. For the second survey see R. A. Kulka and J. B. Kessler, "Is Justice Really Blind?—The Influence of Litigant Physical Attractiveness on Juridical Judgment," *Journal of Applied Social Psychology*, 1978, *8*, 366–381. For car theft see N. L. Kerr, "Beautiful and Blameless: Effects of Victim Attractiveness and Responsibility on Mock Jurors' Verdicts," *Personality and Social Psychology Bulletin*, 1978, *4*, 479–482.

22. H. Sigall and N. Ostrove, "Beautiful but Dangerous: Effects of Offender Attractiveness and Nature of Crime on Juridic Judgment," *Journal of Personality and Social Psychology*, 1975, *31*, 410–414.

23. For burglary case see M. R. Solomon and J. Schopler, "The Relationship of Physical Attractiveness and Punitiveness: Is the Linearity Assumption out of Line?" *Personality and Social Psychology Bulletin*, 1978, *4*, 483–486. For rape cases see S. R. Deitz, M. Littman, and B. J. Bently, *op. cit.*; C. Seligman, J. Brickman, and D. Koulack, "Rape and Physical Attractiveness: Assigning Responsibility to Victims," *Journal of Personality*, 1977, *45*, 554–563.

24. R. M. Friend and M. Vinson, "Leaning Over Backwards: Jurors' Responses to Defendants' Attractiveness," *Journal of Communication*, 1974, *24*, 124–129.

25. M. G. Efran and E. W. J. Patterson, "Voters Vote Beautiful: The Effect of Physical Appearance on a National Election," *Canadian Journal of Behavioral Science*," 1974, *6*, 352–356.

26. P. A. Goldberg, M. Gottesdiener, and P. R. Abramson, "Another Put-Down of Women?: Perceived Attractiveness as a Function of Support for the Feminist Movement," *Journal of Personality and Social Psychology,* 1975, *32,* 113–115.

27. On the interview see T. F. Cash, J. A. Kehr, J. Polyson, and V. Freeman, "Role of Physical Attractiveness in Peer Attribution of Psychological Disturbance," *Journal of Consulting and Clinical Psychology,* 1977, *45,* 987–993. On the photograph study see W. H. Jones, R. O. Hansson, and A. L. Phillips, "Physical Attractiveness and Judgments of Psychopathology," *Journal of Social Psychology,* 1978, *105,* 79–84.

28. On judgment by others see R. Barocas and F. L. Vance, "Physical Appearance and Personal Adjustment Counseling," *Journal of Counseling Psychology,* 1974, *21,* 96–100; R. O. Hansson and B. J. Duffield, "Physical Attractiveness and the Attribution of Epilepsy," *Journal of Social Psychology,* 1976, *99,* 233–240; S. E. Hobfoll and L. A. Penner, "Effect of Physical Attractiveness on Therapists' Initial Judgments of a Person's Self-Concept," *Journal of Consulting and Clinical Psychology,* 1978, *46,* 200–201; P. J. Martin, M. H. Friedmeyer, and J. E. Moore, "Pretty Patient—Healthy Patient? A Study of Physical Attractiveness and Psychopathology," *Journal of Clinical Psychology,* 1977, *33,* 990–994; A. G. Miller, "Social Perception of Internal-External Control," *Psychological Reports,* 1970, *30,* 103–109; T. Napoleon, L. Chassin, and R. D. Young, "A Replication and Extension of 'Physical Attractiveness and Mental Illness'," *Journal of Abnormal Psychology,* 1980, *89,* 250–253. On self-judgment see K. E. O'Grady, "Sex, Physical Attractiveness, and Perceived Risk for Mental Illness," *Journal of Personality and Social Psychology,* 1982, *43,* 1064–1071.

29. T. F. Cash, P. J. Begley, D. A. McCown, and B. C. Weise, "When Counselors Are Heard but Not Seen: Initial Impact of Physical Attractiveness," *Journal of Counseling Psychology,* 1975, *22,* 273–279.

30. K. N. Lewis and W. B. Walsh, "Physical Attractiveness: Its Impact on the Perception of a Female Counselor," *Journal of Counseling Psychology,* 1978, *25,* 210–216; A. M. Vargas and J. G. Borkowski, "Physical Attractiveness and Counseling Skills," *Journal of Counseling Psychology,* 1982, *29,* 246–255; T. F. Cash and J. Kehr, "Influence of Nonprofessional Counselors' Physical Attractiveness and Sex on Perceptions of Counselor Behavior," *Journal of Counseling Psychology,* 1978, *25,* 336–342; T. F. Cash and R. F. Salzbach, "The Beauty of Counseling: Effects of Counselor Physical Attractiveness and Self-Disclosure on Perceptions of Counselor Behavior," *Journal of Counseling Psychology,* 1978, *25,* 283–291.

31. J. A. Carter, "Impressions of Counselors as a Function of Counselor Physical Attractiveness," *Journal of Counseling Psychology,* 1978, *25,* 28–34.

32. P. L. Benson, S. A. Karabenick, and R. M. Lerner, "Pretty Please: The Effects of Physical Attractiveness, Race, and Sex on Receiving Help," *Journal of Experimental Social Psychology,* 1976, *12,* 409–415.

33. On the dime study see R. Sroufe, A. Chaikin, R. Cook, and V. Freeman, "The Effects of Physical Attractiveness on Honesty: A Socially Desirable Response," *Personality and Social Psychology Bulletin*, 1977, *3*, 59–62. On the letter study see D. W. Wilson, "Helping Behavior and Physical Attractiveness," *Journal of Social Psychology*, 1978, *104*, 313–314. On the tetanus shot study see S. G. West and T. J. Brown, "Physical Attractiveness, the Severity of the Emergency and Helping: A Field Experiment and Interpersonal Simulation," *Journal of Experimental Social Psychology*, 1975, *11*, 531–538.

34. R. J. Pellegrini, R. A. Hicks, S. Meyers-Winton, and B. G. Antal, "Physical Attractiveness and Self-Disclosure in Mixed-Sex Dyads," *Psychological Record*, 1978, *28*, 509–516; L. E. Brundage, V. J. Derlega, and T. F. Cash, "The Effects of Physical Attractiveness and Need for Approval on Self-Disclosure," *Personality and Social Psychology Bulletin*, 1977, *3*, 63–66; C. C. Kunin and M. J. Rodin, "The Interactive Effects of Counselor Gender, Physical Attractiveness and Status on Client Self-Disclosure," *Journal of Clinical Psychology*, 1982, *38*, 84–90.

35. On speed limits see M. Snyder and M. Rothbart, "Communicator Attractiveness and Opinion Change," *Canadian Journal of Behavioral Science*, 1971, *3*, 377–387. On the petition see S. Chaiken, "Communicator Physical Attractiveness and Persuasion," *Journal of Personality and Social Psychology*, 1979, *37*, 1387–1397; J. Horai, N. Naccari, and E. Fatoullah, "The Effects of Expertise and Physical Attractiveness upon Opinion Agreement and Liking," *Sociometry*, 1974, *37*, 601–606. On messages without thought see J. E. Maddux and R. W. Rogers, "Effects of Source Expertness, Physical Attractiveness, and Supporting Arguments on Persuasion: A Case of Brains over Beauty," *Journal of Personality and Social Psychology*, 1980, *39*, 235–244; R. Norman, "When What Is Said Is Important: A Comparison of Expert and Attractive Sources," *Journal of Experimental Social Psychology*, 1976, *12*, 294–300; S. R. Pallak, "Salience of a Communicator's Physical Attractiveness and Persuasion: A Heuristic Versus Systematic Processing Interpretation," *Social Cognition*, 1983, *2*, 158–170; S. R. Pallak, E. Murroni, and J. Koch, "Communicator Attractiveness and Expertise, Emotional Versus Rational Appeals, and Persuasion: A Heuristic Versus Systematic Processing Interpretation," *Social Cognition*, 1983, *2*, 122–141.

36. H. Sigall, R. Page, and A. C. Brown, "Effort Expenditure as a Function of Evaluation and Evaluator Attractiveness," *Representative Research in Social Psychology*, 1971, *2*, 19–25; H. Sigall and E. Aronson, "Liking for an Evaluator as a Function of Her Physical Attractiveness and Nature of the Evaluations," *Journal of Experimental Social Psychology*, 1969, *5*, 93–100; A. Kahn, J. Hottes, and W. L. Davis, "Cooperation and Optimal Responding in the Prisoner's Dilemma Game: Effects of Sex and Physical Attractiveness," *Journal of Personality and Social Psychology*, 1971, *17*, 267–279.

37. M. Snyder, E. D. Tanke, and E. Berscheid, *op. cit.*

38. On the study with children see K. K. Dion and E. Berscheid, "Physical Attractiveness and Peer Perception Among Children," *Sociometry*," 1974, *37*, 1–12; R. M. Lerner and J. V. Lerner, "Effects of Age, Sex, and Physical Attractiveness on Child-Peer Relations, Academic Performance, and Elementary School Adjustment," *Developmental Psychol-*

ogy, 1977, *13,* 585–590; L. E. Styczynski and J. H. Langlois, "The Effects of Familiarity on Behavioral Stereotypes Associated with Physical Attractiveness in Young Children," *Child Development,* 1977, *48,* 1137–1141. On the study with adolescent boys see R. E. Kleck, S. A. Richardson, and L. Ronald, "Physical Appearance Cues and Interpersonal Attraction in Children," *Child Development,* 1974, *45,* 305–310. On the study with fifth and eleventh graders see N. Cavior and P. R. Dokecki, "Physical Attractiveness, Perceived Attitude Similarity, and Academic Achievement as Contributors to Interpersonal Attraction Among Adolescents," *Developmental Psychology,* 1973, *9,* 44–54. On the study with adolescents see R. B. Felson and G. W. Bohrnstedt, "Are the Good Beautiful or the Beautiful Good?: The Relationship Between Children's Perceptions of Ability and Perceptions of Physical Attractiveness," *Social Psychology Quarterly,* 1979, *42,* 386–392.

39. On the fifth grader see M. M. Clifford and E. Walster, "The Effect of Physical Attractiveness on Teacher Expectations," *Sociology of Education,* 1973, *46,* 248–257. On first graders see M. M. Clifford, "Physical Attractiveness and Academic Performance," *Child Study Journal,* 1975, *5,* 201–209. On test of teachers see R. M. Lerner and J. V. Lerner, *op. cit.*

40. K. K. Dion, "Physical Attractiveness and Evaluation of Children's Transgressions," *Journal of Personality and Social Psychology,* 1972, *24,* 207–213.

41. K. K. Dion, "Children's Physical Attractiveness and Sex as Determinants of Adult Punitiveness," *Developmental Psychology,* 1974, *10,* 772–778.

42. J. Rich, "Effects of Children's Physical Attractiveness on Teachers' Evaluations," *Journal of Educational Psychology,* 1975, *67,* 599–609.

43. On attractive people see M. Dermer and D. L. Thiel, "When Beauty May Fail," *Journal of Personality and Social Psychology,* 1975, *31,* 1168–1176; C. L. Kleinke and R. A. Staneski, "First Impressions of Female Bust Size," *Journal of Social Psychology,* 1980, *110,* 123–143; D. Krebs and A. A. Adinolfi, *op. cit.* On attractive women see T. F. Cash, "The Interface of Sexism and Beautyism: A Review," mimeographed paper, Old Dominion University, 1982; C. L. Kleinke, R. A. Staneski, and D. E. Berger, *op. cit.;* C. L. Kleinke, R. A. Staneski, and S. L. Pipp, *op. cit.;* L. Scherwitz and R. Helmreich, "Interactive Effects of Eye Contact and Verbal Content on Interpersonal Attraction," *Journal of Personality and Social Psychology,* 1973, *25,* 6–14; T. F. Cash and R. F. Salzbach, *op. cit.;* C. L. Kleinke and M. L. Kahn, "Perceptions of Self-Disclosers: Effects of Sex and Physical Attractiveness," *Journal of Personality,* 1980, *48,* 190–205.

44. G. Maruyama and N. Miller, "Physical Attractiveness and Personality," in B. A. Maher and W. B. Maher (eds.), *Progress in Experimental Personality Research,* Vol. 10 (New York: Academic Press, 1981); S. Sussman, K. T. Mueser, B. W. Grau, and P. R. Yarnold, "Stability of Females' Facial Attractiveness During Childhood," *Journal of Personality and Social Psychology,* 1983, *44,* 1231–1233. See also G. R. Adams, "Physical Attractiveness Research: Toward a Developmental and Social Psychology of Beauty," *Human Development,* 1977, *20,* 217–239.

45. W. Goldman and P. Lewis, "Beautiful Is Good: Evidence that the Physically Attract-ive are More Socially Skillful," *Journal of Experimental Social Psychology,* 1977, *13,* 125–130; P. A. Pilkonis, "The Behavioral Consequences of Shyness," *Journal of Personality,* 1977, *45,* 596–611.

46. On men see H. T. Reis, J. Nezlek, and L. Wheeler, "Physical Attractiveness in So-cial Interaction," *Journal of Personality and Social Psychology,* 1980, *38,* 604–617; H. T. Reis, L. Wheeler, N. Spiegel, M. H. Kernis, J. Nezlek, and M. Perri, "Physical Attractiveness in Social Interaction: II. Why Does Appearance Affect Social Experience?" *Journal of Per-sonality and Social Psychology,* 1982, *43,* 979–996. On women see D. S. Glenwick, L. A. Jason, and D. Elman, "Physical Attractiveness and Social Contact in the Singles Bar," *Journal of Social Psychology,* 1978, *105,* 311–312.

47. D. J. Jackson and T. L. Huston, "Physical Attractiveness and Assertiveness," *Journal of Social Psychology,* 1975, *96,* 79–84.

48. T. F. Cash and D. Soloway, "Self-Disclosure Correlates of Physical Attractiveness: An Exploratory Study," *Psychological Reports,* 1975, *36,* 579–586.

49. K. K. Dion and S. Stein, "Physical Attractiveness and Interpersonal Influence," *Journal of Experimental Social Psychology,* 1978, *14,* 97–108.

50. S. Chaiken, *op. cit.*

51. D. T. Larrance and M. Zuckerman, "Facial Attractiveness and Vocal Likability as Determinants of Nonverbal Sending Skills," *Journal of Personality,* 1981, *49,* 349–362.

52. G. R. Kaats and K. E. Davis, "The Dynamics of Sexual Behavior of College Stu-dents," *Journal of Marriage and the Family,* 1970, *32,* 390–399; E. W. Mathes and A. Kahn, "Physical Attractiveness, Happiness, Neuroticism, and Self-Esteem," *Journal of Psychology,* 1975, *90,* 27–30; G. R. Adams, "Physical Attractiveness, Personality, and Social Reactions to Peer Pressure," *Journal of Psychology,* 1977, *96,* 287–296; E. Berscheid, E. Walster, and R. Campbell, "Grow Old Along with Me," mimeographed paper, University of Minne-sota, 1972.

53. A. Farina, E. H. Fischer, S. Sherman, W. T. Smith, T. Groh, and P. Mermin, "Phys-ical Attractiveness and Mental Illness," *Journal of Abnormal Psychology,* 1977, *86,* 510–517.

54. S. Hansell, J. Sparacino, and D. Ronchi, "Physical Attractiveness and Blood Pressure: Sex and Age Differences," *Personality and Social Psychology Bulletin,* 1982, *8,* 113–121.

55. N. Cavior and I. R. Howard, "Facial Attractiveness and Juvenile Delinquency Among Black and White Offenders," *Journal of Abnormal Child Psychology,* 1973, *1,* 202–213; J. H. Langlois and A. C. Downs, "Peer Relations as a Function of Physical Attractiveness: The Eye of the Beholder or Behavioral Reality?" *Child Development,* 1979, *50,* 409–418.

56. On people see R. Anderson, "Physical Attractiveness and Locus of Control," *Journal of Social Psychology,* 1978, *105,* 213–216; T. F. Cash and P. J. Begley, "Internal-External

Control, Achievement Orientation and Physical Attractiveness of College Students," *Psychological Reports,* 1976, *38,* 1205–1206; T. F. Cash and E. Smith, "Physical Attractiveness and Personality Among American College Students," *Journal of Psychology,* 1982, *111,* 183–191; J. Shea, S. M. Crossman, and G. R. Adams, "Physical Attractiveness and Personality Development," *Journal of Psychology,* 1978, *99,* 59–62. On men see D. Krebs and A. A. Adinolfi, "Physical Attractiveness, Social Relations, and Personality Style," *Journal of Personality and Social Psychology,* 1975, *31,* 245–253. On children see G. Maruyama and N. Miller, *op. cit.*

57. On children see M. M. Clifford, *op. cit.;* G. Maruyama and N. Miller, *op. cit.* On college students see J. Sparacino and S. Hansell, "Physical Attractiveness and Academic Performance: Beauty Is Not Always Talent," *Journal of Personality,* 1979, *47,* 447–469.

58. P. L. Benson and S. Vincent, "Development and Validation of the Sexist Attitudes Toward Women Scale (SATWS)," *Psychology of Women Quarterly,* 1980, *5,* 276–291; S. M. Andersen and S. L. Bem, "Sex Typing in Dyadic Interaction: Individual Differences in Responsiveness to Physical Attractiveness," *Journal of Personality and Social Psychology,* 1981, *41,* 74–86; J. C. Touhey, "Sex-Role Stereotyping and Individual Differences in Liking for the Physically Attractive," *Social Psychology Quarterly,* 1979, *42,* 285–289.

59. K. J. Gergen, "Social Psychology as History," *Journal of Personality and Social Psychology,* 1973, *26,* 309–320.

60. On self-esteem see S. J. Morse, J. Gruzen, and H. T. Reis, "The 'Eye of the Beholder': A Neglected Variable in the Study of Physical Attractiveness," *Journal of Personality,* 1976, *44,* 209–225; S. J. Morse, H. T. Reis, J. Gruzen, and E. Wolff, "The 'Eye of the Beholder': Determinants of Physical Attractiveness Judgments in the U. S. and South Africa," *Journal of Personality,* 1974, *42,* 528–542. On experience see D. T. Kenrick and S. E. Gutierres, "Contrast Effects and Judgments of Physical Attractiveness: When Beauty Becomes a Social Problem," *Journal of Personality and Social Psychology,* 1980, *38,* 131–140.

61. On costs see R. J. Pellegrini, R. A. Hicks, and S. Meyers-Winton, "Self-Evaluations of Attractiveness and Perceptions of Mate-Attraction in the Interpersonal Marketplace," *Perceptual and Motor Skills,* 1980, *50,* 812–814. On availability see J. W. Pennebaker, M. A. Dyer, R. S. Caulkins, D. L. Litowitz, P. L. Ackreman, B. D. Anderson, and K. M. McGraw, "Don't the Girls Get Prettier at Closing Time: A Country and Western Application to Psychology," *Personality and Social Psychology Bulletin,* 1979, *5,* 122–125; M. Gilley, "Don't the Girls All Get Prettier at Closing Time," in *The Best of Mickey Gilley,* Vol. 2, 1975, Columbia. Written by Baker Knight, Singleton Music Company: BMI; S. Sprecher, J. DeLamater, N. Neuman, M. Neuman, P. Kahn, D. Orbuch, and K. McKinney, "Asking Questions in Bars: The Girls (and Boys) May Not Get Prettier at Closing Time and Other Interesting Results," *Personality and Social Psychology Bulletin,* 1984, *10,* 482–488. See also S. A. Nida and J. Koon, "They Get Better Looking at Closing Time Around Here, Too," *Psychological Reports,* 1983, *52,* 657–658.

62. J. W. Thibaut and H. W. Riecken, "Some Determinants and Consequences of the Perception of Social Causality," *Journal of Personality,* 1955, *24,* 113–133; J. Mills and

E. Aronson, "Opinion Change as a Function of the Communicator's Attractiveness and Desire to Influence," *Journal of Personality and Social Psychology,* 1965, *1,* 173–177; M. R. Solomon and J. Schopler, *op. cit.*

CHAPTER 4

1. E. Berscheid and E. Walster, "Physical Attractiveness," in L. Berkowitz (ed.), *Advances in Experimental Social Psychology,* Vol. 7 (New York: Academic Press, 1974).

2. T. F. Cash and D. Soloway, "Self-Disclosure Correlates of Physical Attractiveness: An Exploratory Study," *Psychological Reports,* 1975, *36,* 579–586; W. Goldman and P. Lewis, "Beautiful Is Good: Evidence that the Physically Attractive Are More Socially Skillful," *Journal of Experimental Social Psychology,* 1977, *13,* 125–130; B. I. Murstein and P. Christy, "Physical Attractiveness and Marriage Adjustment in Middle-Aged Couples," *Journal of Personality and Social Psychology,* 1976, *34,* 537–542; W. Stroebe, C. A. Insko, V. D. Thompson, and B. D. Layton, "Effects of Physical Attractiveness, Attitude Similarity, and Sex on Various Aspects of Interpersonal Attraction," *Journal of Personality and Social Psychology,* 1971, *18,* 79–91.

3. C. L. Kleinke, "Self-Ratings of Physical Attractiveness by 100 College Men and 100 College Women," unpublished data, Boston College, 1980.

4. F. A. Perrin, "Physical Attractiveness and Repulsiveness," *Journal of Experimental Psychology,* 1921, *4,* 203–217.

5. R. M. Lerner and S. A. Karabenick, "Physical Attractiveness, Body Attitudes, and Self-Concept in Late Adolescents," *Journal of Youth and Adolescence,* 1974, *3,* 307–316; R. M. Lerner, S. A. Karabenick, and J. L. Stuart, "Relations Among Physical Attractiveness, Body Attitudes, and Self-Concept of Male and Female College Students," *Journal of Psychology,* 1973, *85,* 119–129.

6. On men see J. Liggett, *The Human Face* (New York: Stein and Day, 1974), p. 146. On women see E. Wagatsuma and C. L. Kleinke, "Ratings of Facial Beauty by Asian-American and Caucasian Females," *Journal of Social Psychology,* 1979, *109,* 299–300.

7. On color preferences see S. Feinman and G. W. Gill, "Sex Differences in Physical Attractiveness Preferences," *Journal of Social Psychology,* 1978, *105,* 43–52. On features see J. C. McCullers and J. Staat, "Draw an Ugly Man: An Inquiry into the Dimensions of Physical Attractiveness," *Personality and Social Psychology Bulletin,* 1974, *1,* 33–35. See also J. F. Cross and J. Cross, "Age, Sex, Race, and the Perception of Facial Beauty," *Developmental Psychology,* 1971, *5,* 433–439; J. T. Milord, "Aesthetic Aspects of Faces: A (Somewhat) Phenomenological Analysis Using Multidimensional Scaling Methods," *Journal of Personality and Social Psychology,* 1978, *36,* 205–216. On facial "character" see L. L. Light, "Recognition Memory for Typical and Unusual Faces," *Journal of Experimental Psychology: Human Learning and Memory,* 1979, *5,* 212–228; L. L. Light, S. Hollander, and F. K. Stuart, "Why Attractive People Are Harder to Remember," *Personality and Social Psychology Bulletin,* 1981, *7,* 269–276.

8. E. Wagatsuma and C. L. Kleinke, op. cit.; J. Liggett, op. cit.

9. On children see H. C. Foot, A. J. Chapman, and J. R. Smith, "Friendship and Social Responsiveness in Boys and Girls," Journal of Personality and Social Psychology, 1977, 35, 401–411. On college students see A. R. D'Augelli, "Nonverbal Behavior of Helpers in Initial Helping Interactions," Journal of Counseling Psychology, 1974, 21, 360–363. On college women see S. Thayer and W. Schiff, "Eye-Contact, Facial Expression, and the Experience of Time," Journal of Social Psychology, 1975, 95, 117–124. On inducing liking see H. M. Rosenfeld, "Instrumental Affiliative Functions of Facial and Gestural Expressions," Journal of Personality and Social Psychology, 1966, 4, 65–72. On roles see R. M. Eisler, M. Hersen, P. M. Miller, and E. B. Blanchard, "Situational Determinants of Assertive Behaviors," Journal of Consulting and Clinical Psychology, 1975, 43, 330–340. On expressing popular views see D. O. Jorgenson, "Nonverbal Assessment of Attitudinal Affect with the Smile Return Technique," Journal of Social Psychology, 1978, 106, 173–179. On enhancing conversation see L. J. Brunner, "Smiles Can Be Back Channels," Journal of Personality and Social Psychology, 1979, 37, 728–734.

10. J. T. Milord, op. cit.; K. T. Mueser, B. W. Grau, S. Sussman, and A. J. Rosen, "You're Only as Pretty as You Feel: Facial Expression as a Determinant of Physical Attractiveness," Journal of Personality and Social Psychology, 1984, 46, 469–478; R. L. Terry, "Further Evidence on Components of Facial Attractiveness," Perceptual and Motor Skills, 1977, 45, 130. See also C. L. Kleinke and J. H. Walton, "Influence of Reinforced Smiling on Affective Responses in an Interview," Journal of Personality and Social Psychology, 1982, 42, 557–565.

11. On the newscaster see J. W. Tankard, J. S. McCleneghan, V. Ganju, E. B. Lee, C. Olkes, and D. DuBose, "Nonverbal Cues and Television News," Journal of Communication, 1977, 27, 106–111. On electric shocks see J. C. Savitsky, C. E. Izard, W. E. Kotsch, and L. Christy, "Aggressor's Response to the Victim's Facial Expression of Emotion," Journal of Research in Personality, 1974, 7, 346–357.

12. On assertiveness see R. M. Eisler, M. Hersen, P. M. Miller, and E. B. Blanchard, op. cit. On women see R. M. Adams and B. Kirkevold, "Looking, Smiling, Laughing, and Moving in Restaurants: Sex and Age Differences," Environmental Psychology and Nonverbal Behavior, 1978, 3, 117–121; I. H. Frieze and S. J. Ramsey, "Nonverbal Maintenance of Traditional Sex Roles," Journal of Social Issues, 1976, 32, 133–141. On college students see C. C. McClintock and R. G. Hunt, "Nonverbal Indicators of Affect and Deception in an Interview Setting," Journal of Applied Social Psychology, 1975, 5, 54–67. On psychiatric patients see L. A. Fairbanks, M. T. McGuire, and C. J. Harris, "Nonverbal Interaction of Patients and Therapists During Psychiatric Interviews," Journal of Abnormal Psychology, 1982, 91, 109–119.

13. On moods see A. Schiffenbauer, "Effect of Observer's Emotional State on Judgments of the Emotional State of Others," Journal of Personality and Social Psychology, 1974, 30, 31–35. On expectations see A. Schiffenbauer and A. Babineau, "Sex Role Stereotypes and the Spontaneous Attribution of Emotion," Journal of Research in Personality, 1976, 10, 137–145.

14. J. M. Haviland, "Sex-Related Pragmatics in Infants' Nonverbal Communication," *Journal of Communication*, 1977, *27*, 80–84.

15. P. Ekman, W. V. Friesen, and P. C. Ellsworth, *Emotion in the Human Face* (Elmsford, N.Y.: Pergamon Press, 1972).

16. *Ibid.;* P. Ekman, "Universals and Cultural Differences in Facial Expressions of Emotion," in J. Cole (ed.), *Nebraska Symposium on Motivation* (Lincoln: University of Nebraska Press, 1972).

17. *Ibid.*

18. *Ibid.*

19. G. Gubar, "Recognition of Human Facial Expressions Judged Live in a Laboratory Setting," *Journal of Personality and Social Psychology*, 1966, *4*, 108–111.

20. J. T. Lanzetta and R. E. Kleck, "Encoding and Decoding of Nonverbal Affect in Humans," *Journal of Personality and Social Psychology*, 1970, *16*, 12–19. See also C. I. Notarius and R. W. Levenson, "Expressive Tendencies and Physiological Response to Stress," *Journal of Personality and Social Psychology*, 1979, *37*, 1204–1210.

21. On slot machines see R. E. Miller, A. J. Giannini, and J. M. Levine, "Nonverbal Communication in Man with a Cooperative Conditioning Task," *Journal of Social Psychology*, 1977, *103*, 101–113. On slides and television see R. W. Buck, R. E. Miller, and W. F. Caul, "Sex, Personality, and Physiological Variables in the Communication of Affect via Facial Expression," *Journal of Personality and Social Psychology*, 1974, *30*, 587–596; R. W. Buck, V. J. Savin, R. E. Miller, and W. F. Caul, "Communication of Affect through Facial Expressions in Humans," *Journal of Personality and Social Psychology*, 1972, *23*, 362–371; M. Zuckerman, J. A. Hall, R. S. DeFrank, and R. Rosenthal, "Encoding and Decoding of Spontaneous and Posed Facial Expressions," *Journal of Personality and Social Psychology*, 1976, *34*, 966–977.

22. D. E. Bugental, L. R. Love, and R. M. Gianetto, "Perfidious Feminine Faces," *Journal of Personality and Social Psychology*, 1971, *17*, 314–318; D. E. Bugental, J. W. Kaswan, and L. R. Love, "Perception of Contradictory Meanings Conveyed by Verbal and Nonverbal Channels," *Journal of Personality and Social Psychology*, 1970, *16*, 647–655.

23. D. E. Bugental, L. R. Love, J. W. Kaswan, and C. April, "Verbal-Nonverbal Conflict in Parental Messages to Normal and Disturbed Children," *Journal of Abnormal Psychology*, 1971, 77, 6–10.

24. H. S. Friedman, "The Interactive Effects of Facial Expressions of Emotion and Verbal Messages on Perceptions of Affective Meaning," *Journal of Experimental Social Psychology*, 1979, *15*, 453–469.

25. R. S. Feldman and J. B. White, "Detecting Deception in Children," *Child Development*, 1980, *30*, 121–128.

26. P. Ekman and W. V. Friesen, "Felt, False, and Miserable Smiles," *Journal of Nonverbal Behavior*, 1982, *6*, 238–252; R. E. Riggio and H. S. Friedman, "Individual Differences and Cues to Deception," *Journal of Personality and Social Psychology*, 1983, *45*, 899–915; M. Zuckerman, R. S. DeFrank, J. A. Hall, D. T. Larrance, and R. Rosenthal, "Facial and Vocal Cues of Deception and Honesty," *Journal of Experimental Social Psychology*, 1979, *15*, 378–396. See also B. M. DePaulo and R. Rosenthal, "Telling Lies," *Journal of Personality and Social Psychology*, 1979, *37*, 1713–1722.

27. P. Ekman and W. V. Friesen, "Detecting Deception from the Body or Face," *Journal of Personality and Social Psychology*, 1974, *29*, 288–298; P. Ekman, W. V. Friesen, and K. R. Scherer, "Body Movement and Voice Pitch in Deceptive Interaction," *Semiotica*, 1976, *16*, 23–27. On first-grade children see R. S. Feldman, L. Jenkins, and O. Popoola, "Detection of Deception in Adults and Children via Facial Expressions," *Child Development*, 1979, *50*, 350–355. On convincing others see B. M. DePaulo and R. Rosenthal, *op. cit.*; J. P. Forgas, K. V. O'Connor, and S. L. Morris, "Smile and Punishment: The Effects of Facial Expression on Responsibility Attribution by Groups and Individuals," *Personality and Social Psychology Bulletin*, 1983, *9*, 587–596. See also B. M. DePaulo, K. Lanier, and T. Davis, "Detecting the Deceit of the Motivated Liar," *Journal of Personality and Social Psychology*, 1983, *45*, 1096–1103.

28. On body language and tone of voice see B. M. DePaulo, R. Rosenthal, R. A. Eisenstat, P. L. Rogers, and S. Finkelstein, "Decoding Discrepent Nonverbal Cues," *Journal of Personality and Social Psychology*, 1978, *36*, 313–323; M. Zuckerman, N. H. Spiegel, B. M. DePaulo, and R. Rosenthal, "Nonverbal Strategies for Decoding Deception," *Journal of Nonverbal Behavior*, 1982, *6*, 171–187. On accuracy see M. Zuckerman, R. Koestner, and A. O. Alton, "Learning to Detect Deception," *Journal of Personality and Social Psychology*, 1984, *46*, 519–528. On lie detection see B. M. DePaulo and R. Rosenthal, *op. cit.*; G. Littlepage and T. Pineault, "Verbal, Facial, and Paralinguistic Cues to the Identification of Truth and Lying," *Personality and Social Psychology Bulletin*, 1978, *4*, 461–464; B. M. DePaulo and R. Rosenthal, *op. cit.*; M. Zuckerman, R. Loestner, M. J. Colella, and A. O. Alton, "Anchoring in the Detection of Deception and Leakage," *Journal of Personality and Social Psychology*, 1984, *47*, 301–311.

29. P. Ekman and W. V. Friesen, "Felt, False, and Miserable Smiles." See also P. Ekman and W. V. Friesen, "Measuring Facial Movement," *Environmental Psychology and Nonverbal Behavior*, 1976, *1*, 56–75; P. Ekman and W. V. Friesen, *Facial Action Coding System* (Palo Alto, Calif.: Consulting Psychologists Press, 1978).

30. R. M. Lerner and S. A. Karabenick, *op. cit.*; R. M. Lerner, S. A. Karabenick, and J. L. Stuart, *op. cit.*

31. K. T. Strongman and C. J. Hart, "Stereotyped Reactions to Body Build," *Psychological Reports*, 1968, *23*, 1175–1178; W. Wells and B. Siegel, "Stereotyped Somatypes," *Psychological Reports*, 1961, *8*, 77–78.

32. On ratings by school boys see J. R. Staffieri, "A Study of Social Stereotypes of Body Image in Children," *Journal of Personality and Social Psychology*, 1967, *7*, 101–104. On rat-

ings by males see R. M. Lerner, "The Development of Stereotyped Expectancies of Body Build Behavior Relations," *Child Development,* 1969, *40,* 137–141.

33. J. B. Cortés and F. M. Gatti, "Physique and Self-Description of Temperament," *Journal of Consulting Psychology,* 1965, *29,* 432–439.

34. P. J. Lavrakas, "Female Preferences for Male Physiques," *Journal of Research in Personality,* 1975, *9,* 324–334.

35. A. G. Gitter, J. Lomranz, and L. Saxe, "Factors Affecting Perceived Attractiveness of Male Physiques by American and Israeli Students," *Journal of Social Psychology,* 1982, *118,* 167–175.

36. R. A. Staneski, R. J. Pellegrini, and B. G. Antal, "Effects of Body Build and Attitude Similarity on Interpersonal Attraction," paper presented at the Meeting of the Western Psychological Association, Sacramento, Calif., 1975.

37. On men's preferences see J. S. Wiggins, N. Wiggins, and J. C. Conger, "Correlates of Heterosexual Somatic Preference," *Journal of Personality and Social Psychology,* 1968, *10,* 82–90. On women's preferences see S. B. Beck, C. I. Ward-Hull, and P. M. McLear, "Variables Related to Women's Somatic Preferences of the Male and Female Body," *Journal of Personality and Social Psychology,* 1976, *43,* 1200–1210.

38. On college students see A. G. Gitter, J. Lomranz, L. Saxe, and Y. Bar-Tal, "Perceptions of Female Physique Characteristics by American and Israeli Students," *Journal of Social Psychology,* 1983, *121,* 7–13. On women see S. M. Jourard and P. F. Secord, "Body-Cathexis and the Ideal Female Figure," *Journal of Abnormal and Social Psychology,* 1955, *50,* 243–246.

39. C. L. Kleinke and R. A. Staneski, "First Impressions of Female Bust Size," *Journal of Social Psychology,* 1980, *110,* 123–134.

40. W. J. Cahnman, "The Stigma of Obesity," *Sociological Quarterly,* 1968, *9,* 283–299.

41. On school children see S. A. Richardson, N. Goodman, A. H. Hastorf, and S. M. Dornbusch, "Cultural Uniformity in Reactions to Physical Disabilities," *American Sociological Review,* 1961, *26,* 241–247. On adults see N. Goodman, S. M. Dornbusch, S. A. Richardson, and A. H. Hastorf, "Variant Reactions to Physical Disabilities," *American Sociological Review,* 1968, *28,* 429–435. On children see R. M. Lerner, S. A. Karabenick, and M. Meisels, "Effect of Age and Sex on the Development of Personal Space Schemata Towards Body Build," *Journal of Genetic Psychology,* 1975, *127,* 91–101; R. M. Lerner, J. Venning, and J. R. Knapp, "Age and Sex Effects on Personal Space Schemata Toward Body Build in Late Childhood," *Developmental Psychology,* 1975, *11,* 855–856.

42. R. M. Lerner and E. Gellert, "Body Build Identification, Preference, and Aversion in Children," *Developmental Psychology,* 1969, *1,* 456–462; R. M. Lerner and C. Schroeder, "Physique Identification, Preference, and Aversion in Kindergarten Children," *Developmental Psychology,* 1971, *5,* 538. See also R. M. Lerner and S. J. Korn, "The Development of Body Build Stereotypes in Males," *Child Development,* 1972, *43,* 908–920.

43. On college students see P. R. Wilson, "Perceptual Distortion of Height as a Function of Ascribed Academic Status," *Journal of Social Psychology*, 1968, *74*, 97–102. On student nurses see W. D. Dannenmaier and F. J. Thuman, "Authority Status as a Factor in Perceptual Distortion of Size," *Journal of Social Psychology*, 1964, *63*, 361–365.

44. On Kennedy-Nixon election see H. H. Kassarjian, "Voting Intention and Political Perception," *Journal of Psychology*, 1963, *56*, 85–88. On Johnson see C. Ward, "Own Height, Sex, and Liking in the Judgment of the Heights of Others," *Journal of Personality*, 1967, *35*, 381–401.

45. P. R. Bleda, "Perception of Height as a Linear Function of Attitude Similarity," *Psychonomic Science*, 1972, *27*, 197–198; P. R. Bleda and S. E. Bleda, "Attitude Similarity, Attraction, Perception of Height, and Judgment of Agreement," *Representative Research in Social Psychology*, 1977, *8*, 57–61. See also D. Koulack and J. A. Tuthill, "Height Perception: A Function of Social Distance," *Canadian Journal of Behavioral Science*, 1972, *4*, 50–53.

46. E. E. Rump and P. S. Delin, "Differential Accuracy in the Status-Height Phenomenon and an Experimenter Effect," *Journal of Personality and Social Psychology*, 1973, *28*, 343–347. See also R. M. Lerner and T. Moore, "Sex and Status Effects on Perception of Physical Attractiveness," *Psychological Reports*, 1974, *34*, 1047–1050.

47. M. L. Knapp, *Nonverbal Communication in Human Interaction* (New York: Holt, Rinehart, and Winston, 1978), p. 167.

48. W. Graziano, T. Brothen, and E. Berscheid, "Height and Attraction: Do Men and Women See Eye-to-Eye?" *Journal of Personality*, 1978, *46*, 128–145; A. G. Prieto and M. C. Robbins, "Perceptions of Height and Self-Esteem," *Perceptual and Motor Skills*, 1975, *40*, 395–398.

49. C. L. Kleinke, "Choices by College Students of Ideal Height for an Opposite-Sex Dating Partner," unpublished data, Boston College, 1980.

50. L. B. Rosenfeld and T. G. Plax, "Clothing as Communication," *Journal of Communication*, 1977, *27*, 24–31.

51. P. Hamid, "Changes in Perception as a Function of Dress," *Perceptual and Motor Skills*, 1969, *29*, 191–194; R. D. Coursey, "Clothes Doth Make the Man, in the Eye of the Beholder," *Perceptual and Motor Skills*, 1973, *36*, 1259–1264.

52. S. Amira and S. I. Abramowitz, "Therapeutic Attraction as a Function of Therapist Attire and Office Furnishings," *Journal of Counsulting and Clinical Psychology*, 1979, *47*, 198–200; M. A. Hubble and C. J. Gelso, "Effect of Counselor Attire in an Initial Interview," *Journal of Counseling Psychology*, 1978, *25*, 581–584; B. A. Kerr and D. M. Dell, "Perceived Interviewer Expertness and Attractiveness: Effects of Interviewer Behavior and Attire and Interview Setting," *Journal of Counseling Psychology*, 1976, *23*, 553–556; J. M. Littrell and M. A. Littrell, "Preferences for Counselors: Effects of Counselor Dress and Sex," *Journal of Counseling Psychology*, 1982, *29*, 48–57; M. A. Littrell, J. M. Littrell, and A. Kuznik, "Formal/Informal Dimension in Perceptions of Counselors' Dress," *Per-*

ceptual and Motor Skills, 1981, *53*, 751–757; L. D. Schmidt and S. R. Strong, "'Expert' and 'Inexpert' Counselors," *Journal of Counseling Psychology*, 1970, *17*, 115–118; S. Stillman and H. Resnick, "Does Counselor Attire Matter?" *Journal of Counseling Psychology*, 1972, *19*, 347–348.

53. On pedestrians see M. Lefkowitz, M. Blake, and J. Mouton, "Status Factors in Pedestrian Violation of Traffic Signals," *Journal of Abnormal and Social Psychology*, 1955, *51*, 704–706. On people in stations and airports see L. Bickman, "The Effect of Social Status on the Honesty of Others," *Journal of Social Psychology*, 1971, *85*, 87–92. On requests see C. L. Kleinke, "Effects of Dress on Compliance to Requests in a Field Setting," *Journal of Social Psychology*, 1977, *101*, 223–224; R. S. Schiavo, B. Sherlock, and G. Wicklund, "Effect of Attire on Obtaining Directions," *Psychological Reports*, 1974, *34*, 245–246. On petitions et al. see N. J. Bryant, "Petitioning: Dress Congruence Versus Belief Consistency," *Journal of Applied Social Psychology*, 1975, *5*, 144–149; J. M. Darley and J. Cooper, "The 'Clean for Gene' Phenomenon: The Effects of Students' Appearance on Political Campaigning," *Journal of Applied Social Psychology*, 1972, *2*, 24–33; H. Giles and W. Chavasse, "Communication Length as a Function of Dress Style and Social Status," *Perceptual and Motor Skills*, 1975, *40*, 961–962; C. B. Keasey and C. Thomlinson-Keasey, "Petition Signing in a Naturalistic Setting," *Journal of Social Psychology*, 1973, *89*, 313–314; S. Lambert, "Reactions to Strangers as a Function of Style of Dress," *Perceptual and Motor Skills*, 1972, *35*, 711–712; B. Raymond and R. Unger, "The Apparel Oft Proclaims the Man," *Journal of Social Psychology*, 1972, *87*, 75–82. On librarians see H. W. Kroll and D. K. Moren, "Effect of Appearance on Requests for Help in Libraries," *Psychological Reports*, 1977, *40*, 129–130.

54. L. Bickman, "The Effect of Social Status on the Honesty of Others"; M. Lefkowitz, M. Blake, and J. Mouton, *op. cit.*; C. L. Kleinke, "Effects of Dress on Compliance to Requests in a Field Setting"; B. Raymond and R. Unger, *op. cit.*; R. S. Schiavo, B. Sherlock, and G. Wicklund, *op. cit.*; P. Suedfeld, S. Bochner, and C. Matas, "Petitioner's Attire and Petition Signing by Peace Demonstrators—A Field Experiment," *Journal of Applied Social Psychology*, 1971, *1*, 278–283; T. Emswiller, K. Deaux, and J. E. Willits, "Similarity, Sex, and Requests for Small Favors," *Journal of Applied Social Psychology*, 1971, *1*, 284–291. See also W. E. Hensley, "The Effects of Attire, Location, and Sex on Aiding Behavior: A Similarity Explanation," *Journal of Nonverbal Behavior*, 1981, *6*, 3–11; W. P. Green and H. Giles, "Reactions to a Stranger as a Function of Dress Style: The Tie," *Perceptual and Motor Skills*, 1973, *37*, 676.

55. F. A. Deseran and C. S. Chung, "Appearance, Role-Taking, and Reactions to Deviance: Some Experimental Findings," *Social Psychology Quarterly*, 1979, *42*, 426–430; D. J. Steffensmeier and R. L. Terry, "Deviance and Respectability: An Observational Study of Reactions to Shoplifting," *Social Forces*, 1973, *51*, 417–426.

56. L. Bickman, "The Social Power of a Uniform," *Journal of Applied Social Psychology*, 1974, *4*, 47–61.

57. J. Liggett, *op. cit.*, p. 96.

58. On eight men see R. J. Pellegrini, "Impressions of the Male Personality as a Function of Beardedness," *Psychology,* 1973, *10,* 29–33. On college students see C. T. Kenny and D. Fletcher, "Effects of Beardedness on Person Perception," *Perceptual and Motor Skills,* 1973, *37,* 413–414. On college women see S. Feinman and G. W. Gill, "Females' Response to Males' Beardedness," *Perceptual and Motor Skills,* 1977, *44,* 533–534.

59. G. Thorton, "The Effect of Wearing Glasses upon Judgments of Personality Traits of Persons Seen Briefly," *Journal of Applied Psychology,* 1944, *28,* 203–207; W. Manz and H. E. Lueck, "Influence of Wearing Glasses on Personality Ratings: Crosscultural Validation of an Old Experiment," *Perceptual and Motor Skills,* 1968, *27,* 704; M. Argyle and R. McHenry, "Do Spectacles Really Affect Judgments of Intelligence?" *British Journal of Social and Clinical Psychology,* 1971, *10,* 27–29. See also R. L. Terry and D. L. Kroger, "Effects of Eye Correctives on Ratings of Attractiveness," *Perceptual and Motor Skills,* 1976, *42,* 562; R. L. Terry and C. S. Brady, "Effects of Framed Spectacles and Contact Lenses on Self-Ratings of Facial Attractiveness," *Perceptual and Motor Skills,* 1976, *42,* 789–790.

60. W. McKeachie, "Lipstick as a Determiner of First Impressions of Personality: An Experiment for the General Psychology Course," *Journal of Social Psychology,* 1952, *36,* 241–244.

61. D. H. McBurney, J. M. Levine, and P. H. Cavanaugh, "Psychophysical and Social Ratings of Human Body Odor," *Personality and Social Psychology Bulletin,* 1977, *3,* 135–138.

62. R. A. Baron, "'Sweet Smell of Success?' The Impact of Pleasant Artificial Scents on Evaluations of Job Applicants," *Journal of Applied Psychology,* 1983, *68,* 709–713.

63. R. E. Kleck and A. Strenta, "Perceptions of the Impact of Negatively Valued Physical Characteristics on Social Interaction," *Journal of Personality and Social Psychology,* 1980, *39,* 861–873.

64. R. J. Pellegrini, R. A. Hicks, and S. Meyers-Winton, "Self-Evaluations of Attractiveness and Perceptions of Mate-Attraction in the Interpersonal Marketplace," *Perceptual and Motor Skills,* 1980, *50,* 812–814; P. J. McDonald and V. C. Eilenfield, "Physical Attractiveness and the Approach/Avoidance of Self-Awareness," *Personality and Social Psychology Bulletin,* 1980, *6,* 391–395; H. Sigall and J. Michela, "I'll Bet You Say That to All the Girls: Physical Attractiveness and Reactions to Praise," *Journal of Personality,* 1976, *44,* 611–626.

65. T. F. Cash and D. W. Cash, "Women's Use of Cosmetics: Psychosocial Correlates and Consequences," *International Journal of Cosmetic Science,* 1982, *4,* 1–14; J. A. Graham and A. J. Jouhar, "The Effects of Cosmetics on Person Perception," *International Journal of Cosmetic Science,* 1981, *3,* 199–210; T. F. Cash and D. W. Cash, *op. cit.*

66. T. F. Cash and C. E. Horton, "Aesthetic Surgery: Effects of Rhinoplasty on the Social Perception of Patients by Others," *Plastic and Reconstructive Surgery,* 1983, *72,*

543–548. See also R. L. Kurtzberg, H. Safar, and N. Cavior, "Surgical and Social Rehabilitation of Adult Offenders," *Proceedings of the 76th Annual Convention of the American
Psychological Association,* 1968, *3,* 649–650.

CHAPTER 5

1. D. Archer and R. M. Akert, "Words and Everything Else: Verbal and Nonverbal
Cues in Social Interpretation," *Journal of Personality and Social Psychology,* 1977, *35,*
443–449.

2. P. Ekman and W. V. Friesen, "The Repertoire of Nonverbal Behavior: Categories,
Origins, Usage, and Coding," *Semiotica,* 1969, *1,* 49–98; P. Ekman and W. V. Friesen,
"Hand Movements," *Journal of Communication,* 1972, *22,* 353–374.

3. L. Carmichael, S. Roberts, and N. Wessell, "A Study of the Judgment of Manual
Expression as Presented in Still and Motion Pictures," *Journal of Social Psychology,* 1937, *8,*
115–142. See also S. G. Watson, "Judgment of Emotion From Facial and Contextual Cue
Combinations," *Journal of Personality and Social Psychology,* 1972, *24,* 334–342.

4. H. G. Johnson, P. Ekman, and W. V. Friesen, "Communicative Body Movements:
American Emblems," *Semiotica,* 1975, *15,* 335–353.

5. L. Kumin and M. Lazar, "Gestural Communication in Preschool Children," *Perceptual
and Motor Skills,* 1974, *38,* 707–710; G. Michael and F. N. Willis, "The Development of
Gestures as a Function of Social Class, Education, and Sex," *Psychological Record,* 1968, *18,*
515–519.

6. For southern Italians see D. Efron, *Gesture, Race, and Culture* (The Hague: Mouton,
1972). For Americans and Colombians see R. Saitz and E. Cervenka, *Colombian and North
American Gestures* (The Hague: Mouton, 1973). For Europeans see D. Morris, P. Collett,
P. Marsh, and M. O'Shaughnessy, *Gestures, Their Origins and Distribution* (New York:
Stein and Day, 1979).

7. W. La Barre, "The Cultural Basis of Emotions and Gestures," *Journal of Personality,*
1947, *16,* 49–68.

8. M. A. Jancovic, S. Devoe, and M. Wiener, "Age-Related Changes in Hand and Arm
Movements as Nonverbal Communication: Some Conceptualizations and an Empirical
Exploration," *Child Development,* 1975, *46,* 922–928. See also A. A. Cohen and R. P. Har-
rison, "Intentionality in the Use of Hand Illustrators in Face-to-Face Communication Sit-
uations," *Journal of Personality and Social Psychology,* 1973, *28,* 276–279; A. Kendon, "Some
Relationships Between Body Motion and Speech," in A. W. Siegman and B. Pope (eds.),
Studies in Dyadic Communication (Elmsford, N.Y.: Pergamon Press, 1972).

9. A. T. Dittmann and L. G. Llewellyn, "Relationships Between Vocalizations and Head
Nods as Listener Responses," *Journal of Personality and Social Psychology,* 1968, *9,* 79–84;
A. T. Dittmann and L. G. Llewellyn, "Body Movement and Speech Rhythm in Social
Conversation," *Journal of Personality and Social Psychology,* 1969, *11,* 98–106.

10. D. Efron, *op. cit.*

11. D. Schiffrin, "Handwork as Ceremony: The Case of the Handshake," *Semiotica,* 1974, *12,* 189–202; M. L. Knapp, R. P. Hart, G. W. Fredrich, and G. M. Shulman, "The Rhetoric of Goodbye: Verbal and Nonverbal Correlates of Human Leave-Taking," *Speech Monographs,* 1973, *40,* 182–198.

12. S. D. Duncan and G. Niederehe, "On Signalling that It's Your Turn to Speak," *Journal of Experimental Social Psychology,* 1974, *10,* 234–247; J. M. Wiemann and M. L. Knapp, "Turn-Taking in Conversations," *Journal of Communication,* 1975, *25,* 75–92.

13. P. Ekman and W. V. Friesen, "Nonverbal Behavior in Psychotherapy Research," in J. M. Shlien (ed.), *Research in Psychotherapy,* Vol. 3 (Washington, D.C.: American Psychological Association, 1968).

14. A. T. Dittmann, "The Relationship Between Body Movements and Moods in Interviews," *Journal of Consulting Psychology,* 1956, *20,* 480; P. Sainesbury, "Gestural Movement During Psychiatric Interviews," *Psychosomatic Medicine,* 1955, *17,* 458–469; J. C. Baxter and R. M. Rozelle, "Nonverbal Expression as a Function of Crowding During a Simulated Police-Citizen Encounter," *Journal of Personality and Social Psychology,* 32, 40–54.

15. N. Freedman, T. Blass, A. Rifkin, and F. Quitkin, "Body Movements and the Verbal Encoding of Aggressive Affect," *Journal of Personality and Social Psychology,* 1973, *26,* 72–85.

16. M. Krout, "An Experimental Attempt to Determine the Significance of Unconscious Manual Symbolic Movements," *Journal of General Psychology,* 1954, *51,* 121–152; M. Krout, "An Experimental Attempt to Produce Unconscious Manual Symbolic Movements," *Journal of General Psychology,* 1954, *51,* 93–120.

17. D. K. Fromme and C. K. Schmidt, "Affective Role Enactment and Expressive Behavior," *Journal of Personality and Social Psychology,* 1972, *24,* 413–419.

18. On arguing see A. Mehrabian, "Nonverbal Betrayal of Feeling," *Journal of Experimental Research in Personality,* 1971, *5,* 64–73. On lying see C. C. McClintock and R. G. Hunt, "Nonverbal Indicators of Affect and Deception in an Interview Setting," *Journal of Applied Social Psychology,* 1975, *1,* 54–67; R. E. Riggio and H. S. Friedman, "Individual Differences in Cues to Deception," *Journal of Personality and Social Psychology,* 1983, *45,* 899–915; P. Ekman and W. V. Friesen, "Hand Movements." On persuasive speech see A. Mehrabian and M. Williams, "Nonverbal Concomitants of Perceived and Intended Persuasiveness," *Journal of Personality and Social Psychology,* 1969, *13,* 37–58.

19. P. Ekman and W. V. Friesen, "Nonverbal Leakage and Clues to Deception," *Psychiatry,* 1969, *32,* 88–106; P. Ekman and W. V. Friesen, "Detecting Deception from the Body or Face," *Journal of Personality and Social Psychology,* 1974, *29,* 288–298. See also P. Ekman, "Differential Communication of Affect by Head and Body Cues," *Journal of Personality and Social Psychology,* 1965, *2,* 726–735; P. Ekman and W. V. Friesen, "Head and Body

Cues in the Judgment of Emotion: A Reformulation," *Perceptual and Motor Skills,* 1967, *24,* 711–724.

20. G. F. Mahl, "Gestures and Body Movements in Interviews," in J. Shlien (ed.), *Research in Psychotherapy,* Vol. 3 (Washington, D. C.: American Psychological Association, 1968). See also A. Mehrabian, "Verbal and Nonverbal Interaction of Strangers in a Waiting Situation," *Journal of Experimental Research in Personality,* 1971, *5,* 127–138.

21. A. Mehrabian, "Significance of Posture and Position in the Communication of Attitude and Status Relationships," *Psychological Bulletin,* 1969, *71,* 359–372.

22. On approaching a known person see A. Mehrabian, "Inference of Attitudes from the Posture, Orientation, and Distance of a Communicator," *Journal of Consulting and Clinical Psychology,* 1968, *32,* 296–308; A. Mehrabian, "Relationship of Attitude to Seated Posture, Orientation, and Distance," *Journal of Personality and Social Psychology,* 1968, *10,* 26–30. On approaching a stranger see H. M. Rosenfeld, "Approval-Seeking and Approval-Inducing Functions of Verbal and Nonverbal Responses in the Dyad," *Journal of Personality and Social Psychology,* 1966, *4,* 597–605; H. M. Rosenfeld, "Instrumental Affiliative Functions of Facial and Gestural Expressions," *Journal of Personality and Social Psychology,* 1966, *4,* 65–72.

23. A. Mehrabian, "Inference of Attitudes from the Posture, Orientation, and Distance of a Communicator"; A. Mehrabian and J. T. Friar, "Encoding of Attitude by a Seated Communicator via Posture and Position Cues," *Journal of Consulting and Clinical Psychology,* 1969, *33,* 330–336.

24. J. Spiegel and P. Machotka, *Messages of the Body* (New York: Free Press, 1974); P. Machotka, "Body Movement as Communication," *Dialogues: Behavioral Science Research* (Boulder, Colo.: Western Interstate Commission for Higher Education, 1965), pp. 33–65.

25. J. Spiegel and P. Machotka, *op. cit.*

26. G. L. Clore, N. H. Wiggins, and S. Itkin, "Judging Attraction from Nonverbal Behavior: The Gain Phenomenon," *Journal of Consulting and Clinical Psychology,* 1975, *43,* 491–497; G. L. Clore, N. H. Wiggins, and S. Itkin, "Gain and Loss in Attraction: Attributions from Nonverbal Behavior," *Journal of Personality and Social Psychology,* 1975, *31,* 706–712.

27. W. S. Royce and R. L. Weiss, "Behavioral Cues in the Judgment of Marital Satisfaction: A Linear Regression Analysis," *Journal of Consulting and Clinical Psychology,* 1975, *43,* 816–824.

28. S. S. Smith-Hanen, "Effects of Nonverbal Behaviors on Judged Levels of Counselor Warmth and Empathy," *Journal of Counseling Psychology,* 1977, *24,* 87–91.

29. A. Mehrabian, "Orientation Behaviors and Nonverbal Attitude Communication," *Journal of Communication,* 1967, *17,* 324–332; M. Reece and R. Whitman, "Expressive Movements, Warmth, and Verbal Reinforcement," *Journal of Abnormal and Social Psychology,* 1962, *64,* 234–236.

30. H. McGinley, R. Lefevre, and P. McGinley, "The Influence of a Communicator's Body Position on Opinion Change in Others," *Journal of Personality and Social Psychology*, 1975, *31*, 686–690; A. S. Imada and M. D. Hakel, "Influence of Nonverbal Communication and Rater Proximity on Impressions and Decisions in Simulated Employment Interviews," *Journal of Applied Psychology*, 1977, *62*, 295–300.

31. B. R. Fretz, R. Corn, J. M. Tuemmler, and W. Bellet, "Counselor Nonverbal Behaviors and Client Evaluations," *Journal of Counseling Psychology*, 1979, *26*, 304–311; J. C. Siegel and J. M. Sell, "Effects of Objective Evidence of Expertness and Nonverbal Behavior on Client-Perceived Expertness," *Journal of Counseling Psychology*, 1978, *25*, 188–192.

32. G. L Trager, "Paralanguage: A First Approximation," *Studies in Linguistics*, 1958, *13*, 1–12.

33. On whispered speech see N. J. Lass, K. R. Hughes, M. D. Bowyer, L. T. Waters, and V. T. Broune, "Speaker Sex Identification from Voiced, Whispered, and Filtered Isolated Vowels," *Journal of the Acoustical Society of America*, 1976, *59*, 675–678. On age et al. see P. B. Davis, *An Investigation of the Suggestion of Age Through Voice in Interpretative Reading*, Masters Thesis, University of Denver, 1949, cited in M. L. Knapp, *Nonverbal Communication in Human Interaction* (New York: Holt, Rinehart, and Winston, 1978), p. 339; L. S. Harms, "Listener Judgments of Status Cues in Speech," *Quarterly Journal of Speech*, 1961, *47*, 164–168; N. J. Lass and M. Davis, "An Investigation of Speaker Height and Weight Identification," *Journal of the Acoustical Society of America*, 1976, *60*, 700–703; N. J. Lass and L. A. Harvey, "An Investigation of Speaker Photograph Identification," *Journal of the Acoustical Society of America*, 1976, *59*, 1232–1236. On people unseen see P. Fay and W. Middleton, "Judgments of Occupation from the Voice as Transmitted over a Public Address System and over a Radio," *Journal of Applied Psychology*, 1939, *23*, 586–601; P. Fay and W. Middleton, "Judgment of Intelligence from the Voice as Transmitted over a Public Address System," *Sociometry*, 1940, *3*, 186–191; P. Fay and W. Middleton, "The Ability to Judge Rested or Tired Condition of a Speaker from His Voice as Transmitted over a Public Address System," *Journal of Applied Psychology*, 1940, *24*, 645–650; P. Fay and W. Middleton, "The Ability to Judge Sociability from the Voice as Transmitted over a Public Address System," *Journal of Social Psychology*, 1941, *13*, 303–309; P. Fay and W. Middleton, "The Ability to Judge Truth Telling or Lying from the Voice as Transmitted over a Public Address System," *Journal of Applied Psychology*, 1941, *24*, 211–215; P. Fay and W. Middleton, "Judgment of Leadership from Transmitted Voice," *Journal of Social Psychology*, 1943, *17*, 99–102. On physical prediction see E. Kramer, "Judgment of Personal Characteristics and Emotions from Nonverbal Properties," *Psychological Bulletin*, 1963, *60*, 408–420; E. Kramer, "Personality Stereotypes in Voice: A Reconsideration of the Data," *Journal of Social Psychology*, 1964, *62*, 247–251.

34. K. R. Scherer, "Judging Personality from Voice: A Cross-Cultural Approach to an Old Issue in Person Perception," *Journal of Personality*, 1972, *40*, 191–210.

35. D. W. Addington, "The Relationship of Selected Vocal Characteristics to Personality Perception," *Speech Monographs*, 1968, *35*, 492–503.

36. H. Giles and P. F. Powesland, *Speech Style and Social Evaluation* (New York: Academic Press, 1975); W. E. Lambert, H. Frankel, and G. R. Tucker, "Judging Personality Through Speech: A French-Canadian Example," *Journal of Communication*, 1966, *16*, 305–321. On Jewish accents see M. Anisfeld, N. Bogo, and W. Lambert, "Evaluation Reactions to Accented English Speech," *Journal of Abnormal and Social Psychology*, 1962, *65*, 223–231. On varied accents see A. Bradford, D. Ferror, and G. Bradford, "Evaluation Reactions of College Students to Dialect Differences in the English of Mexican-Americans," *Language and Speech*, 1974, *17*, 255–270; J. Buck, "The Effects of Negro and White Dialectical Variations upon Attitudes of College Students," *Speech Monographs*, 1968, *35*, 181–186; A. Mulac, T. D. Hanley, and D. Y. Prigge, "Effects of Phonological Speech Foreignness upon Three Dimensions of Attitude of Selected American Listeners," *Quarterly Journal of Speech*, 1974, *60*, 411–420. On black accents see T. K. Crowl and W. H. MacGinitie, "The Influence of Students' Speech Characteristics on Teachers' Evaluations of Oral Answers," *Journal of Educational Psychology*, 1974, *66*, 304–308; R. C. Granger, M. Mathews, L. C. Quay, and R. Verner, "Teacher Judgments of the Communication Effectiveness of Children Using Different Speech Patterns," *Journal of Educational Psychology*, 1977, *69*, 793–796.

37. E. B. Ryan and M. A. Carranza, "Evaluative Reactions of Adolescents Toward Speakers of Standard English and Mexican American Accented English," *Journal of Personality and Social Psychology*, 1975, *31*, 855–863.

38. A. Mulac, "Assessment and Application of the Revised Speech Dialect Attitudinal Scale," *Communication Monographs*, 1976, *43*, 238–245.

39. F. E. Aboud, R. Clement, and D. M. Taylor, "Evaluational Reactions to Discrepancies Between Social Class and Language," *Sociometry*, 1974, *37*, 239–250; H. Giles and P. F. Powesland, *op. cit.*, p. 108.

40. On the first technique see J. R. Davitz and L. Davitz, "Correlates of Accuracy in the Communication of Feelings," *Journal of Communication*, 1959, *9*, 110–117. On the second technique see P. L. Rogers, K. R. Scherer, and R. Rosenthal, "Content Filtering Human Speech: A Simple Electronic System," *Behavior Research Methods and Instrumentation*, 1971, *3*, 16–18; J. Starkweather, "The Communication Value of Content-Free Speech," *American Journal of Psychology*, 1956, *69*, 121–123. On the third technique see K. R. Scherer, "Randomized Splicing: A Note on a Simple Technique for Masking Speech Content," *Journal of Experimental Research in Personality*, 1971, *5*, 155–159.

41. J. R. Davitz and L. Davitz, "Correlates of Accuracy in the Communication of Feelings"; J. R. Davitz and L. Davitz, "The Communication of Feelings by Content-Free Speech," *Journal of Communication*, 1959, *9*, 6–13.

42. M. Beldoch, "Sensitivity to Expression of Emotional Meaning in Three Modes of Communication," in J. R. Davitz (ed.), *The Communication of Emotional Meaning* (New York: McGraw-Hill, 1964), chap. 3; E. A. Levitt, "The Relationship Between Abilities to Express Emotional Meanings Vocally and Facially," in J. R. Davitz (ed.), *op. cit.,* chap. 7; P. K. Levy, "The Ability to Express and Perceive Vocal Communications of Feeling," in J. R. Davitz (ed.), *op. cit.,* chap. 4; J. R. Davitz, "Personality, Perceptual, and Cognitive Correlates of Emotional Sensitivity," in J. R. Davitz (ed.), *op. cit.,* chap. 5.

43. L. Dimitrovsky, "The Ability to Identify the Emotional Meaning of Vocal Expressions at Successive Age Levels," in J. R. Davitz (ed.), *op. cit.,* chap. 6; S. Blau, "An Ear for an Eye: Sensory Compensation and Judgments of Affect by the Blind," in J. R. Davitz (ed.), *op. cit.,* chap. 9; J. B. Turner, "Schizophrenics as Judges of Vocal Expressions of Emotional Meaning," in J. R. Davitz (ed.), *op. cit.,* chap. 10.

44. J. R. Davitz, "Auditory Correlates of Vocal Expressions of Emotional Meanings," in J. R. Davitz (ed.), *op. cit.,* chap. 8.

45. G. Fairbanks and L. W. Hoaglin, "An Experimental Study of the Durational Characteristics of the Voice During Expression of Emotion," *Speech Monographs,* 1941, 8, 85–90; G. Fairbanks and W. Provonost, "An Experimental Study of the Pitch Characteristics of the Voice During the Expression of Emotion," *Speech Monographs,* 1939, 6, 87–104.

46. E. G. Beier and A. J. Zautra, "Identification of Vocal Communication of Emotions Across Cultures," *Journal of Consulting and Clinical Psychology,* 1972, 39, 166.

47. J. R. Davitz, "Minor Studies and Some Hypotheses," in J. R. Davitz (ed.), *op. cit.,* chap. 11.

48. H. J. Berman, A. D. Shulman, and S. J. Marwit, "Comparison of Multidimensional Decoding of Affect from Audio, Video, and Audiovideo Recordings," *Sociometry,* 1976, 39, 83–89; K. L. Burns and E. G. Beier, "Significance of Vocal and Visual Channels in the Decoding of Emotional Meaning," *Journal of Communication,* 1973, 23, 118–130; A. Mehrabian and S. Ferris, "Inference of Attitudes from Nonverbal Communication in Two Channels," *Journal of Consulting Psychology,* 1967, 31, 248–252; S. Zaidel and A. Mehrabian, "The Ability to Communicate and Infer Positive and Negative Attitudes Facially and Vocally," *Journal of Experimental Research in Personality,* 1969, 3, 233–241.

49. P. Ekman, W. V. Friesen, M. O'Sullivan, and K. Scherer, "Relative Importance of the Face, Body, and Speech in Judgments of Personality and Affect," *Journal of Personality and Social Psychology,* 1980, 38, 270–277. See also M. Zuckerman, D. T. Larrance, N. H. Spiegel, and R. Klorman, "Controlling Nonverbal Displays: Facial Expressions and Tone of Voice," *Journal of Experimental Social Psychology,* 1981, 17, 506–524; P. Ekman and W. V. Friesen, "Nonverbal Leakage and Clues to Deception."

50. H. J. Berman, A. D. Shulman, and S. J. Marwit, *op. cit.;* P. Ekman, W. V. Friesen, M. O'Sullivan, and K. Scherer, *op. cit.*

51. D. J. Kiesler, *The Process of Psychotherapy: Empirical Foundations and Systems of Analysis* (Chicago: Aldine, 1973), pp. 128–146.

52. A. A. Harrison, M. Hwalek, D. F. Raney, and J. G. Fritz, "Cues to Deception in an Interview Situation," *Social Psychology*, 1978, *41*, 156-161; L. A. Streeter, R. M. Krauss, V. Geller, C. Olson, and W. Apple, "Pitch Changes During Attempted Deception," *Journal of Personality and Social Psychology*, 1977, *35*, 345-350; M. Zuckerman, R. S. DeFrank, J. A. Hall, D. T. Larrance, and R. Rosenthal, "Facial and Vocal Cues of Deception and Honesty," *Journal of Experimental Social Psychology*, 1979, *15*, 378-396. See also B. M. DePaulo, K. Lanier, and T. Davis, "Detecting Deceit of the Motivated Liar," *Journal of Personality and Social Psychology*, 1983, *45*, 1096-1103; P. J. Lavrakas and R. A. Maier, "Differences in Human Ability to Judge Veracity from the Audio Medium," *Journal of Research in Personality*, 1979, *13*, 139-153; M. Zuckerman, R. S. DeFrank, J. A. Hall, D. T. Larrance, and R. Rosenthal, *op. cit.*

53. R. M. Eisler, M. Hersen, P. M. Miller, and E. B. Blanchard, "Situational Determinants of Assertive Behaviors," *Journal of Consulting and Clinical Psychology*, 1975, *43*, 330-340; D. B. Bugental, B. Henker, and C. K. Whalen, "Attributional Antecedents of Verbal and Vocal Assertiveness," *Journal of Personality and Social Psychology*, 1976, *34*, 405-411.

54. D. B. Bugental and L. Love, "Nonassertive Expression of Parental Approval and Disapproval and Its Relationship to Child Disturbance," *Child Development*, 1975, *46*, 747-752.

55. R. A. Page and J. L. Balloun, "The Effect of Voice Volume on the Perception of Personality," *Journal of Social Psychology*, 1978, *105*, 64-72; M. Natale, "Convergence of Mean Vocal Intensity in Dyadic Communication as a Function of Social Desirability," *Journal of Personality and Social Psychology*, 1975, *32*, 790-804.

56. On speech disruptions see L. M. Horowitz, D. Weckler, A. Saxon, J. D. Livaudais, and L. I. Boutacoff, "Discomforting Talk and Speech Disruptions," *Journal of Consulting and Clinical Psychology*, 1977, *45*, 1036-1042; S. V. Kasl and G. F. Mahl, "The Relationship of Disturbances and Hesitations in Spontaneous Speech to Anxiety," *Journal of Personality and Social Psychology*, 1965, *1*, 425-433; G. F. Mahl, "Disturbances and Silences in the Patient's Speech in Psychotherapy," *Journal of Abnormal and Social Psychology*, 1956, *53*, 1-15. On rate of speech see F. H. Kanfer, "Verbal Rate, Content, and Adjustment Ratings in Experimentally Structured Interviews," *Journal of Abnormal and Social Psychology*, 1959, *58*, 305-311; A. W. Siegman and B. Pope, "The Effects of Ambiguity and Anxiety on Interviewee Verbal Behavior," in A. W. Siegman and B. Pope (eds.), *Studies in Dyadic Communication* (Elmsford, N.Y.: Pergamon Press, 1972).

57. M. H. L. Hecker, K. N. Stevens, G. von Bismark, and C. E. Williams, "Manifestations of Task-Induced Stress in the Acoustic Speech Signal," *Journal of the Acoustical Society of America*, 1968, *44*, 993-1001; C. E. Williams and K. N. Stevens, "On Determining the Emotional State of Pilots During Flight: An Exploratory Study," *Aerospace Medicine*, 1969, *40*, 1369-1372. See also P. Ekman, W. V. Friesen, and K. Scherer, "Body Movements and Voice Pitch in Deceptive Interaction," *Semiotica*, 1976, *16*, 23-27; F. H. Kanfer, "Effect of Warning Signal Preceding a Noxious Stimulus on Verbal Rate and Heart Rate," *Journal of Experimental Psychology*, 1958, *55*, 73-80.

58. S. Weitz, "Attitude, Voice, and Behavior: A Repressed Affect Model of Interracial Interaction," *Journal of Personality and Social Psychology,* 1972, *24,* 14–21; C. O. Word, M. P. Zanna, and J. Cooper, "The Nonverbal Mediation of Self-Fulfilling Prophecies in Interracial Interaction," *Journal of Experimental Social Psychology,* 1974, *10,* 109–120.

59. On positive roles see R. M. Eisler, M. Hersen, P. M. Miller, and E. B. Blanchard, *op. cit.* On interviewers see C. L. Kleinke, R. A. Staneski, and D. E. Berger, "Evaluation of an Interviewer as a Function of Interviewer Gaze, Reinforcement of Subject Gaze, and Interviewer Attractiveness," *Journal of Personality and Social Psychology,* 1975, *31,* 115–122; B. Pope and A. W. Siegman, "Relationship and Verbal Behavior in the Initial Interview," in A. W. Siegman and B. Pope (eds.), *Studies in Dyadic Communication* (Elmsford, N.Y.: Pergamon Press, 1972). On contagious warmth see C. L. Kleinke, "Effects of False Feedback About Response Lengths on Subjects' Perception of an Interview," *Journal of Social Psychology,* 1975, *95,* 99–104.

60. E. G. Beier, *The Silent Language of Psychotherapy: Social Reinforcement of Unconscious Processes* (Chicago: Aldine, 1966).

61. S. Duncan, L. N. Rice, and J. M. Butler, "Therapists' Paralanguage in Peak and Poor Psychotherapy Hours," *Journal of Abnormal Psychology,* 1968, *73,* 566–570.

62. D. T. Tepper and R. F. Haase, "Verbal and Nonverbal Communication of Facilitative Conditions," *Journal of Counseling Psychology,* 1978, *25,* 35–44.

63. C. L. Kleinke and T. B. Tully, "Influence of Talking Level on Perceptions of Counselors," *Journal of Counseling Psychology,* 1979, *26,* 23–29; F. R. Staples, R. B. Sloane, and A. H. Cristol, "Truax Variables, Speech Characteristics, and Therapeutic Outcome," *Journal of Nervous and Mental Disease,* 1976, *163,* 135–140; M. Scher, "Verbal Activity, Sex, Counselor Experience, and Success in Counseling," *Journal of Counseling Psychology,* 1975, *22,* 97–101.

64. D. J. Stang, "Effect of Interaction Rate on Ratings of Leadership and Liking," *Journal of Personality and Social Psychology,* 1973, *27,* 405–408; R. T. Stein and T. Heller, "An Empirical Analysis of the Correlations Between Leadership Status and Participation Rates Reported in the Literature," *Journal of Personality and Social Psychology,* 1979, *37,* 1993–2002. See also R. M. Sorrentino and R. G. Boutillier, "The Effect of Quantity and Quality of Verbal Interaction on Ratings of Leadership Ability," *Journal of Experimental Social Psychology,* 1975, *11,* 403–411. On task orientation see H. P. Sims and C. C. Manz, "Observing Leader Verbal Behavior: Toward Reciprocal Determinism Leadership Theory," *Journal of Applied Psychology,* 1984, *69,* 222–232; R. T. Stein and T. Heller, *op. cit.;* G. Gintner and S. Lindskold, "Rate of Participation and Expertise as Factors Influencing Leader Choice," *Journal of Personality and Social Psychology,* 1975, *32,* 1085–1089; M. Wish, R. B. D'Andrade, and J. E. Goodnow, "Dimensions of Interpersonal Communication: Correspondences Between Structures for Speech Acts and Bipolar Scales," *Journal of Personality and Social Psychology,* 1980, *39,* 848–860; H. P. Sims and C. C. Manz, *op. cit.* On facilitators see R. F. Bales, "Task Roles and Social Roles in Problem-Solving Groups," in E. E. Maccoby, T. M. Newcomb, and F. L. Hartley (eds.), *Readings in Social Psychology*

(New York: Holt, Rinehart, and Winston, 1958); R. F. Bales, *Personality and Interpersonal Behavior* (New York: Holt, Rinehart, and Winston, 1970); A. P. Hare, *Handbook of Small Group Research* (New York: Free Press, 1976).

65. K. R. Scherer, H. London, and J. J. Wolf, "The Voice of Confidence: Paralinguistic Cues and Audience Evaluation," *Journal of Research in Personality*, 1973, 7, 31–44; W. Apple, L. A. Streeter, and R. M. Krauss, "Effects of Pitch and Speech Rate on Personal Attributions," *Journal of Personality and Social Psychology*, 1979, 37, 715–727; J. A. Hall, "Voice Tone and Persuasion," *Journal of Personality and Social Psychology*, 1980, 38, 924–934. See also W. Apple, L. A. Streeter, and R. M. Krauss, *op. cit.*; L. A. Streeter, R. M. Krauss, V. Geller, C. Olson, and W. Apple, *op. cit.*

66. L. M. Horowitz, D. Weckler, A. Saxon, J. D. Livaudais, and L. I. Boutacoff, *op. cit.*; G. R. Miller and M. A. Hewgill, "The Effect of Variations of Noninfluency on Audience Ratings of Source Credibility," *Quarterly Journal of Speech*, 1964, 50, 36–44; K. K. Sereno and G. J. Hawkins, "The Effect of Variations in Speakers' Noninfluency upon Audience Ratings of Attitude Toward Speech Topic and Speakers' Credibility," *Speech Monographs*, 1967, 34, 58–64. See also A. A. Harrison, M. Hwalek, D. F. Raney, and J. G. Fritz, *op. cit.*; J. D. Matarazzo, A. N. Wiens, and T. S. Manaugh, "IQ Correlates of Speech and Silence Behavior Under Three Dyadic Speaking Conditions," *Journal of Consulting and Clinical Psychology*, 1975, 43, 198–204.

67. K. R. Scherer, H. London, and J. J. Wolf, *op. cit.*; W. Apple, L. A. Streeter, and R. M. Krauss, *op. cit.*; S. Feldstein and B. Sloan, "Actual and Stereotyped Speech Tempos of Extroverts and Introverts," *Journal of Personality*, 1984, 52, 188–204; B. L. Smith, B. L. Brown, W. J. Strong, and A. C. Rencher, "Effects of Speech Rate on Personality Perception," *Language and Speech*, 1975, 18, 145–152; N. Miller, G. Maruyama, R. J. Beaber, and K. Valone, "Speed of Speech and Persuasion," *Journal of Personality and Social Psychology*, 1976, 34, 615–624.

68. J. M. Conley, W. M. O'Barr, and E. A. Lind, "The Power of Language: Presentational Style in the Courtroom," *Duke Law Journal*, 1978, 6, 1375–1399; B. Erickson, E. A. Lind, B. C. Johnson, and W. M. O'Barr, "Speech Style and Impression Formation in a Court Setting: The Effects of 'Powerful' and 'Powerless' Speech," *Journal of Experimental Social Psychology*, 1978, 14, 266–279.

69. *Ibid.*

CHAPTER 6

1. B. M. Bass and S. Klubeck, "Effects of Seating Arrangements on Leaderless Group Discussions," *Journal of Abnormal and Social Psychology*, 1952, 47, 724–727; R. Sommer, "Leadership and Group Geography," *Sociometry*, 1961, 24, 99–110; F. Strodtbeck and L. Hook, "The Social Dimensions of a Twelve Man Jury Table," *Sociometry*, 1961, 24, 397–415; C. Ward, "Seating Arrangements and Leadership Emergence in Small Discussion Groups," *Journal of Social Psychology*, 1968, 74, 83–90.

2. A. Hare and R. F. Bales, "Seating Position and Small Group Interaction," *Sociometry,* 1963, *26,* 480–486; L. T. Howells and S. W. Becker, "Seating Arrangement and Leadership Emergence," *Journal of Abnormal and Social Psychology,* 1962, *64,* 148–150; C. H. Silverstein and D. J. Stang, "Seating Position and Interaction in Triads: A Field Study," *Sociometry,* 1976, *39,* 166–170. See also D. F. Lott and R. Sommer, "Seating Arrangements and Status," *Journal of Personality and Social Psychology,* 1967, 7, 90–94; R. J. Pellegrini, "Some Effects of Seating Position on Social Perception," *Psychological Reports,* 1971, *28,* 887–893.

3. G. Hearn, "Leadership and the Spatial Factor in Small Groups," *Journal of Abnormal and Social Psychology,* 1957, *54,* 269–272; B. Steinzor, "The Spatial Factor in Face to Face Discussion Groups," *Journal of Abnormal and Social Psychology,* 1950, *45,* 552–555. See also M. Cook, "Experiments on Orientation and Proxemics," *Human Relations,* 1970, *23,* 61–76; R. Sommer, "Further Studies of Small Group Ecology," *Sociometry,* 1965, *28,* 337–348.

4. M. Cook, *op. cit.;* R. Sommer, *op. cit.* See also J. J. Seta, P. B. Paulus, and J. K. Schkade, "Effects of Group Size and Proximity Under Cooperative and Competitive Conditions," *Journal of Personality and Social Psychology,* 1976, *34,* 47–53.

5. R. Sommer, *Personal Space* (Englewood Cliffs, N.J.: Prentice-Hall, 1969); R. Sommer, *Design Awareness* (San Francisco: Rinehart Press, 1972); R. Sommer, *Tight Spaces: Hard Architecture and How to Humanize It* (Englewood Cliffs, N.J.: Prentice-Hall, 1974).

6. M. W. Segal, "Alphabet and Attraction: An Unobtrusive Measure of the Effect of Propinquity in a Field Setting," *Journal of Personality and Social Psychology,* 1974, *30,* 654–657; L. Festinger, S. Schachter, and K. Back, *Social Pressures in Informal Groups: A Study of Human Factors in Housing* (New York: Harper and Row, 1950); L. Nahemow and M. P. Lawton, "Similarity and Propinquity in Friendship Formation," *Journal of Personality and Social Psychology,* 1975, *32,* 205–213; R. F. Priest and J. Sawyer, "Proximity and Peership: Bases of Balance in Interpersonal Attraction," *American Journal of Sociology,* 1967, *72,* 633–649.

7. A. Mehrabian and S. G. Diamond, "The Effects of Furniture Arrangement, Props, and Personality on Social Interaction," *Journal of Personality and Social Psychology,* 1971, *20,* 18–20; A. Mehrabian and S. G. Diamond, "Seating Arrangement and Conversation," *Sociometry,* 1971, *34,* 281–289.

8. On the elderly see R. Sommer and H. Ross, "Social Interaction on a Geriatrics Ward," *International Journal of Social Psychiatry,* 1958, *4,* 128–133. On psychiatric patients see C. J. Holahan, "Seating Patterns and Patient Behavior in an Experimental Dayroom," *Journal of Abnormal Psychology,* 1972, *80,* 115–124. On college students see C. J. Holahan, "Consultation in Environmental Psychology: A Case Study of a New Counseling Role," *Journal of Counseling Psychology,* 1977, *24,* 251–254.

9. R. Sommer, *Personal Space;* A. I. Schwebel and D. L. Cherlin, "Physical and Social Distancing in Teacher-Pupil Relationships," *Journal of Educational Psychology,* 1972, *63,* 543–550.

10. R. Zweigenhaft, "Personal Space in the Faculty Office: Desk Placement and the Student-Faculty Interaction," *Journal of Applied Psychology*, 1976, *61*, 529–532; A. G. White, "The Patient Sits Down: A Clinical Note," *Psychosomatic Medicine*, 1953, *15*, 256–257; R. Widgery and C. Stackpole, "Desk Position, Interviewee Anxiety, and Interviewer Credibility: An Example of Cognitive Balance in a Dyad," *Journal of Counseling Psychology*, 1972, *19*, 173–177.

11. A. H. Maslow and N. L. Mintz, "Effects of Esthetic Surroundings: I. Initial Effects of Three Esthetic Conditions upon Perceiving 'Energy' and 'Well-Being' in Faces," *Journal of Psychology*, 1956, *41*, 247–254; N. L. Mintz, "Effects of Esthetic Surroundings: II. Prolonged and Repeated Experience in a 'Beautiful' and 'Ugly' Room," *Journal of Psychology*, 1956, *41*, 459–466.

12. D. C. Murray and H. L. Deabler, "Colors and Mood-Tones," *Journal of Applied Psychology*, 1957, *41*, 279–283; L. B. Wexner, "The Degree to Which Colors (Hues) Are Associated with Mood-Tones," *Journal of Applied Psychology*, 1954, *38*, 432–435.

13. On evaluating strangers see W. Griffitt, "Environmental Effects of Interpersonal Affective Behavior: Ambient Effective Temperature and Attraction," *Journal of Personality and Social Psychology*, 1970, *15*, 240–244; W. Griffitt and R. Veitch, "Hot and Crowded: Influence of Population Density and Temperature on Interpersonal Affective Behavior," *Journal of Personality and Social Psychology*, 1971, *17*, 92–98. See also R. A. Baron, "Aggression as a Function of Ambient Temperature and Prior Anger Arousal," *Journal of Personality and Social Psychology*, 1972, *21*, 183–189; R. A. Baron and P. A. Bell, "Aggression and Heat: Mediating Effects of Prior Provocation and Exposure to an Aggressive Model," *Journal of Personality and Social Psychology*, 1975, *31*, 825–832; R. A. Baron and P. A. Bell, "Aggression and Heat: The Influence of Ambient Temperature, Negative Affect, and a Cooling Drink on Physical Aggression," *Journal of Personality and Social Psychology*, 1976, *33*, 245–255. On riots see J. M. Carlsmith and C. A. Anderson, "Ambient Temperature and the Occurrence of Collective Violence: A New Analysis," *Journal of Personality and Social Psychology*, 1979, *37*, 337–344.

14. L. Bickman, A. Teger, T. Gabriele, C. McLaughlin, M. Berger, and E. Sunaday, "Dormitory Density and Helping Behavior," *Environment and Behavior*, 1973, *5*, 465–490.

15. E. T. Hall, *The Hidden Dimension* (New York: Doubleday, 1966).

16. F. D. Kelly, "Communicational Significance of Therapist Proxemic Cues," *Journal of Consulting and Clinical Psychology*, 1972, *39*, 345; A. Mehrabian, "Inference of Attitude from the Posture, Orientation, and Distance of a Communicator," *Journal of Consulting and Clinical Psychology*, 1968, *32*, 296–308. See also M. L. Patterson and L. B. Sechrest, "Interpersonal Distance and Impression Formation," *Journal of Personality*, 1970, *38*, 161–166.

17. On men and women see C. L. Kleinke, R. A. Staneski, and S. L. Pipp, "Effects of Gaze, Distance, and Attractiveness on Males' First Impressions of Females," *Representative Research in Social Psychology*, 1975, *6*, 7–12. On strangers see A. Kahn and T. A.

McGaughey, "Distance and Liking: When Moving Close Produces Increased Liking," *Sociometry*, 1977, *40*, 138–144.

18. On psychiatric patients see C. L. Lassen, "Effect of Proximity on Anxiety and Communication in the Initial Psychiatric Interview," *Journal of Abnormal Psychology*, 1973, *81*, 226–232. On students see G. L. Stone and C. J. Morden, "Effect of Distance on Verbal Productivity," *Journal of Counseling Psychology*, 1976, *23*, 486–488; N. G. Dinges and E. R. Oetting, "Interaction Distance Anxiety in the Counseling Dyad," *Journal of Counseling Psychology*, 1972, *19*, 146–149; P. H. Knight and C. K. Blair, "Degree of Client Comfort as a Function of Dyadic Interaction Distance," *Journal of Counseling Psychology*, 1976, *23*, 13–16.

19. S. Albert and J. M. Dabbs, "Physical Distance and Persuasion," *Journal of Personality and Social Psychology*, 1970, *15*, 265–270; R. E. Kleck, "Interaction Distance and Non-Verbal Agreeing Responses," *British Journal of Social and Clinical Psychology*, 1970, *9*, 180–182.

20. L. R. Greene, "Effects of Verbal Evaluative Feedback and Interpersonal Distance on Behavioral Compliance," *Journal of Counseling Psychology*, 1977, *24*, 10–14.

21. S. Milgram, "Some Conditions of Obedience and Disobedience to Authority," *Human Relations*, 1965, *18*, 57–76.

22. On strangers see M. L. Patterson, "Compensation in Nonverbal Immediacy Behaviors: A Review," *Sociometry*, 1973, *36*, 237–252. See also N. J. Felipe and R. Sommer, "Invasions of Personal Space," *Social Problems*, 1966, *14*, 206–214; E. R. Mahoney, "Compensatory Reactions to Spatial Immediacy," *Sociometry*, 1974, *37*, 423–431; M. L. Patterson, S. Mullens, and J. Romano, "Compensatory Reactions to Spatial Intrusion," *Sociometry*, 1971, *34*, 114–121; R. Sommer, *Personal Space*. On pedestrians see V. Konečni, L. Libuser, H. Morton, and E. Ebbesen, "Effects of a Violation of Personal Space on Escape and Helping Responses," *Journal of Experimental Social Psychology*, 1975, *11*, 288–299; R. J. Smith and E. S. Knowles, "Attributional Consequences of Personal Space Invasions," *Personality and Social Psychology Bulletin*, 1978, *4*, 429–433.

23. On students see D. P. Barash, "Human Ethology: Personal Space Reiterated," *Environment and Behavior*, 1973, *5*, 67–73. On adults see A. M. Fry and F. N. Willis, "Invasion of Personal Space as a Function of the Age of the Invader," *Psychological Record*, 1971, *21*, 385–389. On women see J. M. Dabbs, "Sex, Setting, and Reactions to Crowding on Sidewalks," *Proceedings of the 80th Annual Convention of the American Psychological Association*, 1972, 205–206; E. Sundstrom and M. G. Sundstrom, "Personal Space Invasions: What Happens When the Invader Asks Permission?" *Environmental Psychology and Nonverbal Behavior*, 1977, *2*, 76–82.

24. J. D. Fisher and D. Byrne, "Too Close for Comfort: Sex Differences in Response to Invasions of Personal Space," *Journal of Personality and Social Psychology*, 1975, *32*, 15–21.

25. J. B.Calhoun, "Population Density and Social Pathology," *Scientific American*, 1962, *206*, 139–148; A. Ellis, *Reason and Emotion in Psychotherapy* (New York: Lyle Stuart, 1962); D. Meichenbaum, *Cognitive-Behavior Modification* (New York: Plenum, 1977); R. M.

Baron and S. P. Needel, "Toward an Understanding of the Differences in the Responses of Humans and Other Animals to Density," *Psychological Review*, 1980, *87*, 320–326.

26. J. L. Freedman, *Crowding and Behavior* (San Francisco: W. H. Freeman, 1975). See also J. Rodin and A. Baum, "Crowding and Helplessness: Potential Consequences of Density and Loss of Control," in A. Baum and Y. M. Epstein (eds.), *Human Response to Crowding* (Hillsdale, N.J.: Erlbaum, 1978); S. Worchel, "The Experience of Crowding: An Attributional Analysis," in A. Baum and Y. M. Epstein (eds.), *op. cit.*

27. J. Schopler and J. E. Stockdale, "An Interference Analysis of Crowding," *Environmental Psychology and Nonverbal Behavior*, 1977, *1*, 81–88. See also P. C. Cozby, "Effects of Density, Activity, and Personality, on Environmental Preferences," *Journal of Research in Personality*, 1973, *7*, 45–60; Y. M. Epstein and R. A. Karlin, "Effects of Acute Experimental Crowding," *Journal of Applied Social Psychology*, 1975, *5*, 34–53.

28. J. F. Heller, B. D. Groff, and S. H. Solomon, "Toward an Understanding of Crowding: The Role of Physical Interaction," *Journal of Personality and Social Psychology*, 1977, *35*, 183–190; E. Sundstrom, "An Experimental Study of Crowding: Effects of Room Size, Intrusion, and Goal Blocking on Nonverbal Behavior, Self-Disclosure, and Self-Reported Stress," *Journal of Personality and Social Psychology*, 1975, *32*, 645–654.

29. D. E. Schmidt and J. P. Keating, "Human Crowding and Personal Control: An Integration of the Research," *Psychological Bulletin*, 1979, *86*, 680–700. On elevator riders see J. Rodin, S. K. Solomon, and J. Metcalf, "Role of Control in Mediating Perceptions of Density," *Journal of Personality and Social Psychology*, 1978, *36*, 988–999.

30. R. M. Baron, D. R. Mandel, C. A. Adams, and L. M. Griffen, "Effects of Social Density in University Residential Environments," *Journal of Personality and Social Psychology*, 1976, *34*, 434–446.

31. A. Baum, J. R. Aiello, and L. E. Calesnick, "Crowding and Personal Control: Social Density and the Development of Learned Helplessness," *Journal of Personality and Social Psychology*, 1978, *36*, 1000–1011; A. Baum and R. J. Gatchel, "Cognitive Determinants of Reaction to Uncontrollable Events: Development of Reactance and Learned Helplessness," *Journal of Personality and Social Psychology*, 1981, *40*, 1078–1089.

32. V. C. Cox, P. B. Paulus, and G. McCain, "Prison Crowding Research," *American Psychologist*, 1984, *39*, 1148–1160; P. B. Paulus, G. McCain, and V. C. Cox, "Death Rates, Psychiatric Commitments, Blood Pressure and Perceived Crowding as a Function of Institutional Crowding," *Environmental Psychology and Nonverbal Behavior*, 1978, *3*, 107–116.

33. J. R. Aiello, D. T. DeRisi, Y. M. Epstein, and R. A. Karlin, "Crowding and the Role of Interpersonal Distance Preference," *Sociometry*, 1977, *40*, 271–282; P. C. Cozby, *op. cit.* See also B. J. Carducci and A. W. Webber, "Shyness as a Determinant of Interpersonal Distance," *Psychological Reports*, 1979, *44*, 1075–1078; E. T. Hall, *op. cit.*

34. A. Baum and G. E. Davis, "Reducing the Stress of High-Density Living: An Architectural Intervention," *Journal of Personality and Social Psychology*, 1980, *38*, 471–481.

35. K. Klein and B. Harris, "Disruptive Effects of Disconfirmed Expectancies About Crowding," *Journal of Personality and Social Psychology*, 1979, *37*, 769–777; A. Baum and C. I. Greenberg, "Waiting for a Crowd: The Behavioral and Perceptual Effects of Anticipated Crowding," *Journal of Personality and Social Psychology*, 1975, *32*, 671–679.

36. R. McCallum, C. E. Rusbult, G. K. Hong, T. A. Walden, and J. Schopler, "Effects of Resource Availability and Importance of Behavior on the Experience of Crowding," *Journal of Personality and Social Psychology*, 1979, *37*, 1304–1313.

37. A. Baum, L. E. Calesnick, G. E. Davis, and R. J. Gatchel, "Individual Differences in Coping with Crowding: Stimulus Screening and Social Overload," *Journal of Personality and Social Psychology*, 1982, *43*, 821–830.

38. A. Baum, J. D. Fisher, and S. K. Solomon, "Type of Information, Familiarity, and the Reduction of Crowding Stress," *Journal of Personality and Social Psychology*, 1981, *40*, 11–23; E. J. Langer and S. Saegert, "Crowding and Cognitive Control," *Journal of Personality and Social Psychology*, 1977, *35*, 175–182.

39. A. Baum and S. Korman, "Differential Response to Anticipated Crowding: Psychological Effects of Social and Spatial Density." *Journal of Personality and Social Psychology*, 1976, *34*, 526–536.

40. E. T. Hall, *op. cit.;* N. M. Sussman and H. M. Rosenfeld, "Influence of Culture, Language, and Sex on Conversational Distance," *Journal of Personality and Social Psychology*, 1982, *42*, 66–74; O. M. Watson, *Proxemic Behavior: A Cross-Cultural Study* (The Hague: Mouton, 1970).

41. On zoo visitors see J. C. Baxter, "Interpersonal Spacing in Natural Settings," *Sociometry*, 1970, *33*, 444–456. On college students see F. N. Willis, "Initial Speaking Distance as a Function of the Speakers' Relationship," *Psychonomic Science*, 1966, *5*, 221–222. On school children see J. R. Aiello and S. E. Jones, "Field Study of the Proxemic Behavior of Young School Children in Three Subcultural Groups," *Journal of Personality and Social Psychology*, 1971, *19*, 351–356; S. E. Jones and J. R. Aiello, "Proxemic Behavior of Black and White First-, Third-, and Fifth-Grade Children," *Journal of Personality and Social Psychology*, 1973, *25*, 21–27.

42. S. E. Scherer, "Proxemic Behavior of Primary School Children as a Function of their Socioeconomic Class and Subculture," *Journal of Personality and Social Psychology*, 1974, *29*, 800–805.

43. J. R. Aiello and T. D. Aiello, "The Development of Personal Space: Proxemic Behavior in Children 6 Through 16," *Human Ecology*, 1974, *2*, 177–189; G. H. Tennis and J. M. Dabbs, "Sex, Setting, and Personal Space: First Grade Through College," *Sociometry*, 1975, *38*, 385–394. See also G. W. Evans and R. B. Howard, "Personal Space," *Psychological Bulletin*, 1973, *80*, 334–344.

44. L. M. Dean, F. N. Willis, and J. Hewitt, "Initial Interaction Distance Among Individuals Equal and Unequal in Military Rank," *Journal of Personality and Social Psychology*,

1975, *32*, 294–299. See also J. M. Dabbs and N. A. Stokes, "Beauty Is Power: The Use of Space on the Sidewalk," *Sociometry*, 1975, *38*, 551–557; M. J. White, "Interpersonal Distance as Affected by Room Size, Status, and Sex," *Journal of Social Psychology*, 1975, *95*, 241–249; D. O. Jorgenson, "Field Study of the Relationship Between Status Discrepancy and Proxemic Behavior," *Journal of Social Psychology*, 1975, *97*, 173–179.

45. M. A. Wittig and P. Skolnick, "Status Versus Warmth as Determinants of Sex Differences in Personal Space," *Sex Roles*, 1978, *4*, 491–503.

46. A. Mehrabian, "Inference of Attitudes from the Posture, Orientation, and Distance of a Communicator," *Journal of Consulting and Clinical Psychology*, 1968, *32*, 296–308; A. Mehrabian, "Relationship of Attitude to Seated Posture, Orientation, and Distance," *Journal of Personality and Social Psychology*, 1968, *10*, 26–30; A. Mehrabian and J. T. Friar, "Encoding of Attitude by a Seated Communicator via Posture and Position Cues," *Journal of Consulting and Clinical Psychology*, 1969, *33*, 330–336. See also H. M. Rosenfeld, "Effect of an Approval-Seeking Induction on Interpersonal Proximity," *Psychological Reports*, 1965, *17*, 120–122; S. Heshka and Y. Nelson, "Interpersonal Speaking Distance as a Function of Age, Sex, and Relationship," *Sociometry*, 1972, *35*, 491–498; F. N. Willis, *op. cit.*

47. On students see J. R. Aiello and R. E. Cooper, "Use of Personal Space as a Function of Social Affect," *Proceedings of the 80th Annual Convention of the American Psychological Association*, 1972, 207–208. On couples see D. Byrne, C. R. Ervin, and J. Lamberth, "Continuity Between the Experimental Study of Attraction and Real-Life Computer Dating," *Journal of Personality and Social Psychology*, 1970, *16*, 157–165. On attitudes see A. R. Allgeier and D. Byrne, "Attraction Toward the Opposite Sex as a Determinant of Physical Proximity," *Journal of Social Psychology*, 1973, *90*, 213–219. On children see M. G. King, "Interpersonal Relations in Preschool Children and Average Approach Distance," *Journal of Genetic Psychology*, 1966, *109*, 109–116. On pedestrians see S. Thayer and L. Alban, "A Field Experiment of the Effect of Political and Cultural Factors on the Use of Personal Space," *Journal of Social Psychology*, 1972, *88*, 267–272.

48. M. A. Dosey and M. Meisels, "Personal Space and Self-Protection," *Journal of Personality and Social Psychology*, 1969, *11*, 93–97; W. E. Leipold, *Psychological Distance in a Dyadic Interview*, unpublished doctoral dissertation, University of North Dakota, 1963; C. L. Kleinke, R. A. Staneski, and D. E. Berger, "Evaluation of an Interviewer as a Function of Interviewer Gaze, Reinforcement of Subject Gaze, and Interviewer Attractiveness," *Journal of Personality and Social Psychology*, 1975, *31*, 115–122.

49. S. A. Karabenick and M. Meisels, "Effects of Performance Evaluation on Interpersonal Distance," *Journal of Personality*, 1972, *40*, 275–286; J. F. Tedesco and D. K. Fromme, "Cooperation, Competition and Personal Space," *Sociometry*, 1974, *37*, 116–121.

50. R. E. Kleck, "Physical Stigma and Nonverbal Cues Emitted in Face-to-Face Interaction," *Human Relations*, 1969, *22*, 51–60. See also B. A. Barrios, L. C. Corbitt, J. P. Estes, and J. S. Topping, "Effect of Social Stigma on Interpersonal Distance," *Psychological Record*, 1976, *26*, 343–348; R. E. Kleck, P. L. Buck, W. L. Goller, R. S. London, J. R.

Pfeiffer, and D. P. Vukcevic, "Effect of Stigmatizing Conditions on the Use of Personal Space," *Psychological Reports*, 1968, *23*, 111–118.

51. M. Meisels and M. A. Dosey, "Personal Space, Anger-Arousal, and Psychological Defense," *Journal of Personality*, 1971, *39*, 333–344; D. K. Fromme and C. K. Schmidt, "Affective Role Enactment and Expressive Behavior," *Journal of Personality and Social Psychology*, 1972, *24*, 413–419; P. G. Zimbardo, "The Psychology of Police Confessions," *Psychology Today*, June, 1967, p. 16; P. G. Zimbardo, "Toward a More Perfect Justice," *Psychology Today*, July, 1967, p. 44.

CHAPTER 7

1. L. K. Frank, "Tactile Communication," *Genetic Psychology Monographs*, 1957, *56*, 209–255, p. 211.

2. M. F. A. Montagu, *Touching: The Human Significance of the Skin* (New York: Harper and Row, 1971), p. 332.

3. S. M. Jourard, "An Exploratory Study of Body-Accessibility," *British Journal of Social and Clinical Psychology*, 1966, *5*, 221–231, p. 221.

4. On college students see *Ibid.*; L. B. Rosenfeld, S. Kartus, and C. Ray, "Body Accessibility Revisited," *Journal of Communication*, 1976, *26*, 27–30. See also E. L. Cowen, R. P. Weissberg, and B. S. Lotyczewski, "Physical Contact in Helping Interactions with Young Children," *Journal of Consulting and Clinical Psychology*, 1982, *50*, 219–225; S. Goldberg and M. Lewis, "Play Behavior in the Year Old Infant: Early Sex Differences," *Child Development*, 1969, *40*, 21–31; M. Lewis, "Parents and Children: Sex-Role Development," *School Review*, 1972, *80*, 229–240; M. Lewis and S. Goldberg, "Perceptual-Cognitive Development in Infancy: A Generalized Expectancy Model as a Function of the Mother-Infant Interaction," *Merrill-Palmer Quarterly*, 1969, *15*, 81–100; V. P. Perdue and J. M. Connor, "Patterns of Touching Between Preschool Children and Male and Female Teachers," *Child Development*, 1978, *49*, 1258–1262. For the 1976 study see L. B. Rosenfeld, S. Kartus, and C. Ray, *op. cit.* On Japanese students see D. C. Barnlund, "Communicative Styles in Two Cultures: Japan and the United States," in A. Kendon, R. M. Harris and M. R. Key (eds.), *Organization of Behavior in Face-to-Face Interaction* (The Hague: Mouton, 1975).

5. P. A. Andersen and K. Leibowitz, "The Development and Nature of the Construct Touch Avoidance," *Environmental Psychology and Nonverbal Behavior*, 1978, *3*, 89–106; R. Heslin, T. D. Nguyen, and M. L. Nguyen, "Meaning of Touch: The Case of Touch from a Stranger or Same Sex Person," *Journal of Nonverbal Behavior*, 1983, *7*, 147–157.

6. On school children see F. N. Willis and G. E. Hofmann, "Development of Tactile Patterns in Relation to Age, Sex, and Race," *Developmental Psychology*, 1975, *11*, 866; F. N. Willis and D. L. Reeves, "Touch Interactions in Junior High Students in Relation to Sex and Race," *Developmental Psychology*, 1976, *12*, 91–92. On the airport study see R. Heslin and D. Boss, "Nonverbal Intimacy in Airport Arrival and Departure," *Personal-*

ity and Social Psychology Bulletin, 1980, *6,* 248–252. On nursing home residents see C. M. Rinck, F. N. Willis, and L. M. Dean, "Interpersonal Touch Among Residents of Homes for the Elderly," *Journal of Communication,* 1980, *30,* 44–47.

7. M. L. Nguyen, R. Heslin, and T. D. Nguyen, "The Meaning of Touch as a Function of Sex and Marital Status," *Representative Research in Social Psychology,* 1976, *7,* 13–18; T. D. Nguyen, R. Heslin, and M. L. Nguyen, "The Meaning of Touch: Sex Differences," *Journal of Communication,* 1975, *25,* 92–103.

8. C. L. Kleinke, F. B. Meeker, and C. La Fong, "Effects of Gaze, Touch, and Use of Name on Evaluation of 'Engaged' Couples," *Journal of Research in Personality,* 1974, *7,* 368–373; R. A. Staneski, C. L. Kleinke, and F. B. Meeker, "Effects of Ingratiation, Touch, and Use of Name on Evaluation of Job Applicants and Interviewers," *Social Behavior and Personality,* 1977, *5,* 13–19.

9. B. Major and R. Heslin, "Perceptions of Cross-Sex and Same-Sex Nonreciprocal Touch: It Is Better to Give than to Receive," *Journal of Nonverbal Behavior,* 1982, *6,* 148–162; C. A. Florez and M. Goldman, "Evaluation of Interpersonal Touch by the Sighted and the Blind," *Journal of Social Psychology,* 1982, *116,* 229–234.

10. On the slide study see C. Silverthorne, C. Noreen, T. Hunt, and L. Rota, "The Effects of Tactile Stimulation on Visual Experience," *Journal of Social Psychology,* 1972, *88,* 153–154. On problem solving see N. M. Sussman and H. M. Rosenfeld, "Touch, Justification, and Sex: Influence on the Aversiveness of Spatial Violations," *Journal of Social Psychology,* 1978, *106,* 215–225. On handshakes see C. Silverthorne, J. Micklewright, M. O'Donnell, and R. Gibson, "Attribution of Personal Characteristics as a Function of the Degree of Touch on Initial Contact and Sex," *Sex Roles,* 1976, *2,* 185–193.

11. On the male interviewer see S. M. Jourard and R. Friedman, "Experimenter-Subject 'Distance' and Self-Disclosure," *Journal of Personality and Social Psychology,* 1970, *15,* 278–282. On female counseling clients see J. E. Pattison, "Effects of Touch on Self-Exploration and the Therapeutic Relationship," *Journal of Consulting and Clinical Psychology,* 1973, *40,* 170–175. On the twenty-five-minute interview see F. J. Alagna, S. J. Whitcher, J. D. Fisher, and E. A. Wicas, "Evaluative Reaction to Interpersonal Touch in a Counseling Interview," *Journal of Counseling Psychology,* 1979, *26,* 465–472. On the fifty-minute interview see S. R. Stockwell and A. Dye, "Effects of Counselor Touch on Counseling Outcome," *Journal of Counseling Psychology,* 1980, *27,* 443–446. On warmth see G. Breed and J. S. Ricci, "'Touch Me, Like Me': Artifact?" *Proceedings of the 81st Annual Convention of the American Psychological Association,* 1973, *8,* 153–154. On encounter group members see R. R. Dies and B. Greenberg, "Effects of Physical Contact in an Encounter Group Context," *Journal of Consulting and Clinical Psychology,* 1976, *44,* 400–405.

12. S. M. Jourard, *The Transparent Self* (New York: Van Nostrand, 1964); S. J. Whitcher and J. D. Fisher, "Multidimensional Reaction to Therapeutic Touch in a Hospital Setting," *Journal of Personality and Social Psychology,* 1979, *39,* 87–96.

13. J. D. Fisher, M. Rytting, and R. Heslin, "Hands Touching Hands: Affective and Evaluative Effects of an Interpersonal Touch," *Sociometry*, 1976, *39*, 416–421.

14. C. L. Kleinke, "Compliance to Requests Made by Gazing and Touching Experimenters in Field Settings," *Journal of Experimental Social Psychology*, 1977, *13*, 218–223.

15. F. N. Willis and H. K. Hamm, "The Use of Interpersonal Touch in Securing Compliance," *Journal of Nonverbal Behavior*, 1980, *5*, 49–55. See also R. Heslin, A. Rodolfo, and T. Whittler, "An Experimental Study of Customer Reactions to Being Touched by a Salesperson," *Purdue Papers in Consumer Psychology*, paper no. 176, 1983; D. E. Smith, J. A. Gier, and F. N. Willis, "Interpersonal Touch and Compliance with a Marketing Request," *Basic and Applied Social Psychology*, 1982, *3*, 35–38.

16. R. A. Baron, "Invasions of Personal Space and Helping: Mediating Effects of Invader's Apparent Need," *Journal of Experimental Social Psychology*, 1978, *14*, 304–312; C. L. Kleinke, "Interaction Between Gaze and Legitimacy of Request on Compliance in a Field Setting," *Journal of Nonverbal Behavior*, 1980, *5*, 3–12.

17. N. M. Henley, "Status and Sex: Some Touching Observations," *Bulletin of the Psychonomic Society*, 1973, *2*, 91–93; N. M. Henley, "The Politics of Touch," in P. Brown (ed.), *Radical Psychology* (New York: Harper and Row, 1973); N. M. Henley, *Body Politics* (Englewood Cliffs, N.J.: Prentice-Hall, 1977). See also A. Leffler, D. L. Gillespie, and J. C. Conaty, "The Effects of Status Differentiation on Nonverbal Behavior," *Social Psychology Quarterly*, 1982, *45*, 153–161.

18. D. S. Stier and J. A. Hall, "Gender Differences in Touch: An Empirical and Theoretical Review," *Journal of Personality and Social Psychology*, 1984, *47*, 440–459.

19. A. Kendon, "Some Functions of Gaze-Direction in Social Interaction," *Acta Psychologica*, 1967, *26*, 22–63. See also J. S. Efran, "Looking for Approval: Effects on Visual Behavior of Approbation from Persons Differing in Importance," *Journal of Personality and Social Psychology*, 1968, *10*, 21–25; R. V. Exline, "Visual Interaction: The Glances of Power and Preference," in J. K. Cole (ed.), *Nebraska Symposium on Motivation*, Vol. 19 (Lincoln: University of Nebraska Press, 1971); R. V. Exline and L. C. Winters, "Affective Relations and Mutual Glances in Dyads," in S. S. Tomkins and C. E. Izard (eds.), *Affect, Cognition, and Personality* (New York: Springer, 1965).

20. P. C. Ellsworth, J. M. Carlsmith, and A. Henson, "The Stare as a Stimulus to Flight in Human Subjects: A Series of Field Experiments," *Journal of Personality and Social Psychology*, 1972, *21*, 302–311.

21. R. V. Exline, *op cit.*; M. Argyle, L. M. Lefebvre, and M. Cook, "The Meaning of Five Patterns of Gaze," *European Journal of Social Psychology*, 1974, *4*, 125–136.

22. C. L. Kleinke, F. B. Meeker, and C. La Fong, *op cit.*; T. H. Naiman and G. Breed, "Gaze Duration as a Cue for Judging Conversational Tone," *Representative Research in Social Psychology*, 1974, *5*, 115–122; S. Thayer and W. Schiff, "Gazing Patterns and Attribution of Sexual Involvement," *Journal of Social Psychology*, 1977, *101*, 235–246. See also

A. Mehrabian, "Inference of Attitudes from the Posture, Orientation, and Distance of a Communicator," *Journal of Consulting and Clinical Psychology*, 1968, *32*, 296–308; S. Thayer and W. Schiff, "Observer Judgment of Social Interaction: Eye Contact and Relationship Inferences," *Journal of Personality and Social Psychology*, 1974, *30*, 110–114.

23. On counselors see B. R. Fretz, R. Corn, J. M. Tuemmler, and W. Bellet, "Counselor Nonverbal Behaviors and Client Evaluations," *Journal of Counseling Psychology*, 1979, *26*, 304–311; R. F. Haase and D. T. Tepper, "Nonverbal Components of Empathic Communication," *Journal of Counseling Psychology*, 1972, *19*, 417–424; E. W. Kelly and J. H. True, "Eye Contact and Communication of Facilitation Conditions," *Perceptual and Motor Skills*, 1980, *51*, 815–820; M. B. LaCrosse, "Nonverbal Behavior and Perceived Counselor Attractiveness and Persuasiveness," *Journal of Counseling Psychology*, 1975, *22*, 563–566; R. M. Tipton and R. A. Rymer, "A Laboratory Study of the Effects of Varying Levels of Counselor Eye Contact on Client-Focused and Problem-Focused Counseling Styles," *Journal of Counseling Psychology*, 1978, *25*, 200–204. On interviewers see C. L. Sodikoff, I. J. Firestone, and K. J. Kaplan, "Distance Matching and Distance Equilibrium in the Interview Dyad," *Personality and Social Psychology Bulletin*, 1974, *1*, 243–245; R. Tessler and L. Sushelsky, "Effects of Eye Contact and Social Status on the Perception of a Job Applicant in an Employment Interviewing Situation," *Journal of Vocational Behavior*, 1978, *13*, 338–347; R. W. Wheeler, J. C. Baron, S. Michell, and H. J. Ginsburg, "Eye Contact and the Perception of Intelligence," *Bulletin of the Psychonomic Society*, 1979, *13*, 101–102.

24. G. D. Hemsley and A. N. Doob, "The Effect of Looking Behavior on Perceptions of a Communicator's Credibility," *Journal of Applied Social Psychology*, 1978, *8*, 136–144.

25. M. Cook and M. C. Smith, "The Role of Gaze in Impression Formation," *British Journal of Social and Clinical Psychology*, 1975, *14*, 19–25; J. W. Stass and F. N. Willis, "Eye-Contact, Pupil Dilation, and Personal Preference," *Psychonomic Science*, 1967, *7*, 375–376. See also C. L. Kleinke, R. A. Staneski, and D. E. Berger, "Evaluation of an Interviewer as a Function of Interviewer Gaze, Reinforcement of Subject Gaze, and Interviewer Attractiveness," *Journal of Personality and Social Psychology*, 1975, *31*, 115–122; L. Scherwitz and R. Helmreich, "Interactive Effects of Eye Contact and Verbal Content on Interpersonal Attraction in Dyads," *Journal of Personality and Social Psychology*, 1973, *25*, 6–14.

26. L. Scherwitz and R. Helmreich, *op. cit.*; P. C. Ellsworth, H. S. Friedman, D. Perlick, and M. E. Hoyt, "Some Effects of Gaze on Subjects Motivated to Seek or to Avoid Social Comparison," *Journal of Experimental Social Psychology*, 1978, *14*, 69–87.

27. G. Breed, "The Effect of Intimacy: Reciprocity or Retreat?" *British Journal of Social and Clinical Psychology*, 1972, *11*, 135–142; E. W. Kelly, "Effects of Counselor's Eye Contact on Student-Clients' Perceptions," *Perceptual and Motor Skills*, 1978, *46*, 627–632; C. L. Kleinke, R. A. Staneski, and D. E. Berger, *op. cit.* See also J. R. Aiello, "A Further Look at Equilibrium Theory: Visual Interaction as a Function of Interpersonal Distance," *Environmental Psychology and Nonverbal Behavior*, 1977, *1*, 122–140; P. C. Ellsworth and J. M. Carlsmith, "Effects of Eye Contact and Verbal Content on Affective Response to a Dyadic Interaction," *Journal of Personality and Social Psychology*, 1968, *10*, 15–20.

28. On legitimate requests see R. C. Ernest and R. E. Cooper, "'Hey Mister, Do You Have Any Change?': Two Real World Studies of Proxemic Effects on Compliance with a Mundane Request," *Personality and Social Psychology Bulletin,* 1974, *1,* 158–159; C. L. Kleinke, "Compliance to Requests Made by Gazing and Touching Experimenters in Field Settings"; C. L. Kleinke and D. A. Singer, "Influence of Gaze on Compliance with Demanding and Conciliatory Requests in a Field Setting," *Personality and Social Psychology Bulletin,* 1979, *5,* 387–390; M. Snyder, J. Grether, and K. Keller, "Staring and Compliance: A Field Experiment on Hitchhiking," *Journal of Applied Social Psychology,* 1974, *4,* 165–170. On illegitimate requests see H. T. Reis and A. Werner, "Some Inter- and Intrapersonal Consequences of Eye Contact," paper presented at the meeting of the Eastern Psychological Association, Philadelphia, 1974.

29. C. L. Kleinke, "Interaction Between Gaze and Legitimacy of Request on Compliance in a Field Setting."

30. P. C. Ellsworth and E. J. Langer, "Staring and Approach: An Interpretation of the Stare as a Nonspecific Activator," *Journal of Personality and Social Psychology,* 1976, *33,* 117–122.

31. P. C. Ellsworth, J. M. Carlsmith, and A. Henson, *op. cit.;* P. Greenbaum and H. M. Rosenfeld, "Patterns of Avoidance in Response to Interpersonal Staring and Proximity: Effects of Bystanders on Drivers at a Traffic Intersection," *Journal of Personality and Social Psychology,* 1978, *36,* 575–587.

32. P. C. Ellsworth, J. M. Carlsmith, and A. Henson, *op. cit.;* D. Elman, D. C. Schulte, and A. Bukoff, "Effects of Facial Expression and Stare Duration on Walking Speed: Two Field Experiments," *Environmental Psychology and Nonverbal Behavior,* 1977, *2,* 93–99; C. Kmiecik, P. Mausar, and G. Banziger, "Attractiveness and Interpersonal Space," *Journal of Social Psychology,* 1979, *108,* 277–278.

33. J. D. Scheman and J. S. Lockard, "Development of Gaze Aversion in Children," *Child Development,* 1979, *50,* 594–596.

34. R. V. Exline, *op. cit.;* S. Thayer, "The Effect of Interpersonal Looking Duration on Dominance Judgments," *Journal of Social Psychology,* 1969, *79,* 285–286; P. C. Ellsworth and J. M. Carlsmith, "Eye Contact and Gaze Aversion in an Aggressive Encounter," *Journal of Personality and Social Psychology,* 1973, *28,* 280–292.

35. J. Hughes and M. Goldman, "Eye Contact, Facial Expression, Sex, and the Violation of Personal Space," *Perceptual and Motor Skills,* 1978, *46,* 579–584; D. R. Buchanan, M. Goldman, and R. Juhnke, "Eye Contact, Sex, and the Violation of Personal Space," *Journal of Social Psychology,* 1977, *103,* 19–25; M. G. Efran and J. A. Cheyne, "Affective Concomitants of the Invasion of Shared Space: Behavioral, Physiological, and Verbal Indicators," *Journal of Personality and Social Psychology,* 1974, *29,* 219–226.

36. C. L. Kleinke and P. D. Pohlen, "Affective and Emotional Responses as a Function of Other Person's Gaze and Competitiveness in a Two-Person Game," *Journal of Personality and Social Psychology,* 1971, *17,* 308–313.

37. On couples see C. L. Kleinke, A. A. Bustos, F. B. Meeker, and R. A. Staneski, "Effects of Self-Attributed and Other-Attributed Gaze on Interpersonal Evaluations Between Males and Females," *Journal of Experimental Social Psychology,* 1973, *9,* 154–163. On men see E. E. Maccoby and C. N. Jacklin, *The Psychology of Sex Differences* (Stanford, Calif.: Stanford University Press, 1974). On women see P. C. Ellsworth and L. Ross, "Intimacy in Response to Direct Gaze," *Journal of Experimental Social Psychology,* 1975, *11,* 592–613; S. Thayer and W. Schiff, "Gazing Patterns and Attribution of Sexual Involvement."

38. C. L. Kleinke, M. S. Desautels, and B. E. Knapp, "Adult Gaze and Affective and Visual Responses of Preschool Children," *Journal of Genetic Psychology,* 1977, *131,* 321–322; B. Post and E. M. Hetherington, "Sex Differences in the Use of Proximity and Eye Contact Judgments of Affiliation in Preschool Children," *Developmental Psychology,* 1974, *10,* 881–889.

39. M. L. Knapp, *Nonverbal Communication in Human Interaction* (New York: Holt, Rinehart, and Winston, 1978), p. 313.

40. On couples see M. A. Goldstein, M. C. Kilroy, and D. Van de Voort, "Gaze as a Function of Conversation and Degree of Love," *Journal of Psychology,* 1976, *92,* 227–234; Z. Rubin, "Measurement of Romantic Love," *Journal of Personality and Social Psychology,* 1970, *16,* 265–273. On children see L. M. Coutts and F. W. Schneider, "Affiliative Conflict Theory: An Investigation of the Intimacy Equilibrium and Compensation Hypothesis," *Journal of Personality and Social Psychology,* 1976, *34,* 1135–1142; N. F. Russo, "Eye Contact, Interpersonal Distance, and the Equilibrium Theory," *Journal of Personality and Social Psychology,* 1975, *31,* 497–502. On people see A. Mehrabian, "Inference of Attitudes from the Posture, Orientation, and Distance of a Communicator"; A. Mehrabian, "Relationship of Attitude to Seated Posture, Orientation, and Distance," *Journal of Personality and Social Psychology,* 1968, *10,* 26–30. See also L. M. Lefebvre, "Encoding and Decoding of Ingratiation in Modes of Smiling and Gaze," *British Journal of Social and Clinical Psychology,* 1975, *14,* 33–42; R. J. Pellegrini, R. A. Hicks, and L. Gordon, "The Effect of an Approval-Seeking Induction on Eye-Contact in Dyads," *British Journal of Social and Clinical Psychology,* 1970, *9,* 373–374.

41. On the experimenter see D. Nevill, "Experimental Manipulation of Dependency Motivation and its Effects on Eye Contact and Measures of Field Dependency," *Journal of Personality and Social Psychology,* 1974, *29,* 72–79. On girls see L. Harris, "Looks by Preschoolers at the Experimenter in a Choice-of-Toys Game: Effects of Experimenter and Age of Child," *Journal of Experimental Child Psychology,* 1968, *6,* 493–500. On boys see *Ibid.;* C. L. Kleinke, M. S. Desautels, and B. E. Knapp, *op. cit.*

42. J. A. Burns and B. L. Kintz, "Eye Contact While Lying During an Interview," *Bulletin of the Psychonomic Society,* 1976, *7,* 87–89; A. Mehrabian, "Nonverbal Betrayal of Feeling," *Journal of Experimental Research in Personality,* 1971, *5,* 64–73; A. Mehrabian and M. Williams, "Nonverbal Concomitants of Perceived and Intended Persuasiveness," *Journal of Personality and Social Psychology,* 1969, *13,* 37–58; S. C. Sitton and S. T. Griffin,

"Detection of Deception from Clients' Eye Contact Patterns," *Journal of Counseling Psychology*, 1981, *28*, 269–271; B. Timney and H. London, "Body Language Concomitants of Persuasiveness and Persuasibility in Dyadic Interaction," *International Journal of Group Tensions*, 1973, *3*, 48–67.

43. C. E. Kimble, R. A. Forte, and J. C. Yoshikawa, "Nonverbal Concomitants of Enacted Emotional Intensity and Positivity: Visual and Vocal Behavior," *Journal of Personality*, 1981, *49*, 271–283; C. E. Kimble and D. A. Olszewski, "Gaze and Emotional Expression: The Effects of Message Positivity-Negativity and Emotional Intensity," *Journal of Research in Personality*, 1980, *14*, 60–69.

44. C. O. Word, M. P. Zanna, and J. Cooper, "The Nonverbal Mediation of Self-Fulfilling Prophecies in Interracial Interaction," *Journal of Experimental Social Psychology*, 1974, *10*, 109–120; G. N. Hobson, K. T. Strongman, D. Bull, and G. Craig, "Anxiety and Gaze Aversion in Dyadic Encounters," *British Journal of Social and Clinical Psychology*, 1973, *12*, 122–129.

45. M. Natale, "Induction of Mood States and Their Effect on Gaze Behaviors," *Journal of Consulting and Clinical Psychology*, 1977, *45*, 960; P. Waxer, "Nonverbal Cues for Depression," *Journal of Abnormal Psychology*, 1974, *83*, 319–322; B. J. Zimmerman and G. H. Brody, "Race and Modeling Influences on the Interpersonal Play Patterns of Boys," *Journal of Educational Psychology*, 1975, *67*, 591–598.

46. J. M. Jellison and W. J. Ickes, "The Power of the Glance: Desire to See and Be Seen in Cooperative and Competitive Situations," *Journal of Experimental Social Psychology*, 1974, *10*, 444–450.

47. S. J. Carr and J. M. Dabbs, "The Effects of Lighting, Distance, and Intimacy of Topic on Verbal and Visual Behavior," *Sociometry*, 1974, *37*, 592–600; R. J. Edelmann and S. E. Hampson, "Changes in Non-Verbal Behaviour During Embarrassment," *British Journal of Social and Clinical Psychology*, 1979, *18*, 385–390; R. J. Edelmann and S. E. Hampson, "Embarrassment in Dyadic Interaction," *Social Behavior and Personality*, 1981, *9*, 171–177; R. V. Exline, D. Gray, and D. Schuette, "Visual Behavior in a Dyad as Affected by Interview Content and Sex of Respondent," *Journal of Personality and Social Psychology*, 1965, *3*, 201–209; R. Schulz and J. Barefoot, "Non-Verbal Responses and Affiliative Conflict Theory," *British Journal of Social and Clinical Psychology*, 1974, *13*, 1–7. See also A. Modigliani, "Embarrassment, Facework, and Eye Contact: Testing a Theory of Embarrassment," *Journal of Personality and Social Psychology*, 1971, *17*, 15–24.

48. R. V. Exline and L. C. Winters, *op. cit.;* N. A. Walsh, L. A. Meister, and C. L. Kleinke, "Interpersonal Attraction and Visual Behavior as a Function of Perceived Arousal and Evaluation by an Opposite Sex Person," *Journal of Social Psychology*, 1977, *103*, 65–74.

49. On people see J. S. Efran, *op. cit.;* J. S. Efran and A. Broughton, "Effect of Expectancies for Social Approval on Visual Behavior," *Journal of Personality and Social Psychology*, 1966, *4*, 103–107; S. S. Fugita, "Effects of Anxiety and Approval on Visual Interaction,"

Journal of Personality and Social Psychology, 1974, *29,* 586–592; A. Mehrabian and J. T. Friar, "Encoding of Attitude by a Seated Communicator via Posture and Position Cues," *Journal of Consulting and Clinical Psychology,* 1969, *33,* 330–336. On college men see R. E. Kleck and C. Rubenstein, "Physical Attractiveness, Perceived Attitude Similarity, and Interpersonal Attraction in an Opposite Sex Encounter," *Journal of Personality and Social Psychology,* 1975, *31,* 107–114.

50. W. Mischel, *Personality and Assessment* (New York: Wiley, 1968). See also R. J. Daniel and P. Lewis, "Stability of Eye Contact and Physical Distance Across a Series of Structured Interviews," *Journal of Consulting and Clinical Psychology,* 1972, *39,* 172; W. L. Libby, "Eye Contact and Direction of Looking as Stable Individual Differences," *Journal of Experimental Research in Personality,* 1970, *4,* 303–312; M. L. Patterson, "Stability of Nonverbal Immediacy Behaviors," *Journal of Experimental Social Psychology,* 1973, *9,* 97–109.

51. On nurturance et al, see M. Argyle and M. Cook, *Gaze and Mutual Gaze* (Cambridge, England: Cambridge University Press, 1976), p. 141; R. V. Exline, "Explorations in the Process of Person Perception: Visual Interaction in Relation to Competition, Sex, and Need for Affiliation," *Journal of Personality,* 1963, *31,* 1–20; R. V. Exline, D. Gray, and D. Schuette, *op. cit.;* R. V. Exline and D. Messick, "The Effects of Dependency and Social Reinforcement upon Visual Behaviour During an Interview," *British Journal of Social and Clinical Psychology,* 1967, *6,* 256–266; R. V. Exline, J. Thibaut, C. B. Hickey, and P. Gumpert, "Visual Interaction in Relation to Machiavellianism and an Unethical Act," in R. Christie and F. L. Geis (eds.), *Studies in Machiavellianism* (New York: Academic Press, 1970); M. LaFrance and B. Carmen, "The Nonverbal Display of Androgyny," *Journal of Personality and Social Psychology,* 1980, *38,* 36–49; W. L. Libby and D. Yaklevich, "Personality Determinants of Eye Contact and Direction of Gaze Aversion," *Journal of Personality and Social Psychology,* 1973, *27,* 197–206. On control and desirability see J. S. Efran, *op. cit.;* J. S. Efran and A. Broughton, *op. cit.;* A. Kendon and M. Cook, "The Consistency of Gaze Patterns in Social Interaction," *British Journal of Psychology,* 1969, *60,* 481–494; H. M. Lefcourt and J. Wine, "Internal versus External Control of Reinforcement and the Development of Attention in Experimental Situations," *Canadian Journal of Behavioral Science,* 1969, *1,* 167–181.

52. O. M. Watson, *Proxemic Behavior: A Cross-Cultural Study* (The Hague: Mouton, 1970); M. Argyle and M. Cook, *op cit.,* pp. 29–33; M. LaFrance and C. Mayo, "Racial Differences in Gaze Behavior During Conversations: Two Systematic Observational Studies," *Journal of Personality and Social Psychology,* 1976, *33,* 547–552.

53. M. Argyle and M. Cook, *op. cit.,* p. 147; I. H. Frieze and S. J. Ramsey, "Nonverbal Maintenance of Traditional Sex Roles," *Journal of Social Issues,* 1976, *32,* 133–141; M. S. Cary, "Does Civil Inattention Exist in Pedestrian Passing?" *Journal of Personality and Social Psychology,* 1978, *36,* 1185–1193; N. M. Henley, *Body Politics.*

54. M. Argyle and J. Dean, "Eye-Contact, Distance, and Affiliation," *Sociometry,* 1965, *28,* 289–304; M. Argyle and M. Cook, *op. cit.,* pp. 63–74. See also J. N. Cappella, "Mutual

Influence in Expressive Behavior: Adult-Adult and Infant-Adult Dyadic Interaction," *Psychological Bulletin,* 1981, *89,* 101–132.

55. On people see M. Argyle and J. Dean, *op. cit.;* M. Argyle and M. Cook, *op. cit.;* L. M. Coutts and M. Ledden, "Nonverbal Compensatory Reactions to Changes in Interpersonal Proximity," *Journal of Social Psychology,* 1977, *102,* 283–290; L. M. Coutts and F. W. Schneider, "Visual Behavior in an Unfocused Interaction as a Function of Sex and Distance," *Journal of Experimental Social Psychology,* 1975, *11,* 64–77; G. N. Goldberg, C. A. Kiesler, and B. E. Collins, "Visual Behavior and Face-to-Face Distance During Interaction," *Sociometry,* 1969, *32,* 43–53; M. L. Patterson, "Interpersonal Distance, Affect, and Equilibrium Theory," *Journal of Social Psychology,* 1977, *101,* 205–214; R. Schulz and J. Barefoot, *op. cit.* On reciprocation see S. J. Carr and J. M. Dabbs, *op. cit.;* C. L. Kleinke, R. A. Staneski, and S. L. Pipp, "Effects of Gaze, Distance, and Attractiveness on Males' First Impressions of Females," *Representative Research in Social Psychology,* 1975, *6,* 7–12. On women participants see J. R. Aiello, "A Test of Equilibrium Theory: Visual Interaction in Relation to Orientation, Distance, and Sex of Interactants," *Psychonomic Science,* 1972, *27,* 335–336; J. R. Aiello, "A Further Look at Equilibrium Theory: Visual Interaction as a Function of Interpersonal Distance"; J. R. Aiello, "Visual Interaction at Extended Distances," *Personality and Social Psychology Bulletin,* 1977, *3,* 83–86.

56. C. F. Johnson and J. M. Dabbs, "Self-Disclosure in Dyads as a Function of Distance and the Subject-Experimenter Relationship," *Sociometry,* 1976, *39,* 257–263. See also S. J. Carr and J. M. Dabbs, *op. cit.;* L. M. Coutts, M. Irvine, and F. W. Schneider, "Nonverbal Adjustments to Changes in Gaze and Orientation," *Psychology,* 1977, *14,* 28–32; M. L. Goldberg and A. R. Wellens, "A Comparison of Nonverbal Compensatory Behaviors Within Direct Face-to-Face and Television-Mediated Interviews," *Journal of Applied Social Psychology,* 1979, *9,* 250–260; M. L. Patterson, "Interpersonal Distance, Affect, and Equilibrium Theory"; E. Sundstrom, "A Test of Equilibrium Theory: Effects of Topic Intimacy and Proximity on Verbal and Nonverbal Behavior in Pairs of Friends and Strangers," *Environmental Psychology and Nonverbal Behavior,* 1978, *3,* 3–16.

57. G. Breed, "The Effect of Intimacy: Reciprocity or Retreat?" *British Journal of Social and Clinical Psychology,* 1972, *11,* 135–142; C. L. Kleinke, "Gaze and Eye Contact: A Research Review," *Psychological Bulletin,* 1986, in press. See also M. Argyle and M. Cook, *op. cit.,* p. 67; C. L. Kleinke, "Effects of Personal Evaluations," in G. J. Chelune and Associates, *Self-Disclosure: Origins, Patterns, and Implications of Openness in Interpersonal Relations* (San Francisco: Jossey-Bass, 1979).

58. M. L. Patterson, "An Arousal Model of Interpersonal Intimacy," *Psychological Review,* 1976, *83,* 235–245. See also C. L. Kleinke, "A Note on the Relationship Between Gaze and Arousal," paper presented at the meeting of the Western Psychological Association, Los Angeles, 1981; C. L. Kleinke, "Gaze and Eye Contact: A Research Review."

59. M. L. Patterson, "A Sequential Functional Model of Nonverbal Exchange," *Psychological Review,* 1982, *89,* 231–249; M. L. Patterson, *Nonverbal Behavior: A Functional Perspective* (New York, Springer, 1983).

60. M. Cook and M. C. Smith, *op. cit.;* C. L. Kleinke, "A Note on the Relationship Between Gaze and Arousal"; C. L. Kleinke and J. H. Walton, "Influence of Reinforced Smiling on Affective Responses in an Interview," *Journal of Personality and Social Psychology,* 1982, *42,* 557–565.

CHAPTER 8

1. J. T. Cacioppo and R. E. Petty, "The Need for Cognition," *Journal of Personality and Social Psychology,* 1982, *42,* 116–131.

2. V. L. Hamilton, "Intuitive Psychologist or Intuitive Lawyer? Alternative Models of the Attribution Process," *Journal of Personality and Social Psychology,* 1980, *39,* 767–772.

3. F. Heider, *The Psychology of Interpersonal Relations* (New York: Wiley, 1958).

4. E. E. Jones and K. E. Davis, "From Acts to Dispositions: The Attribution Process in Person Perception," in L. Berkowitz (ed.), *Advances in Experimental Social Psychology,* Vol. 2 (New York: Academic Press, 1965).

5. I. Ajzen, "Attribution of Dispositions to an Actor: Effects of Perceived Decision Freedom and Behavioral Utilities," *Journal of Personality and Social Psychology,* 1971, *18,* 144–156; C. H. Lay, D. F. Burron, and D. N. Jackson, "Base Rates and Informational Value in Impression Formation," *Journal of Personality and Social Psychology,* 1973, *28,* 390–395.

6. E. E. Jones and D. McGillis, "Correspondent Inferences and the Attribution Cube: A Comparative Reappraisal," in J. H. Harvey, W. J. Ickes, and R. F. Kidd (eds.), *New Directions in Attribution Research,* Vol. 1 (Hillsdale, N.J.: Erlbaum, 1976).

7. E. J. Kepka and P. Brickman, "Consistency versus Discrepency as Clues in the Attribution of Intelligence and Motivation," *Journal of Personality and Social Psychology,* 1971, *20,* 223–229.

8. E. E. Jones, S. Worchel, G. R. Goethals, and J. F. Grumet, "Prior Expectancy and Behavioral Extremity as Determinants of Attitude Attribution," *Journal of Experimental Social Psychology,* 1971, *7,* 59–80.

9. E. E. Jones and S. Berglas, "A Recency Effect in Attitude Attribution," *Journal of Personality,* 1976, *44,* 433–448.

10. E. E. Jones and D. McGillis, *op. cit.*

11. J. Mills and J. M. Jellison, "Effect of Opinion Change on How Desirable the Communication Is to the Audience the Communicator Addressed," *Journal of Personality and Social Psychology,* 1967, *6,* 98–101.

12. E. E. Jones, K. E. Davis, and K. J. Gergen, "Role Playing Variations and Their Informational Value," *Journal of Abnormal and Social Psychology,* 1961, *63,* 302–310.

13. E. E. Jones and K. E. Davis, *op. cit.;* M. E. Enzle, M. D. Harvey, and E. T. Wright, "Personalism and Distinctiveness," *Journal of Personality and Social Psychology,* 1980, *39,* 542–552; E. E. Jones and R. deCharms, "Changes in Social Perception as a Function of the Personal Relevance of Behavior," *Sociometry,* 1957, *20,* 75–85.

14. E. E. Jones and K. E. Davis, *op. cit.;* K. J. Gergen and E. E. Jones, "Mental Illness, Predictability, and Affective Consequences as Stimulus Factors in Person Perception," *Journal of Abnormal and Social Psychology,* 1963, *67,* 95–105.

15. D. Newston, "Dispositional Inference from Effects of Actions: Effects Chosen and Effects Foregone," *Journal of Experimental Social Psychology,* 1974, *10,* 489–496.

16. M. L. Snyder, R. E. Kleck, A. Strenta, and S. J. Mentzer, "Avoidance of the Handicapped: An Attributional Ambiguity Analysis," *Journal of Personality and Social Psychology,* 1979, *37,* 2297–2306.

17. W. G. Stephan, "Actor vs Observer: Attributions to Behavior with Positive or Negative Outcomes and Empathy for the Other Role," *Journal of Experimental Social Psychology,* 1975, *11,* 205–214.

18. On the covariation model see H. H. Kelley, "Attribution Theory in Social Psychology," in D. Levine (ed.), *Nebraska Symposium on Motivation,* Vol. 15 (Lincoln: University of Nebraska Press, 1967); H. H. Kelley, "The Process of Causal Attribution," *American Psychologist,* 1973, *28,* 107–128. On the causal schemata model see *Ibid.;* H. H. Kelley, *Causal Schemata and the Attribution Process* (Morristown, N.J.: General Learning Press, 1972).

19. L. Z. McArthur, "The How and What of Why: Some Determinants and Consequences of Causal Attribution," *Journal of Personality and Social Psychology,* 1972, *22,* 171–193; L. Z. McArthur, "The Lesser Influence of Consensus than Distinctiveness Information on Causal Attributions: A Test of the Person-Thing Hypothesis," *Journal of Personality and Social Psychology,* 1976, *33,* 733–742. See also D. N. Ruble and N. S. Feldman, "Order of Consensus, Distinctiveness, and Consistency Information and Causal Attributions," *Journal of Personality and Social Psychology,* 1976, *34,* 930–937; M. Zuckerman, "Actions and Occurrences in Kelley's Cube," *Journal of Personality and Social Psychology,* 1978, *36,* 647–656; M. Zuckerman and L. S. Feldman, "Actions and Occurrences in Attribution Theory," *Journal of Personality and Social Psychology,* 1984, *46,* 541–550; A. W. Kruglanski, I. A. Hamel, S. A. Maides, and J. M. Schwartz, "Attribution Theory as a Special Case of Lay-Epistemology," in J. H. Harvey, W. J. Ickes, and R. F. Kidd (eds.), *New Directions in Attribution Research,* Vol. 2 (Hillsdale, N.J.: Erlbaum, 1978).

20. V. Karaz and D. Perlman, "Attribution at the Wire: Consistency and Outcome Finish Strong," *Journal of Experimental Social Psychology,* 1975, *11,* 470–477.

21. B. R. Orvis, J. D. Cunningham, and H. H. Kelley, "A Closer Examination of Causal Inference: The Roles of Consensus, Distinctiveness, and Consistency Information," *Journal of Personality and Social Psychology,* 1975, *32,* 605–616.

22. D. J. Pruitt and C. A. Insko, "Extension of the Kelley Attribution Model: The Role of Comparison-Object Consensus, Target-Object Consensus, Distinctiveness, and Consistency," *Journal of Personality and Social Psychology,* 1980, *39,* 39–58.

23. B. R. Orvis, J. D. Cunningham, and H. H. Kelley, *op. cit.*

24. H. H. Kelley, "The Process of Causal Attribution"; H. H. Kelley, *Causal Schemata and the Attribution Process.* A critical analysis of Kelley's Causal Schemata Model can be found in K. Fiedler, "Causal Schemata: Review and Criticism of Research on a Popular Construct," *Journal of Personality and Social Psychology,* 1982, *42,* 1001–1013. See also E. R. Smith and F. D. Miller, "Attributional Information Processing: A Response Time Model of Causal Subtraction," *Journal of Personality and Social Psychology,* 1979, *37,* 1723–1731.

25. H. H. Kelley, "The Process of Causal Attribution"; H. H. Kelley, *Causal Schemata and the Attribution Process.*

26. *Ibid.*

27. D. S. Cordray and J. I. Shaw, "An Empirical Test of the Covariation Analysis in Causal Attribution," *Journal of Experimental Social Psychology,* 1978, *14,* 280–290. See also T. Pyszcynski and J. Greenberg, "Determinants of Reduction in Intended Effort as a Strategy for Coping with Anticipated Failure," *Journal of Research in Personality,* 1983, *17,* 412–422.

28. H. H. Kelley, "The Process of Causal Attribution"; H. H. Kelley and J. L. Michela, "Attribution Theory and Research," in M. R. Rosenzweig and L. W. Porter (eds.), *Annual Review of Psychology,* Vol. 31 (Palo Alto, Calif.: Annual Reviews, 1980).

29. *Ibid.*

30. S. Wimer and H. H. Kelley, "An Investigation of the Dimensions of Causal Attribution," *Journal of Personality and Social Psychology,* 1982, *43,* 1142–1162.

31. J. H. Harvey, K. L. Yarkin, J. M. Lightner, and J. P. Town, "Unsolicited Interpretation and Recall of Interpersonal Events," *Journal of Personality and Social Psychology,* 1980, *38,* 551–568; P. T. P. Wong and B. Weiner, "When People Ask 'Why' Questions, and the Heuristics of Attributional Research," *Journal of Personality and Social Psychology,* 1981, *40,* 650–663.

32. E. J. Langer, "Rethinking the Role of Thought in Social Interaction," in J. H. Harvey, W. Ickes, and R. F. Kidd (eds.), *New Directions in Attribution Research,* Vol. 2 (Hillsdale, N.J.: Erlbaum, 1978); E. J. Langer, A. Blank, and B. Chanowitz, "The Mindlessness of Ostensibly Thoughtful Action: The Role of 'Placebic' Information in Interpersonal Interaction," *Journal of Personality and Social Psychology,* 1978, *36,* 635–642.

33. *Ibid.*

34. *Ibid.*

35. *Ibid.;* E. Berscheid, W. Graziano, T. Monson, and M. Dermer, "Outcome Dependency: Attention, Attribution, and Attraction," *Journal of Personality and Social Psychology,* 1976, *34,* 978–989; J. H. Harvey, K. L. Yarkin, J. M. Lightner, and J. P. Town, *op. cit.;* E. J. Langer and L. Imber, "Role of Mindlessness in the Perception of Deviance," *Journal of Personality and Social Psychology,* 1980, *39,* 360–367; T. A. Pyszcynski and J. Greenberg, "Role of Disconfirmed Expectancies in the Instigation of Attributional Processing," *Journal of Personality and Social Psychology,* 1981, *40,* 31–38.

36. T. S. Pittman and N. L. Pittman, "Deprivation of Control and the Attribution Process," *Journal of Personality and Social Psychology,* 1980, *39,* 377–389; S. E. Taylor and S. T. Fiske, "Salience, Attention, and Attribution: Top of the Head Phenomena," in L. Berkowitz (ed.), *Advances in Experimental Social Psychology,* Vol. 11 (New York: Academic Press, 1978); R. Hastie, "Causes and Effects of Causal Attribution," *Journal of Personality and Social Psychology,* 1984, *46,* 44–56.

37. For a more technical review of current issues in attribution theory and research see J. H. Harvey and G. Weary, "Current Issues in Attribution Theory and Research," in M. R. Rosenzweig and L. W. Porter (eds.), *Annual Review of Psychology,* Vol. 35 (Palo Alto, Calif.: Annual Reviews, 1984). For a summary of the process see R. D. Hansen, "Commonsense Attribution," *Journal of Personality and Social Psychology,* 1980, *39,* 996–1009.

CHAPTER 9

1. E. Burns, *Theatricality: A Study of Convention in the Theatre and in Social Life* (New York: Harper and Row, 1973), p. 37; W. Shakespeare, "As You Like It," (New York: Pocket Books, 1959), act II, scene VII; B. R. Schlenker, *Impression Management* (Monterey, Calif.: Brooks/Cole, 1980), p. 6; R. F. Baumeister, "A Self-Presentational View of Social Phenomena," *Psychological Bulletin,* 1982, *91,* 3–26.

2. V. J. Derlega and J. Grzelak, "Appropriateness of Self-Disclosure," in G. J. Chelune and Associates, *Self-Disclosure: Origins, Patterns, and Implications of Openness in Interpersonal Relationships* (San Francisco: Jossey–Bass, 1979), chap. 6; G. J. Chelune, "Measuring Openness in Interpersonal Communication," in G. J. Chelune and Associates, *op. cit.,* chap. 1. On the study see Z. Rubin, "Disclosing Oneself to a Stranger: Reciprocity and its Limits," *Journal of Experimental Social Psychology,* 1975, *11,* 233–260.

3. V. J. Derlega, M. S. Harris, and A. L. Chaikin, "Self-Disclosure Reciprocity, Liking, and the Deviant," *Journal of Experimental Social Psychology,* 1973, *9,* 277–284.

4. V. J. Derlega and A. L. Chaikin, "Norms Affecting Self-Disclosure in Men and Women," *Journal of Consulting and Clinical Psychology,* 1976, *44,* 376–380; G. J. Chelune, "Reactions to Male and Female Disclosure at Two Levels," *Journal of Personality and Social Psychology,* 1976, *34,* 1000–1003.

5. C. L. Kleinke and M. L. Kahn, "Perceptions of Self-Disclosers: Effects of Sex and Physical Attractiveness," *Journal of Personality,* 1980, *48,* 190–205.

6. A. L. Chaikin and V. J. Derlega, "Variables Affecting the Appropriateness of Self-Disclosure," *Journal of Consulting and Clinical Psychology*, 1974, *42*, 588–593; D. M. Daher and P. G. Banikiotes, "Interpersonal Attraction and Rewarding Aspects of Disclosure Content and Level," *Journal of Personality and Social Psychology*, 1976, *33*, 492–496; W. Lawless and S. Nowicki, "Role of Self-Disclosure in Interpersonal Attraction," *Journal of Consulting and Clinical Psychology*, 1972, *38*, 300; A. L. Chaikin and V. J. Derlega, "Liking for the Norm-Breaker in Self-Disclosure," *Journal of Personality*, 1974, *42*, 117–129.

7. B. C. Certner, "The Exchange of Self-Disclosure in Same-Sexed Groups of Strangers," *Journal of Consulting and Clinical Psychology*, 1973, *40*, 292–297; M. Worthy, A. L. Gary, and G. M. Kahn, "Self-Disclosure as an Exchange Process," *Journal of Personality and Social Psychology*, 1969, *13*, 59–63. See also E. E. Jones and R. L. Archer, "Are There Special Effects of Personalistic Self-Disclosure?" *Journal of Experimental Social Psychology*, 1976, *12*, 180–193.

8. I. Altman and D. Taylor, *Social Penetration: The Development of Interpersonal Relationships* (New York: Holt, Rinehart, and Winston, 1973); C. B. Wortman, P. Adesman, E. Herman, and R. Greenberg, "Self-Disclosure: An Attributional Perspective," *Journal of Personality and Social Psychology*, 1976, *33*, 184–191. On early disclosure see E. E. Jones and E. M. Gordon, "Timing of Self-Disclosure and Its Effects on Personal Attraction," *Journal of Personality and Social Psychology*, 1972, *24*, 358–365; R. L. Archer and J. A. Burleson, "The Effects of Timing of Self-Disclosure on Attraction and Reciprocity," *Journal of Personality and Social Psychology*, 1980, *38*, 120–130. On counselors and therapists see M. A. Hoffman-Graff, "Interviewer Use of Positive and Negative Self-Disclosure and Interviewer-Subject Sex Pairing," *Journal of Counseling Psychology*, 1977, *24*, 184–190.

9. C. L. Kleinke, "Effects of Personal Evaluations," in G. J. Chelune and Associates, *op. cit.*, chap. 3.

10. M. Wiener and A. Mehrabian, *Language Within Language: Immediacy, a Channel in Verbal Communication* (New York: Appleton-Century-Crofts, 1968).

11. *Ibid.*

12. A. Mehrabian, "Attitudes Inferred from Non-Immediacy of Verbal Communications," *Journal of Verbal Learning and Verbal Behavior*, 1967, *6*, 294–295; A. Mehrabian and M. Wiener, "Non-Immediacy Between Communicator and Object of Communication in a Verbal Message: Application to the Inference of Attitudes," *Journal of Consulting Psychology*, 1966, *30*, 420–425; A. Mehrabian, "Attitudes in Relation to the Forms of Communicator-Object Relationship in Spoken Communications," *Journal of Personality*, 1966, *34*, 80–93; A. Mehrabian, "Communication Length as an Index of Communicator Attitude," *Psychological Reports*, 1965, *17*, 519–522; A. N. Wiens, R. H. Jackson, T. S. Manaugh, and J. D. Matarazzo, "Communication Length as an Index of Communicator Attitude: A Replication," *Journal of Applied Psychology*, 1969, *53*, 264–266.

13. R. Gottlieb, M. Wiener, and A. Mehrabian, "Immediacy, DRQ, and Content in Verbalizations about Positive and Negative Experiences," *Journal of Personality and Social Psy-*

chology, 1967, *7,* 266–274; A. Mehrabian and M. Wiener, *op. cit.* See also H. Wagner and K. Pease, "The Verbal Communication of Inconsistency Between Attitudes Held and Attitudes Expressed," *Journal of Personality,* 1976, *44,* 1–15; D. Kuiken, "Nonimmediate Language Style and Inconsistency Between Private and Expressed Evaluations," *Journal of Experimental Social Psychology,* 1981, *17,* 183–196.

14. A. Mehrabian, "Attitudes Inferred from Neutral Verbal Communications," *Journal of Consulting Psychology,* 1967, *31,* 414–417; A. Mehrabian, "Immediacy: An Indicator of Attitudes in Linguistic Communication," *Journal of Personality,* 1966, *34,* 26–34.

15. C. L. Kleinke, "Perceived Approbation in Short, Medium, and Long Letters of Recommendation," *Perceptual and Motor Skills,* 1978, *46,* 119–122.

16. On accuracy see B. Ackerman and B. R. Schlenker, "Self-Presentation: Attributes of the Actor and Audience," paper presented at the 83rd annual meeting of the American Psychological Association, Chicago, Sept., 1975; R. F. Baumeister and E. E. Jones, "When Self-Presentation Is Constrained by the Target's Knowledge: Consistency and Compensation," *Journal of Personality and Social Psychology,* 1978, *36,* 608–618; B. R. Schlenker, "Self-Presentation: Managing the Impression of Consistency When Reality Interferes with Self-Enhancement," *Journal of Personality and Social Psychology,* 1975, *32,* 1030–1037. On amplification see B. R. Schlenker and M. R. Leary, "Audiences' Reactions to Self-Enhancing, Self-Derogating, and Accurate Self-Presentations," *Journal of Experimental Social Psychology,* 1982, *18,* 89–104; B. R. Schlenker, *Impression Management,* p. 193.

17. L. K. Stires and E. E. Jones, "Modesty Versus Self-Enhancement as Alternative Forms of Ingratiation," *Journal of Experimental Social Psychology,* 1969, *5,* 172–188; P. M. Blau, "A Theory of Social Integration," *American Journal of Sociology,* 1960, *65,* 545–557; E. E. Jones, K. J. Gergen, and R. G. Jones, "Tactics of Ingratiation among Leaders and Subordinates in a Status Hierarchy," *Psychological Monographs,* 1963, *77,* Whole No. 566.

18. R. B. Cialdini, R. J. Borden, A. Thorne, M. R. Walker, S. Freeman, and L. R. Sloan, "Basking in Reflected Glory: Three (Football) Field Studies," *Journal of Personality and Social Psychology,* 1976, *34,* 366–375.

19. R. B. Cialdini and K. D. Richardson, "Two Indirect Tactics of Image Management: Basking and Blasting," *Journal of Personality and Social Psychology,* 1980, *39,* 406–415.

20. J. Cooper and E. E. Jones, "Opinion Divergence as a Strategy to Avoid Being Miscast," *Journal of Personality and Social Psychology,* 1969, *13,* 23–30.

21. D. Carnegie, *How to Win Friends and Influence People* (New York: Pocket Books, 1972), p. 130. Originally published in 1936.

22. E. E. Jones and E. M. Gordon, *op. cit.*

23. E. Aronson, B. Willerman, and J. Floyd, "The Effect of a Pratfall on Increasing Interpersonal Attractiveness," *Psychonomic Science,* 1966, *4,* 227–228.

24. R. Helmreich, E. Aronson, and J. LeFan, "To Err is Humanizing—Sometimes: Effects of Self-Esteem, Competence, and a Pratfall on Interpersonal Attraction," *Journal of Personality and Social Psychology,* 1970, *16,* 259–264; D. R. Mettee and P. C. Wilkins, "When Similarity 'Hurts': The Effects of Perceived Ability and a Humorous Blunder upon Interpersonal Attractiveness," *Journal of Personality and Social Psychology,* 1972, *22,* 246–258.

25. W. R. Gove, M. Hughes, and M. R. Geerken, "Playing Dumb: A Form of Impression Management with Undesirable Side Effects," *Social Psychology Quarterly,* 1980, *43,* 89–102.

26. L. W. Heath and S. B. Gurwitz, "Self-Presentation and Stereotypes: Is It Smart to Play Dumb?", paper presented at the 85th annual meeting of the American Psychological Association, San Francisco, Sept., 1977; M. P. Zanna and S. J. Pack, "On the Self-Fulfilling Nature of Apparent Sex Differences in Behavior," *Journal of Experimental Social Psychology,* 1975, *11,* 583–591.

27. C. R. Snyder and H. L. Fromkin, *Uniqueness: The Human Pursuit of Difference* (New York: Plenum, 1980), p. 79.

28. E. E. Jones and S. Berglas, "Control of Attributions About the Self Through Self-Handicapping Strategies: The Appeal of Alcohol and the Role of Underachievement," *Personality and Social Psychology Bulletin,* 1978, *4,* 200–206; C. R. Snyder and T. W. Smith, "Symptoms as Self-Handicapping Strategies: The Virtues of Old Wine in a New Bottle," in G. Weary and H. L. Mirels (eds.), *Integrations of Clinical and Social Psychology* (New York: Oxford University Press, 1982). See also S. Berglas and E. E. Jones, "Drug Choice as a Self-Handicapping Strategy in Response to Noncontingent Success," *Journal of Personality and Social Psychology,* 1978, *36,* 405–417.

29. *Ibid.*

30. On psychiatric patients see B. Braginsky, D. Braginsky, and K. Ring, *Methods of Madness: The Mental Hospital as a Last Resort* (New York: Holt, Rinehart, and Winston, 1969); A. F. Fontana, E. B. Klein, E. Lewis, and L. Levine, "Presentation of Self in Mental Illness," *Journal of Consulting and Clinical Psychology,* 1968, *32,* 110–119. On students see T. W. Smith, C. R. Snyder, and M. M. Handelsman, "On the Self-Serving Function of an Academic Wooden Leg: Test Anxiety as a Self-Handicapping Strategy," *Journal of Personality and Social Psychology,* 1982, *42,* 314–321.

31. C. R. Snyder and T. W. Smith, *op. cit.*

32. The ideas in this section were suggested by G. Weary and R. M. Arkin, "Attributional Self-Presentation," in J. H. Harvey, W. Ickes, and R. F. Kidd (eds.), *New Directions in Attribution Research,* Vol. 3 (Hillsdale, N.J.: Erlbaum, 1981).

CHAPTER 10

1. D. Carnegie, *How to Win Friends and Influence People* (New York: Pocket Books, 1972), p. 39. Originally published in 1936.

2. E. E. Jones, *Ingratiation: A Social Psychological Analysis* (New York: Appleton-Century-Crofts, 1964); E. E. Jones and C. Wortman, *Ingratiation: An Attributional Approach* (Morristown, N.J.: General Learning Press, 1973); E. E. Jones and C. Wortman, *op. cit.*, p. 2.

3. D. Carnegie, *op. cit.*, p. 31; D. Byrne and R. Rhamey, "Magnitude of Positive and Negative Reinforcements as a Determinant of Attraction," *Journal of Personality and Social Psychology*, 1965, 2, 884–889; C. Gouaux and K. Summers, "Interpersonal Attraction as a Function of Affective State and Affective Change," *Journal of Research in Personality*, 1973, 7, 254–260; H. McGinley and P. McGinley, "Attraction Toward a Stranger as a Function of Direct and Vicarious Reinforcement," *Journal of Research in Personality*, 1972, 6, 60–68; N. A. Walsh, L. A. Meister, and C. L. Kleinke, "Interpersonal Attraction and Visual Behavior as a Function of Perceived Arousal and Evaluation by an Opposite Sex Person," *Journal of Social Psychology*, 1977, 103, 65–74; K. W. Wyant and G. W. Gardner, "Interpersonal Evaluations, Attitudes, and Attraction," *Journal of Research in Personality*, 1977, 11, 356–367. See also D. R. Mettee and E. Aronson, "Affective Reactions to Appraisal from Others," in T. L. Huston (ed.), *Foundations of Interpersonal Attraction* (New York: Academic Press, 1974).

4. E. E. Jones and C. Wortman, *op cit.*

5. M. Deutsch and L. Solomon, "Reactions to Evaluation by Others as Influenced by Self-Evaluation," *Sociometry*, 1959, 22, 93–112.

6. R. C. Howard and L. Berkowitz, "Reactions to the Evaluators of One's Performance," *Journal of Personality*, 1958, 26, 496–506.

7. D. G. Dutton and A. J. Arrowood, "Situational Factors in Evaluation Congruency and Interpersonal Attraction," *Journal of Personality and Social Psychology*, 1971, 18, 222–229.

8. H. Dickoff, "Reactions to Evaluations by Another Person as a Function of Self-Evaluation and the Interaction Context," unpublished doctoral dissertation, Duke University, 1961. Cited in E. E. Jones and C. Wortman, *op. cit.*, p. 7; C. A. Lowe and J. W. Goldstein, "Reciprocal Liking and Attributions of Ability: Mediating Effects of Perceived Intent and Personal Involvement," *Journal of Personality and Social Psychology*, 1970, 16, 291–297.

9. D. Drachman, A. DeCarufel, and C. A. Insko, "The Extra Credit Effect in Interpersonal Attraction," *Journal of Experimental Social Psychology*, 1978, 14, 458–465.

10. E. E. Jones and C. Wortman, *op. cit.*

11. E. Walster and L. Festinger, "The Effectiveness of 'Overheard' Persuasive Communications," *Journal of Abnormal and Social Psychology*, 1962, 65, 395–402.

12. D. Landy and E. Aronson, "Liking for an Evaluator as a Function of His Discernment," *Journal of Personality and Social Psychology*, 1968, *9*, 133–141; E. E. Jones and C. Wortman, *op. cit.*, p. 11; D. A. Potter, "Personalism and Interpersonal Attraction," *Journal of Personality and Social Psychology*, 1973, *28*, 192–198.

13. E. E. Jones, *op. cit.*, p. 30; E. Aronson, "Some Antecedents of Interpersonal Attraction," in W. J. Arnold and D. Levine (eds.), *Nebraska Symposium on Motivation* (Lincoln: University of Nebraska Press, 1969); E. Aronson and D. Linder, "Gain and Loss of Esteem as Determinants of Interpersonal Attractiveness," *Journal of Experimental Social Psychology*, 1965, *1*, 156–172.

14. D. R. Mettee and E. Aronson, *op. cit.*; E. E. Jones and C. Wortman, *op. cit.*, p. 11; D. R. Mettee and E. Aronson, *op. cit.*, p. 276.

15. E. Berscheid, T. Brothen, and W. Graziano, "Gain-Loss Theory and the 'Law of Infidelity': Mr. Doting versus the Admiring Stranger," *Journal of Personality and Social Psychology*, 1976, *33*, 709–718.

16. R. E. Farson, "Praise Reappraised," *Harvard Business Review*, 1963, *41*, 61–66; E. E. Jones and C. Wortman, *op. cit.*, p. 15.

17. E. E. Jones and C. Wortman, *op. cit.*, p. 12.

18. A. Pepitone and J. Sherberg, "Intentionality, Responsibility, and Interpersonal Attraction," *Journal of Personality*, 1957, *25*, 757–766.

19. The ideas in this section were suggested by D. E. Kanouse, P. Gumpert, and D. Canavan-Gumpert, "The Semantics of Praise," in J. H. Harvey, W. Ickes, and R. F. Kidd (eds.), *New Directions in Attribution Research*, Vol. 3 (Hillsdale, N.J.: Erlbaum, 1981).

20. E. E. Jones and C. Wortman, *op. cit.*, p. 22.

21. V. D. Thompson, W. Stroebe, and J. Schopler, "Some Situational Determinants of the Motives Attributed to the Person Who Performs a Helping Act," *Journal of Personality*, 1971, *39*, 460–472; P. Brounstein and H. Sigall, "Effects of Dependence and Timing of a Favor on Liking for a Favor Doer," *Representative Research in Social Psychology*, 1977, *8*, 118–127; J. W. Thibaut and H. W. Riecken, "Some Determinants and Consequences of the Perception of Social Causality," *Journal of Personality*, 1955, *24*, 113–133.

22. S. B. Kiesler, "The Effect of Perceived Role Requirements on Reactions to Favor Doing," *Journal of Experimental Social Psychology*, 1966, *2*, 198–210; J. Schopler and V. D. Thompson, "Role of Attribution Processes in Mediating Amount of Reciprocity for a Favor," *Journal of Personality and Social Psychology*, 1968, *10*, 243–250.

23. M. S. Greenberg and D. M. Frisch, "Effect of Intentionality on Willingness to Reciprocate a Favor," *Journal of Experimental Social Psychology*, 1972, *8*, 99–111; C. Nemeth, "Effects of Free versus Constrained Behavior on Attraction," *Journal of Personality and Social Psychology*, 1970, *15*, 302–311.

24. J. W. Brehm and A. H. Cole, "Effect of a Favor Which Reduces Freedom," *Journal of Personality and Social Psychology*, 1966, *3*, 420–426.

25. E. T. Webb and J. B. Morgan, *Strategy in Handling People* (Garden City, N.Y.: Garden City Publishing Company, 1930), p. 8; G. L. Clore, *Interpersonal Attraction—An Overview* (Morristown, N.J.: General Learning Press, 1975), p. 24.

26. On residents see J. L. Freedman and S. C. Fraser, "Compliance Without Pressure: The Foot-in-the-Door Technique," *Journal of Personality and Social Psychology*, 1966, *4*, 195–202. On pedestrians see M. B. Harris, "The Effects of Performing One Altruistic Act on the Likelihood of Performing Another," *Journal of Social Psychology*, 1972, *88*, 65–73. On the cancer donations see P. Pliner, H. Hart, J. Kohl, and D. Saari, "Compliance Without Pressure: Some Further Data on the Foot-in-the-Door Technique," *Journal of Experimental Social Psychology*, 1974, *10*, 17–22. On students see M. B. Harris, *op. cit.* On neighborhood residents see R. P. Lowman, "Recycling Refuse: The Effect of the Foot-in-the-Door Technique on Attitude and Repetitive Behavior," unpublished doctoral dissertation, Claremont Graduate School, 1972. On arguments see D. L. McMillen and R. L. Helmreich, "The Effectiveness of Several Types of Ingratiation Techniques Following Argument," *Psychonomic Science*, 1969, *15*, 207–208.

27. M. Snyder and M. R. Cunningham, "To Comply or Not Comply: Testing the Self-Perception Explanation of the 'Foot-in-the-Door' Phenomenon," *Journal of Personality and Social Psychology*, 1975, 31, 64–67.

28. A. L. Beaman, C. M. Cole, M. Preston, B. Klentz, and N. M. Steblay, "Fifteen Years of Foot-in-the-Door Research: A Meta-Analysis," *Personality and Social Psychology Bulletin*, 1983, *9*, 181–196; W. DeJong, "An Examination of the Self-Perception Mediation of the Foot-in-the-Door Effect," *Journal of Personality and Social Psychology*, 1979, *37*, 2221–2239; C. L. Kleinke, *Self-Perception: The Psychology of Personal Awareness* (San Francisco: W. H. Freeman, 1978), chap. 5.

29. J. W. Brehm, *A Theory of Psychological Reactance* (New York: Academic Press, 1966); S. S. Brehm and J. W. Brehm, *Psychological Reactance: A Theory of Freedom and Control* (New York: Academic Press, 1981).

30. On the camera see D. Regan, M. Williams, and S. Sparling, "Voluntary Expiation of Guilt: A Field Experiment," *Journal of Personality and Social Psychology*, 1972, *24*, 42–45. On the bag see D. Regan, "Guilt, Perceived Injustice, and Altruistic Behavior," *Journal of Personality and Social Psychology*, 1971, *18*, 124–132. On the cards see J. L. Freedman, S. A. Wallington, and E. Bless, "Compliance Without Pressure: The Effect of Guilt," *Journal of Personality and Social Psychology*, 1967, *7*, 117–124.

31. E. I. Rawlings, "Witnessing Harm to Other: Reassessment of the Role of Guilt on Altruistic Behavior," *Journal of Personality and Social Psychology*, 1968, *10*, 377–380; J. M. Carlsmith and A. E. Gross, "Some Effects of Guilt on Compliance," *Journal of Personality and Social Psychology*, 1969, *11*, 232–239; R. B. Darlington and C. E. Macker, "Displace-

ment of Guilt-Produced Altruistic Behavior," *Journal of Personality and Social Psychology,* 1966, *4,* 442–443.

32. C. M. Steele, "Name-Calling and Compliance," *Journal of Personality and Social Psychology,* 1975, *31,* 361–369.

33. S. B. Gurwitz and B. Topol, "Determinants of Confirming and Disconfirming Responses to Negative Social Labels," *Journal of Experimental Social Psychology,* 1978, *14,* 31–42.

34. C. L. Kleinke, *op. cit.,* chap. 4.

35. E. E. Jones, R. G. Jones, and K. J. Gergen, "Some Conditions Affecting the Evaluation of a Conformist," *Journal of Personality,* 1963, *31,* 270–288; E. E. Jones, L. K. Stires, K. G. Shaver, and V. A. Harris, "Evaluation of an Ingratiator by Target Persons and Bystanders," *Journal of Personality,* 1968, *36,* 349–385. See also G. L. Clore and B. Baldridge, "Interpersonal Attraction: The Role of Agreement and Topic Interest," *Journal of Personality and Social Psychology,* 1968, *9,* 340–346; E. E. Jones and C. Wortman, *op. cit.,* p. 19.

36. H. B. Gerard and C. W. Greenbaum, "Attitudes Toward an Agent of Uncertainty Reduction," *Journal of Personality,* 1962, *30,* 485–495; J. C. Stapert and G. L. Clore, "Attraction and Disagreement-Produced Arousal," *Journal of Personality and Social Psychology,* 1969, *13,* 64–69. See also E. E. Jones and G. Wein, "Attitude Similarity, Expectancy Violation, and Attraction," *Journal of Experimental Social Psychology,* 1972, *8,* 222–235.

37. H. Sigall, "Effects of Competence and Consensual Validation on a Communicator's Liking for the Audience," *Journal of Personality and Social Psychology,* 1970, *16,* 251–258.

38. J. P. Lombardo, R. F. Weiss, and W. Buchanan, "Reinforcing and Attracting Functions of Yielding," *Journal of Personality and Social Psychology,* 1972, *21,* 359–368.

39. S. L. Braver, D. E. Linder, T. T. Corwin, and R. B. Cialdini, "Some Conditions that Affect Admissions of Attitude Change," *Journal of Experimental Social Psychology,* 1977, *13,* 565–576.

40. D. Carnegie, *op. cit.,* p. 110.

41. C. L. Kleinke, R. A. Staneski, and P. Weaver, "Evaluation of a Person Who Uses Another's Name in Ingratiating and Noningratiating Situations," *Journal of Experimental Social Psychology,* 1972, *8,* 457–466.

42. *Ibid.*

43. R. A. Staneski, C. L. Kleinke, and F. B. Meeker, "Effects of Ingratiation, Touch, and Use of Name on Evaluation of Job Applicants and Interviewers," *Social Behavior and Personality,* 1977, *5,* 13–19.

CHAPTER 11

1. H. C. Smith, *Sensitivity Training: The Scientific Understanding of Individuals* (New York: McGraw-Hill, 1973).

2. R. F. Dymond, "A Scale for the Measurement of Emphatic Ability," *Journal of Consulting Psychology*, 1949, *13*, 127–133; R. F. Dymond, "Personality and Empathy," *Journal of Consulting Psychology*, 1950, *14*, 343–350.

3. L. J. Cronbach, "Processes Affecting Scores on 'Understanding of Others' and 'Assumed Similarity,'" *Psychological Bulletin*, 1955, *52*, 177–193; E. E. Jones, "A Conversation with Edward E. Jones and Harold H. Kelley," in J. H. Harvey, W. J. Ickes, and R. F. Kidd (eds.), *New Directions in Attribution Research*, Vol. 2 (Hillsdale, N.J.: Erlbaum, 1978). A report of research in which Cronbach's controls were taken into account can be found in V. B. Cline, "Interpersonal Perception," in B. A. Maher (ed.), *Progress in Experimental Personality*, Vol. 1 (New York: Academic Press, 1964).

4. W. Mischel, *Personality and Assessment* (New York: Wiley, 1968).

5. B. R. Forer, "The Fallacy of Personal Validation: A Classroom Demonstration of Gullibility," *Journal of Abnormal and Social Psychology*, 1949, *44*, 118–123.

6. R. E. Ulrich, T. J. Stachnik, and N. R. Stainton, "Student Acceptance of Generalized Personality Interpretations," *Psychological Reports*, 1963, *13*, 831–843; C. R. Snyder, R. J. Shenkel, and C. R. Lowery, "Acceptance of Personality Interpretations: The 'Barnum Effect' and Beyond," *Journal of Consulting and Clinical Psychology*, 1977, *45*, 104–114.

7. P. E. Meehl, "Wanted—A Good Cookbook," *American Psychologist*, 1956, *11*, 263–272; C. R. Snyder, R. J. Shenkel, and C. R. Lowery, *op. cit.*; R. W. Collins, V. M. Dmitruk, and J. T. Ranney, "Personal Validation: Some Empirical and Ethical Considerations," *Journal of Consulting and Clinical Psychology*, 1977, *45*, 70–77.

8. C. R. Snyder and R. J. Shenkel, "Astrologers, Handwriting Analysts, and Sometimes Psychologists use . . . the P. T. Barnum Effect," *Psychology Today*, 1975, *8*, 52–54.

9. C. L. Kleinke, unpublished data, Boston College, 1980.

10. D. R. Atkinson and G. Carskaddon, "A Prestigious Introduction, Psychological Jargon, and Perceived Counselor Credibility," *Journal of Counseling Psychology*, 1975, *22*, 180–186; C. R. Snyder, "Why Horoscopes Are True: The Effects of Specificity on Acceptance of Astrological Interpretations," *Journal of Clinical Psychology*, 1974, *30*, 577–580.

11. L. J. Chapman and J. P. Chapman, "Genesis of Popular but Erroneous Psychodiagnostic Observations," *Journal of Abnormal Psychology*, 1967, *72*, 193–204; L. J. Chapman and J. P. Chapman, "Illusory Correlation as an Obstacle to the Use of Valid Psychodiagnostic Signs," *Journal of Abnormal Psychology*, 1969, *74*, 271–280.

12. B. F. Skinner, *About Behaviorism* (New York: Knopf, 1974); B. F. Skinner, *Contingencies of Reinforcement: A Theoretical Analysis* (New York: Appleton-Century-Crofts, 1969).

13. G. J. Gaeth and J. Shanteau, "Training to Reduce the Use of Irrelevant Information in Personnel Selection," Psychology Report #81–12, Kansas State University, 1981.

14. D. Kahneman and A. Tversky, "On the Psychology of Prediction," *Psychological Review*, 1973, *80*, 237–251; A. Tversky and D. Kahneman, "Judgment under Uncertainty: Heuristics and Biases," *Science*, 1974, *185*, 1124–1131.

15. E. Borgida, "Scientific Deduction—Evidence Is not Necessarily Informative: A Reply to Wells and Harvey," *Journal of Personality and Social Psychology,* 1978, *36,* 477–482; R. E. Nisbett and E. Borgida, "Attribution and the Psychology of Prediction," *Journal of Personality and Social Psychology,* 1975, *32,* 932–943.

16. S. Oskamp, "Confidence in Case Study Judgments," *Journal of Consulting Psychology,* 1965, *29,* 261–265.

17. On availability bias see A. Tversky and D. Kahneman, *op. cit.* On buying a car see R. E. Nisbett, E. Borgida, R. Crandall, and H. Reed, "Popular Induction: Information Is not Always Informative," in J. Carroll and J. Payne (eds.), *Cognitive and Social Behavior* (Hillsdale, N.J.: Erlbaum, 1976).

18. E. Borgida and R. E. Nisbett, "The Differential Impact of Abstract vs. Concrete Information on Decisions," *Journal of Applied Social Psychology,* 1977, *7,* 258–271; R. Hamil, T. D. Wilson, and R. E. Nisbett, "Insensitivity to Sample Bias: Generalizing from Atypical Cases," *Journal of Personality and Social Psychology,* 1980, *39,* 578–589.

19. E. Borgida and N. Brekke, "The Base Rate Fallacy in Attribution and Prediction," in J. H. Harvey, W. Ickes, and R. F. Kidd (eds.), *New Directions in Attribution Research,* Vol. 3 (Hillsdale, N.J.: Erlbaum, 1981); S. M. Kassin, "Consensus Information, Prediction, and Causal Attribution: A Review of the Literature and Issues," *Journal of Personality and Social Psychology,* 1979, *37,* 1966–1981; S. E. Taylor and S. C. Thompson, "Stalking the Elusive 'Vividness' Effect," *Psychological Review,* 1982, *89,* 155–181.

20. On logical explanation see R. E. Nisbett and T. D. Wilson, "Telling More than We Can Know: Verbal Reports on Mental Processes," *Psychological Review,* 1977, *84,* 231–259. On traits see R. E. Nisbett and N. Bellows, "Verbal Reports about Causal Influences on Social Judgments: Private Access versus Public Theories," *Journal of Personality and Social Psychology,* 1977, *35,* 613–624.

21. R. E. Nisbett and T. D. Wilson, "The Halo Effect: Evidence for Unconscious Alteration of Judgments," *Journal of Personality and Social Psychology,* 1977, *35,* 250–256.

22. J. Sabini and M. Silver, "Introspection and Causal Accounts," *Journal of Personality and Social Psychology,* 1981, *40,* 171–179; E. Smith and F. Miller, "Limits on Perception of Cognitive Processes: A Reply to Nisbett and Wilson," *Psychological Review,* 1978, *85,* 355–362.

23. All three experiments in T. D. Wilson and R. E. Nisbett, "The Accuracy of Verbal Reports about the Effects of Stimuli on Evaluations and Behavior," *Social Psychology,* 1978, *41,* 118–131.

24. L. Ross, "The Intuitive Psychologist and His Shortcomings: Distortions in the Attribution Process," in L. Berkowitz (ed.), *Advances in Experimental Social Psychology,* Vol. 10 (New York: Academic Press, 1977); J. H. Harvey, J. P. Town, and K. L. Yarkin, "How Fundamental Is 'The Fundamental Attribution Error'?" *Journal of Personality and Social Psychology,* 1981, *40,* 346–349.

25. On the essay see E. E. Jones, "The Rocky Road from Acts to Dispositions," *American Psychologist,* 1979, *34,* 107–117. On the speech see A. G. Miller, "Constraint and Target Effects in the Attribution of Attitude," *Journal of Experimental Social Psychology,* 1976, *12,* 325–339; M. L. Snyder and E. E. Jones, "Attitude Attribution When Behavior Is Constrained," *Journal of Experimental Social Psychology,* 1974, *10,* 585–600.

26. B. Yandell and C. A. Insko, "Attribution of Attitudes to Speakers and Listeners under Assigned-Behavior Conditions: Does Behavior Engulf the Field?" *Journal of Experimental Social Psychology,* 1977, *13,* 269–278; I. Ajzen, C. A. Dalto, and D. P. Blyth, "Consistency and Bias in the Attribution of Attitudes," *Journal of Personality and Social Psychology,* 1979, *37,* 1871–1876.

27. B. F. Skinner, *Science and Human Behavior* (New York: Macmillan, 1953).

28. M. L. Snyder and E. E. Jones, *op. cit.*

29. D. A. Napolitan and G. R. Goethals, "The Attribution of Friendliness," *Journal of Experimental Social Psychology,* 1979, *15,* 105–113; L. Ross, *op. cit.*

30. S. E. Taylor and S. T. Fiske, "Salience, Attention, and Attribution: Top of the Head Phenomena," in L. Berkowitz (ed.), *Advances in Experimental Social Psychology,* Vol. 11 (New York: Academic Press, 1978); S. E. Taylor, J. Crocker, S. T. Fiske, M. Sprinzen, and J. D. Winkler, "The Generalizability of Salience Effects," *Journal of Personality and Social Psychology,* 1979, *37,* 357–368; E. R. Smith and F. D. Miller, "Salience and the Cognitive Mediation of Attribution," *Journal of Personality and Social Psychology,* 1979, *37,* 2240–2252. On seating see S. E. Taylor and S. T. Fiske, "Point of View and Perceptions of Causality," *Journal of Personality and Social Psychology,* 1975, *32,* 439–445. On uniqueness see S. E. Taylor, S. T. Fiske, M. Close, C. Anderson, and A. Ruderman, "Solo Status as a Psychological Variable: The Power of Being Distinctive," unpublished paper, University of California, Los Angeles, 1974. On lighting see L. Z. McArthur and D. L. Post, "Figural Emphasis and Person Perception," *Journal of Experimental Social Psychology,* 1977, *13,* 520–535.

31. R. M. Arkin and S. Duval, "Focus of Attention and Causal Attributions of Actors and Observers," *Journal of Experimental Social Psychology,* 1975, *11,* 427–438.

32. L. Ross, *op. cit.;* L. Ross, T. M. Amabile, and J. L. Steinmetz, "Social Roles, Social Control, and Biases in Social Perception Processes," *Journal of Personality and Social Psychology,* 1977, *35,* 485–494.

33. E. J. Langer and A. Benevento, "Self-Induced Dependence," *Journal of Personality and Social Psychology,* 1978, *36,* 886–893.

34. L. Ross, *op. cit.;* L. Ross, D. Greene, and P. House, "The False Consensus Phenomenon: An Attributional Bias in Self-Perception and Social Perception Processes," *Journal of Experimental Social Psychology,* 1977, *13,* 279–301.

35. L. Ross, *op. cit.;* T. Gilovich, D. L. Jennings, and S. Jennings, "Causal Focus and Estimates of Consensus: An Examination of the False-Consensus Effect," *Journal of Personality*

and Social Psychology, 1983, *45*, 550–559; M. Zuckerman and R. W. Mann, "The Other Way Around: Effects of Causal Attributions on Estimates of Consensus, Distinctiveness, and Consistency," *Journal of Experimental Social Psychology*, 1979, *15*, 582–597; S. J. Sherman, C. C. Presson, L. Chassin, E. Corty, and R. Olshavsky, "The False Consensus Effect in Estimates of Smoking Prevalence: Underlying Mechanisms," *Personality and Social Psychology Bulletin*, 1983, *9*, 197–207.

36. L. Ross, *op. cit.*

37. H. J. Einhorn and R. M. Hogarth, "Confidence in Judgment: Persistence of the Illusion of Validity," *Psychological Review*, 1978, *85*, 395–416; P. C. Wason, "On the Failure to Eliminate Hypotheses in a Conceptual Task," *Quarterly Journal of Experimental Psychology*, 1960, *12*, 129–140.

38. M. Snyder, "Seek and Ye Shall Find: Testing Hypotheses about Other People," in E. T. Higgins, C. P. Herman, and M. P. Zanna (eds.), *Social Cognition: The Ontario Symposium on Personality and Social Psychology* (Hillsdale, N.J.: Erlbaum, 1980).

39. D. L. Hamilton, "A Cognitive-Attributional Analysis of Stereotyping," in L. Berkowitz (ed.), *Advances in Experimental Social Psychology*, Vol. 12 (New York: Academic Press, 1979). See also D. L. Hamilton and T. L. Rose, "Illusory Correlation and the Maintenance of Stereotypic Beliefs," *Journal of Personality and Social Psychology*, 1980, *39*, 832–845.

40. W. B. Swann, T. Giuliano, and D. M. Wegner, "Where Leading Questions Can Lead: The Power of Conjecture in Social Interaction," *Journal of Personality and Social Psychology*, 1982, *42*, 1025–1035.

41. L. Ross, M. R. Lepper, and M. Hubbard, "Perseverance in Self-Perception and Social Perception: Biased Attributional Processes in the Debriefing Paradigm," *Journal of Personality and Social Psychology*, 1975, *32*, 880–892.

42. L. Ross, M. R. Lepper, F. Strack, and J. L. Steinmetz, "Social Explanation and Social Expectation: Effects of Real and Hypothetical Explanations on Subjective Likelihood," *Journal of Personality and Social Psychology*, 1977, *35*, 817–829.

43. B. Fischoff, "Hindsight ≠ Foresight: The Effect of Outcome Knowledge on Judgment Under Uncertainty," *Journal of Experimental Psychology: Human Perception and Performance*, 1975, *1*, 288–299.

44. B. Fischoff and R. Beyth, "'I Knew It Would Happen' Remembered Probabilities of Once-Future Things," *Organizational Behavior and Human Performance*, 1975, *13*, 1–16; M. Rothbart, M. Evans, and S. Fulero, "Recall for Confirming Events: Memory Processes and the Maintenance of Social Stereotypes," *Journal of Experimental Social Psychology*, 1979, *15*, 343–355.

CHAPTER 12

1. E. E. Jones and R. E. Nisbett, *The Actor and the Observer: Divergent Perceptions of the Causes of Behavior* (Morristown, N.J.: General Learning Press, 1971).

2. R. E. Nisbett, C. Caputo, P. Legant, and J. Marecek, "Behavior as Seen by the Actor and as Seen by the Observer," *Journal of Personality and Social Psychology*, 1973, *27*, 154–164.

3. D. Bar-Tal and I. H. Frieze, "Attributions of Success and Failure for Actors and Observers," *Journal of Research in Personality*, 1976, *20*, 256–265; S. B. Gurwitz and L. Panciera, "Attributions of Freedom by Actors and Observers," *Journal of Personality and Social Psychology*, 1975, *32*, 531–539; A. G. Miller, "Actor and Observer Perceptions of the Learning of a Task," *Journal of Experimental Social Psychology*, 1975, *11*, 95–111.

4. B. R. Schlenker, T. V. Bonoma, and D. R. Forsyth, "The Attributional 'Double Standard': Actor-Observer Differences in Predicting the Relationship Between Attitudes and Behaviors," *Representative Research in Social Psychology*, 1977, *8*, 108–117.

5. R. E. Nisbett, C. Caputo, P. Legant, and J. Marecek, *op. cit.*

6. S. G. West, S. P. Gunn, and P. Chernicky, "Ubiquitous Watergate: An Attributional Analysis," *Journal of Personality and Social Psychology*, 1975, *32*, 55–65.

7. S. D. Herzberger and G. L. Clore, "Actor and Observer Attributions in a Multitrait-Multimethod Matrix," *Journal of Research in Personality*, 1979, *13*, 1–15.

8. L. R. Goldberg, "Unconfounding Situational Attributions from Uncertain, Neutral, and Ambiguous Ones: A Psychometric Analysis of Descriptions of Oneself and Various Types of Others," *Journal of Personality and Social Psychology*, 1981, *41*, 517–552; A. R. Buss, "Causes and Reasons in Attribution Theory: A Conceptual Critique," *Journal of Personality and Social Psychology*, 1978, *36*, 1311–1321; A. R. Buss, "On the Relationship Between Causes and Reasons," *Journal of Personality and Social Psychology*, 1979, *37*, 1458–1461; D. Locke and D. Pennington, "Reasons and Other Causes: Their Role in Attribution Processes," *Journal of Personality and Social Psychology*, 1982, *42*, 212–223.

9. T. C. Monson and M. Snyder, "Actors, Observers, and the Attribution Process: Toward a Reconceptualization," *Journal of Experimental Social Psychology*, 1977, *13*, 89–111; T. C. Monson, E. D. Tanke, and J. Lund, "Determinants of Social Perception in a Naturalistic Setting," *Journal of Research in Personality*, 1980, *14*, 104–120.

10. L. G. Bell, R. A. Wicklund, G. Manko, and C. Larkin, "When Unexpected Behavior Is Attributed to the Environment," *Journal of Research in Personality*, 1976, *10*, 316–327; D. T. Regan, E. Straus, and R. Fazio, "Liking and the Attribution Process," *Journal of Personality and Social Psychology*, 1974, *10*, 385–397; S. E. Taylor and J. H. Koivumaki, "The Perception of Self and Others: Acquaintanceship, Affect, and Actor-Observer Differences," *Journal of Personality and Social Psychology*, 1976, *33*, 403–408. On explaining judgments see G. L. Wells, R. E. Petty, S. G. Harkins, D. Kagehiro, and J. H. Harvey, "Anticipated Discussion of Interpretation Eliminates Actor-Observer Differences in the Attribution of Causality," *Sociometry*, 1977, *40*, 247–253.

11. C. R. Snyder, R. J. Shenkel, and A. Schmidt, "Effects of Role Perspective and Client Psychiatric History on Locus of Problem," *Journal of Consulting and Clinical Psychology*, 1976, *44*, 467–472.

12. E. J. Langer and R. P. Abelson, "A Patient by any Other Name . . . : Clinical Group Difference in Labeling Bias," *Journal of Consulting and Clinical Psychology*, 1974, *42*, 4-9; C. R. Snyder, R. J. Shenkel, and A. Schmidt, *op. cit.*

13. D. T. Miller, S. A. Norman, and E. Wright, "Distortion in Person Perception as a Consequence of the Need for Effective Control," *Journal of Personality and Social Psychology*, 1978, *36*, 598-607.

14. On self-serving bias see G. W. Bradley, "Self-Serving Biases in the Attribution Process: A Reexamination of the Fact or Fiction Question," *Journal of Personality and Social Psychology*, 1978, *36*, 56-71; D. T. Miller and M. Ross, "Self-Serving Biases in the Attribution of Causality: Fact or Fiction?" *Psychological Bulletin*, 1975, *82*, 213-225; M. Zuckerman, "Attributions of Success and Failure Revisited, or: The Motivational Bias Is Alive and Well in Attribution Theory," *Journal of Personality*, 1979, *47*, 245-287. On taking credit see J. H. Harvey, B. Harris, and R. D. Barnes, "Actor-Observer Differences in the Perceptions of Responsibility and Freedom," *Journal of Personality and Social Psychology*, 1975, *32*, 22-28. On attributing success to skill see J. H. Harvey, R. M. Arkin, J. M. Gleason, and S. Johnston, "Effect of Expected and Observed Outcome of an Action on the Differential Causal Attributions of Actor and Observer," *Journal of Personality*, 1974, *42*, 62-77; M. L. Snyder, W. G. Stephan, and D. Rosenfeld, "Egotism and Attribution," *Journal of Personality and Social Psychology*, 1976, *33*, 435-441. On accountability see M. Zuckerman, *op. cit.*

15. R. E. Nisbett, C. Caputo, P. Legant, and J. Marecek, *op. cit.;* D. Watson, "The Actor and the Observer: How Are Their Perceptions of Causality Divergent?" *Psychological Bulletin*, 1982, *92*, 682-700. See also L. R. Goldberg, "Differential Attribution of Trait-Descriptive Terms to Oneself as Compared to Well-Liked, Neutral, and Disliked Others: A Psychometric Analysis," *Journal of Personality and Social Psychology*, 1978, *36*, 1012-1028.

16. On the game see D. T. Miller and S. A. Norman, "Actor-Observer Differences in Perceptions of Effective Control," *Journal of Personality and Social Psychology*, 1975, *31*, 503-515. On electric shocks see M. R. Wolfson and G. R. Salancik, "Observer Orientation and Actor-Observer Differences in Attributions for Failure," *Journal of Experimental Social Psychology*, 1977, *13*, 441-451.

17. M. D. Storms, "Videotape and the Attribution Process: Reversing Actors' and Observers' Points of View," *Journal of Personality and Social Psychology*, 1973, *27*, 165-175.

18. S. S. Brehm and D. Aderman, "On the Relationship Between Empathy and the Actor-Observer Hypothesis," *Journal of Research in Personality*, 1977, *11*, 340-346; R. E. Galper, "Turning Observers into Actors: Differential Causal Attributions as a Function of 'Empathy,'" *Journal of Research in Personality*, 1976, *10*, 323-335; R. Gould and H. Sigall, "The Effects of Empathy and Outcome on Attribution: An Examination of the Divergent-Perspective Hypothesis," *Journal of Experimental Social Psychology*, 1977, *13*, 480-491; D. M. Wegner and K. Finstuen, "Observers' Focus of Attention in the Simulation of Self-Perception," *Journal of Personality and Social Psychology*, 1977, *35*, 56-62. See

also R. J. Wolosin, J. Esser, and G. A. Fine, "Effects of Justification and Vocalization on Actors' and Observers' Attributions of Freedom," *Journal of Personality*, 1975, *43*, 612–633.

19. B. S. Moore, D. R. Sherrod, T. J. Liu, and B. Underwood, "The Dispositional Shift in Attribution over Time," *Journal of Experimental Social Psychology*, 1979, *15*, 553–569.

20. M. Ross and F. Sicoly, "Egocentric Biases in Availability and Attribution," *Journal of Personality and Social Psychology*, 1979, *37*, 322–336; S. C. Thompson and H. H. Kelley, "Judgments of Responsibility for Activities in Close Relationships," *Journal of Personality and Social Psychology*, 1981, *41*, 469–477. On happy couples see S. C. Thompson and H. H. Kelley, *op. cit.*

21. B. R. Orvis, H. H. Kelley, and D. Butler, "Attributional Conflict in Young Couples," in J. H. Harvey, W. J. Ickes, and R. F. Kidd (eds.), *New Directions in Attribution Research*, Vol. 1 (Hillsdale, N.J.: Erlbaum, 1976). See also A. L. Sillars, "Attributions and Interpersonal Conflict Resolution," in J. H. Harvey, W. Ickes, and R. F. Kidd (eds.), *New Directions in Attribution Research*, Vol. 3 (Hillsdale, N.J.: Erlbaum, 1981).

22. J. H. Harvey, G. L. Wells, and M. D. Alvarez, "Attribution in the Context of Conflict and Separation in Close Relationships," in J. H. Harvey, W. J. Ickes, and R. F. Kidd (eds.), *New Directions in Attribution Research*, Vol. 2 (Hillsdale, N.J.: Erlbaum, 1978).

23. F. B. Meeker and C. La Fong, "Brokenhearts: Dissolution of Romantic Relationships," paper presented at the meeting of the Western Psychological Association, San Francisco, 1978.

24. C. L. Kleinke, "Assignment of Responsibility for Marital Conflict to Husbands and Wives: Sex Stereotypes or a Double Standard?" *Psychological Reports*, 1977, *41*, 219–222.

25. R. I. Edelson and E. Seidman, "Use of Videotaped Feedback in Altering Interpersonal Perceptions of Married Couples: A Therapy Analogue," *Journal of Consulting and Clinical Psychology*, 1975, *43*, 244–250.

26. U. Bronfenbrenner, "The Mirror Image in Soviet-American Relations: A Social Psychologist's Report," *Journal of Social Issues*, 1961, *17*, 45–56; S. Oskamp, "Attitudes Toward U.S. and Russian Actions: A Double Standard," *Psychological Reports*, 1965, *16*, 43–46.

27. M. J. Lerner, *The Just World Hypothesis* (New York: Plenum, 1980); M. J. Lerner, "The Justice Motive: Some Hypotheses as to Its Origins and Forms," *Journal of Personality*, 1977, *45*, 1–52; M. J. Lerner and D. T. Miller, "Just World Research and the Attribution Process: Looking Back and Ahead," *Psychological Bulletin*, 1978, *85*, 1030–1051.

28. Z. Rubin and A. Peplau, "Belief in a Just World and Reaction to Another's Lot: A Study of Participants in the National Draft Lottery," *Journal of Social Issues*, 1973, *29*, 73–93; Z. Rubin and A. Peplau, "Who Believes in a Just World?" *Journal of Social Issues*, 1975, *31*, 65–81.

29. You may wish to read Robert Jay Lifton's analysis of the motives and rationalizations of Nazi doctors who worked in concentration camps. R. J. Lifton, "Medicalized Killing in Auschwitz," *Psychiatry*, 1982, *45*, 283–297.

30. On the status of the victim see C. Jones and E. Aronson, "Attribution of Fault to a Rape Victim as a Function of Respectability of the Victim," *Journal of Personality and Social Psychology*, 1973, *26*, 415–419. On acquaintance with the assailant see R. E. Smith, J. P. Keating, R. K. Hester, and H. E. Mitchell, "Role and Justice Considerations in the Attribution of Responsibility to a Rape Victim," *Journal of Research in Personality*, 1976, *10*, 346–357. On unplanned pregnancy see D. Stokols and J. Schopler, "Reactions to Victims under Conditions of Situational Detachment: The Effects of Responsibility, Severity, and Expected Future Interaction," *Journal of Personality and Social Psychology*, 1973, *25*, 199–209. On completed rape see J. E. Krulewitz and J. E. Nash, "Effects of Rape Victim Resistance, Assault Outcome, and Sex of Observer on Attributions about Rape," *Journal of Personality*, 1979, *47*, 557–574.

31. W. Ryan, *Blaming the Victim* (New York: Random House, 1971).

32. B. Weiner, "A Theory of Motivation for Some Classroom Experiences," *Journal of Educational Psychology*, 1979, *71*, 3–25; B. Weiner, I. Frieze, A. Kukla, L. Reed, S. Rest, and R. M. Rosenbaum, *Perceiving the Causes of Success and Failure* (Morristown, N.J.: General Learning Press, 1971); B. Weiner, D. Russell, and D. Lerman, "Affective Consequences of Causal Ascriptions," in J. H. Harvey, W. Ickes, and R. F. Kidd (eds.), *New Directions in Attribution Research*, Vol. 2 (Hillsdale, N.J.: Erlbaum, 1978); B. Weiner, D. Russell, and D. Lerman, "The Cognition-Emotion Process in Achievement-Related Contexts," *Journal of Personality and Social Psychology*, 1979, *37*, 1211–1220.

33. B. Weiner, I. Frieze, A. Kukla, L. Reed, S. Rest, and R. M. Rosenbaum, *op. cit.;* I. H. Frieze, "Causal Attributions and Information Seeking to Explain Success and Failure," *Journal of Research in Personality*, 1976, *10*, 293–305.

34. On school children see G. R. Andrews and R. L. Debus, "Persistence and the Causal Perception of Failure: Modifying Cognitive Attributions," *Journal of Educational Psychology*, 1978, *70*, 154–166; C. S. Dweck, "The Role of Expectations and Attributions in the Alleviation of Learned Helplessness," *Journal of Personality and Social Psychology*, 1975, *31*, 674–685. On freshmen see T. D. Wilson and P. W. Linville, "Improving the Academic Performance of College Freshmen: Attribution Theory Revisited," *Journal of Personality and Social Psychology*, 1982, *42*, 367–376.

35. B. Weiner, D. Russell, and D. Lerman, "Affective Consequences of Causal Ascriptions"; B. Weiner, D. Russell, and D. Lerman, "The Cognition-Emotion Process in Achievement-Related Contexts."

36. B. Weiner and A. Kukla, "An Attributional analysis of Achievement Motivation," *Journal of Personality and Social Psychology*, 1970, *15*, 1–20.

37. J. T. Lanzetta and T. E. Hannah, "Reinforcing Behavior of 'Naive' Trainers," *Journal of Personality and Social Psychology*, 1969, *11*, 245–252.

38. G. S. Leventhal and J. W. Michaels, "Locus of Cause and Equity Motivation as Determinants of Reward Allocation," *Journal of Personality and Social Psychology*, 1971, *17*, 229–235.

39. B. F. Skinner, *Beyond Freedom and Dignity* (New York: Knopf, 1971).

Name Index

Subject Index